THE AMAZIGH
REVIVAL

THE AMAZIGH REVIVAL

A Memoir of Its Birth and Progression

BRAHIM AKHIATE

Translated from Arabic by Paul Raymond

GEORGETOWN UNIVERSITY PRESS / WASHINGTON, DC

The publisher is not responsible for third-party websites or their content. URL links were active at time of publication.

This series is made possible by the generous support of the Robert Lemelson Foundation.

Cataloging-in-Publication Data is on file with the Library of Congress

978-1-64712-651-3 (hardcover)
978-1-64712-652-0 (paperback)
978-1-64712-653-7 (ebook)

♾ This paper meets the requirements of ANSI/NISO Z39.48-1992 (Permanence of Paper).

26 25   9 8 7 6 5 4 3 2   First printing

Printed in the United States of America

Cover design by TG Design Studio
Interior design by Westchester Publishing Services

CONTENTS

PREFACE

Brahim El Guabli and Aomar Boum, series editors

We are delighted to open the Georgetown University Press's Amazigh Studies series with Brahim Akhiate's magisterial book *The Amazigh Revival*. Titled *al-Nahḍa al-amāzīghiyya kama 'ishtu mīlādahā wa-taṭawwurahā* (The Amazigh Renaissance as I lived its birth and development) in Arabic, Akhiate's book is anything but an ordinary memoir. It is, rather, a historical document that bears witness to the crucial period when the Amazigh Cultural Movement (ACM) in Morocco and in Tamazgha (broader North Africa) emerged in the postcolonial period. Akhiate returns to the humble beginnings of the ACM in Rabat and takes you on a journey inside the inner workings of Amazigh activism during the painful "Years of Lead" (1956–1999), which were characterized by state violence and political repression. *The Amazigh Revival* is not solely about Akhiate and his activism but also about an entire historical period marred by political repression of difference.

The Amazigh Revival could be the foundational text about Amazigh cultural and political activism in Morocco—not because it contains almost everything that you need to know about Imazighen and their history but because Akhiate, probably more than anyone else, was a fixture of the ACM. He and several of his companions founded *al-Jam'iyya al-maghribiyya li-al-baḥt wa-al-tabādul al-thaqāfī* (The Moroccan Association for Research and Cultural Exchange, or AMREC, as it is known by its French acronym) in 1967, and Akhiate was at the helm of the organization until his death in 2018. During that time, he was at the center of the synergies that were developed to advocate for Imazighen's linguistic and cultural rights. His multi-decade involvement in Amazigh advocacy earned him the privileged position of a maverick figure among the Moroccan conservative political parties whose leaders opposed Amazigh rights as a post-independence national priority. This same position elicited criticism from Amazigh groups that disagreed with his acceptance of a gradual transformation of the state of Tamazight, the Amazigh language. As you will discover in reading *The Amazigh Revival*, however, Akhiate never deviated from his fundamental goal to see Tamazight recognized and rehabilitated.

In bequeathing us this memoir, Akhiate achieves several things at once. His work demonstrates how the author was central to many initiatives that aimed to push the Moroccan state to end the marginalization of Amazigh language and culture. He was involved in the establishment of the Agadir Summer School, which organized several seminal seminars that have become foundational for Amazigh literature and thought; he helped create a musical band to renew Amazigh music; and he was at the center of the Agadir Charter, which has defined the goals and the strategies of collective Amazigh activism since 1991. Akhiate was a multifaceted person navigating the demands and pressures of his era in ways that made sense to him in his own context. Thus, his views and actions reflect the desire to rally support from conservative ideologues and political parties and help them see Tamazight as a matter of democratization and cultural pluralism rather than a colonial Trojan horse aimed at attacking Morocco's Islamic and Arab identities. Throughout his book, Akhiate chronicles the history of a movement and of Morocco's postcolonial era while documenting his own actions in response to the explicit denial of Morocco's Indigenous identity following independence.

It also gives insight into the intricacies of the activism required to build and sustain the ACM. As a witness, Akhiate cites names, dates, and little-known enterprises to demonstrate that a strategy to assert Amazigh rights underpinned every action undertaken by AMREC. For instance, activists infiltrated Moroccan radio and recorded musical sessions in Akhiate's house and broadcasted them on air without the knowledge of the Moroccan state. No one, other than the witness, would know this significant detail. Likewise, he tells of the involvement of wealthy Amazigh entrepreneurs who supported the movement financially without participating in its activities, for fear of retaliation by the Moroccan state. This would not be known without the testimony of a stakeholder like Akhiate. Finally, AMREC leveraged the soft power of Amazigh employees working inside different administrations as a source of information that helped AMREC strategize and prepare the responses that foiled state policies. Again, Akhiate's memoir uncovers important aspects of the ACM that academic studies cannot access without witness accounts. Although he was not the sole witness to these events, he is the only one who authored a lengthy memoir about them for the future Amazigh generations.

Akhiate's candor in his memoir is clear; he shares his positions vis-à-vis ideas or notions from others in the organization that did not align with his vision for Amazigh activism. The lawyers Ahmed Dghirni and Hassan Id Balkassam represented the Tamaynut Association (also known as the New Association for Culture and Arts, founded in 1978) at the 1993 United Nations World Conference on Human Rights in Vienna. Upon their return, Dghirni and Id Balkassam introduced to the Moroccan Amazigh activists the concept of indigeneity as a potential way to connect Imazighen to other Indigenous people worldwide. But after accusations leveled by the conservative parties against indigeneity, Akhiate distanced the AMREC from the concept, demonstrating a limited understanding of its decolonial significance. This seems surprising to us today, but Akhiate's position was the product of the sociopolitical climate of the 1990s. It does not seem that he changed course or evolved despite the inroads that indigeneity made globally with the adoption of the United Nations Declaration on the Rights of Indigenous Peoples in 2007. That said, Akhiate did not express any public disagreement with Id Balkassam or Dghirni, who promoted the concept of indigeneity. He conceded that terrain to them with a clear division of their roles—he worked on internal and they on transnational forms of activism.

One must acknowledge Akhiate's choice to write the history of a nation from his own position as an Amazigh community leader and activist, a type of historical record rarely left by Moroccan activists and officials. Activists often live, witness significant events, and die, leaving nothing behind to establish true accounts and do them historical justice. Akhiate models a new type of writing in which civil society stakeholders, those who have no official positions in the state, present accounts of their struggle for recognition—in his case, recognition of Amazigh people's rights. He does it with brilliance, enthusiasm, and, most of all, with a clear conviction that he was on the right side of history when the majority of his generation were not even aware that Tamazight was an issue. This precocious consciousness was Akhiate's gift to his generation and to the generations that will claim their Amazighity whether they know his name or not.

As the stories in *The Amazigh Revival* tell us, there is much more to the Amazigh renaissance than what has been so far revealed in secondary sources. The impressive body of primary works produced by Amazigh activists and academics in both Arabic and Tamazight has barely been used in most academic scholarship, which has thus far relied on those available in French and, in very rare cases, in Tamazight. The translation of primary sources produced in Arabic and Tamazight into English is a long-overdue project that we hope will make Amazigh Studies available to a wider Anglophone audience. As we welcome *The Amazigh Revival* to our bookshelves, curricula, and transnational conversations about indigeneity and Indigenous people's activism, our intention, as editors of the series, is to make available as many Amazigh-focused resources as possible. This stems from our belief that every effort to convey the rich Amazigh cultural production and the worldviews of its people is valuable. With this series, we want to build a cutting-edge Amazigh Studies field that will benefit generations of scholars and students in Anglophone academia.

The creation of these resources would not be possible without the support of the staff at Georgetown University Press. Our gratitude goes to Hope LeGro and her colleagues who have shown us their tremendous investment in the launch of the series. We are equally grateful to Dr. Rob Lemelson of the Robert Lemelson Foundation who has awarded us a grant to start the Amazigh Studies Initiative (AMASI). A trained anthropologist, Dr. Lemelson has understood AMASI's scholarly and pedagogical importance and has generously funded our initiative.

TRANSLATOR'S NOTE

Paul Raymond

The challenge facing every translator is that of striking a balance between accuracy—close adherence to the linguistic nuance of the original—and clarity: relaying the content in a style natural to the target language and accessible to the reader.

Akhiate's matter-of-fact prose did not pose major problems in this regard. That said, his book was aimed at an Arabophone audience, so I have felt compelled to provide certain elements of context to guide the Anglophone reader. For the sake of flow, I have briefly explained Arabic terms such as *faqīh* and *dārija* in parentheses within the text. Where more cultural or historical detail is required, I have included an endnote. The preface provides the information necessary for a more holistic understanding of the memoir's historical context.

For the sake of convention and practicality, I have adhered to the International Journal of Middle East Studies (IJMES) system when transliterating Arabic, with three exceptions: the names of people, places, and publications. Many of those mentioned in the book are well known in Morocco, and their names have widely used Latinized spellings, usually based on French, so I have adopted whichever is most common.

I have transliterated Tamazight words as they sound to the English ear. The reader is doubtless familiar with the Amazigh aversion to the disparaging term "Berber," so naturally I have only used that word in direct quotes or translations (e.g., the "Berber decree").

Brahim Akhiate was a meticulous recordkeeper, and his memoir includes detailed roll calls from committee meetings over the decades. To avoid such detours, I have extracted most of these from the body of the text, and they appear as endnotes.

Any errors or inconsistencies in the translation are, of course, entirely my own.

Finally, I would like to thank my many Arabic teachers over the years, particularly those in Leeds and Fes, and my family for their unwavering support.

The Amazigh Revival

Brahim Akhiate

DEDICATION

To my late mother and father, whose absence I have suffered since my early days. I left them at one of the highest peaks of the Lesser Atlas range, heading into the unknown in our nation's cities, in search of ways to help renew the language, culture, and identity of the Amazigh people in its nation.

To my late brother, El-Haj Mohamed, who embraced me and funded and encouraged my education in Rabat; and to his wife, El-Hajja Tlait, who took my hand and surrounded me with her love and support.

To all my comrades in the struggle, who made so many sacrifices and worked tirelessly to bring about the cultural revolution for which we all strove over more than four decades, sharing the suffering and the consequences of bringing it to fruition; we who were lucky enough to enjoy living through these achievements for our nation, as we wait to see what remains to be achieved.

To my wife, and to our daughter, Touf Itri, and our son, Yacine, who learned the language of our forebears and our Amazigh culture, with conviction and awareness fit for the modern era, without being forced or pressured; and to my nephew Lahcene Akhiate, who is like a son to me; I wish them all success and happiness in their family and professional lives.

And to my grandchildren, Simane, Elli, and Ilyasse Lachhab, in the hope that this book will be a message through which they can see the sacrifices our generation made for the Amazigh people of Morocco.

A WORD OF HOMAGE AND ACKNOWLEDGMENT TO MY WIFE

I wish to dedicate an additional note in this memoir to my wife, Mahjouba Ouaziz, in acknowledgment of the unforgettable sacrifices and support she has given me since our marriage. She has shared all my joys and all my crises. From the day she embraced my intellectual convictions, she has spared no effort to accompany me. She has played the role of intellectual critic, challenging my arguments to ensure they are defensible. She has played the role of lookout, drawing my attention to issues I may have missed or ignored. She has managed every aspect of my life, seeking to see me in the best possible spirits, enabling me to shoulder my responsibilities actively and with zeal, building on her own conviction that all these aspects of life have an impact on my morale and my activist work.

I continuously find her to be my greatest supporter, morally and materially, in all endeavors related to the exercise of my struggle. She has never abandoned me for a moment, under any circumstances, as she herself is part of the struggle, and feels that by making these sacrifices she is doing her duty toward the Amazigh cause, in which she believes with every fiber of her being. Alongside all these sacrifices, she follows every development, big or small, by reading widely on the Amazigh cause through newspapers, magazines, and books, and shares her opinions with me on every event. It is only fair, therefore, that I express my deepest gratitude to her in this memoir.

In our family life, it was she who oversaw the upbringing and education of our children when it was impossible for me to give them the necessary attention, so that they would not go astray or become victims of the fact that my attention was elsewhere due to the huge demands of doing my duty and bearing my responsibilities toward the organization of which I am a member.

She took pains to convince our children of the importance of what I was doing, for the future of our Amazigh language, culture, and its manifestations, nurturing their belief in the Amazigh element that plays a fundamental role in our national identity. Thus, they themselves might contribute in the future to spreading this awareness and so they could understand it, despite their youth, and be convinced that what we were doing was neither a waste of time nor money, nor a luxury, so they would bear that conviction and its consequences, even at the expense of their own material needs.

Therefore, it is my duty to dedicate this part of my memoir, simple though it is, to my devoted wife, who has been totally loyal and dedicated to her cause—to our cause. I appeal to her to forgive any rash act of mine that has irritated her. I know the depth of the harm inflicted on her and our children by the financial and moral pressures stemming from my struggle.

Indeed, to give her the credit she is due: I would not have been able to fully continue my struggle for the Amazigh cause if it were not for her constant support, awareness, and intellectual elevation, thanks to which we were able to overcome these difficulties, tensions, and material difficulties that hit us throughout our path of struggle, and for which were paid back in spiritual and moral wealth, due to our conviction and belief in our national cause.

So I offer my deepest respects to my wife, Mahjouba Ouaziz. With this testimony, I hope that we can share the honor of the achievements I recount in this memoir, just as she shared with me the suffering involved in attaining these goals.

INTRODUCTION

I decided to write this memoir now, in the presence of my companions in the Amazigh struggle who are still with us, so that they could be witnesses to what I write. This is partly because I feel the weight of responsibility toward the Amazigh cause, by virtue of having lived with it for more than four decades, and partly because I was keen that the history of this cause would not be afflicted by the distortions that have afflicted the history of our Amazigh people.

The Amazigh cause, in its substance and philosophy, is a deep and quiet cultural revolution. As such, it is also a cultural and political revolution that aspires to provoke change from within: a change of mentalities and a reconsideration of concepts, ideas, and behaviors, not simply an external adjustment or a change of appearance, as in the case of coups or other superficial alterations.

I have long believed in this revolution, the need to bring it to fruition, and the imperative to contribute actively to this in every possible way, with all my determination and strength, whatever huge sacrifices this requires of me. It is a revolution that stems from our society's awareness of its Amazigh self, an awareness built on reason, history, and the humanities, that transcends ideologies based on illusions or on racial, regional, religious, or linguistic discrimination or other forms of racial intolerance.

Through the course of this memoir, I have written about my academic work and the contributions I have been able to make to the cause, both individually and as part of a collective, throughout my long struggle. I have written about the difficulties and dangers I faced, which varied in intensity depending on the political situation at every stage. Yet it never occurred to me, even for a moment, to give up on performing this national duty, a duty that was never waged in opposition to any institution or person. Nor did I ever exploit it to achieve any political goals, or for personal benefit.

In concluding this memoir, I wish to emphasize that I have sincerely aspired to relate the events and situations described within it as faithfully to reality as possible, regardless of myself or my relationship with any particular activist within the Amazigh struggle. I believe that these events and their consequences are the property of this movement and of the people as a whole. Therefore, I have striven for truth and integrity, in respect and appreciation for those responsible for these events, both deceased and living. I also feel a sense of responsibility toward all these matters collectively.

Given this firm conviction of my responsibility, I want to affirm that I have no intention of insulting or harming anyone mentioned in these memoirs, including the many friends and various active figures and personalities who might be vexed by my writing about their positions, or who may differ with my perspectives on a given issue. I assure them that the positions expressed here stem from innocent intentions, led by the strength of the principles that guide me, principles from which I cannot deviate. These are supreme national principles that transcend selfishness, utilitarianism, or malice. However, I affirm that, putting any differences in opinion or stances between us aside, the friendship, respect, and esteem we share toward each other remain steadfast and unwavering, because we all value those with differing opinions, just as we respect the courage they show by expressing it.

—Brahim Akhiate
June 2010

CHAPTER 1

Childhood and Youth
1941–1965

THE AMAZIGH ISSUE IN MY CHILDHOOD

During my childhood, I experienced several surprising events that marked the course of my life. I grew up in two culturally different environments: the countryside, with its simplicity and its cultural and linguistic harmony, and the city, with its cultural diversity and class differences.

I was born in around 1941 in the village of Ikhyaten, in the Anti-Atlas Mountains. I came from the Ait Ouikman clan, part of the broader Ait Souab tribe, and in the ʿumāla (village) of Beikra Ait Baha. This was the village established by my forefathers after they left their old village of Imourghet, of which only the mosque remains. I believe that Imourghet was hit by an epidemic that killed most of its residents, and the few who survived left the village and established Ikhyaten on the slopes of the same mountain. Many stories were told about Imourghet, which became a sacred place for the entire Ait Ouikman tribe. My father, may God have mercy on him, was the oldest of the village's Quran reciters, and our family was known for repeatedly producing such men, as well as religious scholars whose names and merits were much talked of by the tribe.

Imourghet was also the site of an annual gathering by the devout people of the Souss-Massa region. They showed me the old road that everyone would take to reach Imourghet. It was the most elevated area in the region, and there was a saying that went: "*Ana takit I Imourghet aka asaouen*," literally meaning, "No matter from which direction I approach Imourghet, it is higher." This was a way of describing something in which one had no choice. As if to attest to this story, four towers stood on the spot. Nobody knew who had built them, but they belonged to the pious men who gathered there to discuss issues of religion.

During my childhood, I survived two incidents that could have killed me. The first was that I was kicked hard by my father's mule. I passed out and was unconscious for several hours before recovering. The second incident happened when I was playing with a girl around my age. We were gathering the green algae that grew in the village pond. The pond was fairly deep, especially as I could not swim well. As I stretched out on its bank, trying to gather the algae, I rolled down and fell in.

The children started screaming and calling for help. My mother and the women of the village, along with some of the youth, were threshing the summer harvest at the *anrār*, the place designated for that task. My mother and the others heard the screaming and rushed to the spot. Without hesitation, she climbed in to rescue me, heedless of the danger to herself. Seeing this, one of the strong young men threw himself into the pond to rescue us both.

When I remembered this incident, I pondered on the divine kindness that had saved me from many dangers. I realized that this had contributed to my life in the struggle aimed at bringing about the cultural revolution that I shall relate in this book. Indeed, for me, these were major moments in my life that require me, as one who believes in God, to pause and contemplate the divine will in the course of events, especially when we call to mind later developments in the various stages of my life, as will be discussed.

During those early years, living with my parents, they told me I had siblings in "the west." For them, "the west" meant Rabat. I didn't know these siblings, and they were much older than me. They were called Abdellah, Mohammed, and Imhammed. I also had a sister, who was older still, who lived in Al-Qabilah, unlike my brothers, who worked as merchants in Rabat.

My father had produced them with his first wife, who had passed away after a chronic illness. At the time, he was working his trade in Rabat, but he had bad luck with it and was not successful. So he left Rabat and settled in the village, marrying my mother. I was her oldest child, followed by my brother El-Tayyib. My father only settled in the countryside after living a difficult life in exile, marked by deep pain. He had been among the first Moroccan migrants to France, in 1912. He had headed there on foot via Algeria, from the depths of Souss to Oran, then onward to Marseille in France. While there, he worked as a builder, then returned to Morocco to establish himself as a merchant in Fes, then Rabat, which he left after losing both his wife and his business. After some time had passed, his three male children would all return to take his place and reside in Rabat.

The experiences of my half-brothers in Rabat had a deep impact on their understanding of life, the demands of the modern age, and how to face its challenges. It particularly marked their view of the role of education for the coming generations, especially as they had interacted with the people of the city after starting their new life there during the French colonial period. My brother Mohammed, along with some of his friends, became a chef in the homes of French people. Through this, he and his colleagues learned to communicate in French and became convinced of the importance of education in modern life.

This was the impulse behind the decision of my brothers, whom I had not yet met, to bring me to the city, despite my young age. This was a historic and highly important decision in my life, and also in theirs, aware as they were of the need to avoid leaving me to an unknown fate if I stayed in the countryside, despite the pain it would cause my mother for her firstborn to be far away. My father agreed to the decision, given his experience in France, Fes, and Rabat. He was an open-minded man and was also convinced that my half-brothers would treat me like one of their sons.

My journey to Rabat was full of surprises. My father asked one of his friends, a man from Ait Baha called Abhalous, who regularly traveled between the town and Rabat, to look after me and deliver me to my brothers in Rabat. We traveled by bus, crammed with passengers on the inside while others climbed on top with their produce, surrounded by an iron barrier so they would not fall off. Abhalous and I were among those who climbed on top. That image stayed in my mind; Abhalous looked after me carefully, wrapping me in his black camel-hair cloak to protect me from the bitter cold and the strong winds that we endured throughout our journey, all the way from Ait Baha to Rabat.

I remember one of my journeys at this young age. I was riding a mule with my father from Ait Baha toward Al-Douar. I asked him an innocent question, stemming from my ignorance about the bus that would transport us back and forth:

"Father, does this bus know the road on its own from here to the west?"

My father got down from our mule and we sat under an Argan tree, where he explained to me about buses, saying it was a machine driven by a human, with a driver to direct it.

I arrived in Rabat—"the west" in village parlance—and settled at the house of my older half-brother Abdellah, who was the only one of the three brothers who was married. At that time, he had a daughter and a son, so I became the third child of the household. The first thing Abdellah did was enroll me at a Quranic school on Moulay Ibrahim Street in the Old City of Rabat, the closest such school to our home on Avenue des Consuls (the lower market). My arrival in Rabat was a major turning point in my life, firstly due to my young age and also due to the fact that I would now be far away from my mother and father for ten months of the year. My brothers would take me back to my father during the summer holidays for two months. But it was important to integrate me into city life, of which I knew nothing. To do so, they enrolled me at a *kuttāb* (a Quranic school) so I could learn *dārija* (Moroccan colloquial Arabic) and complete the traditional education I had started in Douar with my father and uncle.

My first shock was to discover that the *faqīh* (expert and teacher on Islamic law) at this school spoke no Tamazight. He sat me in front of him, at the request of my brother, because I could not yet speak *dārija*. On one occasion, during my early days at the school, he addressed me in a language and in such a manner that I believed he was reproaching and insulting me; I wasn't sure, as I couldn't understand what he meant. All I could do was throw myself at his feet and deliver him a painful bite, before running out of the school. When my brother Abdellah found out that I was not at the school and did not want to return, he realized that there must be a reason. So he dragged me back to the *faqīh*, who told him what I had done. This early experience has stayed in my mind as my first encounter with another culture. My inability to communicate with the *faqīh* had caused this situation, as I felt he had humiliated me by failing to understand my language, culture, and individual situation, and neglected to treat me with kindness, which would have made it easier for me to integrate. Rather, he had used his power over me, and my reaction had been to defend myself and reject this undidactic behavior. This was my first interaction with the culture of the city, and it would not be the last of its kind, as we shall see throughout this memoir.

I did not stay long with Abdellah, as my other half-brother Imhammed also married, and he brought both his wife and me to live with him in Rabat. I then joined a new Quranic school in Bab al-Mellah, with another Tamazight-speaking *faqīh*.

The second such incident came when I started refusing to move between Quranic schools, as my whole experience there amounted to seeing the *faqīh* filling out the blackboard, of which I had to learn the contents by heart. At the beginning of one academic year, after considering the issue and despite my young age, I decided to revolt against the situation, giving my half-brothers a choice: Either I would join a normal school like my peers or I would return to live with my father in Douar. This was a brave decision that I took by myself, to put an end to the situation I was in. It stemmed from my enthusiasm and desire to learn. It was also a kind of challenge, at a time that I see as my period of integration and of dealing with the social situation where I was living, far from my mother and father, and in which education was the only thing that could prepare me to create a better life. This decision had a major impact on my brothers, and they quickly enrolled me at the Maataouia private school, one of several such institutions founded alongside schools established by the French in various Moroccan cities. I began classes a few days after school had started, so that the head teacher could evaluate which class to place me in. He tested me by asking me to read a text from a reading book, which I was able to do. He placed me in the second grade of primary, as I did not know how to use a quill or write in an exercise book. The teacher ordered that I be placed next to another Amazigh-speaking pupil so that he could help me and show me how to write and to organize my work in the exercise book. The pupil in question helped me immensely, doing a great job of this voluntary task. In the same year, I was able to rise to the next grade, a success that I saw as evidence I had risen to the challenge I had set for myself: to tackle the psychological and linguistic problems I had faced from the moment I moved to the city.

But this success, of joining the school and integrating into the school system, did not end my battle and my problems with my peers, both at school and in life more generally. I had not yet mastered any language other than Amazigh, whose distinctive accent dominated my pronunciation both of formal Arabic and Moroccan *dārija*, and as we were from Souss, we carried the behavior of an ostensibly conservative society, which affected our dress. We wore hats on our heads and baggy *qandrīsī* pants, with characteristic shirts, habits that made us stand out from the other residents of the city. This meant we were often the target of mockery by other residents of Rabat, and our peers would harass us in the street. Such things happened everywhere: in class, in the streets, and when we were playing with the other children. None of these places was free of the manifestations of this cultural struggle, which in truth was a superficial struggle because it was not an ethnic or racial issue as much as a result of the linguistic and cultural diversity of Moroccan society—a society made up of speakers of Amazigh, of *dārija*, and of people educated in Arabic and French, as well as followers of both Islam and Judaism. Each of these social strata had its own sonic signature by which it could be identified, as well as its own social customs. Between the 1950s and the 1970s, radio plays would be broadcast in these different dialects: *al-ʿarūbiyya, shilḥa, fāsiyya,* and *yuhūdiyya* (a Jewish dialect).

Here I shall relate certain events that I recall from this cultural struggle. During my primary education, until secondary school, we Amazigh speakers numbered no more than three or four in my class, which had more than thirty pupils. This situation forced us into solidarity and cooperation in order to confront repeated attacks, as well as the social aspect, by helping each other out in class. We were therefore sometimes able to hide our weakness when confronted with the material resources of the others.

These are just some examples of the confrontations we experienced, both at school and in the street. There were so many that there is no need to relate them all in detail.

After noting some of the events I experienced in my childhood, before even graduating from primary school, I should note that this period was not short on opportunities to make friends, even some hailing from this urban society that treated us with such derision and contempt. In the end, despite this conflict, intimate and deep friendships flourished between me and some of my fellow pupils.

For me, and for many like me, this situation had a major impact that lasted well into the future. We experienced a cultural reality on two levels: the social level in the street and at the educational level. A normal speaker of Amazigh who experienced this conflict on the social level found no explanation for it in his daily life as a trader or worker. He could not explain the reasons and drivers behind his lived reality, so he was forced simply to accept it, only seeking the means by which he could secure a living for himself and his family, divided between the countryside and the city. He would therefore avoid anything that could disturb the peace of his life. A pupil at school would progress through the educational system, experience that cultural struggle, and discover that nothing that he was taught connected him to society. Rather, it failed to tell him anything about the history of his forefathers, men of politics, the educated, writers and scholars; he was taught a fragmented and distorted history of his country. This dual state of school and society sowed in us, at a very young age, a curiosity to learn and find the truth beyond the official school curricula.

These events, which I shared with many others like me who had come from the countryside, brought me to the conclusion that it would not be possible for an Amazigh speaker to have a contemporary awareness of his Amazigh identity and of the dangers facing that identity—particularly its most fundamental component, the Amazigh language—without this migration, which, although it was imposed on him due to the conditions he faced in his rural home, would push him to migrate domestically or to head overseas. Thus, he was forced to choose between submission to this new situation, in which he would hide his Amazigh language, culture, and identity, or living up to this historic challenge of identity and doing what was necessary to achieve the cultural revolution needed to guarantee the survival of that identity, language, culture, and civilization. This challenge was a test whose features would become clear with the rise of a cultural elite, stemming from a nationalist background, who benefited from education and schooling as one of the positive outcomes of that migration.

Having placed these events in the context of my childhood and the imprints it left on my psyche and my personality, I must return to other periods of my youth. A year before I received my primary school certificate, I was living with my half-brother Imhammed, as I have mentioned. During this period, he left Morocco and emigrated to France along with his wife. I was therefore forced to move once again, to live with my other half-brother, Mohammed. He was a coordinator of the *yan wawāl* ("unity") cell linked to the resistance movement in Rabat and was the most politically active of my brothers.

I must emphasize that he had a major influence on me. He embraced me and treated me like his oldest son. He loved me very much and never hesitated to respond to my needs or to support my upbringing. He was helped by his wife Tlait, who was like a second mother to me and made me feel like there was no difference between me and her children, Fatima and Abdellah and later Idriss and Saadiya. This gave me great encouragement to continue my education, and after I had graduated from primary school, I moved on to the Mohammed V school to gain a secondary education.

My high school years were marked by two important things. Firstly, I started taking part in, and became passionate about, youth activities. I volunteered in tree-planting campaigns in 1957–58, shortly after independence, taking buses on the weekends to plant trees in the suburbs of Rabat. I don't recall exactly where we went, but of course this activity was encouraged by my brother, who saw it as a national duty and part of the great enthusiasm he shared with his nationalist companions, who had made major sacrifices for independence. After these outings, we were always invited to take part in various performances and exhibitions organized by His Majesty Mohammed V, especially in Rabat, such as when he departed for the airport, prayed the Friday prayers at the Ahl Fes mosque, or received foreign guests. All these activities were forms of national celebrations of our independence. No sooner had this stage ended than I joined the Hassaniya scouts, part of the Istiqlal (independence) party.

Joining this organization had a major impact on my personal development. It taught me and my colleagues how to depend on ourselves, to endure and be disciplined, to respect leaders and those in positions of responsibility, and how to respect and care for nature and the environment. I rose up through the organization, to the rank of scoutmaster, and took part in a national parade led by the late King Mohammed V in Tangiers in 1957. I only left the organization when the National Union of Popular Forces (UNFP) party was founded, and many of those involved in the nationalist struggle left Istiqlal to join the new party.

No sooner had I left the scouts than I took up the sport of sailing, along with some friends I had made. We did this at a youth naval base and sports complex in Rabat. When I joined, I didn't know what went on at the base. All I wanted was to swim in an organized setting, rather than in the sea off Oudaya (a beachfront neighborhood of Rabat). Once there, I discovered that a few foreigners and a very small number of Moroccans, particularly Jews, were taking sailing lessons. We joined the club and took up the sport in a serious way, until I became champion of Morocco in 1969. I took part in several national and international races, and I represented the club in a display at the Al-Mechouar Square of the royal palace, again in front of the king, marking Youth Day. Before winning the Moroccan championship for sailing, I earned a certificate for swimming one thousand meters in 1961, a kind of swimming in clothes that was organized by the club in the Bou Regreg River. It was not possible to become a sailor without being a good swimmer.

In the summer of 1965, I was selected to represent Morocco, along with my friend Abdul Fattah Fenniche, at an international training course on sea travel, organized in Bretagne, France. We were the only Africans at the training, which lasted ten days. We were trained to sail between several ports in the English Channel, and the trainers were surprised at the presence of Africans at this kind of event. They were even more surprised that we were white: They thought all Africans were Black.

These early experiences allowed me to gain skills in many areas, which I would employ later in life. They also allowed me to make friends, both Amazigh speakers and nonspeakers. The friendships I made grew stronger after we passed through this period, in which we experienced the tensions arising from cultural diversity. We used to visit each other's homes and organize group outings to explore or for fun, without tension or problems. This was reflected in my behavior later in life; I would accept the other, accept differences and diversity, and was able to communicate and coexist without hang-ups, complexes, or feelings of inferiority. I would respect others as much as they respected me, speaking politely and respecting my interlocutors, while adhering to my own intellectual and cultural convictions. I would use logic and reason to resolve problems as they were presented.[1]

In 1966, I started a project to combat illiteracy, based in the annex of the Rabat Chamber of Commerce. I also participated in a trip to Tunis, organized by the Istiqlal party's youth association. A Senegalese participant and

I were the only delegates who were not members of this association. I was signed up for the trip by one of my high school classmates, Ahmed Belmamoun. This journey opened my eyes to the reality of Amazigh culture in the Algerian and Tunisian contexts, the aspect of the trip that most interested me. I was looking for similarities and common elements in our Amazigh civilization across North Africa. I noticed the widespread use of the traditional *tazarzit*, a fibula or brooch worn by women in all these regions. This observation led me to choose it as a symbol for the association I went on to establish in 1967.

I must return once again to the influence my brother had on my upbringing and note that due to his strong involvement in the national movement as a coordinator for *Yan Wawāl*, and his knowledge of the secret opposition's activities, he enabled me to meet many opposition figures at an early age. They included Ahmed El Mrabet, El Hussein El Khudar, and Mohammed Khalil ("Dahmou") as well as Bin El Cheikh ("Outkadourt"), El Mehdi El Sleimani, and Abdellah Masrour.

I saw my brother as my main interlocutor and someone to whom I could direct all my questions at that time. Fortunately for me, he liked to engage in dialogue with me and never belittled me for my age or treated me as a child who should not be concerned with the matters at hand. In fact, in this open environment, I would oppose him in many cases, and he never showed any annoyance about it.

During the wave of celebration that accompanied Mohammed V's return from exile, the nationalist movement organized demonstrations, which we all attended to express our joy. I took part in an Amazigh play about the resistance to French rule. I played the role of an Amazigh child who delivered weapons to resistance fighters. The actors wore Amazigh jewelry and dress belonging to my brother's wife and some of our neighbors. We performed the sketch on a stage set up at Bab Oudaya, in the presence of Othmane Djouriou, the headmaster of the Mohammed V school.

MY POLITICAL AND INTELLECTUAL EDUCATION

My political and intellectual education was not theoretical, solely drawing from the ideological literature that was widespread during my youth, such as Marxism-Leninism or various schools of socialism—nor the Liberalism that opposes both. Rather, I drew my education from my own experiences throughout childhood and into maturity, all of which were linked to the economic, cultural, and social reality of Moroccan society. I drew references from the bitter experiences of certain activists who made great sacrifices in the struggle for independence and were active in politics during the resistance and after independence, whether with Istiqlal or the UNFP. My brother Mohammed was one of these people, and he introduced me to others, as well as to his friends who were teachers, so they could be responsible for my education and guidance. They became my political dictionary, thanks to their vast amounts of knowledge and the things they told me about political events and the positions and history of many political leaders before and after independence. I must particularly note the late Abdellah Masrour, who was active in politics and in resistance to colonialism. He was the younger brother of a fighter who was arrested during the battle of Ait Baha in 1936, when Abdellah was working as a small-scale merchant in the Agdal district. He was under eighteen years of age at the time and was forced to engage a French lawyer to defend his brother. He was respected by the French, who made up most of the residents of Agdal, for his intelligence and liveliness. During the years of struggle for independence, and the birth of the national struggle, his house was a headquarters for political meetings. His car was at the disposal of resistance fighters and the national movement whenever they needed transport, and he made a major contribution to building the Mohammed V school. All these actions prepared him to be on the decision-making committee for militant operations in Rabat. My brother also introduced me to someone else, from the same group of stallholders who were part of the resistance in Rabat, who played a major part in political and union life, especially in the area of commerce. He was called El Haj El Mehdi El Soleimani, and he was from Gdourt, in the region of Tafraoute. He was a former member of parliament representing Chtouka Aït Baha province, for the UNFP. He was also the head of the Rabat Chamber of Commerce, and his shop was hit by an arson attack by the intelligence services, in order to intimidate him into giving up politics and union activity. I also met another of these people, Hajj Belkacem El Four. As well as being a political activist with the Istiqlal party and then the UNFP, he had the distinction of being familiar with Amazigh culture. He rarely expressed a point of view without accompanying it with an Amazigh proverb, a story about the subject, or a few lines of poetry to underline his point. Meetings he attended were never devoid of intellectual enjoyment and pointed jokes, and we benefited from the authenticity of his Amazigh cultural knowledge.

Some of the writings I read were "protected" by political parties, which imposed their view despite everyone else, meaning that nobody could criticize these books. This reality pained me and tore me up over the fate of our generation and the next, given these errors and the intellectual terrorism that afflicted our history, our language, and our culture. I knew we had to seriously consider finding a solution to this grim political and cultural reality.

This is how I arrived at the conclusion that the solution lay in sparking a quiet but radical cultural revolution, in order make the Moroccan people aware of itself and its unique cultural and social character, throwing off any ideological hegemony that does not align with its reality. This revolution would gain ever more determination to achieve development and growth, a radical and difficult process, but one that in the end was necessary to save Moroccan society from the disorientation in which it found itself, as well as from imported ideological tugs-of-war that targeted its very existence.

Therefore, this quiet and radical revolution was necessary to wake the people from its slumber, by teaching it its true history, both ancient and modern, and to confront the linguistic and cultural discrimination that its political and faux-intellectual classes were still imposing on society, both in the cities and the villages. This would require building a new, modern society that believed in cultural pluralism and unity in diversity, and did not discriminate between its citizens, a society in which there would be true citizenship and where all citizens would have equal opportunities to take part in cultural, economic, and social development, while preserving its unique cultural and civilizational character.

NOTE

1. Among my friends were Ali Bennour from Frouga near Marrakech, Omar al-Khalfaoui from Amizmiz, El Araby El Bouri, who was from a well-known Rabat family, El Araby Benoumrou, the brother of a famous actor, and Abdul Fattah Fenniche, also from a Rabat family. Then there was Ahmed El-Jdidi, from El Jedidah, Izkil, Melline and El-Araby Kadeirah, Ibrahim El-Rais, Mohammed El-Maaroufi, and Ahmed Belmamoun.

CHAPTER 2

The Beginnings of Amazigh Collective Action
The Phase of Formation and Preparation, 1965–1979

AUSPICIOUS BEGINNINGS: 1965–1979

From my earliest days of university onward, I was preoccupied by the thoughts that I outlined above and began trying to organize a program for myself through which I could embody those ideas. Something needed to be done to change Morocco's cultural and ideological situation, to save what could be saved from the assault of ideological Arab nationalism on our society, led by a group of people infatuated with that ideology.

The first idea that occurred to me, in 1965, was to organize lessons to fight illiteracy among small-scale traders and their assistants, and among workers. I became enthused about this idea after becoming convinced that all these problems, upon deeper analysis, were simply questions of culture and identity. They were not racial, pitting two or more ethnicities against each other. Rather, this was a cultural struggle between Amazighs who had been "Arabized" and those who had not.

It was, therefore, simply a matter of the cultural, linguistic, and religious diversity within the single people making up the states of North Africa. Thus, the starting point was, in essence, to fight illiteracy, equipping citizens with pedagogical tools to allow them to communicate, through reading and writing, as well as providing them with simple lessons to educate them about their true history and their ancient civilization, so as to deepen their awareness of their Amazigh heritage and strengthen their pride in their identity. To put this into action, I enlisted the help of three friends: Ali Bennour, Omar

Al-Khalfaoui, and Abdellah Jachtimi, who had studied at Al-Karaouine University in Fes after completing his education at the old school in Imi Ogchtim. He was from a learned family in Souss. My strong relationship with members of the Chamber of Commerce also helped, and this relationship was strengthened by my brother Mohammed, who had introduced me to them, given his status first as a trader and also as an active patriot, who commanded respect from everyone. Building on this relationship, I proposed to the Chamber that it allow me to organize night classes to fight illiteracy, at a facility affiliated with the Chamber. I did not go into details with them, so as not to bring any suspicion into their minds about political matters that could have prompted them to reject my request. There was an administrator at the Chamber who was an expert in settling trade disputes, called Mohammed El-Khenboubi. I used to engage in long discussions with him, unlike other members of the Chamber, although I had a close relationship with them all. He stood apart as the most familiar with my ideas about identity and the situation in the country. The Chamber accepted my suggestion, with a condition stipulated by El-Khenboubi: The Chamber's guard would accompany us at all times, open and close the door for us, and monitor our activities at the office, which was small and had little more than a hall, a lobby, and a restroom. The fact was that he had little choice but to impose these conditions, due both to his political experience and my long discussions with him. He understood that everything had a political aspect. So I accepted the Chamber's conditions. But the odd thing was that the guard appointed to accompany us knew me well and trusted me, as well as believing in the ideas that I expressed in my conversations with everyone connected to the Chamber—including the guard, El-Chtouki, who agreed after a short period to simply give me the keys and stop monitoring us, meaning we were now free to act as we pleased.

Our curriculum was revolutionary compared to any official program to combat illiteracy. The state curriculum aimed to teach adults formal or literary Arabic, with the same method used in schools, in contrast to other countries that had campaigns to battle illiteracy among adults who had not been able to attend school. This method required teaching students the Arabic alphabet and how to join it up in order to write down what they could say verbally. This would be done in the language of the citizen receiving the tuition, rather than in any other language. An illiterate person is simply someone who lacks the pedagogical tools that enable him to write down his thoughts or to read what falls into his hands. The idea is not to teach him another language besides his own, and the process does not last more than a few months among other peoples. Yet the planners of campaigns to eradicate illiteracy in Morocco strove, instead, to teach Arabic to citizens who had not yet been Arabized, and to rein them in by imposing other languages and thought systems on them, at an age at which they are incapable of assimilating this process, because doing so requires years. The aim of the process is to confuse the subject and convince him that unless he learns Arabic, he will be worthless, and that no language or culture he has learned from his society will be of any benefit to him, but will rather deepen his inferiority in society.

Our project aimed, then, to teach students the Arabic and Latin alphabets and how to use them to form words and sentences. This would allow them to write down the words they needed in order to write invoices or send messages to their loved ones, or to write checks and read bills, regardless of whether they were written in Amazigh or Arabic. We also taught them addition, subtraction, multiplication, and division. I taught them arithmetic, history, and geography, while Ali Bennour and Omar al-Khalfaoui taught French and Abdellah Jachtimi taught Arabic. What set this process apart was that all the subjects were taught in Amazigh, including history and geography, and instead of writing out lessons and getting the students to memorize them, we taught them in the form of stories, which aimed to make the students aware of their ancient and modern history and enable them to discuss freely and in their own language. Geography was taught through practical, tangible methods, such as presenting a globe in order to demonstrate how day, night, and the four seasons worked, and identifying the continents, down to the level of finding Morocco on the African continent and its neighbors in all directions.

In addition to our literacy program, we used the same hall to screen films, which we borrowed from the French cultural mission. They covered many subjects of potential benefit, including commerce, farming, and so on, which the students would discuss in Tamazight. The experiment was very successful and popular. The process lasted two years with each group, after which the beneficiaries received certificates from the Chamber of Commerce confirming that they had followed this course. To mark the occasion, we organized a reception for them, attended by members of the Chamber. However, two years into the program, Mohammed El-Khenboubi started creating obstacles for us. He finally managed to evict us and shut us down. He claimed that residents of the building were complaining about our presence and our activities, along with similar baseless accusations. We were forced to shut down the experiment at the Chamber's office until we could find another venue.

In 1965, Ahmed Amzal was working at the *tashilhīt* (a dialect of Amazigh) language section of the national radio station, presenting a weekly program called *Anbaki n imalas* (Guest of the week). He happened to host Ali Sidqi Azaykou to discuss a number of ideas. Then came my turn: He hosted me to discuss the same themes, and we found we agreed on many things. After the program, he suggested that the three of us meet again, in front of the national radio headquarters. I agreed. But Amzal did not show up. I recognized Ali only by the fact that he was walking up and down in front of the radio building, as if waiting for someone. I introduced myself and asked if he was Ali Sidqi. He said yes. We left together, and I invited him to the headquarters that we were setting up for the anti-illiteracy campaign so that I could show him our project. After that, he agreed to join it and took on the responsibility of giving history and geography lessons, meaning I was only in charge of teaching arithmetic.

What Mohammed El-Khenboubi had feared was that we might use the Chamber of Commerce hall for political ends. That is indeed what happened. After Ali Sidqi Azaykou joined us, he introduced me to a group of students who had come from the south—Marrakech, Agadir, and Essouira. He would discuss the same ideas with them, and it became clear to him that we were all brought together by the same ambitions. So I suggested to him that we meet them at the headquarters in order to continue our discussions. This is how I got to know Boujoumaa El-Habbaz, Ahmed Boukous, Ahmed Akouaou, Abdel Fadel El-Ghouali, Ali El-Jaoui, and Abdullah Bounfour, who were all students at the Faculty of Arts.

During this period, I began to think about something I felt could make a fundamental impact: Amazigh media, and specifically the radio. I realized the power this device possessed to raise awareness and communicate with the public, the length and breadth of Morocco. My relationship with radio dates back to the late 1950s, when I was involved in children's shows on Amazigh radio. I presented cultural programs for children in Amazigh, adapting material I had learned in school. Later, I developed a close relationship with the radio staff, including Abdullah El-Manouzi, Ahmed Amzal, Lhacen Berhou, Mohammed El-Soussi, and Akhrafi. It occurred to me to form a delegation to meet with radio management and present requests to improve its output and expand the geographical coverage of its broadcasts so that it could better contribute to listeners' social and cultural development.

To make this idea a reality, I sought assistance from traders I had met who were known for their political activity, some of whom I have mentioned above. At that time, the president of the Chamber of Commerce was Hassan Al-Idrissi, who shared his office with Haj Ahmed El-Zakari and Haj Belkassem El-Aouri. I persuaded them to help me by taking part in the delegation I had decided to establish, and, ultimately, they became convinced that the idea was sound. To ensure that the meeting would be a success, I held several preparatory sessions and meetings with staff at the radio station, which, at the time, like the national television service, was directed by Abdelwahab Ben Mansour.

I wrote a letter on the subject, which included requests I felt were important. I asked that they increase the number of hours the station was on air, improve its quality so it could be heard clearly, create a national Amazigh orchestra akin to those established for other forms of music, and allocate a full hour a day for the Amazigh language on television. The delegation that finally set out from the chamber, on January 19, 1966, consisted of me, Haj El-Mehdi El-Suleimani, my older brother Abdullah, and a trader from the central market in Rabat, whose name now escapes me.

Accompanying director Abdelwahab Ben Mansour to the meeting was the secretary-general at the time, Ahmed Rayan. I presented the director with the letter laying out our requests. He engaged me in discussion on each point and was surprised at my knowledge of the radio station's intricacies. I talked to him about the American line that Morocco had rented to broadcast news and programs targeted at Mauritania and asked why it couldn't be used for Amazigh broadcasts. I also mentioned the poor sound quality and shortcomings in terms of equipment. He justified these points by noting the station's lack of resources and the cramped quarters of the radio station, among other unconvincing excuses. Haj Mehdi surprised him by saying, "Ask Ahmed Rayan, who is one of the station's longest-serving members of staff, how it was stronger during the colonial era, when it was broadcasting from the ground floor of the current Ministry of Post. Now you have an entire building full of staff and technicians, and yet even with all these resources, the station has regressed, and its signal has become weaker." Haj Mehdi was well aware of the history of the radio during the colonial era and the early days after independence, as he owned two shops adjacent to the Postal Ministry, whose ground floor was the headquarters of the radio station. One of these shops had been burned down by the intelligence services when he was serving as president of the Chamber of Commerce. When asked about the hours of broadcasting, Ben Mansour resorted to another tired excuse. "We can barely develop television in Arabic, so how can we add broadcasts in Amazigh?" He continued by pointing to the number of Amazigh dialects: "If we allocate an hour for *Tachelhit*, then someone else will come forward demanding an hour for *Atlasi*, and then someone will call asking for an hour in *Tarifit*." I interrupted him to prevent a further litany of such flimsy excuses. "Mr. Director, we are demanding an hour of Amazigh broadcast and leaving it to the radio's staff to manage the distribution of slots." The director repeatedly referred questions to the secretary-general, asking him to record the points we presented. I asked him to set an appointment when he would respond to our requests and tell us which of them would be met. I gave him a week to do so; we had informed him that we came from the south and did not clarify that we were living in Rabat. Subsequently, the hour-long Amazigh news broadcast on the radio was brought forward by more than an hour from its late-night slot, so more listeners could tune in.

However, following this meeting, then–justice minister Abdelhadi Boutaleb was tasked with overseeing the radio and television and writing its bylaws. We contacted him and informed him about what had been agreed upon with Ben Mansour, but we never received a reply.

I decided therefore to focus my efforts on educating citizens and communicating with them directly through the radio, to deepen their awareness of themselves and their Amazigh culture. I made sure that this communication through the radio would not gain too much attention from the authorities, which could reveal its true purpose, meaning we would be banned from using this effective medium. To implement my plan, I was in frequent contact with radio staff and with program presenters. We also recorded many programs on a recording device at my house and provided them to the radio staff, who then broadcast them as part of their schedule. In truth, this was the pinnacle of sacrifice and reflected a sense of duty among these journalist friends, who deserve great appreciation and respect for doing what they did, despite the risks it posed to their jobs. They included Mohammed El-Sousse, Ahmed Amzal, Lahcene Barjou, and Akhrafi. I was overjoyed when I heard programs presented by Lahcene Barjou and Mohammed El-Sousse, being broadcast on air without any sensitivity over which dialect of which language each spoke. These programs were among the first initiatives to unify the Amazigh language through radio broadcasts, countering a plan to deepen the policy of division through dialects that had been forced on us since the colonial period.

Let us return to the founding phase of the association. We had met as volunteers fighting illiteracy and had grown to know one another. We began discussing topics that captured our interest, such as history, language, and anthropology. Each of us had knowledge about one or several of these subjects, according to our specializations. This knowledge of the humanities was something we had lacked throughout our formal education, and now we sought to learn more about our ancient history, which had been completely absent from our school curricula. We aimed to familiarize ourselves with *Tifinagh* script, our intellectual and political leaders from bygone eras, and the achievements of our civilization. Most of this information was brought to us by our friend Ali Sidqi Azaykou, who specialized in history. We were often surprised and pleased when we discovered new information in this area. We also conducted research in the field of linguistics, to define terms and concepts that had been unclear to us, such as the difference between a language and a dialect, and how a dialect within a certain community could evolve into a language. We worked to understand the experiences of other peoples in Europe and Asia who had preceded us in this area, and we were guided by specialists like Ahmed Boukous and Ahmed Akouar. During this period, we also became interested in protecting our intellectual, literary, and linguistic heritage, which is mostly oral, with only a small portion written down, especially in the religious domain.

The discussion of all these topics related to our identity and to our linguistic and intellectual heritage prompted us to consider how we could launch a cultural revolution aimed at deepening our self-awareness and fortifying ourselves against the cultural dispossession that was threatening Moroccan society. This gave rise to the idea of establishing a cultural association, which would provide a legal framework for our work. Some of us believed that it was sufficient to remain at our current level of communication and exchange of information on these issues. However, following this debate, we agreed to establish the Moroccan Association for Research and Cultural Exchange (known by its French acronym, AMREC) to operate openly and within the framework of laws governing public freedoms. To achieve this, we worked hard throughout 1966, and the association's founding general assembly was held on May 10, 1967, at the youth center on Madagascar Street in Rabat.

I believe it is important to pause and reflect on this significant event in the history of our people and in the course of the struggle to deepen awareness of Amazigh identity among all Moroccans. This awareness was set to undergo a transformation, from the prevailing, traditional state to the rise of a modern consciousness among Moroccans. The establishment of the association helped transform Amazigh activism from acts of individual awareness and action to a collective consciousness, which would play a significant role in cultural and political life both at the national level and across the Amazigh homeland of North Africa.

I must also draw attention to a fundamental point relating to the name chosen for the association, which expresses its patriotic nature. It indicates that Amazigh culture is not the concern of one region to the exclusion of another. This is a national issue, not a regional one. Moreover, the association was established in the capital, a meeting place of cultural activities, represented by students hailing from various regions, who agreed to organize themselves within a unified, national framework. The Amazigh language is the language of all Moroccans and is not confined to any region of the country. This fact, and the careful choice of a name echoing this national perspective held by the founders of the association, imbued the Moroccan experience on the Amazigh issue with a mature mentality.

WORK BEGINS AT THE MOROCCAN ASSOCIATION FOR RESEARCH AND CULTURAL EXCHANGE

After establishing this framework on November 10, 1967, we laid out our strategy and identified our priorities. High on the list was the work of collecting Amazigh oral heritage, which was threatened with extinction, through recordings of interviews with the elderly, both women and men. We gathered everything we could relating to this heritage, including poetry, prose, and proverbs, as well as written documents that risked being lost. We mobilized ourselves during the summer holidays and other times to go to our rural areas to undertake this work, which we saw as vital. We also devised a program to deliver lectures in the city of Rabat, at the youth house and at La Source, a dormitory in Agdal that housed a number of incoming students from outside Rabat. We also organized exhibitions at the gate Bab al-Rouah, the entrance to Rabat's Old City, the first such activities of their kind in the capital. We made a lot of effort to ensure they had a substantial impact on the city. In the hall of Bab al-Rouah, we organized an exhibition of Amazigh carpets, jewelry, and paintings reflecting the Amazigh identity in the visual arts. These were made available by the Dutch art historian and anthropologist Bert Flint. We also displayed fixed images in diapositive format in the hall at La Source. This event was where we experienced, for the first time, opposition from some students who raised slogans hostile to us. However, we also organized other activities in Kénitra and Marrakech.

In 1969, most of my friends among the founders of the association had graduated and found jobs as teachers at high schools: Ahmed Boukous and Ali Sidqi Azaykou in Rabat, Abdullah Bounfour in Casablanca, and others at schools that I do not remember. I was in Kénitra, and only a few months had passed since the establishment of the association when a new generation of youth joined us, who would play a significant role in the association's future and in Amazigh activity in general. I particularly remember Essafi Moumen Ali, who joined the association in 1968 after graduating from the Greater Morocco High School, where Ali Sidqi Azaykou met him and his friend Ibrahim Madran. Next, a group of students from the Faculty of Arts in Rabat joined us, namely Lhoucine Jouhadi and Afa Omar, and from the Faculty of

Law, El-Awani El-Hassan and Abakrim El-Hocein, as well as Ali Amjoudh from the Faculty of Sciences. All these would be joined in 1970 by a group from the Faculty of Arts in Rabat, including Lhoucine Ait Bahcine, Hussein Agkoun, Ait Hammou Said, Ajana El-Hassan, and Ahmed El-Ghazali from the Faculty of Law. From Casablanca came Abdelaziz Bourass and Mohamed Moustaoui. From the Faculty of Fes, we were joined by Mohamed Farah, Ahmed Bouzid, and Omar Amarir. These would all play important roles in the Amazigh activities on which we were embarking, as we shall see.

In 1969, Ali Sidqi Azaykou and I agreed to visit France with the aim of making contacts with the Moroccan community there. We agreed that he would join me in the city of Saint-Étienne, where my brother Imhammed was living. I left Morocco, accompanied by this brother of mine, in my little Renault R4. The late Ali Azaykou also joined me, and after spending a few days at my brother's house, we had planned a trip that would cover France, Switzerland, and Germany, with the intention of staying in the Janvilliers district of Paris long enough to make several recordings of workers abroad, witness firsthand their suffering as migrants, and see how they managed and arranged their daily lives throughout the year. Indeed, I bought a large recording device in Germany, which we used in this important work. We spent more than ten days with a group of workers from the Ait Ouakman tribe, some of whom were from my family. They treated us hospitably and facilitated our stay despite the difficult conditions they live in, crammed into small rooms in unbearable living conditions.

During this project, we interviewed them on many subjects. How and why had they left Morocco? Was it because of linguistic and cultural problems, or because of their living conditions? What were their ambitions? Did they want to go back, or would they continue to live in France? We asked many other questions. Some of the workers were talented at playing the loutar or the rabab, traditional stringed instruments, and our meetings would sometimes turn into intimate musical gatherings through which the workers tried to forget their suffering and fatigue from their hard work during the week.

During our visit, Ali produced a poem about the reality they were facing in Janvilliers, naming it after the district. The visit gave us great insight into the problems of our community in Europe and enabled us to connect with it. We were also able to inform them about our interests and the cultural and social project we were embarking on. They were greatly touched that we had made the effort to meet them and to make a detailed record of their situation. We felt a warm bond of shared language and culture throughout our stay with them.

In 1970, the Moroccan Ministry of Culture organized a lecture almost every week. Mohammed El-Fassi was the minister of culture. The ministry would often require staff to attend these lectures. It so happened that the ministry scheduled a lecture by Professor Mohamed El Othmani, a well-known poet at the Taroudant Institute, on the subject of pre-Islamic poetry, at which he would debate with a professor from Fes, called El-Bahbeiti. I should note that the subject was not of interest to us. However, what provoked us was that the ministry did not announce El-Othmani's talk as it did other lectures. We considered this uncivilized behavior an insult to the professor and to us, his fellow Amazigh speakers. To protest this, Abdellah Jachtimi and I asked students from the Faculty of Arts and Law, along with many traders we knew, to attend the lecture. We aimed to take up as many seats in the lecture hall as possible, in defiance of the ministry's behavior. Indeed, the event was well attended and showed great respect to Professor El-Othmani.

The professor's presentation lasted more than two hours. After it ended, I suggested that he and all the other friends present come to my house so that we could have a wide-ranging discussion over tea, to talk about our interests and the cultural work of our association. During this meeting, he told us that he was traveling around Morocco trying to set up a cultural magazine overseen by the religious scholars' association in Souss. He said he was heading to Fes to deliver the same lecture and to make contact with enthusiastic individuals from the southern regions who were interested in getting involved in the project and who could contribute by writing. After he had discussed the project with us and assured us that the magazine would be inclusive, we agreed to join it. Ali, Afa Omar, and I were selected to be part of its editorial committee. However, I later withdrew from it after a fundamental disagreement with the magazine's management.

In 1969, the association organized several cultural days in Marrakech, in cooperation with the Comedia Art Club. The programs included the screening of the film "Sincafay," which addressed the distribution of water in the Amazigh countryside, as well as a presentation on Amazigh dance and music, among other exciting performances. Most of these events took place at the Comedia Club, in Bab Doukkala. It is important to understand here that in the view of the association, which was mostly run by activists who believed in the need to develop popular culture in its various expressions, the prevailing intellectual trend at the time saw popular culture as a revolutionary, populist choice in the face of a scholastic, elite culture that looked down on popular culture. Here lies the parallel between the prevailing popular culture and Amazigh culture. None of us therefore felt any embarrassment or contradiction in this cooperation.

The upshot was that we addressed issues and ideas about Amazigh culture that sparked interest among those concerned, posed them questions, and encouraged them to carry out further research to verify their validity and intellectual depth. Essafi Moumen Ali gave a revealing talk on Amazigh music and, for the first time, performed Amazigh songs he had written. The audience loved them, and they inspired many ideas about the need to update and modernize Amazigh music.

From its 1967 establishment onward, the association began attracting students and professors with a keen interest in the humanities and other fields, and this continued over the years. I remember here that Essafi Moumen Ali's family owned the *Chebab* (youth) café in the old city of Rabat, which had a balcony overlooking Mohammed V Street. We held discussion sessions and meetings there, and it quickly became a melting pot of intellectual exchange. We would meet there every day to exchange ideas and inform each other of what we had discovered or read about various aspects of our history and literature. As the association's headquarters was at the home of my brother Mohammed, where I was living, this was also where its official meetings were held. It also played host to some presentations. Thus, the café was like a club where we held our daily rendezvous. Essafi Moumen Ali, who had obtained his baccalaureate and joined the Faculty of Law, had a special talent for the arts. He was involved with music, cinema, and theater, and was in fact our philosopher, as he was an avid reader of intellectual and philosophical books in general. He was at the origin of many cultural, literary, and intellectual projects. As he was from a conservative family with high morals, my relationship with him developed to a point where we considered ourselves brothers. His mother, may she rest in peace, liked me and encouraged him to deepen our friendship. He was a major asset to the Amazigh cause in Morocco and North Africa in general, for his contributions to Amazigh cultural, political, and associative work and for the richness of his literary and intellectual works.

1970–1980: THE PHASE OF FORMATION AND THE CRYSTALLIZATION OF AMAZIGH DISCOURSE

This period in the history of Morocco saw a number of political and cultural transformations that left major marks on the Amazigh cultural movement. The first was the emergence of signs that the fierce struggle pitting the *Makhzen* (the governing institution of Morocco, centered around the

monarchy) against revolutionary parties with aspirations for power, notably the National Union of Popular Forces (UNFP) and Marxist-oriented
leftist currents, was drawing to an end. The Makhzen managed to turn the
situation to its own interests, laying out a new plan to manage the country's
political affairs by eliminating the UNFP and forcing its more extreme leaders into exile. The rest were persuaded to integrate into political life, on the
condition that they abandoned any armed struggle and created a new party,
the Socialist Union of Popular Forces (USFP), on the rubble of the UNFP.
The Makhzen also began to create and foster parties of its own, which would
energize political life while keeping it under its control.

Secondly, as this power struggle had apparently been resolved, cultural
issues began to surface. Certain party leaders took positions on identity, linguistic diversity, Morocco's history and the origins of its people, and other
cultural and civilizational questions. One example was the speech by the late
Allal El-Fassi, a politician and writer, at the conference of the General Union
of Moroccan Students in Casablanca on August 25–27, 1970:

> As a Muslim nation, Morocco had a degree of civilizational develop-
> ment in its pre-Islamic era that gives it the right to demand recogni-
> tion for its pre-Islamic identity. This was embodied in the struggle of
> its kings to preserve their national identity, and their perpetual strug-
> gle against those who tried to conquer it. This great passion for free-
> dom is what made our people an Amazigh people, which is why they
> accepted and integrated with the Phoenicians. People like Bocchus,
> Jugurtha, Massinissa, Saint Augustine and Kahina all helped pave the
> way for Tariq ibn Ziyad and the other heroes of Muslim Morocco.

This effort to address cultural issues gained momentum with the arrival
of growing numbers of students from Amazigh backgrounds who joined our
association, particularly from Rabat and Fes. Lecturers with political orientations, after they had delivered their presentations and lectures at university
halls or in cultural activities, were confronted with a barrage of challenging
questions on the subject of the Amazigh cause. Consequently, some political
figures started paying attention to the issue, especially left-wing intellectuals
from the Progress and Socialism Party and the Moroccan National Union of
Students. It was the association's student activists who led this campaign on
the university campuses. We had student cells at the University of Rabat, two
at the Agronomic and Veterinary Institute Hassan II, one at the Institute of
Statistics, and one in the Yaqub al Mansour neighborhood, as well as one in
the Hassan neighborhood of Rabat and one in Fes. As interest grew among

students, we began to see psychological and public attacks on Amazigh iden-tity. The media began to exploit the colonial-era Berber Dahir.[1] Many pages were dedicated to this event every May 16, aiming to intimidate activists and to portray any action for the Amazigh cause as a call for separatism and racism, as if the Amazigh were the ones who had written the decree.

It is worth noting the nature of these writings. I can cite, for example, Ahmed Sabri's article in the *Al-Raid* magazine on March 2, 1967, "Until When Will Our Heritage Be a Means of Deception and Foolery?" The late El-Mahjoub El-Safrioui published an article titled "This Aspect of Musical Heritage," in *Mudhakarat El-ʿIlm* on March 22, 1969, to which I responded with an article in the same newspaper on March 31. This article, titled "Ama-zighity Is Our National Identity," was my first media appearance after the founding of the association, and I included it in my book. The late Moham-med Aziz Lahbabi published an article in *Al-ʿAlam* newspaper on Decem-ber 1, 1972, under the title "Man Is an Animal That Speaks." These articles were all modest attempts to start delving into the cultural issue, which was receiving ever more attention from thinkers and political activists across Morocco.

In this context, I also recall an important cultural incident that had a sig-nificant impact on interest in popular culture, particularly Amazigh culture and especially as regards scholarly research. It happened that the Moroccan Writers' Union organized a lecture by Professor Abbas El-Jirari in 1968 and the union's club, which was located in the residence that was replaced by the Arab Maghreb Agency on Allal Ben Abdellah street. This lecture was a pre-sentation of his thesis on popular heritage, which he had completed in Cairo. It coincided with my presentation on "Popular Culture, a National Heritage" at the youth house in Kénitra, the same week. Essafi Moumen Ali, Ibrahim Madran, and I attended. Professor Abbas El-Jirari's presentation was limited to the *malḥūn*,[2] as if this was the sole form of popular heritage in our country. He was surprised by our comments, which criticized this systematic exclu-sion of Amazigh culture in his research. We pointed out all the deficiencies in his thesis, including the musical element of the *malḥūn*, which is, at its core, Amazigh.

El-Jirari admitted that we were right, adding that his thesis had not taken into account the Amazigh aspect of Moroccan heritage. So our observations had an impact on El-Jirari, the first professor of Moroccan literature at the University of Fes. From that time onward, he accepted many requests to supervise university theses on subjects relating to Amazigh culture. Indeed, he oversaw Omar Amarir's thesis on Amazigh resistance literature, as well as Ahmed Bouzid's dissertation on the poetry of Omar Wahrouch. The professor stipulated that they include a sample of the poetry in translation from Amazigh, which was an opportunity for him to become familiar with the contents of this poetry, its genres and objectives.

Thirdly, that period saw discrimination between popular culture, whether expressed in Amazigh or Moroccan *dārija* Arabic, and the "official" culture of the cities. Defense of popular culture was also taken up by the Left, which saw official culture, as promoted through the education system, as being connected to the bourgeoisie and particularly with the Makhzen.

Therefore, our struggle on behalf of Amazigh language, culture, and identity was part of a revolutionary, progressive vision, and gave rise to a clear alliance between us and the proponents of *dārija* throughout this period. We used the expression "popular culture" to refer to Amazigh culture in order to preserve this alliance, which involved poets, artists, and writers. This was the culture of the disadvantaged classes—farmers, workers, and the marginalized in general—and within its intellectual depths lay our values and our unique character; thus, it was a culture of struggle and opposition at this time. In the early 1970s, most of the founders of our association had left for France to complete their education in their respective fields. These fields included linguistics, in the case of Ahmed Boukous and Boujoumaa El-Habbaz, and literature in the case of Ahmed Akouaou. They were influenced by Marxist revolutionary thinking in their analysis of Amazigh language and literature. Ali Sidqi Azaykou left to specialize in history.

The natural alliance between the proponents of Amazigh culture and *dārija*, in opposition to the threats they both faced, persisted into the late 1980s. The question of language was settled, and Amazigh activists began to work in the defense of Amazigh linguistic rights outside the context of popular culture, leading to the issuing of the Agadir Charter of 1991.

Fourthly, following the departure of most of the association's founders to France, I found myself alone in Rabat. However, an influx of university students pumped new blood into its veins, and they gave strong momentum to our work at that time. Many of them were able to play important roles in Amazigh cultural activity through the association. One such example was Lhoucine Ait Bahcine, whose involvement was a huge asset to the Amazigh cause generally and to the association in particular, given his deep belief in and loyalty to the cause, both intellectually and through his activism. He was never absent from a meeting about Amazigh issues and was a lively participant in every debate. I came to think of him as the secretary-general of the association, and its living memory.[3]

Here, I recall a scene that has remained vivid in my memory. Lhoucine Jouhadi and his student colleagues were studying at the school of literature, as I have mentioned. Jouhadi was known for his light-hearted jokes. One day, as we were meeting at my house, he dramatically raised a finger and said, "I hereby announce that I have joined Islam!" This was his way of saying that his life had entered a new phase as he had become involved with the association, and that he was happy to be working with the youthful energy present in the room. Jouhadi lived in Casablanca, and he introduced us to many people there, all of them from a single neighborhood, Aïn Chock. They included Abdelaziz Bourass and Mohammed Khalil, as well as Mohamed Moustaoui and Ibrahim Yacine.

It is also worth mentioning here that the involvement of Abdulaziz Bourass in the association would have a major effect on its future. He was an active member of AMEJ, the Moroccan Association for Youth Education, and at the time he was full of the rhetoric of the USFP. My debates with him were often heated. I tried to convince him of the goals of the association and our ambitions for the future, and he would respond with challenging questions and criticisms so he could extract convincing answers, information, and alternatives to his own ideas. The result of these debates was—and I expressed this view in front of everyone—that Abdulaziz Bourass would play a major role in the association and in the Amazigh cause in the future. With his experience both in the association and in a political organization, he knew the meaning of carrying responsibility and of the art of communication and political debate. That is indeed what happened. He joined the association and devoted himself to it full time, with great loyalty and dedication; the Amazigh struggle became part of his daily life, or even the whole of his life. He confronted difficulties and challenges with courage and boldness, and within the association he stood out for his political skill, which was always present when we took a position on an issue. He was never lenient when it came to people who had taken it upon themselves to harm or undermine the Amazigh cause or its principles, whether from within the association or without. He was a great advocate for the Amazigh cause, wherever he went.

A brief mention of the names of students and scholars who joined us in 1971 and 1972 who would go on to play great roles in support of the Amazigh cause and in political life is enough to show the level of enthusiasm for the association shown by students from across Morocco. They included Ajana Ali, Moubarak El-Ardi, Amhamed El-Daser, Douzerki Jama', Mohanned Aït El-Haj, Badri Mohammed, Saïd Oubahmou, Ibrahim Yacine, El-Houcein Atbaji, Hiddou Ichmalel, Lahcene Anane, Issa El-Saadaoui, Mostafa Barakat, Mohammed El-Aroussi, El-Hassan Amsari, El-Hoceine Barahou, Saïd Amhaouech, and Mohammed Annan. Some of these were studying at the Faculty of Letters in Rabat, while others were at the Agronomic and Veterinary Institute Hassan II. Others were teachers in Casablanca, and some were studying medicine in Rabat. They hailed from all parts of Morocco. The association was not yet four years old, but it had already become a meeting place for all the country's people, from the north, the center, and the south, bringing them together in service of their Amazigh identity, through language, culture, and civilization.

Under these political and cultural circumstances, we laid out a plan for the association that aimed to train activists both intellectually and in terms of the struggle, and to deepen the bonds of communication between different social groups in order to deepen their awareness of Amazigh identity. This strategy aimed to intensify cultural activities and to unify and document our heritage.

In the framework of this training program, we organized our first study days. Abdelmalek Ousaden, a member of the association since 1970 (when Ahmed Bouzid, Omar Amarir, and Mohammed Farah, who were students in Fes at the time, had introduced us), allowed us to hold five days of these courses at his residence in Imouzzer Kandar, in December 1971. We took my Renault 4, and on it we carried our bedding from the Dhar El Mehraz University Campus, where a student strike was underway, without thinking of the risks of this operation. We were carrying things related to it without permission from the manager. These training days were attended by Abed Rabbou and Lhoucine Ait Bahceine, Abdullah El-Rahmani and El-Hoceine Ajkoune from Rabat, as well as by Ahmed Bouzid, Omar Amarir, and Mohammed Farah from Fes. These meetings were discreet and quiet, which allowed us to discuss many ideas and concepts in order to arrive at clear and unified conclusions that we could use in the Amazigh struggle and counter all the challenges we faced. Such meetings had a major impact on us and our personal relationships as well as our intellectual development, and the struggle.

It is worth noting that during the 1970s, a project was proposed to teach Persian and Hebrew at the Faculty of Literature in Fes, in the context of what was labeled "reform" of the faculty's curriculum. Some members of the association and others who were active on Amazigh issues demanded that Amazigh language also be taught, as it was a national language and should be offered before foreign languages.

We also had relationships with many small- and medium-scale business owners. In 1971 such people in Rabat began to be hassled by employment authorities and the ministry of commerce, which exploited the lack of foodstuffs such as milk and other commodities to bully merchants, particularly small-scale business owners. They used all forms of intimidation and imposed fines without any reasonable or convincing justification, to the point where they would take them to police stations and humiliate them, sometimes as a group. The traders could not stand this situation and this irresponsible behavior toward them. We decided to act to resolve this situation. As a group, including El-Mehdi El-Suleimani, Abdulmalek Azdou, and Abdellah Masrour, we undertook to train the federation of small traders on how to defend their interests and to organize their sector. We started by presenting a memorandum to the Chamber of Commerce, which was headed at the time by the late El-Hasan El-Idrissi. I drafted the note myself. It contained all the ideas the small business owners had suggested to resolve the crisis afflicting them. Shortly afterward, we wrote an organizational charter for their new union, the Union of Small and Medium-Scale Merchants. Its founding congress was held at the Fairouz Cinema in Hassan II Street in Rabat on October 29, 1971. I wrote the inaugural speech, which I delivered on behalf of the union's president Sadiqi El-Hajj El-Mahdi El-Suleimani. With that, the union was launched, with the aim of protecting the interests of small-scale traders. The union presented a petition to the local authorities on November 10 of the same year. This had a major impact on the morale of the businessmen concerned, as someone was finally showing them support during the crisis they faced that year. From the start, our work was comprehensive and was not limited to cultural activities. Rather, we aimed to link it to its social and political surroundings so it could have a genuine impact.

In the early 1970s, as I have mentioned, we were very active in many areas, including training, communications, and intellectual work. Yet, during this period, most of the founding members of the association were living outside of the country. Ali Sidqi Azaykou and Boujoumaa El-Habbaz continuously wrote me letters and informed me of the group's awareness-raising activities in France, part of the discussions that took place at Dar El-Maghreb in Paris between members of the association and others who had adhered to different ideologies. Given this situation, we all made use of the summer holidays to renew contact with other members of the association, both inside the country and overseas, to crystallize our ideas and strengthen our relationships.

However, this absence never impacted the work of the association's members. As I have mentioned, a generation of enthusiastic students had joined since its foundation. Through our gatherings at the Youth Café and during the many meetings held at the building on Al-Alouyine Street, which simultaneously served as the association's headquarters, important ideas were conceived that reflected our cultural and political ambitions to serve Amazigh language and culture. We also considered ways to convey our work to the general public, fully aware that this effort would deepen awareness of the Amazigh identity among all Moroccans, Amazigh speakers and non-speakers alike. Among our most important projects in the early seventies, in addition to collecting and documenting heritage, were the following:

Firstly, we filmed a silent short film in response to the idea of an African thinker who said, "When an old African dies, a whole treasury of history and thought perishes with him." We felt that this statement applied to our literature and culture, which was in a precarious state, preserved by elderly men and women, and that the loss of any one of these would result in the disappearance of a vast wealth of our literary heritage and the landmarks of our civilization and our regional history. Therefore, we decided to bring this idea to fruition and bought a Super 8 camera. I had my Renault 4 and a small tent, and in the spring of 1972, we produced the silent film. The screenplay, written by Essafi Moumen Ali, told the story of a university student preparing a thesis on Amazigh literature. He was informed that there was an old man in a nearby village who had memorized much of this inherited literature. The student decided to search for this old man, without even knowing his address, armed only with his picture and the name of his village. Upon arriving at the village, he was shocked to discover that the old man had died that very day, a terrible tragedy. The people who were to make this film agreed that Ibrahim Medran would be the director, and that I would play the lead role, portraying the life of the university student. Ahmed El-Ghazali, Essafi Moumen Ali, Ibrahim Medran, and Mohamed Mastour were also involved; Essafi and Medran would take turns filming. We left from Rabat station and headed to Tiznit and Tafraouent and finally to Imi Ogchtim and the home Ahmed El-Ghazali. The film was indeed shot, and we still have a copy of it. It is the first Amazigh short film ever made, and it aims to draw attention to the threats of extinction and disappearance faced by our language and culture, unless urgent measures are taken to preserve and protect them from the threats they face. We had a lot of fun filming it, and we have beautiful memories of the time, linked to the roles we each played or to our individual characters, which sometimes provoked humor and satire, infusing our lives with an unforgettable flavor and sense of intimacy. I would like to evoke God's mercy on the late mother of my friend Ahmad Al-Ghazali for her efforts during our stay at her home, where she did everything she could to make us comfortable. I also want to thank Daabid, one of the men of Imi Ogchtim who has preserved the history of the region and knows its historical figures. In his youth, he also experienced the arrival of colonialism and the fight against it. He was a guide to us and never failed to provide us with animals and everything else we needed, in a welcoming and hospitable way.

The significance of this experience was that despite our lack of financial resources and the difficult political and cultural situation, all of which worked against us achieving our projects and bringing our ideas to completion, our desire and enthusiasm meant that we could see past all these difficulties. In fact, we were full of joy as we were accomplishing these projects, feeling that we were achieving victories for Amazigh identity and culture and their future.

In 2008, during a personal visit to my friend Ahmed El-Ghazali, who was by then head of the High Authority for Audiovisual Communication, I presented him with a copy of this short, silent film in which he had played a role, as he was then a student and a member of the association. I told him, "This is the association's first audiovisual achievement, accomplished in 1972, and you were an actor in it. Now you're the head of the High Authority for Audiovisual Communication. See how things have changed!" He was very pleased, as it took him totally by surprise; he believed the film had been lost a long time before. It was a rare document that reminded him of an unforgettable period of his life, when he was an active young member of the association.

In 1972, I conceived, along with a group of fellow association members, the idea of preparing some radio programs and recording them on a Grundig cassette recorder that I had purchased from Germany during my visit there with Ali Sidqi Azaykou. We reached an agreement on these lines with some colleagues at the Amazigh radio station, especially for the weekly radio show *Inmougaren Imlass*. These programs covered various subjects of interest to a general audience, including business, culture, and social affairs. Of course, our aim was to use these programs to convey some of our ideas in these areas. We would select our guests and take them to my home, where the recording would take place. Then, we would take these recordings to the radio station, and they would be integrated into the relevant programs. Ahmed Amzal, Hussein Barhou, and Hamid Soussi played a significant role in this process. Among those we interviewed in the field of commerce was El-Mahdi Suleimani, the president of the Rabat Chamber of Commerce from the early 1960s, and Abdul Malek Azdou. The students included Mohamad Ourhou, who was studying management and later joined the military academy in Meknes. I was also among those interviewed, as were other students and professors. This process lasted more than a year, until the machine was moved to the city of Ouarzazate, when Essafi Moumen Ali was appointed as a judge there in 1973. He intended to use it to record the late, great artist Mohamed Bin Yehya Outanaght.

THE SITUATION OF AMAZIGH ACTIVISM

Following from this overview of the association's efforts to attract graduates who would become effective activists for the Amazigh cause, after they had been trained and intellectually developed to empower them to carry out this noble work, we should pause to recall the difficult and dangerous conditions under which we were operating during this period of Morocco's political and cultural history, including prosecutions, abductions, and other abuses.

To understand this situation, suffice to say that some graduates would arrive at meetings held at my house, looking right and left for fear they were being followed by an informant, as if they were coming to a prohibited place or were about to perform a secret, banned act. Sometimes, under certain circumstances, these young men would stop attending at all, to avoid harassment. My friend Essafi Moumen Ali once confided in me that he continued to attend the meetings despite the danger, for fear that I would succumb to a despair that would make me abandon these activities given these terrifying conditions, which often discouraged others from attending scheduled meetings. In response to this situation, I tried to organize some artistic activities, such as theatrical or entertaining performances, to dispel any suspicions about us and give monitors the impression that we were only interested in "folklore," as Amazigh culture was labeled at the time. At the same time, we conducted serious theoretical presentations with intellectual and political content at home, away from the watchful eyes of the censors. These limited presentations contributed significantly to the activists' theoretical and intellectual training, and certain members were tasked with preparing them. All attendees then discussed them, and then they were formulated, especially if they pertained to concepts on which we needed to agree, in order to use them as tools of persuasion in the Amazigh discourse we were in the process of developing, to correct the mixed-up concepts that were prevalent.

As an example of these activities, I recall that Essafi Moumen Ali was one of the first people to take an interest in developing Amazigh songs, by creating a model that bridged the traditional and the modern, so that contemporary Amazigh music could meet the demands of the era and match the tastes of the youth. He was assisted in this by our friend Ibrahim Madran and a group of students who were members of the association. I remember among them El-Hassan Abakrim from the Faculty of Law, Ali Amjoudh from the Faculty of Sciences, El-Hussein Bakenzi from the Mohammadia School of Engineers, and Abdallah Ouamou from the medical school. We all used to meet at the house of El-Hassan Abakrim, in Agdal, to train or to simply enjoy ourselves a little in order to forget our difficult circumstances. This group, led by Essafi Moumen Ali, participated in a concert held at the Mohammadia School of Engineers, by the Amazigh students. All forms of Amazigh art were represented, from Ahidous and Raiss songs to a new style of modern singing presented by the group. All this activity, both in organization and performance, was carried out by Amazigh students from various regions of Morocco.

If one were to try to deduce the state's position on us at the time, I believe there were two possibilities. The first was that maybe, given that the association did not have a name that stirred curiosity, the authorities believed that our interest was purely in culture and were not aware of the political aspect of our work, especially as everyone believed that Arab nationalism had conquered the cultural and political sphere and that supporting the Amazigh cause was to ride against the current or try to raise the dead, an accusation some people used to deploy to mock us. The second possibility was that we were not seen as hostile toward the political system, as we did not get involved in any political activity that indicated such a leaning, which was what mattered to the authorities at the time.

In the midst of this politically charged atmosphere and the intellectual terrorism practiced against us by political parties with nationalist ideologies, who advocated for Arabism in language, culture, and identity, and were opposed to any alternative views, we also faced down the culturally colonized elite. Whether consciously or as hired pens, they served Arab nationalist thought and opposed anything national. They practiced intellectual terrorism against us by labeling us with the ugliest of accusations: We were creating divisions and sowing separatism, supporting colonialism and atheism, calling for a return to the time of pre-Islamic ignorance, and countless other charges. All this was intended to undermine our resolve and stir doubts about our work, deterring students from joining the Amazigh cause and inciting society against us in order to isolate and harm us.

THE PHASE OF DOCUMENTATION AND WRITING

I have mentioned that one of the most important strategic goals the association set for itself was the documentation of oral Amazigh heritage in written form. This was a key historical moment in the history of the Amazigh, as they had long neglected to document their thoughts and creativity in their own Amazigh language, causing the loss of most of our heritage and our artistic, literary, and intellectual creations. All that remained was that which had been preserved in oral narratives over the centuries. The association's effort was thus a strategic, political, and intellectual transformation in the history of our national culture in general and of Amazigh culture in particular, as it would mark the beginning of a new era in which Amazigh culture would be strengthened as an intellectual and material reality in the cognitive and intellectual arenas, and would liberate the national culture from its dependency on other cultures or imported ideological systems.

The association, having decided to gather and document this heritage from the mouths of Amazigh men and women, faced many difficulties: The first was the social aspect. Many people, women and men, were reluctant to have their voices recorded, as some believed that doing so was a religious taboo, while others feared their poetry would be used for political purposes, as it often related to historical events and included certain names that were sensitive to mention. To overcome the challenge of writing the language, the association invented a unique combination of Arabic and Aramaic script, combined with Latin orthographic rules to address problems of shapes. This innovation was the brainchild of my brothers Ali Bennour and Omar Al-Khalfaoui. It was a stopgap measure, as we did not yet know the *Tifinagh* writing system. We called our method the "Arraten" method for writing the Amazigh language.

This was the script we later used in the *Arraten* journal on Amazigh heritage, which I shall discuss later. However, everyone was free to choose between this method and Latin script. Some Amazigh from Europe chose the latter method when they were recording poetry or prose they had collected or created. At this stage, our priority was simply to salvage whatever could be salvaged and documented, to make sure it was preserved first, so it could later become a resource and be made available to students and researchers.

Collecting this oral heritage posed major challenges. During the summer vacation of 1973, I set out to record a collection of poems about the Ait Baha incident, an uprising against French colonialism in March 1936. I was directed to a poet from Ait Bahman, my mother's tribe, who had memorized poems about the uprising. My father had prepared his mule for me to go and meet the man, saying, "You know the way to the oasis of Targua Ntouchka. When you get there, ask someone to guide you out, and then the mule will know the route and will take you to your mother's family's village to contact the poet and persuade him to let you record him." Indeed, I followed my father's instructions, but after I left the oasis, the weather became very hot, and the mule insisted on heading toward any village other than the one I was headed for, seeking rest.

Thus, I visited many villages before finally I reached one where a celebration was taking place. Among the crowd, I found some members of my mother's family, who accompanied me to the sought-after poet. I spent much time with him recording his memories of the Ait Baha event, including poetry that glorified its heroes, as well as mentioning the names of traitors among the elders of tribes that had taken part in the uprising, as well as some individuals who had shown their cowardice on the battlefield.

Upon my return to Rabat, I was informed that the poet had been bombarded with rumors that I would broadcast his poems and that there would be terrible consequences, including that he would be pursued by the grandchildren of the people whose names he had mentioned. Overcome with anxiety, he sent messages to me in Rabat, via my relatives, to plead with me not to use or broadcast the recording. He added that if I wanted more poetry, he was happy to provide it, on the condition that it remained secret. I reassured him by promising not to broadcast the recording nor to disclose the names.

In the academic year 1973–74, the association decided to begin publishing a periodical, the first of its kind in the history of Amazigh activism. The association held a meeting, attended by many activists, to discuss the project and how it would be organized and financed, and the journal published. Among those present were Dr. Abdelmalek Ousaden and Ali Sidqi Azaykou. I mention these two key figures specifically because they proposed that we each contribute three hundred dirhams to fund the project and make it viable. Azaykou suggested we name the journal "The Documentary Bulletin" (*Al-Nashra Al-Wathāʾiqiyya*), as its goal was to collect and document rather than to analyze. Although this meeting marked the launch of the project, turning it into a reality was not as easy as some of us thought. The first difficulty was a lack of commitment by some members to the financing we had agreed on. Regarding the literary aspect, I shuttled between many acquaintances at the association who were interested in collecting this heritage so that they would grant me access to what they had gathered. At times I felt demeaned as I begged them for access, considering the time and energy it consumed. It was during this period that I first met Professor Mohammed Chafik, who used to write about Amazigh literature in the magazine *Āfāq*, which was affiliated with the Moroccan Writers' Union. We had been introduced by my friend Abdelmalek Ousadden. I also met Ahmed Chouki, a professor of Arabic literature at Mohammed V University but originally from Imouzzer Kandar, as well as Nait Abdelhamid from Ahermoumou, and El-Hussein Brahou, who worked at the Amazigh radio station and came from Khenifra. All of them came to collaborate on this project, either as members of, or sympathizers with, the association. I also relied on university students to collect what they could from their regions during vacations, or the proverbs and poetic verses they had memorized, for various purposes.

Despite all the difficulties, we published the first issue of the periodical at the beginning of 1974. We turned to some small traders we had known since the founding of the association, who placed their trust in our work and supported us with twenty or thirty dirhams each to help us get it published. We obtained a duplicating machine from our friend Hassan Ouchakour, the owner of the Scar bookstore, and we bought stencil paper. Aicha Adraz, a member of my family who was an employee at the Ministry of Post, volunteered to carry out the printing process. The duplication was done at my house, assisted by Mohamed Khalil, Abdullah Darqawi (may he rest in peace), and some students. In these challenging conditions, the periodical was published. Its first issue carried the title "The Documentary Bulletin," but we immediately changed the name in the second issue to *Arraten: A Periodic Journal Concerned with Amazigh Culture*, given the contradiction between the Arabic name and the Amazigh content in the first edition.

The publication of this Amazigh journal had a significant impact on the general public and among intellectuals. We were asked many questions by small traders and ordinary people, who had not been aware that the Amazigh language could even be written down. They were surprised to see, in writing, texts that they had previously memorized orally, such as those by Sidi Hemmu Ettaleb and other pioneers of Amazigh poetry. Being written down had added value to these texts; now they could be understood in their documented form. We also found written terminology and ancient proverbs we could hear and memorize for the first time. The journal also became the primary means of communication between the association and a broad readership of students, who saw it as a tool to help them convince others to join this revolutionary cultural project, whether by joining the association or by supporting the publication and helping it reach more readers, or preserving it so it could made it available to everyone, especially research students.

The release of the first and second issues of the journal created a new dynamic among university students and the general public who read it. Some mocked us for our interest in reviving a heritage they deemed outdated and of little value, while others accused those responsible of wanting to return to the pre-Islamic state of ignorance (*jāhiliyya*) and of having what they saw as a regressive longing for the past. These were issues that Amazigh activists had to confront and address with conviction, especially as Moroccan society was dominated by cultural illiteracy and an ignorance of its own Amazigh identity. Given that the vast majority of the society with which we interacted, especially in Rabat, Casablanca, Kénitra, and Marrakech, were from the Souss region, I feared that such judgments and misguided ideas of the association's intentions might reach the religious scholar and leader Sidi El-Hajj El-Habib, the head of the Tanalt school in our region of Ait Souab, and that he might issue a religious ruling against us. This would have a major impact on the general Amazigh public in Souss, as nobody among the general public would contest his opinion.

As my fears mounted, I decided to take preemptive action by visiting him at the old school in Tanalt, to explain our cultural project to the esteemed leader in person. I must note that he had been an advisor to Ahmed El- Haiba, who had led the uprising in Souss that expelled French colonial forces and managed to enter Marrakech before being defeated at Sidi Bou Othman. He had then sought refuge in the Spanish-occupied area to the south, until he was permitted to return to Souss, under house arrest, at the Tanalt school, in our region of Ait Souab. He was a well-known scholar in the Islamic world, a great Sufi who had traveled to the Middle East and debated with scholars from Egypt's Al-Azhar University, as well as visiting India, Bangladesh, and Turkey. He had made his first pilgrimage to the holy places on foot.

In the summer of 1974, I decided to visit Sheikh Hajj El-Habib in Tanalt. Professor Omar Afa, a history teacher at Mohammed V University, accompanied me. We decided to have lunch at a festival organized by El-Hajj Ibrahim Fadhl Kheir, the brother of Idriss El-Hassan who owned the Jour et Nuit café. He too wished to accompany me on the visit to the sheikh, but he wasn't able to. Upon our arrival at the school, we were received by Hamid Outgananine, the sheikh's first assistant, who conveyed to him my desire to speak with him. He instructed us to enter, and we found the sheikh sitting in a corner on the upper floor of the school. He was wrapped in his usual white *izār* (a simple religious garment). He was blind and nearly one hundred years old. I sat to his left and Omar to his right. I introduced myself, and he knew of my father, may God have mercy on him. The Sheikh asked, "Have you come for a visit or something else?"

"Yes, sir, I came for a visit and for something else," I responded.

"What is this other thing?"

I began to explain to him the problems that Amazigh-speaking Moroccans faced within the country and abroad, and the marginalization and suffering afflicting their language and culture. Yet, no sooner had I started describing aspects of this suffering than he grasped the implications of what I was saying. He interrupted me, asking me to wait, and told his assistant to gather the school's teachers. They formed a circle around us. Then the sheikh gestured to me and said, "Start what you were saying again, from the beginning." I began once again to explain to everyone the situation of Amazigh language, culture, and identity, as well as the problems faced by Amazigh speakers in Arabized environments and the ways Amazigh language was excluded from the education system and the media. I explained that this had inspired us to establish an association to preserve our language and culture and to prevent them from disappearing. As I was about to finish my presentation, he started tapping his hand on my knee and appeared visibly relieved. This surprised all the teachers, who were not accustomed to seeing him in such a joyful and comfortable mood. The sheikh then asked Outgananine to take a look at the copies of *Arraten* I had brought with me. Outgananine read some of the titles to him, and then the Sheikh began to speak.

"Know that this country, which you see as barren, and where life is difficult, and where the life people can have is modest, was once a country of scholars in every field of knowledge, from mathematics to astronomy and religious sciences. It is a country of creativity and innovation. However, the Middle East has never seen us like this. Instead, they see themselves as our superiors in everything. I have traveled to Egypt and debated them, to prove to them that our country is one of science and knowledge, more than they appreciate, and that it is linguistically and culturally unique." Here, he paused, then continued. "Know that in the history of nations, as in our current state, circumstances arrive like a layer of dust, trying to obscure the truth or change reality, until time brings salvation, which blows away that dust, allowing the truth to shine forth, evident to all, like a blooming, ripe rose." It was clear to us what he meant: that our work was something that had come to remove the dust, as he put it, with which the opponents of Amazigh identity in Morocco had tried to use to obscure the true nature of our people and change our cultural and civilizational reality. This was his way of endorsing our work and encouraging us to continue, with courage, to remove the dust from our history, defending our national identity in language, culture, and civilization, a national project that would bring good to the country.

After the sheikh had finished talking and we had eaten a meal, Outgananine spoke to me.

"Forgive me," he said. "I didn't know that this matter was as important as the sheikh explained. I will not sleep tonight until I have read both of these issues of *Arraten* from cover to cover."

This meeting gave me a strong impetus to continue with our work. Psychologically, I had been in dire need of such a push. The sheikh was a man of politics, who expressed his deep understanding of our noble goal. I understood from him, as he listened to our explanation, that he had had the same concerns in his youth, taking part in the campaign against French colonialism to protect his nation's distinct identity, and that he was pleased to see people working to save and promote the Amazigh language, which was his everyday language and the language of his education.

Sheikh El-Hajj El-Habib's understanding and enthusiasm for our association's project helped us greatly in countering certain religious scholars who opposed our work out of ignorance, especially those who considered us antireligion or advocates for a return to the *jāhiliyya*.

The following year, I returned to visit the old school in Tanalt, accompanied by Essafi Moumen Ali. After being received by the sheikh, we contacted the scholar Outgananine, who again expressed his admiration for our work. He took us to his room at the school, where he showed us a selection of textbooks for learning foreign languages. From our conversation, we learned that he had traveled extensively in Europe, so we discussed with him the idea of developing the school's educational curriculum and adding some scientific and historical subjects, so that students who had completed their religious studies would have a general culture enabling them to live their lives and integrate easily into society. The scholar told us that he was convinced by the ideas we had presented to him, but he was powerless to implement them at this stage of the school's life. In 1980, I visited the scholar again, this time accompanied by my friend Ibrahim Akdime. He had become the custodian of the old Tanalt school and told us of ongoing difficulties with the local authorities following the death of the sheikh.

Arraten was now launched, and, thanks to the efforts of activists from the association and beyond, it became an important reference for research students. It also played a pioneering role in documenting Amazigh heritage across different regions of Morocco and was a resource for students writing research papers in the social sciences, especially those in the last year of their bachelor's degrees in literature. Dr. Abbas El-Jirari was the first professor to supervise such projects, being a professor of Moroccan literature.

Among the dissertation topics I recall are the following:

- "Popular Poetry in the *Amanūz* Tribe," by Belkassem Chaouan, in the academic year 1975–1976
- "Popular Poetry in the *Znāga* Amazigh Tribe," by Aicha Jaber, 1976–1977
- "A Study on *al-rāisa* Poetry of the *Damsīriyya*," by Ali Id Ali, 1978–1979
- "Amazigh Proverbs: A Collection and Study," by Zahri Mohammed, 1978–1979
- "Analytical Study of the Poetry of Hajj Mohammad Ben Yahya," by student Mohammad El-Khatib, 1979–1980

This last study was the fruit of significant efforts by Essafi Moumen Ali and Imhammed Akram, who were both judges in the city of Ouarzazate. The association had provided them with a tape recorder, and they used the same tapes as I had purchased from Spain during my visit there with Ali Sidqi Azaykou. They used to invite the late Rais Hajj Mohammad Ben Yahya Outazanaght to their home every Friday and record discussions on Amazigh poetry. He would tell them about all his unpublished works and the artists he had known. They were able to record everything the late Rais was able to offer them. These recordings then formed the basis upon which student Mohammad El-Khatib based his research, converting it from oral to written form. He also provided us with a photograph of the artist, something we had not been able to find. I recount this example of our work to demonstrate the major historical contribution these efforts to document and record made to rescuing our literature and arts alike. The judges had hardly completed their project when Rais Mohammad Ben Yahya passed away. He had been a treasure trove of knowledge on oral Amazigh literature and the singers of old. In the middle of 1973, Ali Azaykou and I visited Essafi Moumen Ali and Imhammed Akram, who were newly appointed as judges in Ouarzazate. This wasn't a holiday or a particular occasion, but we had decided to visit to boost their morale, as they were living in quasi-exile in this marginalized city, which had few facilities. We chose the route passing through the city of Midelt, although we took little note of the political conditions and the tension in the region at the time.

We reached the heights of the Middle Atlas at night. The weather was cold, and snow was falling. We came across a military surveillance and gendarmerie checkpoint, where the officers had lit a fire and were gathering around it. They led us to a police station to verify our identities. They were suspicious about us, because it was not a school holiday, and we had introduced ourselves as teachers. They tried to interrogate us to find out where we were going and the real reason for our wanderings through this near-deserted region. The only way we could get ourselves released was by mentioning the name of a prominent figure in the region, who was a university friend of Ali Sidqi Azaykou. Fortunately, the gendarmes knew him. Only after Ali told them his name and described him would they allow us to leave the station and continue our journey in my car, until we reached a café where the truck drivers used to rest. We had now crossed the Atlas Mountains, and we were on the outskirts of Ouarzazate. We spent the night at this stopover, lying on the ground, so we could continue our journey once the sun had risen and we had eaten breakfast at the café.

Before I move on to another topic, I want to mention something else in the context of preserving cultural heritage and the need to document it to prevent it from being lost. Dr. Abdelmalek Ousaden used to hold wonderful poetic gatherings at his home, inviting many *imdiyāzen* (poets) from the region and recording samples of this heritage that they had composed or memorized. He played for me many of those recordings, which numbered in the dozens, and I suggested that we include them in the program we were about to launch, assigning students to incorporate them into their university research. Sadly, however, he did not respond to this suggestion.

In the early 1970s, I met Professor Mohammed Chafik and began to visit him at his home, where he provided me with history books to read and benefit from. Conversations with him were a rich source of ideas and valuable information in all fields. I used to ask him to provide articles for publication in our journals *Arraten* and *al-Tabādul al-Thaqāfi* (Cultural Exchange).

Another aspect of our efforts to document the Amazigh language and transform it from oral to written form was to encourage young people to write in Amazigh, especially the generation who had a university education, in order to overcome the traditional nature of Amazigh culture that was prevalent at the time. Thus, the association began to encourage the youth to create poetic works in Amazigh that were modern, both in content and form. Some wrote in the old style of metered verse, while others wrote free poetry, which had become a phenomenon among poets in Arabic and other languages. This meant that the association produced poets like Ali Sidqi Azaykou, Ahmed Bouzid, Ahmed El-Ghazali, Mohamed Farah, Mohamed Moustaoui, Lhoucine Jouhadi, Essafi Moumen Ali, and Hussein Berhou. We encouraged these poets by providing them with a platform to recite their works at meetings or cultural gatherings in various cities. Building on the association's strategy of encouraging writing in Amazigh, we decided to issue our first Amazigh poetry collection, printing it with stencils, as we had when we published *Arraten*, because we were not yet able to print books due to our limited resources. Thus, the association published the first collective Amazigh poetry book in 1974, under the name *Amouzar*, which included many poems from the association's early members. They included the following:

- The poem *Yan Irzan Zaj Nas*, by Ahmed Bouzid, from Souss, under the pen name Azdoud Hammad
- Two poems by Chouki Mohammed from Imouzzer Marmoucha: *Anzioum* and *Watit Raitoutra Anfarou*

- Two poems by Berhou El-Hassan, from Khenifra: *Ouad Asrouqah Tyoutmin* and *Ais Tmout Ajab*
- The poem *Tazarzit* by Abaamran El-Hussein (Lhoucine Jouhadi) from Souss
- *Imi Mqourn*, by Essafi Moumen Ali, from Souss, writing under the pseudonym Amzal Ali
- *Azru* by Mohamed Farah, under the pseudonym Outznakht Mohamed, from Taznakht
- *Tawada Nik*, by Mohamed Moustaoui, from Souss
- Two poems by Ahmed El-Ghazali from Souss, writing under the pseudonym Asafu Ahmed: *Butayri* and *Dunit*
- Four poems by the author, under the pseudonym Sagho Ibrahim: *Tabrat, Lamsaq n Tabrat, Todrt,* and *Amzwak*
- Three poems by Ali Sidqi Azaykou: *Tamkra n Ijdeiken, Talalit* and *Maryama*

Ahmed Bouzid contributed an extensive introduction to the book, in Arabic, in which he discussed Amazigh poetic meters and the themes covered by the poems in this modern collection, the first of its type in the field of written Amazigh literature. The collection also began with a statement from the association, which read: "This Amazigh poetry collection is part of the authors' selves, and is thus a reflection of their personality and stance on life. From this stems the collection's importance and our encouragement for their writings, in which these authors have crystallized their thoughts and expressed their emotions and pains, as they have sincerely and faithfully expressed their problems and those of their people."

THE ASSOCIATION AND POLITICAL PROJECTS IN THE LATE 1970S

Starting in 1976, after his return from France, our late brother Ali Sidqi Azaykou, who was my deputy on the board of the association, began searching for a new project for himself, something that would provide a framework in which he could practice something closer to political activity, rather than the cultural work in which he had been involved at the association. This began to manifest in his relationships and conversations with some of the association's members, whom he hoped would accompany him in this desire. He also made contacts with others outside the association, particularly in Rabat and Fes. I had introduced him to Dr. Abdelmalek

Ousaden in Fes. Azaykou also began contacting members of the association, especially those from the Atlas, such as Mohammed Aanan, Issa
Aanan, Hassan El-Arrousi, and Ahmed Chouki. He believed that members
from the Atlas region were more inclined toward political activity than the
others, and moreover, as they worked within the state, they had it within their
power to achieve great things for the Amazigh cause. He spoke honestly with
me on this subject. Within the same context, he also made contact with Idriss
El-Khattabi, the son of Mohammed Abdelkrim El-Khattabi, in Fes, as well as
contacting a group led by Ali Oudadis. Mohammed Amhazoun wrote to me
about the subject from Fes on March 8, 1975. Most of these people were
members of the association, with the exception of Idriss El-Khattabi.

Azaykou also attempted to win over other members of the association
in Casablanca, Agadir, and Rabat, but they rejected his offers. In Rabat, he
attended a meeting at the house of Dr. El-Zaki Moubarak. I had been invited
to this meeting but did not attend, asking Lhoucine Jouhadi to go in my place
to find out what would be discussed. The meeting was attended by the late
Lahcen Ismail Chihabi and by Abdellah El-Sanhaji, who were in the process
of preparing to establish the Labor Party. After the meeting, Ali Azaykou got
into an argument with Lhoucine Jouhadi, who had commented on Azaykou's intervention in a way that led Azaykou to believe that Lhoucine Jouhadi
was accusing him of belonging to a political group without the association's
knowledge, and of failing to act transparently. The argument grew heated, as
they made their way to my home, where I had waited up until past midnight,
as Lhoucine was to spend the night there. They arrived in a state of high
tension, exchanging accusations. It reached a point where Ali Azaykou asked
me to call for an extraordinary meeting of the association's council to settle
the dispute and examine what he felt was a serious accusation against him.
However, with the help of Boujoumaa El-Habbaz, I managed to resolve the
dispute, and we agreed that every member of the association has the right to
be politically affiliated and there was nothing to prevent the exercise of this
constitutional right.

In the same context of change, in all directions, Ali Sidqi Azaykou,
Ahmed Chouki, and Idriss El-Khattabi established the Moroccan Association for Knowledge and Culture. It published an Arabic-language periodical,
Tidrine, of which there was only one issue, and which was notable in that all
of its articles were published anonymously. Azaykou continued searching
for a new group that shared his ambition to carry out his project, a group that
he set up outside the association he had helped found and outside the group
with which he had begun his long journey as an activist and intellectual. But
he clashed with his colleagues in setting up the Moroccan Association for

Knowledge and Culture. He had hoped that, with them, he could establish a new project, but ultimately they left him isolated. While some activists entered communal elections or turned to projects aimed at fulfilling their personal ambitions, Azaykou had been thinking of the general good. Idriss El-Khattabi was killed in a traffic accident between Rabat and Casablanca, while Ahmed Chouki was appointed to a job at the office of the minister of transport, El-Mansouri, and worked with him at the Mediterranean Sea Association, a well-known association of the mountains and plains. Chouki completely severed his ties with associative work and did not maintain any connection with Amazigh activism. However, Ali Azaykou remained in contact with our association, although he was always occupied with his political activities. Unfortunately, he continued to choose comrades with this goal in mind, something I discussed with him at length. My stance, in summary, was that our efforts to promote the Amazigh language, culture, and identity, and our work to deepen awareness of our Amazigh self, were a much larger and more political project than the superficial politics in which he was involved. Correct political activity should be built on a foundation of discourse and by preparing suitable men, not through arbitrary and superficial politics as we see today.

However, I would like to express a word of truth about my late friend Ali. He was like a brother to me, and I to him. We considered each other's homes our own. Neither of us needed to ask for permission to enter the other's house. We became like family. His mother was like my own, addressing us both as her sons, and my brother's wife, who was like my mother, saw him as one of the family, affectionately calling him "Ali Boutagourt." He was a man truly committed to his cause and to our collective Amazigh cause, with the faith of the sincere believer. He had no personal ambitions to fulfill through it, and his ascetic behavior and disdain for material things enabled him to dedicate all his intellectual energy to serving his Amazigh language, culture, and identity without self-interested calculations. Throughout our work together, our numerous travels and our deep, ongoing discussions, we never once had a fight or uttered a word against each other. Although he distanced himself from AMREC, which he had cofounded, he never resigned from it, because he belonged to it in spirit and body, and he never uttered a sentence that could harm it or diminish from its pioneering role in defense of the Amazigh cause. All that mattered to him was his obsession with a social program that he was trying to achieve in line with his own ideas. May God have mercy on him: When he passed away, we lost an eloquent poet, a national historian, and a firm believer in the struggle. I will return to him again in this memoir. After returning from France, he was elected to the role of deputy general secretary in June 1974, and did not withdraw from his responsibilities until the general assembly in October 1978.

As the formation of the Liberal Party approached completion in 1974, a general assembly of the new party's membership was held at the house of the late Najem Abaakil, in Casablanca. Most of those present were directors of companies. The meeting was attended by party founder Ahmed Oulhaj Akhannouch, as well as Ibrahim Charfeddine, who was tasked with managing the party's newspaper, *Al-Adalah*. We already knew him, as he was a history professor in Rabat. Wishing to understand the party's direction and its stance on the Amazigh issue, I suggested to Azaykou and Chouki that they accompany me to the meeting, because I was aware of their interest in politics. I also had a good relationship with Akhannouch, having mediated between him and those who wanted to establish the Labor Party, in order to unify them and avoid creating two parties at the same time. I also had a good relationship with the late Najem Abaakil. During the gathering, I asked many questions about the party's manifesto, its projects regarding the Amazigh issue, and the added value that the establishment of a new party would bring to political life in Morocco. Ibrahim Charfeddine gave me unsatisfactory answers on the topic. After we had left the meeting, he told me that he understood the meaning of my question and had been deliberately vague in his answers. I understood his answer and his reluctance to debate with me, as I had no wish to irritate him. Rather, we agreed to arrange a private meeting with him to discuss the possibility of cooperating with the party's newspaper, *Al-Adalah*, and what this platform could offer to the Amazigh cause.

During the mid-1970s, Omar Dahkoun and others went on trial, charged with involvement in an anti-government conspiracy. After the trials ended and Dr. Omar El-Khattabi was released from prison, I was contacted by Mohammed Kaboun, a lawyer at the Rabat court. He had also been among those arrested, for allegedly failing to inform the authorities about Dahkoun's activities. Kaboun had also been my schoolmate at the Mohammed V high school in Rabat, before he moved to Nahda, a district of Salé. He told me about his time in prison, saying that while he was under torture, he and Omar Al-Khattabi both noticed a strange difference in the harsh treatment of detainees from the rural areas, unlike others who were given more privileged conditions, including better food, blankets, and other things. As they were discussing this topic, Kaboun had told Al-Khattabi about me and how, since high school, I would tell my classmates and friends about the Amazigh issue and the marginalization and exclusion affecting Amazigh people, language, and culture, and about the disdain among urban, educated people toward everything Amazigh and generally toward anything associated with the rural areas.

The doctor had then asked him to introduce us after his release from prison, so he asked me to meet him at Kaboun's house in Salé, with just the three of us present. I accepted the invitation. During the meeting, I explained to El-Khattabi that I knew him well, as I was teaching at Attaqadoum High School in Kénitra, and I mentioned many names of my teacher friends and union members who used to visit him regularly. He was surprised that I had never introduced myself to him before. I replied, honestly, that I had met him when he was delivering a fiery speech at an office in Bab Fes, in Kénitra, and that he was totally engrossed in the Palestinian cause and the Middle Eastern and Arab issues, and that he had influenced people with his charisma. I did not appreciate this, as it seemed to me that he was distracted by other people's issues, prioritizing them over what matters to the Moroccan people, who were in dire need of someone to guide them and raise their awareness on the issues that concern them, whether economic, social, political, or cultural. After our discussion, he confirmed to me that he shared my feelings toward the Amazigh cause, saying it was a national issue, and added that from now on, he was ready to meet me at any time and to support the association with all the material and moral resources he had. After this meeting, I started to visit him regularly at his home, which is also his private clinic in Kénitra.

During one of these visits, I was accompanied by Dr. Abdelmalek Ousaden, who at that time was a surgeon at the El-Idrissi Hospital in Kénitra. I introduced him to Dr. Omar Al-Khattabi, as they had not yet met. As we were talking about the Amazigh issue and the activities of the association, I spoke about *Arraten* and particularly the financial problems afflicting it. Dr. Ousaden suggested that the association could approach someone with financial means who could help us. He mentioned the Popular Movement as an example. However, El-Khattabi was outraged at this suggestion and, in his usual manner, slapped the table forcefully, telling Ousaden, "You're wrong! These people are right to do what they're doing and to distance themselves from that party and all other parties, to guarantee their independence and freedom." I met El-Khattabi regularly for the rest of his life, may God have mercy on him. He would often joke with me, asking, "Where is your friend Ousaden?" to remind me about that meeting. I will talk about the doctor again in this memoir, when I discuss how we founded the Prince Mohammed Abdelkrim El-Khattabi Foundation in March 1996.

In 1975, El Houssaïn El Moujahid joined the association as a university student. He would go on to make a significant contribution to the Amazigh cause, becoming an active member who believed in his cause and one of the association's best-versed members in the fields of language, literature, and linguistics. Amazigh activism substantially accelerated in this period, in several key areas, primarily our continued work of documenting Amazigh heritage and the publication of new issues of *Arraten*. We also began to publish another journal called *al-Tabādul al-Thaqāfi* ("Cultural Exchange"). The purpose of this new journal was to nurture the writing skills of our young members who had literary, historical, and social interests so that they could start writing for publication by editing analytical articles on these topics. These journals were distributed by activists in student circles, so no student residence was without an issue—or several, which students passed from hand to hand, as they all represented the efforts and writings of talented youth. The association maintained its constant presence at the heart of societal issues and revived its literacy classes for young traders and workers. It managed to do this after I convinced the late Mahjoub Amdour, the owner of the school where I had received my primary education, to put some classrooms at our disposal, as well as the annex of the Maataouia School in the old city of Rabat. Several students volunteered to help,[4] delivering those lessons in the same way and with the same methodology as we had done at the beginning, back in the mid-1960s. Alongside this, we began to think about how to assist students who had completed university theses on topics related to the Amazigh issue and were keen on publishing them. Our first initiative in this direction was to help Dr. Omar Amarir print his book, *Amazigh Moroccan Poetry*, by extending him financial assistance to that end. In 1976, we also published the anthology *Iskrāf*, by Mohamed Moustaoui, after it had been edited for style and content according to the association's guidelines. Several association members in Casablanca—Lhoucine Jouhadi, Abdelaziz Bourass, Omar Amarir, Mohammed Khalil, and others—helped Moustaoui refine his poetry by shifting it from a traditional to a more modern style, in terms of its objectives, poetic imagery, and thematic unity. Indeed, the period 1974–76 saw the emergence of a generation of young poets, the group who really founded modern standard written Amazigh poetry. We published a collective anthology called *Imouzar*, which includes poems by Ali Sidqi Azaykou, Ahmed Bouzid, Ahmed El-Ghazali, El-Hussein Barhou, Lhoucine Jouhadi, Mohammed Farah, and me. Most of these would go on to write more poetry during the years 1974 to 1978.

In the same vein, in the association's board meeting of June 9, 1976, we agreed to publish the dissertation of Dr. Ahmed Boukous, "Popular

Language and Culture in Morocco," once it was turned from an academic dissertation into a book suitable for the general public. We also published a book on the Malekite school of Islamic jurisprudence, by Abdellah Jachtimi, and in 1978 the association supported the publication of Omar Amarir's book *Amalou*.

In 1976, given the association's strong relationship with jurist Imhammad El-Othmani and his son Saadeddine,[5] we proposed to publish Professor El-Othmani's book *Alwāh Jazūla*, a treatise on the relationship between Amazigh customs and Islam, which had been a dissertation for a diploma in advanced studies at Dar El-Hadith El-Hassania in Rabat, supervised by Allal El-Fassi. The professor accepted our offer, and we agreed to make what we deemed some necessary corrections to some aspects of the thesis. Professor El-Hossein Ouakak made some remarks, and the association tasked Professor Imhammed El-Dasser, a professor at the faculty of law, with reviewing and commenting on the thesis. However, he was suddenly struck by illness, and he sent me a message via one of his sons dated May 7, 1981, asking me to return the research to him for revision and to include the mentioned comments. The professor passed away, may God have mercy on him, leaving the thesis unpublished, but he left the letter with his sons, who later published it.

Prior to this, we had also convinced the late Professor El-Othmani, who had a relationship with the association and great sympathy for its noble goals, to undertake a project to translate the meanings of the Quran into Amazigh. He accepted our suggestion, on the condition that he could find another skilled jurist and theologian, fluent in Amazigh and Arabic, to help him. After some searching, he suggested such a jurist in Ifrane. However, the political situation in the mid-1970s was not conducive to such a project. Some opponents of the Amazigh cause would have considered it politically threatening, because it would allow the Amazigh language to overstep the boundaries that had been imposed on it. Such a translation would imply that the Amazigh language was capable of developing and growing, which was antithetical to the agenda of the Arab nationalists and proponents of cultural uniformity, with whom we were in a showdown. So we decided to postpone this translation until more suitable political conditions prevailed. Imhammad El-Othmani had given me a translation of the *basmala* (the statement: "In the name of God, the Most Gracious, the Most Merciful") as an example. May God have mercy on him, he was lighthearted. Abdellah Jachtimi and I used to visit him regularly at his house in Inezgane, along with other friends. Our sessions with him were enjoyable and humorous, and we used to benefit from his advice. He worked hard to persuade the

Association of Religious Scholars (*'ulamā'*) of Souss to partner with us in the first session of our summer university in Agadir, although his efforts were ultimately unsuccessful.

On top of this strategy of comprehensive work covering all aspects of Amazigh cultural work, the association began collaborating with foreign researchers wishing to conduct university research on topics related to Amazigh culture. One American researcher, Philip Daniel Schuyler, approached the association to ask for assistance in preparing his doctoral research at the University of Washington in the field of ethnomusicology, specifically on the music of the *rwais*, professional Berber musicians from southwestern Morocco. After he had provided me with documents showing this, and we had obtained permission from the Ministry of Interior allowing him to proceed with his project, I wrote to Omar Wahrouch in Marrakech to ask him to assist the researcher in exchange for a small fee, as the research was supported by his university. Schuyler completed his dissertation—the association still has a copy of it—and he is now an associate professor emeritus of ethnomusicology at the University of Washington, Seattle. He stayed in regular correspondence with the association. He was not the only such case: Since 1974, waves of foreign researchers, of various disciplines, have been coming to Morocco to conduct studies on the Amazigh issue.

This surge in documentation and publishing on Amazigh culture was accompanied by another effort of the utmost importance: the continuous training of association staff through a series of lectures and seminars at my house on Damascus Street, which was effectively the association's headquarters. A great number of presentations were given by scholarly members of the association who had graduated or were pursuing their university studies in various fields of humanities, history, literature, and language, as well as political science. We also prepared a list of topics that we felt were priorities for research and discussion, which would contribute to the development of our knowledge in the field of Amazigh culture, as well as the political and social aspects surrounding it. These presentations were given twice a month. I recall some of the following as examples of the topics that were presented at these study circles:

- "The Arabs' Entry into Morocco," by Professor Jamil Dourzaki
- "Full Federation," by Professor Abdulaziz El-Jazouli
- "The Nationalist Experience in the Islamic World," "Arab Nationalism and the Cultural Issue," and "Amazigh Self-Awareness and Its Evolution in the Modern Era," presented by the author

- "Concepts of Culture and their Reflections in Western Reality," presented by Professor Ahmed El-Ghazali
- "Moroccan Amazigh Colloquial Language (Dārija as a Literal Translation of Amazigh)," by Essafi Moumen Ali
- "Reasons for the Loss of Amazigh Poetry," by Professor Lhoucine Jouhadi
- "The Project to Unify the Amazigh Language," by Essafi Moumen Ali

I will not cite all the topics covered in these presentations during this period, but I want to demonstrate that the association sought, throughout the late 1970s, to intensify its training activities to enable it to formulate an Amazigh discourse capable of responding to any question on an academic level, as well as in the context of political debates within social organizations at the time, giving activists the knowledge to face challenges competently and have a significant impact on society, deepening awareness of Amazigh identity among all Moroccans.

Before I address other periods of the history of Amazigh activism, it is my duty to mention those who devoted their efforts to this work within the framework of the association's offices between 1967 to 1978.

Founding Board, November 1967

Name	Position	Profession	Place of origin
Brahim Akhiate	President	Teacher	Aït Souab
Ahmed Boukous	Vice-president in charge of literature and cultural exchange	Teacher	Bouizakarne
Abdelfadhel El-Ghouli	Vice-president in charge of social affairs	Student	Essouaira
Abdellah Bounfour	Vice-president in charge of folklore	Student	Marrakech
Ali Sidqi Azaykou	General secretary	Student	Tafingoult
Ahmed Akouaou	Assistant general secretary	Student	Aït Baha
Omar al-Khalfaoui	Treasurer	Civil servant	Amizmiz
Ali El Jaoui	Assistant treasurer	Student	Imouzzer Fes

Elected Board, October 1969

Name	Position	Profession	Place of origin
Brahim Akhiate	President	Teacher	
Abdelfadhel El-Ghouli	Vice-president		
Abdellah Bounfour	Vice-president		
Ali Sidqi Azaykou	General secretary		
Boujemâa Hebbaz	Assistant general secretary	Teacher	Imini
Omar al-Khalfaoui	Treasurer		
Amhammad El Dasser	Deputy treasurer	Salé	

Elected Central Committee, December 1970

Name	Position	Profession	Place of origin
Brahim Akhiate	President	Teacher	
Boujemâa Hebbaz	Vice-president in charge of literature	Teacher	Imini
Essafi Moumen Ali	Vice-president in charge of the arts	Student	Ait Mzal
Ali Amjehdi	Vice-president in charge of history	Student	Imintanoute
Ahmed El-Ghazali	General secretary	Student	Rabat
Amhammad El Dasser	Assistant general secretary	Student	Salé
Lahcen Abakrim	Treasurer	Civil servant	Aït Baâmrane

Elected Central Committee, December 1971

Name	Position	Profession	Place of origin
Brahim Akhiate	President	Teacher	
Ibrahim Madran	Vice-president and chair of Artistic Committee	Student	Rabat
Ahmed El Ghazali	Vice-president and chair of Literary Committee	Student	Rabat
Essafi Moumen Ali	General secretary	Civil servant	
Said Aït Hammou	Assistant general secretary	Student	Imintanoute
Lahcen Abakrim	Treasurer	Civil servant	

Elected Central Committee, January 1974

Name	Position	Profession	Place of origin
Ahmed El-Ghazali	President	Student	
Lhoucine Ait Bahcine	Vice president in charge of literature	Student	M'Zouda
Ibrahim Madran	Vice president in charge of the arts		
Said Aït Hammou	Secretary-general	Student	Imintanoute
Mostafa Essadaoui	Deputy secretary-general		Ait Youssi
Mohammed Ouanan	Treasurer	Engineer	Imouzzer Marmoucha

Elected Central Committee, June 1974

Name	Position	Profession	Place of origin
Brahim Akhiate	President	Teacher	
Ali Sidqi Azaykou	Vice president		Tafingoult
Imhammad El Dasser	Vice president	Teacher	Salé
Omar Amarir	Treasurer	Teacher	Argana
Lahcen Laaroussi	Vice treasurer	Student	Sefrou

Elected Central Committee, October 1978

Name	Position	Profession	Place of origin
Brahim Akhiate	Secretary-general	Administrative director	
Mohammed Errami	Vice secretary-general	Student	Guercif
Mohammed Boutkhidouch	Vice secretary-general	Civil servant	El Hoceima
Abdullah Balkmir	Treasurer	Student	Aït Toufaout
Lhoucine Ait Bahcine	Vice treasurer	Teacher	

THE FIRST SIGNS OF THE INTELLECTUAL
CONTEST OVER AMAZIGH IDENTITY

The return from France of our activists, who had completed their postgraduate studies in linguistics, history, and literature, had a significant impact within the universities of Rabat and Fes. There, they began to express their new ideas in their respective fields. These ideas were entirely in opposition to the prevailing ideas promoted by proponents of Arabism and the Islamist current, who neglected modern cultural concepts as well as rejecting linguistic and cultural diversity or the very principle of pluralism within society. By default, this meant that they disseminated ideas and ideologies opposed to Amazigh language, culture, and identity. As these returning scholars[6] secured positions at universities, they began to face all manner of attacks and criticism in response to the new ideas they proposed, whether in the fields of linguistics, history, or literature. These attacks extended to the question of promotions and a reluctance to appoint them to academic positions for which they were qualified. However, a generation of students was influenced by them, and they started to form an intellectual cadre with modern orientations.

Therefore, from the mid-1970s onward, as these people joined the universities, a new phase of Amazigh activism began, on two main battlefields. The first was the academic world, where intellectual and ideological camps wrestled with each other, and each intellectual school tried to impose its supremacy over a department, to the exclusion of others. The second was in society at large, where various entities and social organizations struggled to win over the public.

Hence, the association's intellectual and activist work to train activists, our publications, printing, and constant communicative work all diversified our means of communication and influence. This included combating illiteracy, lectures, creating the Ousmane band, producing radio programs, and numerous other activities. All this generated significant reactions, including plenty of attacks against Amazigh identity, especially in the written media. These attacks often focused on the Berber Decree, or covered subjects such as history and language, all with the aim of imposing an exclusive Arabist and Islamic view in the press and in academic writings, in order to thwart and obstruct the rising Amazigh tide. But our presence had grown at the universities and gained a foothold in the public cultural arena, thanks to the expansion of work by Amazigh associations and to the heated debates at the universities of Rabat, Fes, and Casablanca.

THE OUSMANE BAND AND THE GREAT ARTISTIC REVOLUTION

Ousmane and the Challenges of the Period

Starting in the late 1960s, the association grew aware of the need to develop Amazigh music, both in terms of the literary nature of song lyrics and the music itself. This idea particularly occupied the mind of my dear friend Essafi Moumen Ali, who was then a university student and had recently joined the association. He was enrolled at the National Conservatory in Rabat and was receiving lessons in modern music and the guitar. He and Ibrahim Madran started to become increasingly keen on the idea of developing Amazigh music, due to serious concern for its fate in the absence of the kind of care that would mean it was heard around the world, especially as it has all the qualities needed for such popularity.

Essafi Moumen Ali gave his first performance to the public when the association organized a cultural week in Marrakech in February 1969, in cooperation with the Comedia Club in Bab Doukkala, Marrakech. He presented modern forms of Amazigh music in the framework of the development of the Amazigh song. His performance was much appreciated and sparked a lively discussion between him and the audience, who had never heard Amazigh songs performed this way. The association's cultural week was the association's first major cultural activity outside Rabat since its founding on November 11, 1967. It included many cultural activities covering various subjects including the Sufi *zāwiya* in Moroccan society, a photo exhibition about rural dyeing by art researcher Bert Flint, as well as two Moroccan films, *Sedinkafay* and *Tarfaya*. Ahmed Boukous, Boujoumaa El-Habbaz, and Abdellah Bounfour, all members of the association, took part alongside me and Essafi Moumen Ali.

Around the same time, certain members of the association in Fes demonstrated similar interests. Ahmed Bouzid had an excellent grip on the meters and rhythms of traditional Amazigh music; he attempted to deploy these skills by composing modern poems of his own creation and presented them to his friends at student events.

One of these Amazigh cultural evenings was for the students of the Mohammadia School of Engineers, in the spring of 1972. It was the second time Essafi Moumen Ali had performed, and he delighted the students' ears with these modern Amazigh songs, all of his own composition, and either using his own lyrics or those of other members of the association, such as Ibrahim Madran or a group of students including Lahcen Abakrim, Aamou

Abdallah, Ali Amjout, Saïd Bijaadh, and Bakenzi Lahcen. This concert was where I met the late Atbaji El Hussein for the first time.

We continued like this. Some of us wrote committed modern poetry, and Essafi took on the task of putting it to music and performing it, with the help of Ibrahim Madran and Bijaadh Saïd. We reached the point where we had a respectable collection of songs, which were recorded on tape so they wouldn't be lost. Then, however, Essafi was appointed as a judge in Ouarzazate, and we were no longer able to continue without the key element—the performer, composer, and the person who had had the vision in the first place. In response, we began to search for a professional composer who shared our vision and our enthusiasm for the project. We were initially frustrated, as we had taken upon ourselves the responsibility of making this revolutionary project a success, aware that it would be a huge leap in the Amazigh arts, aiming to change the demeaning and derogatory view perpetuated by traditional media against our music and poetry alike, yet we had few material or human resources to achieve this goal. In the absence of Essafi Moumen Ali, we tried to contact a band from Salé, through our friend in the association, Ahmed Zakri. They had no base where they could practice, so we proposed to provide them with a headquarters and some of the equipment they lacked, and in exchange, they would produce an album of Amazigh songs for the association. We even offered to give up our copyright in exchange for their accomplishment of this work, as our only goal was to see these songs performed and produced so that Amazigh audiences in particular, and Moroccans in general, could experience this creativity and this revolutionary form of Berber music. The band from Salé agreed to the offer, and we provided them with everything we had promised, including a rental space, electricity, and everything else they needed. However, upon returning from a trip with Azaykou to visit Essafi Moumen Ali in Ouarzazate, I was surprised to find that the group had left the place and even taken some of the equipment we provided for them. Ultimately, it became clear that they too disdained the Amazigh language and were not happy to be performing Amazigh songs.

We did not despair in the face of this racist behavior. Instead, we turned to another group that had worked with Bijaadh. They were different from the first group, as they had a headquarters in the El-Akkari district of Rabat. I set up a meeting so they could hear my presentation on the topic and I could attempt to convince them to perform the songs that were already composed and ready. This group, unlike the first, sang both modern Moroccan songs and songs from the Arab east, performing at weddings and events. I tried hard to convince and enthuse them about this new and unique project, which would give them a boost and enable their group to transform from a cover band into a creative and unique band with its own personality. I said it would open up limitless opportunities for them, and that our association would support them logistically and with the media. They repeatedly said that all this was good and important, and that they would discuss it among themselves. However, I was disappointed once again. Bijaadh told me not to waste my energy on them, as they could not be convinced. Their view of Amazigh culture was just like that of the last group and of other artists of the time, who saw performing Amazigh music as an artistic adventure full of risks, as they could be ridiculed and mocked by audiences.

These two experiences revealed the extent of the intellectual and ideological subjugation that had afflicted the minds of Moroccans and the degree to which they had become culturally, artistically, and politically subjugated to the Arab *Mashreq*, resulting in negative attitudes and behaviors toward national culture and art in all its forms. This had ingrained an inferiority complex into the Moroccan consciousness and a derogatory view toward the self and to everything distinctly Moroccan. A look back at the dominant artistic and musical scene of the period shows that promoters of music from the Mashreq or the West music totally dominated the Moroccan music scene.

Yet we did not despair in the face of all these difficulties and challenges but continued to explore and search for solutions. One day, I personally discovered an amazing voice from the heart of Souss, specifically from Taroudant. I met Ammouri Mbarek at the wedding party of one of my friends, a private tutor in Tiznit, in the summer of 1973. It caught my attention that after his band, the "Souss Five," had finished playing, he performed a solo with Amazigh lyrics and a Western-influenced melody. I told him I was curious to know why he had performed the Amazigh song in this modern style. His answers told me that I had found my sought-after treasure, and I proposed that he collaborate on our project. He agreed in principle. At the beginning of 1974, I met him by chance at the Jour et Nuit café in Rabat.

I suggested that he live with me, to provide him with the conditions that would allow him to devote himself to serious work toward our grand project of serving and developing Amazigh music and songs in particular, preserving their authenticity while renewing them and absorbing modern musical trends.

Now, we felt that we had to make up for lost time. I introduced Ammouri to the other musicians, namely Bijaadh Saïd, Said Butrufin, and Belaid El-Akkaf. They were later joined by Tarik El-Maaroufi and Lyazed Qorfi. We were also helped by the late Abdellah Jachtimi, Mohamed Moustaoui, Omar

Amarir, and many others. Within a few weeks of intensive rehearsals, they were ready to perform a set list of songs on the guitar, drums, violin, and accordion, and the association had sought out the necessary sound equipment. With this, we finally started to feel optimistic that our project would come to fruition, despite the setbacks. People also started becoming enthusiastic, competing to write the best lyrics on a multitude of topics. Ammouri worked hard to showcase his talent for composition, which was reflected in the excellent standard of the resulting songs.

Before the band had finished preparing a set of seven songs, I invited them to my house (the association's headquarters) on Alaouiyine Street to showcase the work to several of our members. Everyone appreciated the group's efforts, and several made observations about how it could be improved and connected more deeply to its Amazigh roots as well as keeping it open to modern influences to appeal to the youth, who were eager for development in this field.

One of those present at the session was a friend of the association and the son of a businessman. He was the first to invite the group to perform at a family party at his house. We were happy to oblige, as this would be the first opportunity to showcase the group's music to an audience, even a small one. This pushed me to source special clothes for the group, similar to those worn by modern bands at the time. We worked against the clock to achieve all this. We decided to call the band "Yah," and we chose a Saturday for the event, with a performance in the afternoon for the women and one in the afternoon for the men. Omar Amarir was the host for the group, reading the words and introducing the band members. The women, who had already listened to a group of old women singing, enjoyed the performance even before the men started arriving. But our joy at this response from the audience did not last long. A security official, Commissioner Jalal, appeared on the scene. It turned out he was in charge of everything happening at the house, managing the household, regardless of the desires of its owner and his son. The commissioner was surprised by our arrival and insisted that we stop what we were doing. To achieve this, he used a trick, sending the old women back to the stage after having convinced us to stop playing for dinner. We only realized afterward that his aim had been to prevent us from continuing our performance. I protested to him several times over this, until he rudely told us we had to leave, claiming that our presence was not desired and that the audience didn't like us, even though the opposite was clearly true. None of the women had left the event: They had stayed and were clearly looking forward to the group's performance. I tried to speak with the owner of the house, who seemed overwhelmed and unaware of what was happening in

his own house. It appeared that everything was controlled by this commissioner, who had no relation to the family except for his role in the intelligence services in family and business circles. There were many people like
this among that class at the time. Thus, the homeowner left me to confront
the commissioner, who abruptly told me: "Get your stuff and leave, we only
want the *sheikhāt* (old women)."

As several of our friends were there, including Ali Sidqi Azaykou,
Ahmed Chouki, and Abdelmalek Azdou, our argument with this officer
could have escalated, had it not been for our self-control. But we understood the situation we were in. After all our attempts to change the officer's mind failed, with pain and frustration tearing at my insides, I asked
the band members to gather their instruments to leave, due to oppressive
police behavior in the house of this overwhelmed individual. However, the
situation quickly changed. As soon as they began to gather the instruments,
the women in the audience became aware of what was happening and of
the commissioner's attempt to deprive them of enjoying the band's performance, which they had been eagerly awaiting. The women responded
by erupting into a noisy rebellion against him, demanding the immediate
halt of the *sheikhāt*, and for our band to resume its performance, whether
he liked it or not. The commissioner glared at us and immediately came up
with another plot to achieve his goal of stopping people hearing Amazigh
music at any cost. He created a power cut, knowing that most of the sound
equipment was electrical. This was the level he stooped to in order to stop
us playing, hoping that we would be frustrated and give up, thus achieving
his vile goal.

However, we stood firm in the face of all these behaviors, foiling all his
attempts through strong cooperation between us. We did everything we
could to encourage the band members to overcome this ordeal, boosting
their morale and explaining to them that everything that was happening was
a test of their resilience, the strength of their will, and their conviction in
the path they had chosen, and that therefore, they should not fall into the
trap set by this vandal. After we had arranged everything, the band started
playing again, albeit with some tension due to what had happened. However,
the event turned into an enthusiastic, wild party. Everyone danced, both
women and men, and the celebration continued until dawn. This restored
the confidence of the band members. We had emerged triumphantly from
this difficult test, without succumbing to despair or giving up in the face of
a crisis that could have jeopardized all our efforts and hopes. As Ammouri
and I returned to my home, I had the idea of changing the band's name from
Yah to Ousmane. The performance had shown that the original name did

not resonate with the audience, while Ousmane had a beautiful musical tone and would be more harmonious with this type of modern music.

The band's second performance before an audience took place at the house of El-Hajj Taysir, in Casablanca, shortly after the soirée in Rabat. Those in attendance at this family event were predominantly businessmen, politicians, and a selection of intellectuals from various parts of Morocco. I was fascinated to see how the audience members were quickly captivated as they heard the songs sung in Tamazight, and the new melodies. They started emerging from under the marquees erected in the garden and drew closer to the stage to hear this new genre of Amazigh song, a style they had never heard before. Among those whom I remember expressing their admiration were the late Ahmed Oulhaj Akhannouch, Najem Abaakil, Abdulkarim El-Khatib, and El-Haj Abdullah Essouairi, as well as many others whose names escape me now.

This successful concert marked the beginning of a good relationship with the business sector. I now began to receive many calls on the subject, and word of the band began to spread among families in this milieu. Yet, while it was a success, the event did not mark the end of the challenges we faced in the form of attempts to sabotage our work. That said, the Casablanca evening was a success, not least thanks to the technical and organizational efforts of our dear friend El-Youtanan Mohammed Arhou, who took time out of his vacation to accompany us from Rabat to Casablanca for the show.

Just days later, we were invited to Taroudant to play two concerts at the city's annual exhibition. These events turned out to be glaring examples of the challenges we faced. I loaded my car with all the musical equipment, accompanied by a band member, while the others took public transport. As usual, at the first performance of the group, I greeted the audience and the attendees and recited the association's anthem. The event was attended by some local government officials and a cultured audience of lawyers and professors. After I left the stage, Ammouri Mbarek began performing his first song. However, a group of his acquaintances were in the audience, and they did not appreciate him returning to the city to surprise them with his remarkable achievement, seeing it as a victory for him compared with their failures. He had left them in a different way and made himself into someone, and moreover, he had done so in Tamazight. They started therefore to demand Arabic songs of their choice. Ammouri did not comply with their requests, as the band did not play covers—it had its own album to perform. Every time they interrupted him, he repeated the song lyrics again, until their patience ran out. Now they started shouting, declaring they did not want to hear the Amazigh language. They even started shouting: "We are Arabs, not

Amazigh!" Yet despite all their efforts to provoke him and to sabotage his performance, this isolated group in the back of the tent did not manage to ruin the Ousmane concert. The rest of the audience took no notice; they wanted to hear and enjoy this new sound, and their enthusiasm thwarted the hecklers' efforts to undermine the band.

After the concert in Taroudant, I left at 2:00 a.m., with all the equipment in my car. While some of the group also returned, Ammouri and some others stayed a few more days. The hecklers at the concert used this opportunity to contact the band members who had stayed. They shifted from their failed strategy at the concert, this time casting doubt on the band's convictions and choices. They argued that there was no point in nurturing Amazigh culture, which they deemed backward and folkloric. They tried to persuade Ammouri and the others to abandon their project, warning it could be dangerous for their future. They argued that our association was racist and sought to sow divisions among Moroccans, favoring Amazigh culture over other cultures, and claimed that as art is a universal language, artists should not be confined to any particular identity. They used these and any number of other flimsy arguments in their attempts to sway the band members from their course. I was surprised by the extent of the impact this visit had on the band's thinking and how confused they had become as a result, despite all the efforts we had made with them. I realized all this when we met back at my house. They arrived more than an hour and a half late, unusually tense and disturbed. I soon grasped the seriousness of the problem. I was kind with them and tried to extend the meeting to create a warm atmosphere between us that would facilitate communication. Later, I tried to reaffirm the principles and goals we had set. We were not able to achieve this goal until we had spent more than five hours in frank and constructive talk and discussion. With that, we were able to remove all the doubts and confusion that had begun to creep into the minds of some of the band's members, and to overcome the situation and regain awareness of our responsibilities. We agreed to set out a timeline for the group's work and to resume their rehearsal with determination and enthusiasm.

This incident marked the turning point between the early hesitancy among members of Ousmane and their determined launch along their path. Having overcome their lingering confusion after that visit to Taroudant, they performed at a few more family and private gatherings before shooting to fame and becoming a household name across Morocco. Their success and the great turnout at their shows was crowned by their first interview on national television. Their songs were included in the World Music section of the national radio and became hugely popular. All this encouraged the band to face the reactions, both positive and negative, to themselves and to Amazigh culture, particularly in the newspapers. The battle had moved from behind the scenes to the public sphere, becoming an open intellectual and ideological showdown.

Ousmane's relationship with the visual and written media began with a press conference I organized in the band's name at the house of Hajj Mohammed Abasour, in the Hay El-Limoun district of Rabat, with a number of journalists in attendance.[7] This media campaign, which targeted audio, visual, and written outlets, along with an intensive schedule of concerts in numerous locations, had a significant impact on the public both inside Morocco and further afield. This led a certain company to sign a deal with us for a tour in France and Belgium. The band performed at L'Olympia in Paris on February 5 and 6, 1977, and at the Lehman Center in Brussels on February 18, 1977. The success of the tour, as well as the accompanying publicity, played a major role in the band's clear victory over its critics and naysayers, and the victory of Amazigh art in general. It shattered the long-held contempt toward Amazigh musical and expressive arts that had dominated Morocco from independence until that time.

I have no intention of retelling everything that Ousmane did and listing all their achievements, as this has been documented by other researchers. However, I wanted to focus briefly on specific events, told from the battlefield where they, and everyone who helped us, waged this struggle, experiencing these events from the inside and feeling the difficulties that accompanied these battles. Without understanding this struggle, it is not possible to explain how the group—and through it, Amazigh music—were able to break the shackles. Through all this, I hope I have shown that that the matter was not as simple as it may seem. From the beginning, it was not just about a group or an individual; rather, it was a matter of self-assertion by all possible means. As we have seen from the anecdotes above, it could not have happened without the stirring of bold and conscious intellectual debates that were able to persist and to influence people as individuals and as groups.

Our work was crowned with great pride and honor when the doors of the Mohammed V Theater swung wide open for a historic public concert by Ousmane on March 19, 1977. It was an evening of Amazigh music the likes of which Rabat had never seen before. By this time, the band had signed a deal with a music promoter, and I gradually began to distance myself from managing their affairs, as they had become highly skilled and capable of managing their own business. I began instead to devote more time to my responsibilities with the association. In fact, I had been reluctant to attend the Rabat concert, due to a principled disagreement over the agreement with that promoter, as he had reneged on previous commitments to release the group's recordings.

Therefore, I was taken by surprise when the band members arrived unannounced at my house shortly before the concert and swore that they would not perform there unless I accompanied them. Faced with their insistence, and without time even to change into more suitable clothes for the occasion, we headed to the theater. We entered through the back door and headed straight to the stage. The concert opened with a surprise that I saw as the gift of a lifetime, from the audience to the band, and to everyone who had contributed to this achievement and to the Amazigh cause. No sooner had the master of ceremonies delivered a few mocking words in Arabic than the sides of the theater shook with boos from the crowd, rejecting this in one voice and demanding that he speak in his native Amazigh language or leave the hall. They waved their handkerchiefs and shouted at him, threatening chaos unless he complied. As all hell threatened to break loose, he appealed to me to intervene to address the audience in Tamazight to avert disaster. It seemed clear that this was a natural response from the audience, showing that they had understood our message. It was an honest expression of their self-awareness.

I addressed the audience, and silence pervaded the theater in anticipation. All I could do was repeat the anthem of the association, sincerely expressing the feelings that stirred in our hearts and theirs alike:

My gathered brothers and sisters,
The echoes of bygone centuries have called us,
We follow the message for which our for great forebears died,
The road revealed by the wind has been covered,
We will reveal it again so everyone can see it.

I had barely finished reading these verses when the theater shook with cries of "*tghazant akma!*" ("You speak the truth, my brother!").

The theater was nearly full, and more than a third of those present were educated Moroccans and non-Amazigh speakers, attending through a desire to see for themselves this phenomenon that they had heard about in the media, especially after the band's return from France and Belgium. The story was a true epic, a struggle of will and perseverance against marginalization and exclusion, all for the purpose of raising awareness about the Amazigh identity among all Moroccans through art and honest speech. This resounding victory, and the opening of the theater to Amazigh culture, which had long been kept out in the cold, sparked a vivid public debate. Public performances of Berber music had been a rare event. Some politicians who had been present on the night said they had never imagined that they would one day hear such strong expressions from the public declaring their non-Arab identity as they had at the theater. Reactions in the press varied from joy to rejection. The most bizarre example was the title of Mustafa Arzouzi's column in the *El-Fann* ("Art") newspaper on September 23, 1978: "Reviving the Berber Decree Through Singing."

Ousmane left a pioneering and profound mark on Moroccan music, as evidenced by the genre it created. The band's members continued to innovate with it. Ammouri Mbarek released several recordings in the genre, and Belaid El-Akkaf continued to shine with his musical efforts, attempting to fuse Amazigh music with its counterparts worldwide. Other bands also emerged in different regions of Morocco, following in Ousmane's footsteps, such as Yun Amazigh in the Rif and Amazighen in Khemisset.

Ousmane therefore deserves recognition not only from the state, or from experts and music connoisseurs, for its wonderful works and the individual and collective sacrifices made by those involved, but also from everyone passionate about Amazigh language and music, to whom they opened doors that had long been closed, giving a new burst of hope and resilience to both young and old. The band's work gave us sustenance and fuel to continue along our path.

Therefore I present my sincere gratitude and appreciation to all members of this group and their families, with whom I shared meaningful and memorable moments that have left their mark on us and on our struggle, deepening our awareness of our Amazigh identity within Moroccan society, both individually and collectively, helping free it from cultural dependence and alienation, and propelling it powerfully along the path of development and creativity, with its own unique identity.

POLITICAL AND GRASSROOTS REACTIONS TO AMAZIGH ACTIVISM IN THE LATE 1970S AND EARLY 1980S

1. The Political Level

In the late 1970s, in light of the factors mentioned above, several transformations took place around the Amazigh issue, both at the universities and concerning activism, as well as in terms of intellectual engagement with writing on cultural diversity and on national and linguistic issues in Morocco and North Africa more generally.

In 1977, this situation forced the government of Prime Minister Ahmed Osman to acknowledge Amazigh culture, even indirectly, using the phrase *al-aṣāla al-maghribiyya* (Moroccan authenticity), in a statement to parliament on November 1, 1977. This prompted the scholar and royal advisor Mohamed Moatassim, on behalf of the Moroccan Authenticity and Social Justice bloc, to declare in the subsequent discussion that: "At a time when our country has achieved its political unity and is fighting for its territorial unity, and has chosen to build the new Morocco, the Morocco of the Green March and army conscription, our bloc wishes that special importance be given to preserving Amazigh language and culture." He went on to say, "Our bloc, Mr. Prime Minister, reiterates the importance you have placed on Moroccan authenticity and social justice within your program, and supports the project to establish an institute for Amazigh language and culture, whose role will be to protect and to conduct social and cultural research in this field, which remains for us a source of pride in our national artistic genius, and a subject of scholarly admiration."[8]

On the same topic, a sharp debate took place between Mahjoubi Aherdane, the minister of state for the post office, and cabinet member Amhammed El-Douiri, after the Ministry of Public Works adopted the Arabic language (replacing French). Similar intense discussions about identity and linguistic issues soon mushroomed throughout the corridors of government, which had not happened since Morocco's independence in 1956 until the late 1970s. Interior Minister Driss Basri, following royal instructions, now asked Professor Mohammed Chafik to prepare a report on the subject. On April 26, 1978, Chafik presented his report, including the following points:

- Tamazight is a language that contributed to the spread of the Islamic faith.
- A significant segment of Moroccan public opinion continues to wonder why the Amazigh language has been totally neglected.
- Every nation of the world cares about all elements of its heritage. Preserving Tamazight will bring Morocco political benefits in North Africa and the Sahel countries.

Following this discussion within the state apparatus, a government charter was drafted for an Institute for Amazigh Studies. A draft decree was presented to the House of Representatives in the October 1978 session, aiming to supplement the decree of October 17, 1957, which defined the competencies of academic institutions. Article 11 bis. would establish an institute for study and research of the Amazigh language, entrusting that institute with the task of preserving the language, developing it and perpetuating it as an integral part of the modern national heritage.[9]

Following a discussion on the establishment of an institute for linguistic studies, Moulay Ahmed El-Allaoui wrote two editorials, in the newspapers *Le Matin* and *Le Maroc soir*. The title of the first was "Yes to Amazigh Studies," in which he expounded at length on the importance of the Amazigh language and its study and development. He also dedicated a full page to the ancient kings of Morocco. El-Allaoui received numerous responses warning about the dangers of promoting this language, which compelled him to write another editorial titled "Yes to Amazigh Studies, No to Amazighization," in which he clarified his stance, explaining that he was not calling for the adoption or development of the Amazigh language, but rather for Amazigh culture to be promoted through other languages. I met El-Allaoui one morning in Khemisset, shortly after these articles were published. He was coming from Fes. I expressed my interest in the topic and noted his courage in tackling it. He told me that he had not received any reactions from readers about his writings, supportive or critical, and commented that Moroccans "are all talk." He asked why they didn't write and express their opinions on whether he was right or wrong. I responded that not all Moroccans were aware of the issue. I realized that he was suggesting that his editorials had been intended to gauge public opinion on an institute for Amazigh studies.

While the government was doing this, political parties and organizations also started taking an interest and addressing or using the Amazigh issue in their electioneering and media outlets, in some cases to win over voters. Brahim Abbad became the first candidate to use Tamazight on an election poster, in the Chtouka Ait Baha district, after asking me to compose the text. At the same time, a debate was raging in the newspapers over the question of Arabization. One editorial in the Popular Movement's newspaper was titled "Arabization and Double Standards." There was also a debate over the social aspects of the Amazigh issue. The late Hassan Ismail El-Chihabi, from the Labor Party, spoke out on the issues facing Morocco's marginalized rural areas. Parliamentarians began drawing attention to the lack of public media in Tamazight. Mohamed Moatassim asked the minister of information in a verbal query, "How do you explain the fact that television programming is offered in three foreign languages, but not in the Berber language?"[10]

Yet despite these developments on the governmental level during Ahmed Osman's tenure, none of these projects ever came to light. The prime minister himself responded to this observation during a meeting the board of our association held with him as part of meetings with political parties and unions many years later, in 1996. During these meetings at his house, also attended by members of the political bureau of the National Rally of Independents (including former Minister of the Interior Mohamed Haddou Chiguer and the director of the party newspaper), Osman told us of his regret over the issue. While he had been able to start preparing the way for these projects, he said conflicts among the parties in the governing coalition at the time meant he had not been able to complete them.

These were some of the political responses to the growth of the Amazigh cause socially, culturally, and politically. They stirred significant activity in the media, from those who opposed to the idea of this identity growing and taking root in cultural circles and the general public. The following are headlines from national newspapers in this regard:

- "Conditions for the Revival of National Culture," by Mohamed Zniber, *Al-Hurriya*, November 12, 1975
- "On the Margins of Language Sovereignty," by El Yazid El Barka, *Al-Hurriya*, March 13, 1977
- "The Moroccan Personality," by Abdelkrim Ghallab, *Al-Alam*, October 12, 1977
- "Culture and Society in Western History," by Mohamed Ziyane, *Al-Hurriya*, October 18, 1977
- "Oui à la berbéritude, non au berbérisme," by Ahmed Alaoui, *Le Matin*, June 4, 1978
- "Reviving the Berber Decree Through Singing," by Mustafa Arzouzi, *Al-Muharrir*, March 23, 1978
- "The Moroccan Throne Established a Maghreb-Mashreq Company. The Mashreq Offered Its Best: Islam and Arabism, and the Maghreb Gave What It Had: Land and People. An Interview with Ahmed Bouzfour," *Al-Mithaq Al-Watani*, 1978
- "Is There Linguistic Sectarianism in Morocco?" By Mohamed Bennice, *Al-Nahar Al-Arabi Wal-Duwali*, November 8, 1978
- "Suspicious Symposiums Aiming to Harm the Arabic Language," *Al-Mithaq Al-Watani*, July 20, 1978

These are just some examples of articles that all intended to counter Moroccans' growing awareness of their Amazigh identity. The issue was now sparking heated debates within political parties and at the official level. But rather than achieving their intended results, these attacks encouraged and inspired us; instead of abandoning the cause, we gave more thought to drumming up ideas and ways to expedite the realization of our cultural project.

One factor that should not be overlooked in the context of the growing interest in the Amazigh issue during this period among government officials and the cultural class, including political party activists, was the question of the Moroccan Sahara. The late King Hassan II urged all Moroccans to close ranks and rally behind this central national cause. To do so, he ended the isolation of the south, by launching major development and urbanization projects in Marrakech and Souss, as well as opening new roads to integrate the Sahara with the rest of Morocco's national territory. His initiative also aimed to show Sahrawis the development that awaited the region once it had been reclaimed. He also sought to reassure Sahrawis that the central government was committed to preserving local linguistic and cultural characteristics, through cultural projects. Indirectly, then, the issue of the Moroccan Sahara contributed to the launch of cultural projects to preserve and promote Amazigh language and culture during the late 1970s. The fact that these projects were not realized indicates that they were merely part of the state's tactics for managing the situation, and not a true strategic goal.

2. At the Level of Activism

After his return from America, Mohamed Benaissa organized the second Asilah Cultural Festival, in 1979. Given the growing interest in Amazigh culture and in popular culture in general, he decided to dedicate two days of the event to Amazigh culture. His first idea was to ask Mahjoubi Aherdane's office at the Ministry of Post to propose a set of suggestions and names to take part. At a meeting with some of the ministry's staff, he promised to organize several different shows. However, just a week before the event, when he went to ask how things were progressing, he found that none of these promises had been fulfilled. Fortunately, he met a friend of the late Abdellah Jachtimi, a certain Hossein Amer, and told him about the issue with the minister's office. Amer promised to solve the crisis and contacted us via Jachtimi. We discussed the situation at my house, and I proposed several items on the various aspects of Amazigh culture, with artistic segments that would fill and enrich the two days allotted to Amazigh culture. Benaissa was pleased with this, and we scheduled a show on the topic of "Awareness of Authenticity," which I presented myself, as well as a presentation about Amazigh women, by Naima Al-Murabit; and an artistic evening introducing Amazigh music, presented by Omar Amarir, with the Rwais band led by the late Omar Wahrouch. This was where I first met Hassan Id Balkassam, who engaged me in debate over several points in the presentation. He did not introduce himself, and he had not known me previously. At the end of my presentation, which was chaired by Benaissa, he commented, saying, "We're all Amazigh, and the city of Asilah has an Amazigh name. These presentations are successful because they're provocative, they present unexpected questions and ideas. They give added value because they're out of the ordinary." Consequently, the association and I developed a good relationship with Benaissa. We went on to meet on many other occasions, which I will mention later on in these memoirs.

THE FIFTH CONFERENCE OF THE ARAB MUSIC ACADEMY IN RABAT

Efforts continued to link Moroccan culture with the Arab *Mashreq*, bolstered by a painstaking search for evidence to prove this connection and exert psychological pressure on citizens to embrace this trend and believe in it as a natural reality. On October 22–27, 1977, the Ministry of State for Cultural Affairs held a conference attended by delegations from twelve Arabic-speaking countries.

Among the presentations offered on Moroccan music were the following:

- "Sources of Popular Moroccan Music," by Ahmed Aouatif
- "The Influence of Andalusian Music on Popular Songs," by Idris Benjelloun
- "Melodic-Rhythmic Models in Various Types of Popular Moroccan Music," by Idris El Charradi
- "Glossary of Technical Terms in *malḥūn* Music," by Dr. Abbas El-Jirari"
- "Moroccan Popular Music," by Abdelaziz Ben Abdeljalil
- "Lyrics and Performance in Souss Songs," by Abdullah Maawi
- "Amazigh Popular Songs in Morocco," by Omar Amarir
- "The *ahāzīj* (folk songs or *aḥwāsh*) of Souss," by Mohammed Abou Drar
- "The Popular *ahāzīj* of the Sebou Basin," by Mohammed El-Raisi
- "Music and Language in *gnāwa* Songs," by Philip Schuyler (University of Washington)

What I am trying to point out here is that there were three participants from within the Amazigh struggle who had been trained as part of the colossal efforts undertaken by Amazigh activists: Omar Amarir, Abdullah Maoui, and Philip Schuyler from the University of Washington, whom I have mentioned previously and whom the association helped with his PhD research.

My second observation is that all the presentations that did *not* involve Amazigh artists were very poorly attended, to the point that Arab researchers from the Middle East would often arrive late to seminars or performances of Andalusian music to find the halls almost empty, but could freely choose their seats in the front rows. We in the association noticed this phenomenon. Myself and Jachtimi took it upon ourselves to spread the word in the old city and at the university that Omar Wahrouch was to perform, introduced by Dr. Omar Amarir. The Arabs from the Middle East were shocked to find the hall completely full, and were unable to find seats. They started to wonder why. They later learned the reason: that authentic Moroccan art is Amazigh art, the art of the bulk of the population. After every one of Wahrouch's songs, the women would ululate to express their satisfaction, naturally creating an atmosphere of joy and happiness, which was not the case at the other performances. Our work at such occasions primarily built on the psychological and emotional aspects of this cultural struggle, as we encouraged artists, so they would not feel shocked or neglected, rather sending a strong and clear message to Middle Easterners that this country has its own distinctive and deeply rooted cultural and civilizational characteristics.

THE PUBLICATION OF "CULTURAL EXCHANGE"

After the publication of *Arraten* and of several books by researchers at the association, as mentioned above, we had a deep and pointed discussion on the idea of the association publishing a new periodical. Throughout 1977, we debated its importance, its intended goals, the languages to be used, and the financial resources that would be needed. Finally we decided, at a meeting on November 18, 1977, to publish a new journal in three languages: Arabic, Tamazight, and French. The aim was to provide a platform for students to express their opinions and publish their articles on topics related to Amazigh culture. It would also include indexes of research previously published in this field and translations of useful material from other languages into Tamazight or Arabic.[11]

In 1978, serious discussions began within the association about the need to learn and write in the Amazigh script, Tifinagh. Some members also started calling for more attention to other aspects of Amazigh culture that the society had not addressed until that point. Lhoucine Ait Bahcine championed the need to document and photograph all aspects of Amazigh life, including rituals and clothing, and argued that we should consider promoting Amazigh theater as a component of Amazigh culture and a tool in its development.[12]

A MEETING AT DR. ABDELMALEK OUSADEN'S HOUSE IN 1978

The association's intensive activities throughout the late 1970s had a major impact on the political and intellectual situation in Morocco. This was evident in the government's public statements after Ahmed Osman's appointment as prime minister, his aborted moves to create an institute for Amazigh studies, and the growing number of articles about history and language as they concerned issues of identity, cultural diversity, the relationship between the Maghreb and the Arab East, as well as other topics directly or indirectly related to the Amazigh issue. It was in this context that, in late 1977, Dr. Abdelmalek Ousaden invited us to his house in Fes for an Iftar meal, as it was Ramadan. Accompanying me was Mohammed El-Kebir Errami from Guercif—specifically Ait Ouarayn—who was my deputy at the association's national office. Mohammed Chafik was also invited. After we had broken fast, Chafik explained the motives for the meeting. He said the time had come to do something with greater impact than the cultural work we had been practicing until now. Ousaden then expanded on the subject, finally proposing the creation of a national association, in which they would represent the Middle Atlas region and we would represent Souss. He added that he might contact members of the Intilaqa Cultural Association in Nador to represent the Rif region. This was their perception of the situation, and this was their proposal on how to deal with it at that time. I spoke next, responding to their proposal and questioning their stance toward the association and their attempt to bypass it. I explained that the association, as its name indicates, is a Moroccan society, meaning it is for all Moroccans, and that Ousaden himself had been a member since the early 1970s. I asked why they considered it a society concerned with Souss, simply because I am from Souss; Mohammed Errami, who was with me, was from Ait Ouarayn, and the society had dozens of members from all regions of Morocco and did not discriminate on the basis of its members' origins. Therefore, I rejected their regionalist suggestion on principle, saying it would further fragment the unity of the various components of the Amazigh Moroccan people. I added that what was now required was to encourage the creation of local Amazigh associations in each region of Morocco, to deepen awareness of the Amazigh issue and thus the scope of Amazigh activity. Only then would circumstances arise that would require us to act or coordinate according to the demands of the day, depending on the options available and the various developments that would result from the associative efforts of all those components. But for now, I said, we were fulfilling our national duty toward the Amazigh cause, with our modest capabilities.

Everyone dispersed, and they did not contact me again on the subject, nor did they contact the Intilaqa group in Nador. They began preparing to create the new association, under the name "Amazigh Association."[13] The only activity this association undertook was to organize a cultural event at the Hassan Hotel, where the former president of Senegal, Léopold Sédar Senghor, gave a lecture on "Arab (Berber) Civilization." Shortly afterward, in 1980, Ali Sidqi Azaykou would be arrested, a topic I will address later.

The association held a special meeting on January 12, 1979, to discuss the proposal to establish an Institute of Amazigh Studies. We addressed all aspects of the project and the possibilities it raised. We particularly focused on the intentions behind the state's announcement at that time specifically. Was it to gauge citizens' opinions and their reactions to the idea? Or did the authorities want to implement a project of this kind in order to alleviate the tensions stemming from regional demands for linguistic and cultural rights, particularly among associations and university students, before things took a turn for the worse?

Everyone concluded in this discussion that the association should adopt a cautious approach to the project, even if—despite our doubts—it was a serious proposal, in order to contribute to any possible gains for the Amazigh cause. However, everyone agreed that the state's project in this official framework could not meet the association's aspirations and the ambitions of the Amazigh for the development and enhancement of the Amazigh language and culture.[14]

MARRIAGE AND ITS RELATIONSHIP TO THE ACTIVIST'S STRUGGLE

Since I had been appointed as a secondary school teacher in Kénitra and found a permanent job in that role, I began thinking about marriage, in order to start my own small family, like any young man who reaches this stage of maturity and financial stability. I began giving serious thought to the matter, and as is natural for any young man in this situation, I began looking for a person to be my life partner.

However, my situation was not typical in this regard. I was engaged, active, and a passionate member of an association with goals toward which it was working. We, as activists, believed in these goals and committed our-selves to achieving them, to the extent that our personal lives had become hostages to the realization of these goals.

My role in this struggle was fraught with risks, as these goals were regarded with suspicion by the authorities, political parties, and thinkers managing public affairs and formulating cultural, economic, and social pol-icies. The situation meant that everyone connected to me, particularly my spouse and my children, could face discrimination in their lives due to my involvement in this activism. This sense of responsibility toward the person I would take as my life partner led me to conclude that this partner must meet several conditions for our marriage to be successful.

Firstly, from a cultural and social perspective, it was essential to me that my wife shared my cultural outlook, to avoid contradictions and intellectual differences in the way we lived our lives as a couple, in all its manifestations of lifestyle and raising children. Secondly, my wife should be educated, to ensure that she was financially independent and could protect herself and our children from all life's risks, were I to come to any harm due to my intel-lectual and political convictions. Thirdly, we should come from similar social environments, to ensure harmony between our families.

These were the main conditions I set as I tried to choose a spouse. It took me several years to find someone who met these conditions, due to my caution, rational decision-making, and consideration of all the relevant fac-tors before I would thrust anyone—particularly my future children—into a risky fate. I set these conditions because I had witnessed the experiences of several friends whose choice of spouse only met emotional criteria, without considering the other aspects I have described. This resulted in them being separated, and the children being lost between the spouses. These cases were caused either by a lack of cultural harmony or by class disparity, or some-times both.

Someone who champions a cause considered taboo, like the Amazigh issue at that time, is different from an ordinary person who does not bear similar responsibilities. An activist carries two burdens simultaneously: con-cern for the cause and concern for his family. If the two are not in harmony, one risks losing both the cause and the family. Achieving this balance is not easy.

Thank God, I had the good fortune to find a wife who met these criteria, as well as the emotional aspect, which is the gateway to all those other con-ditions. I met her at the Attaqadoum High School in Kénitra, where I taught. I got to know all her family members, and after ensuring that all she fulfilled my conditions, I proposed to her.

After several meetings, she also got to know my family very well, and agreed to marry me. One day when we were talking about our future life together, I playfully said to her, "Don't be shocked if I tell you I'm already married, and that this wife comes first in my life and I will never abandon her, no matter what. If you agree with this, we can continue, but if not, there's no need to go on." She was startled and thought, "What a catastrophe, how can I accept having a co-wife?" But instead of letting her thoughts wander too far, I said, "This wife is the Amazigh cause. For me, it's a cause I cannot abandon. It accompanies me wherever I go, it's with me at home, at work, and on the street. This reality must not surprise you in our married life. I don't want to hide from you what it will cost me in terms of time, and material and intellectual effort. This is a cause we share, and I hope it brings strength to our marriage until we achieve its goals together, whether in our lives or through our children."

Addressing my fiancée with this level of honesty gave me a shortcut to the depths of her emotions, because I felt that she shared my sentiments and the same deep feelings for our shared Amazigh identity, even though—up until that point—she had not fully grasped all the theoretical aspects of the issue, in terms of our language, culture, and what it would require in terms of effort, time, and sacrifice to achieve our goals of deepening awareness of Amazigh identity among all Moroccans.

Finally then, I married Mahjouba Ouaziz, of the Idaouzakri tribe in Irherm, near Taroudant. She had grown up in Kénitra and graduated in law at Mohammed V University in Rabat. Our wedding ceremony, on August 7, 1976, was very modest. However, it was marked by a performance by Ousmane, who volunteered to play for free, and was attended by many of the friends I have mentioned previously in these memoirs, including Dr. Omar El-Khattabi, activists Mohammed Mrabet and Abdullah Masrour (all now deceased), El Mehdi Slimani, and several friends from the association including Essafi Moumen Ali, Ibrahim Madran, and Lahcen Ait Nasser. The wedding was also special because I had written the invitations in Amazigh. We were blessed with our first daughter Touf Itri in 1977 and our son Yacine in 1986.

THE AMAZIGH CAUSE AND PROFESSIONAL HARDSHIPS

Before moving on to the eventful decade of the 1980s, I would like to conclude this chapter on the 1970s by talking about the impact that our concern for the Amazigh cause, and our efforts to expand and deepen awareness of it, had on our professional careers. Each one of us, activist teachers in particular, whether in secondary or university education, suffered opposition from our administrative and professional colleagues, who were intellectually opposed to the Amazigh cause. We also suffered from exclusion and antagonism by the management, intended to deprive us of our rights, such as promotions or positions, even when we were better qualified than other candidates. All these practices aimed to confront Amazigh demands for rights and decrease interest in the cause, by attacking the messengers in order to discourage them or persuade them to give up their intellectual convictions.

In the academic year 1967–1968, I was appointed as a teacher of mathematics and applied sciences at the Teacher Training School in Kénitra. However, I had only worked there for a few months when a teacher I knew from my previous employer, the Attaqadoum High School, approached me to request that we swap places. I agreed to this because I preferred teaching at the high school, where I could instruct students on modern mathematics, unlike during my teacher training.

The Attaqadoum High School was managed by the late Ahmed Belhaj, a prominent figure from the Istiqlal Party. Like the Mohammed V Schools in Rabat also run by the party, it was a free school. Its director was married to the sister of the opposition figure Moumen Diouri, who was in France. A street in Kénitra was named after their father, Hajj Mohamed Diouri, who played a role in Morocco's independence struggle. The director's political status and party affiliations meant he behaved as if he owned the school, imposing his own system upon it. He exercised a kind of paternal and authoritarian behavior over the teachers, unlike at other schools in Kénitra. It didn't help that some of the teachers were his former students at the school, and dared not oppose him or discuss teaching matters with him. However, I was part of a group of teachers who had graduated from the École Normale Supérieure (a teacher training college in Rabat) and had no prior relationship with the school. We had more courage than the others to express our opinions and perform our duties at the school according to Morocco's education law, with less regard for the director's political and family status. We also insisted on maintaining a relationship of mutual respect. I used to travel frequently between Rabat and Kénitra because I did not live in the city, although I had been provided with an apartment at the city's education department as a reward for accepting to swap places with Professor Ibrahimi, who was also a friend of the deputy education minister.

Before moving to the high school, I had asked Ibrahimi—who is also Amazigh—to give me the names of the Amazigh-speaking teachers at the high school and to describe each one, so that I could surprise them by directly addressing them by their names and their tribe or area. He was happy to oblige. So I approached each of them in the teachers' lounge in the early days of my time there, calling them by their names and adding that they were from such and such a place. They were surprised by this information, which I presented to them in Tamazight, and then I would introduce myself and where I was from. This approach to introducing myself, speaking Tamazight, provoked some people, but it changed the atmosphere and people's behavior in the staff room, where Arabic had been the only language spoken, as no one had dared to express their Amazigh identity. One of the teachers was an Egyptian professor who belonged to the Muslim Brotherhood and had moved from Egypt to Morocco. He was a preacher at a mosque in Kénitra and had married a Moroccan woman. He taught Arabic language and literature. My method revealed that there were at least three Tamazight-speaking teachers. From then on, I addressed them only in Tamazight in the teachers' lounge, which caused some irritation among the management, including the director and administrators. I paid no attention to these reactions. During my early years in this job, my friend Ahmed Mzal published his poetry collection, *Amānār*. It was the first written collection of Amazigh verse dedicated to the poetry of the ancient *rwais* (wandering performers). I often read from it with Mohammed Lbib, a social studies teacher, who was very in tune with what I was doing; whenever we came across a verse that he liked, he would exclaim in admiration, "What a marvelous verse!" or "What eloquence!" These comments intrigued others, especially the Egyptian professor, who would ask for explanations, asking, "Is this Berber?" Instead of stopping, the professor continued reading and commenting. In this way, we stood out from the other teachers, even the Amazigh-speaking ones, who expressed some sympathies or revealed their Amazigh identity through our conversations.

While this was going on in the teachers' lounge, in this challenging way, I behaved differently in the classroom. At the beginning of each academic year, I always introduced myself to my students with my full name, mentioning that I spoke Tamazight fluently. This kind of introduction gave confidence to the Amazigh students and helped them get over their feelings of inferiority or deficiency. I also formed a branch of our association in Kénitra with some of these students, as well as some teachers and educators I met in the city, headed by Hassan Fardous.

Despite the reservations of the director and administration, I managed to organize a series of activities at the school, in collaboration with certain teachers. My first presentation was about Amazigh arts, particularly focusing on dyeing and the visual arts. We were supported by Danish anthropologist

Bert Flint, who was an expert in this field. He provided me with photographs of various examples of art like decorated panels and ornate ceilings adorned with ancient Amazigh designs, and made a presentation on the subject and on Berber dyeing. Saïd Soussan, the school's art teacher, also helped me put together the exhibition, which was attended by the director and teachers. They were impressed, as they had previously been unaware of these forms of Amazigh art. I also supervised students as they transformed small images into large paintings for public display. These students, whose hobby was art, produced many beautiful works that are still in the association's safekeeping. I tasked them with collecting whatever items of heritage they could from their mothers' and grandmothers' stories. Some wrote about their tribes, specific rituals, or customs unique to their towns. These activities at the high school and at the nearby Ain Sebaa youth center enabled the association to establish itself in the community, particularly among the parents and families of students who shared with them their achievements in Amazigh literature and art, as well as becoming more deeply self-aware as Amazigh. My strategy at the school was to secure my presence there by performing my teaching duties with dedication and perseverance, meaning the headteacher and my opponents could not find any reason to criticize me. I helped my students achieve the highest grades and success rates in the school, to the point where the director enrolled his own children in my classes. However, he was not happy with me, due to my cultural activities. His opposition to me grew after the science teachers unanimously elected me as their representative, in opposition to his preferred candidate, who received no votes apart from that of the director. After that, and partly as a punishment for my beliefs, he consistently rejected my requests to move to Rabat, even though I was achieving top grades for the school. Soon after this, an incident took place at the school that marked a turning point, after which neither of us could tolerate the other's behavior. One of the science teachers, Mohammed Sehnoun—who was my close friend and former university colleague, and was living with me at the apartment provided by the delegation—collapsed in the classroom as he was teaching. The school guards carried him to the teachers' lounge but didn't call an ambulance or take him to the hospital, despite having cars available. In response, I submitted a note of protest to the director, on the request of the teachers, as I was their representative. The director was displeased by this, seeing it as damaging the school's reputation, and he held several meetings with the other teachers, in my absence, to persuade them to take a stance against me. Ultimately however, he met with a shock that caused him to faint as well: Most of the teachers supported me and agreed that my actions were correct. During his arguments, as he tried to convince them, he insisted that he had a file on me, saying I had come to the school to cause disturbances and racism among the students and teachers, and similar accusations. However, the teachers rejected all his claims, and he himself fainted, as I said. Finally he was taken home without achieving his goal of turning the teachers against me.

Faced with this charged atmosphere and the director's stubborn refusal to allow me to transfer to Rabat, despite my participation in the transfer process again in the same year as the incident, I decided not to return to the high school. At the start of the school year in September 1971, I resolved not to go back to the school, regardless of the consequences. Even though the director had presented me with a work plan, I gave him no notice of my intention to leave or of my ongoing communications, so as to avoid giving him an opportunity to thwart my plans. It occurred to me to approach El-Faqih El-Badrari, who would go on to be the imam leading prayers during the Green March in November 1975. He was Amazigh, from Souss, and was a parliamentary representative for Taroudant. He was also the son-in-law of Mohamed Fadhel Ben Achour, the former Mufti of Tunisia, and knew me well, understanding my intellectual convictions. We had often met, along with many traders in Rabat. When I met him, he immediately accompanied me to the education ministry. It was around 6:00 p.m., and the staff were heading home. Outside the ministry, we met a certain Dr. Chiadmi, who was then director of education and was covering for the secretary-general of the ministry, who was on vacation at the time. El-Badrari explained my situation to him, and, after asking some questions about me, Chiadmi beckoned me over. I explained to him that I wanted to transfer to Rabat, and that I taught mathematics and spoke both Arabic and French. Chiadmi seemed pleased with this and said, "We need people like you. We ask France to send us teachers, but they usually send us the worst ones." He suggested I come to his office in the morning to register for an appointment. The next day, when I went to his office, the *chawich* (reception clerk) brought in a card. Chiadmi wrote on the back his instructions to the official in the human resources department. I was appointed that same day of October 1971 to a school in Skheirat. Since Skheirat fell under the Rabat district, the employee in charge committed to transferring me to Rabat within a year, so in the next academic term. Thus, I joined the Idrissi preparatory school in Skheirat, where I spent an academic year. I was then appointed to Ibn Rushd High School in the Yaacoub Al-Mansour district of Rabat, in October 1972.

I joined the school, which was in a very downtrodden district, with shacks made out of sheet metal on one side and piles of rocks and rubble on the other. Given the social situation of the residents, the dropout rates were high, and the students often went on strike to protest the neglect and poor management they faced. When I began teaching, I was the only Moroccan teacher who taught mathematics there in French, as all the other teachers of scientific subjects were French. Thus, in my move from Kénitra to Skheirat and Rabat, the language I used in my lessons changed from Arabic to French.

I had barely settled in and started teaching when I noticed the principal's dissatisfaction toward me. This was because, during a general meeting of mathematics teachers, I had objected to a list of excessive demands of students, including books and stationery. I suggested that they could do without some of these materials if the teachers made a modest effort. The students were from very poor families, and some did not even have electricity at home. How could we demand they bring all these tools and books when teachers could simply photocopy mathematical exercises for the students? In the principal's eyes, however, this position made me a revolutionary, unlike the French teachers.

The disputes didn't stop there. I began organizing science teachers to demand a say in managing the school's educational affairs, especially regarding our guidelines, so that we could work to understand pupils' problems instead of confronting them with violence and heavy discipline. My efforts bore fruit, as students kept attending the classes I taught, and stopped going absent, after I explained to them the negative consequences of unnecessary absenteeism. The principal soon noticed this change and found out what was going on. He was not pleased. At the end of the academic year, the district usually sent counselors to guide students to the final preparatory classes. Before I joined the school, the principal would usually meet alone with each counselor and decide the fate of each student, more than ten a day, without considering the teachers' opinions. I managed to get the science teachers to agree that we should change the methodology, by studying each case and considering the teacher's views on each student. Parents were also present at these sessions. This was what happened, and the principal was thus forced to adhere to this methodology, which he disliked and considered an intrusion into the high school, as well as a violation of the hegemonic authority he had previously enjoyed. What delighted me most in this process was the great joy expressed by the parents and guardians, and the response from the students after these long meetings to decide their future paths.

However, my popularity at school drove the principal to look for any mistake he could exploit to harm me and eventually get rid of me. He frequently sent inspectors to attend my lessons, and he fabricated propaganda against me, as he knew of my intellectual convictions. I always filled out the absentee form if I was to be away from the school, as per the rules. On November 15,

1973, I was surprised when one of the guards came into my classroom bearing an order to strike me off the public service register for "abandoning post." I did not leave the classroom immediately, but rather, finished delivering the lesson. At 12:00 noon, I went to the principal to ask him why this decision had been taken, who was behind it, and when I had been absent from work. He started mumbling and trembling, and was, of course, unable to answer. The irony was that the decision to sack me for absenteeism had been delivered as I was in the classroom doing my job.

I did not bother myself to argue with the headteacher, because I knew well that he hated me and that he was the one who had orchestrated this farce. In the afternoon, I went to the ministry to ask officials there about the reasons behind the decision. The official at the human resources department responded, "Aren't you doing your job?" "Of course, and this decision reached me in the classroom, not at my house," I said. "Did you bother yourselves, as is usual when laying someone off, to write to me at my residence to verify my actual situation?" The official asked me for a work certificate from the principal. I told him I would bring one, as I was still going to work.

Indeed, I approached the principal and asked him for a work certificate. He started telling me, "You were absent on such and such days." I interrupted him and said, "Give me a list of all my absences during the two years I've spent at the school, along with my work certificate, because I am doing my job." The principal was forced to hand me the work certificate and the list of absences, which did not exceed four or five days over the two years, all of which were justified and accompanied by doctors' notes. Through it, I discovered that the last one was the Monday following my trip to Ouazarzate with Ali Sidqi Azaykou, when we had visited Essafi Moumen Ali and Mohammed Akram. This absence, despite the fact I had justified it, was what the principal had used to inform the administration that I had stopped showing up for work. Certain employees at the ministry had colluded with him to issue this decision against me without carrying out the usual legal measures in such cases. I delivered the work certificate to the ministry. The official there was shocked at the behavior of the headteacher, who had told the ministry that I was not showing up to work, and then issued me a work certificate. The official started cursing the principal for the embarrassment he had caused the department. However, I had to stop working and my salary was suspended for almost a year, the time it would take to rectify my situation. I stayed at home without work for more than six months. After completing the necessary procedures, I was summoned to the ministry to receive my new appointment. The employee told me I would be sent to some city far from Rabat, I forget where. I told him bluntly, "If you represent the ministry, and if the ministry has any self-respect, it should appoint me to replace the principal who mocked you and the ministry. Otherwise, you should give me a job close to my home. I won't accept any other location." The ministry was now embarrassed and was forced to give me a temporary job at the Hassan II school, close to my house. When the next academic term came around, they found me a school close to my home in Rabat; I was given a job at the Collège Attadili, where I stayed until I quit teaching entirely. This was the price I paid for my steadfastness and for defending my intellectual positions, which I never hesitated to express wherever I settled or traveled.

NOTES

1. Translator's note: The Berber Dahir was a French colonial-era decree that placed Berber-speaking-majority areas under a separate legal system, prompting a backlash from Moroccans who saw it as an attempt to divide and de-Islamize the country. This fueled the rise of the Moroccan nationalist movement.
2. Translator's note: a form of melodic poem in Moroccan Arabic and sometimes Hebrew.
3. Others who joined us from 1970 onward included Lhoucine Jouhadi, Lahcene El-Aouad, Ahmed Zakri, Ali Amjahdi, Dr. Osaden, and Afa Omar. They were also joined by El-Hoceine Ajkoune, Aït Hammou Saïd, Ajana Lahcene, Amarir Omar, Ahmed Bouzid, El-Ghazali Ahmed, Bourasse Abdulaziz, Mohamed Moustaoui, and Farah Mohammed, in 1971.
4. They included Lhoucine Ait Bahcine, El-Hussein Ajkoun, Abdellah Jachtimi, Omar Al-Khalfaoui, and Abedrabbou.
5. Translator's note: Saadeddine El-Othmani would go on to become prime minister of Morocco from 2017 to 2021.
6. They included Ahmed Boukous, Ali Sidqi Azaykou, Ahmed Akouaou, Abdellah Bounfour, Mohammed El-Shamy, Qadi Qaddour, Marzouq El Ouariachi, and El Houssaïn El Moujahid.
7. We invited several journalists, including Said El-Jadidi from Spanish-language Moroccan Radio, Mekki Bartal from the French section, Mohammed Nabzir from Al Muharrir newspaper, and Mounir Hamouni and a friend of his from L'Opinion. Accompanying me from the association were the late Abdellah Jachtimi and Amhammad El Dasserm as well as the members of the band: Ammouri Mbarek, Said Bijaadh, Said Butrufin, Lyazed Qorfi, and Tarik el-Maaroufi.
8. Publications of the Moroccan Authenticity and Social Justice team, No. 111/77, Thursday, November 17, 1977.
9. See Lahcine Ouazi, Nash'at al-ḥarakah al-thaqāfiyyah (The emergence of the cultural movement), 180–181.
10. Manshūrāt al-Farīq al-Ḥarakī, 1978–1979.
11. The meeting was attended by me, Ahmed Boukous, Mohamed Mezouar, Ahmed El Ghazali, Mohammed Khalil, Amhammad El Dasser, Omar Amarir, Mohamed Moustaoui, El-Hoceine Amsari, and El-Hoceine El-Moudjahed. Among those who wrote in

the journal were me, Mohamed Moustaoui, Ouakka Mohammed, Fatima Boukhriss, Naima Al-Murabit, Abdellah Belgmir, El-Hoceine Amsari, Dr. Bouhamdi, Mohammed Chafik, El-Hoceine El-Moudjahed, Mohammed Boutkhidouch, Belgassem Achouan, and Lhoucine Jouhadi El-Baamrani. The French section was managed by Mohamed Mezouar. Four issues of this journal were published, starting from the beginning of 1978.

12. This suggestion came during an association on August 25, 1978, attended by Moham-med Errami, Amhammad El Dasser, Mohammed Ait El Haj, Mohamed Moustaoui, Abdellah Jachtimi, Mohammed Oukouk, Hammad El-Hadiki, Mohammed Khalil, Abdelaziz Bourass, Lhoucine Ait Bahcine, and me.

13. Its president was Abdulhamid El-Zammouri, a national figure and the first governor of Casablanca following independence. Its members included: Ahmed Chafik; Ali Sidqi Azaykou; El-Tahami Ammar, a former minister of agriculture; Yahya Ben Toumert, former secretary general of the Interior Ministry and former director of the Treasury; Dr. Ousaden; Amhammed El Kifani, who was an officer attached to the Interior Minis-try; and others.

14. Participants in this discussion included association members Ahmed Akouaou, Rachid Belhaj, Mohamed Boulouz, Ahmed Boukous, Abdelaziz El-Jazouli, Mohammed Khalil, Mohammed Boutkhidouch, Lahcen Abakrim, and Abdellah Jachtimi.

CHAPTER 3

Activist and Cultural Initiatives

A Period of Intellectual Decisions for Amazigh Activism, 1980–1990

ESTABLISHING THE AGADIR SUMMER UNIVERSITY

The establishment of the Agadir Summer University was a major historical and intellectual development in the late 1970s. It was one of the most significant results of our dedicated efforts during this phase of our political, cultural, and social action. It also paid testimony to the great ambition that drove the association toward achieving our noble goals regarding our identity, language, and culture. Our dreams also fit with the context of North Africa at the time; political and cultural circumstances at the local and regional levels, as well as our deep desire and determination, all worked together to bring about this event, whose importance we shall see below. It was to have a major political and cultural impact on the present and future of the Amazigh cause, both in Morocco and beyond.

In the summer of 1979, I went to Agadir with my wife and our three-year-old daughter, Touf Itri, for the summer vacation. We chose to stay at the Camping International d'Agadir resort. While wandering around the city, visiting its various landmarks, markets, cafés, and meeting my acquaintances there, I observed that the city was in a poor condition and that its young people seemed lost.

As I returned and reached the edge of the city's port, my wife noticed tears in my eyes. When she asked why, I began to explain to her the conclusions I had drawn from this visit and my deep sorrow about the state of the city.

As soon as I returned to Rabat, I began contacting colleagues in the association to discuss the topic. I spoke to Ahmed Boukous, Ahmed El-Ghazali, Abdelaziz El-Jazouli, Lhoucine Ait Bahcine, El Houssaïn El Moujahid, and others. After several meetings in Rabat, I went to Casablanca to discuss the issue with members of that branch, such as Abdelaziz Bourass, Lhoucine Jouhadi, and Mohammed Khalil.

My idea was to organize a major series of cultural activities over the summer vacation, along a line stretching from Essaouira to Marrakech and southward. These events would encompass all aspects of Amazigh culture, from theoretical presentations to art exhibitions. Such an ambitious undertaking would exceed the modest capabilities of the association, so I began to reach out to people outside the association to persuade them to contribute to the project, whose contours were yet to be defined. I contacted a number of educated individuals working in the private sector, all hailing from southern Morocco, to try to convince them of the importance of the project. I also engaged with a group of intellectuals at the university of Rabat and government departments in the city. I wanted to mobilize them all to realize a project that would benefit the southern region and Amazigh culture. I was able to convene the first meeting of all these capable people at my house. I also invited some people from Agadir, led by Lahcen Kahmou. All the members of the Rabat and Casablanca branches of the association attended, as did others from outside, such as Ibrahim Akdime, an expert in accounting, teacher Mohammed Ben Yehia El-Ouajani, and Ahmed Al-Saif, the director of a research office. It was also the first time I met the brilliant poet and writer Mohammed Khaïr-Eddine, and it was an honor to host him at my house. The architect Ahmed El-Hariri, accountant Saïd Al-Raji, researcher El Karim Lahcene, and university lecturer Ahmed El-Aouad were also there. After I had laid out my proposal and my vision for the project, it became clear to everyone that it was impossible to reach this entire region, and that we would need to focus on a location that could serve as a launching point for the expansion we hoped to see over time. We agreed on Agadir and the surrounding district as the venue. Ahmed El-Hariri suggested that the project could be a summer university, serving as a gathering for cultural actors over the summer, with a defined cultural program. This idea was partly inspired by a summer university in Tunis, although the latter was touristic rather than cultural. This was the first time I had heard of such a project. The discussion continued until it was agreed to add the word "Association" to the term "Summer University," to avoid any confusion between it and the touristic summer university. The purpose of the project was now clear. As it was centered on Agadir, Kahmo began making contacts to round up volunteers and people to be involved, particularly those from the Socialist Union of Popular Forces (USFP), which dominated the municipal council. We also started preparing a founding charter, agreed to by consensus, laying out the objectives and intellectual orientations of the Summer University Association. I now found myself shuttling between Rabat, Casablanca, and Agadir to bring together different viewpoints and ease the fears of USFP members in Agadir over the project and its true objectives. Their apprehensions stemmed from the possibility that this cultural endeavor could be used by external parties to infiltrate their region. Eventually, an agreement was reached on the foundational document and the association's basic rules. The first general assembly was held at Kahmou's house in the Swiss City district of Agadir on December 16, 1979. We soon managed to turn this framework into a reality, a project that was to make major contributions to advancing the Amazigh cause. We decided to hold the first session of the university from August 18 to 31, 1980, under the slogan "Popular Culture and Unity in Diversity."

Oversight committees were formed early in 1980 to prepare for the session, which would be of unprecedented scale in the history of Amazigh cultural activity. The association mobilized all its resources to ensure that the event would be organized to the best organizational and academic standards. Three committees were formed for this purpose.[1]

The following is the founding document, agreed upon by all contributors to the creation of the Summer University Association in Agadir:

> The establishment of a summer university in Agadir has become an imperative; it is something demanded by the broad base of inhabitants from this region, who have been force-fed ignorance, and deprived, for various reasons, of the cultural and intellectual resources fitting of the role to which they should be able to aspire, as it had been throughout the region's history, both nationally and at the African level.

> - Nobody can deny the cultural role that the Southern Region has played on the intellectual level and in preserving the authenticity of our national thought throughout the ages.
> - This project is an extension of this role historically played by the South, starting from its unique historical, geographical, economic and architectural characteristics, which have always highlighted its dynamic presence throughout Moroccan history, and which must be stressed in order to demonstrate the degree to which this region has contributed to shaping our national identity.

- The Summer University does not present itself as an alternative to the efforts that should be made to create universities and cultural institutions fitting with the region's role, especially given that it has now become the link joining up our nation after the territories that were under colonial occupation have been restored.
- All this gives rise to the idea of creating a summer university in Agadir, to bring the youth of the region and other enthusiastic young Moroccans face to face with their responsibility to contribute to the positive development of the region's intellectual and cultural life, and to alleviate the severe deprivation that has weighed on this area since colonialism landed on its soil, undermining its historical role and cultural radiance and forcing it to lag behind the country's more fortunate regions, on all levels.
- The region's role as a destination for tourism, a role thrust upon it, seriously threatens to wipe out its unique character, by imposing the alien values of the tourism sector and the drive for quick profit. The Summer University Association must therefore work to ameliorate this sweeping infringement and establish a solid intellectual awareness that places the national interest above all other considerations, and confronts all forms of subjugation we may face.

Although the Summer University Association opposes elitism, exclusivity and all that stems from them, it demands a serious level of culture and education that aligns with its aspirations to be a scholarly reference point for anyone wishing to understand the true potential of this region in various aspects of life.

For all these reasons combined, the Summer University will prioritize the following:

1. Channeling some of the energies of our nation's youth in general, and the youth of the Agadir region in particular, into contributing to the revival of the region and its development in various fields, within the framework of the Summer University.
2. Exerting efforts to benefit from their intellectual energies within the framework of the scholarly research that is the focus of the university, with the aim of raising awareness of the region's economic, intellectual, and cultural potential as well as the economic and social problems from which it suffers.

3. Creating an intellectual and cultural atmosphere to help establish a new approach to cultural interaction, freeing beneficiaries among the general public from the formalities usually imposed at traditional universities.

4. Contributing to addressing the problems facing our national culture in its correct and broader context, and countering attempts, whether conscious and deliberate or otherwise, to distort it.

5. Approaching cultural phenomena through a rigourous and critical approach, rejecting hasty and ignorant unilateral propositions, which are often dictated by preconceived convictions and limited horizons and which hinder any serious scholarship.

6. The Summer University will strive to strengthen the cultural and civilizational bonds that have connected us with our brothers in Africa across the generations, by conducting comparative studies on the cultures of our peoples.

The Summer University is fully aware that it will not be able to achieve all the goals it has set itself, noting the difficulties that will stand in its way. However, it is confident that its early mistakes and its experiences over time will serve as its greatest guide and motivation to achieve the goals for which it was established. Its ambitions will only be realized if it is embraced by productive young people, to whom its curricula offer a scholarly extension to their interests and specialties, thereby allowing everyone to contribute substantively toward building a richer national culture.

I will return to the Summer University, the challenges it faced, what it achieved, and its political and cultural impact, later in this memoir.

PREPARATIONS FOR THE INAUGURAL SESSION, AND ADMINISTRATIVE AND FINANCIAL OBSTACLES

When the association decided to organize the first session of the Summer University, it had no financial resources besides what it could gather from activists and sympathizers with our cause. Naturally, this would not suffice to organize such a major event, lasting twelve days, including three seminars a day and a group trip, among other activities. Our biggest difficulty was securing accommodation for the participants. We also had to allocate the money we had gathered to provide food, posters, and signs. To solve this problem, we lodged a request with the Ministry of Education to see if we could use a teacher training school for accommodation. It is worth noting that the minister of education at that time was Ezzedine El-Iraqi, widely known for his racism and hostility toward the Amazigh cause. The request was made, and I waited for a response, positive or negative. After waiting for a month, as the date of the Summer University approached, it occurred to me to seek help from Dr. Ahmed Ramzi, the minister of Awqaf (Islamic endowments) and Islamic Affairs. He was also the deputy for the city of Agadir in the House of Representatives. Given our good relationship, and his position as the city's representative, I suggested he participate by delivering a lecture at the event. He agreed and chose to speak on "Popular Medicine in the Southern Region."

Dr. Ramzi had been unaware of all aspects of the summer university or its political underpinnings before he agreed to take part, speaking on a medical subject, without considering the consequences of that or of sympathizing with us, especially as a government minister. Sitting in front of me, in his office, he called El-Iraqi to inquire about the delay in responding to our request, informing him that he had joined the association and would participate in the session. For El-Iraqi, this constituted a guarantee, as well as being a responsibility on Ramzi for any consequences the event could have for the authorities and the government, at a time when nobody knew its political nature and what reactions it might generate. I thanked Ramzi for his courage and his help and left. We soon obtained approval to use the teacher training school for accommodation, providing we furnished food and other necessities. I considered this half a solution to the accommodation problem. Next, I started contacting hotel owners in the city, asking if they could provide rooms for teachers who could not be accommodated at the school. I only managed to secure three rooms, at the Al-Najma hotel, owned by the late religious figure Moulay Larbi; three apartments at the Anzi hotel, made available to us by Najem Abaakil; and two rooms at the Arkana Hotel, thanks to Abdellah Essouiri. This was all the accommodation we were able to obtain at the time for that large number of participants. The next problem, after all this effort, was that the teacher training school did not have bathrooms where they could shower. Moreover, the school had not been cleaned since the end of the school term and was in a pitiful state. We had to resort to bringing the conference participants to the hotel rooms so they could shower. Everyone suffered due to the lack of cleanliness and the long duration of the session. These poor conditions forced us to manage the project with strictly limited resources. The only thing the city council provided us was the use of a bus to shuttle us between the city hall, where the activities were held, and the school, where most of the activists were fed and accommodated.

POLITICAL AND INTELLECTUAL OBSTACLES AND PROBLEMS

Despite all this, the university was indeed launched on the scheduled date, with great enthusiasm from cultural figures who came to deliver lectures, and from activists who came from various cities across Morocco to attend the Summer University, as well as the wide audience that gathered in the auditorium at the municipality. This irritated the authorities, who monitored each one of the many seminars, noting the public's interest and the intense debates that ensued from these presentations. This level of engagement was unprecedented for the authorities in this city. When I met the general secretary of the Prefecture at his office so he could review the program, he likened Agadir to the distant, mythical Waq Waq Island referred to in medieval Arabic literature. Some sessions extended very late into the night, and the authorities sent daily reports to the central authorities in Rabat to keep them continuously updated on what was happening and the ideas expressed by both organizers and audience members alike. They were not used to hearing such new and bold ideas.

However, the main problem we faced from the start was that certain elements from the USFP party tried to sabotage the event. They sent a group of activists to thwart it, despite the fact that we had agreed with the party on a cultural and theoretical foundation affirming the necessity of such intellectual events to break the isolation of the city and the region, which had been dismissed as nothing more than a tourist destination. Even though the program started with a lecture by Professor Omar Boumqas, a party figure originally from the area, the group persistently and violently intervened to shift the direction of the discussion and sow suspicions about the intentions of the organizers and the parties allegedly backing us.

As evidence of this stance, not a single member of the municipal council attended the opening session, so as not to endorse this significant cultural effort, the likes of which the city had never witnessed. Party officials in the region clearly believed and hoped that the university would fail from the start. However, they were to be disappointed, as these people, who had been manipulated and believed what they had been told about us, realized after two or three days of following our program that their leaders had been mistaken. Our strategy was to meet their provocations with calmness. We engaged them in discussion, calmly and logically. We invited them to accompany us throughout the session, during presentations, at meals, and at our more intimate gatherings. We surprised party officials because, within a short time, we managed to win over those misled brothers, and they began to share our intellectual convictions and to defend them in their own interventions and questions. A case in point was Lhoucine Ouaizi, who went on to become a leading activist for the Amazigh cause and an active member of our association, as well as completing his doctorate with a thesis on "The Emergence of the Amazigh Cultural Movement." This was just one of our achievements during this first session of the Summer University, and a victory for the Amazigh movement in its first endeavor on such a scale, winning over significant intellectual cadres thanks to the strength of the association in intellectual and political discussions.

The other issue we faced was the reluctance of religious scholars from the region to participate in the university with lectures on religious topics. Abdellah Jachtimi, who had studied at the famous Al-Qarawiyyin mosque-university in Fes, joined me in sending requests to many clergymen who had graduated from Dar El-Hadith El-Hassania or from other institutes, including Al-Qarawiyyin. Professor Mohammed Al-Othmani, another religious scholar and a graduate of Dar Al-Hadith who had become an inspector of the traditional schools in Souss, and who shared our ideas and convictions, accompanied us to visit these scholars to try to convince them to take part. Yet despite all these efforts, we were unable to sway a single one. We tried, among others, El-Abadi, who was responsible for the municipal treasury in Agadir, Lhoceine Ouajaj, the head of the Association of Religious Scholars of Souss, Abdullah El-Karsifi, and poet Mohammed El-Othmani, who was a professor at the Mohammed V Institute in Taroudant, and the head of its academic council, among others, but to no avail. I believe their refusal to take part, despite all our efforts to convince them, came down to their conviction, ever since they became aware of AMREC and its objectives, that it existed to revive the Amazigh language heritage as in order to do away with the Arabic language and return the country to the pre-Islamic era (*jāhiliyya*). There was also another, more important reason: that they were connected, through their scholarly and administrative duties, to the state, which had not yet taken a position on the project. Therefore, they feared for their positions and were avoiding any action that might jeopardize their interests.

Faced with these scholars' reluctance to take part, we decided to organize a group visit to an ancient school in the vicinity of Agadir, for anyone who was interested. Through this, we aimed to acquaint the visitors with the role of such old schools in preserving religious and cultural heritage, and to introduce them to the school's educational system and curriculum. The visit also included listening to the schoolmaster (*faqīh*) delivering his religious lesson in Tamazight, which he used for teaching the Quran and even for Arabic rhetoric, explaining everything in Tamazight. This idea was a powerful riposte to those who claimed that we were against religious values, or even accused of us being atheists, in order to justify their opposition toward our work to deepen Moroccans' awareness of their Amazigh identity.

Every part of the Summer University's program was carried out as planned. What was striking was the significant turnout by the educated public to attend each session. As I have mentioned, the program was intensive, with three sessions a day—one in the morning and two in the afternoon—which often sparked intense intellectual debates. The session on Saturday, August 23, was the most important of these seminars. It focused on the issues around the Amazigh language, and featured speakers Mohammed El-Chami, Ahmed Boukous, El Houssaïn El Moujahid, Marzouq El Ouariachi, Qadi Qaddour, Abdelrahim El-Daoudi, Lhoucine Ajkoun, and Mohamed Sabri. Given the caliber of the participants, this session was able to address the Amazigh issue in all its aspects: linguistic, social, and historical. The hall was packed to capacity and the weather was hot. The comments and questions from the audience were sometimes chaotic, as some of the participants had not followed the university from the start and were unaware of how discussions were conducted, making their contributions feel out of place and seem, to some, like a call to give up. Who were the hidden forces behind this university? they asked. What was its purpose? These questions showed that they were making their last, desperate effort to sabotage the event, by sowing doubt, accusing us of treason and collusion. Yet the rest of the audience met all their interventions with indifference. Indeed, the seminar was a historic moment, serving as an opening argument on the Amazigh issue and an official announcement that Amazigh discourse had come of age. The professors lived up to their historical and academic responsibilities, delivering convincing and scholarly interventions, with strong arguments free from superficiality and emotion, leaving a positive impression on the audience and forcing the opposition to respect and consider this new reality in dealing with the issue. This seminar marked the first public airing of an Amazigh discourse that had been formulated throughout the 1970s.

On the topic of Amazigh discourse, I wish to highlight the work of Dr. Ahmed Boukous, a founding member of AMREC who also participated in this seminal event in the history of the Amazigh cause. Dr. Boukous is credited with bringing a modern character to Amazigh discourse, starting from the relationship between the Amazigh issue with the struggle of popular culture against the elitist, official culture that had monopolized Morocco's state institutions and held popular language and culture in contempt. During the 1960s and 1970s, as Amazigh discourse was crystallizing, a popular movement was contemporaneously emerging that became a revolutionary trend for change. Dr. Boukous, as an expert on sociolinguistics, was able to formulate a discourse and conceptual framework reflecting the revolutionary but rational nature of Amazigh discourse and its engagement in this broader trend. This modernist approach in Dr. Boukous's lectures and seminars helped enrich the conceptual frameworks of activists within the association. He also left his mark on all the association's activities and publications, with his deep commitment to ensuring precision and clarity in all its projects and publications. Given his status as a scholar within the association, Boukous was able to play a major role in defining the themes and slogans of the Summer University Association, starting from this, the first session.

On the subject of the professors involved in this historic seminar, it would be remiss of me not to mention El Houssaïn El Moujahid. Although he was not a founding member of the association, he came to play a major role within it due to his extensive education in various fields, both in Arabic and French. He also had much to offer due to his early engagement in journalism and writing, before going on to specialize in linguistics. El Moujahid brought these rich experiences and skills to his activism within the association, and to the Amazigh cause in which he deeply believed. As a patient activist, dedicated to his principles and his friendships, and sociable by nature, he never failed to fulfill his duties with enthusiasm and dedication. These qualities combined to shape his thinking and made him an excellent analyst and critic of events and ideas. Throughout his time with the association, he was responsible for editing and drafting most of its writings, including statements, among them the foundational platform for the Summer University and the Agadir Charter.

I would also like to acknowledge the work of Mohammed El-Chami, whom I had the honor of meeting that same year, 1980. He participated in the first Summer University with a lecture that addressed what was, for us, a fundamental issue: "The Problem of Amazigh Writing and the Three Options: Tifinagh, Aramaic Letters, Latin Letters." He extensively explored the Tifinagh script, its history and writing, introducing the Amazigh writing system, which, despite being new to the audience, is a key symbol of Moroccan Amazigh identity. Chami is an activist and a unifying figure by all standards. I admire his courage in taking the initiative and his unreserved engagement in every action or project aimed at promoting and defending Amazigh culture as well as his participation in cultural and intellectual events and his constant contributions to the work of Amazigh associations through the Intilaqa and Elmas cultural associations and the National Coordination of Amazigh Associations in Morocco, and in every serious initiative supporting the Amazigh cause. He has always demonstrated his patience, seriousness, and loyalty in his friendships and commitments.

The presence of individuals like these, alongside other activists throughout this seminar and the entire session, honored the Amazigh struggle and discourse on the national level.

Over the course of the Summer University, various hiccups and some tense moments threatened to disrupt the meeting, which meant I did not have a moment of rest throughout the entire event. I had to be at every location and handle every problem or challenge that arose, as I was the primary responsible person as head of the organizing committee. There were also some funny incidents, which do not merit discussion. The point is that all the activists present were ready and prepared to engage in any battle or intellectual confrontation to achieve the outcomes we sought. Everyone was aware of the need to overcome the negativity and obstacles that could hinder the event or give the opponents of Amazigh culture opportunities to prevent us from reaching our goal. I would also like to acknowledge the role of the late thinker and poet Mohammed Khaïr-Eddine, who constantly wrote for the French-language newspaper *Le Maroc*, which was the mouthpiece of the National Rally of Independents. He wrote articles about the topics discussed at the sessions and expressed his opinion on everything related to Amazigh language and culture at the event. This helped to break the siege imposed by the party press around the Summer University, despite its historic significance and its success.

IMPLICATIONS OF THE SUMMER UNIVERSITY'S SUCCESS

Political Implications and Reactions

I have already noted the political conditions under which we prepared to hold the Summer University. When King Hassan II was asked by a journalist if there was a "Berber" problem in Morocco, he replied in the negative. This came after the events of Tizi Ouzou in Algeria in March 1980, just three or four months before we held the first session of the University in Agadir. We were placing ourselves at risk by insisting on pushing on with our preparations despite the king's denial that there was such a thing as an Amazigh cause in Morocco. We were aware that the minister of the interior at the time, Driss Basri, could have used the king's comments to have us thrown into prison, or at least prevent us from organizing the first such event of its kind in Morocco. However, it may be that officials at the interior ministry were unaware of the content of the event. This is unlikely, as during that era nothing escaped their sight. Another possible factor is the political situation facing Morocco at the time, including threats to its territorial integrity, which may have pushed the ministry to ignore us in order to avoid complicating the situation still further. During the first sessions, the local authorities in Agadir flooded the central government with reports about our activities and informed it of every position stated during our seminars. Indeed, during the inaugural session of the National Debate on Education in Ifrane on Thursday August 28, 1980, in which we played a major role, His Majesty indirectly referred to the Summer University:

> We cannot be satisfied with being stingy, and this will not come unless the foundation is correct. If the foundation is correct, it will draw from the deep well of Moroccan ingenuity, and the structure of Morocco will remain the structure of Morocco, and it will not be blown about by whirlwinds or damaged by hurricanes. Therefore we must preserve our authenticity, our heritage and our components. There is a heritage committee at the Moroccan Academy that is studying heritage, and will present its findings at its next session in November. Its recommendations, in summary, are intended to revive Berber heritage at the universities. We must not neglect this at the universities. We should study our history and the fundamentals of our civilization, which have enabled us to stand up to those who attack us. We do not have a deficiency complex, unlike some countries. Thank God, we took the vaccine for this in 1930 and 1937.
>
> Whatever is said about this issue, which has taken on a political meaning, Morocco is vaccinated and has protection and immunity. This issue is not a problem for Morocco. Rather, it is a horizon that we can open before us without fear, because the Moroccan family is integrated, and this is something that people see as the face of Morocco, which is distinguished by this unique integration.
>
> Therefore, we must preserve this authenticity and this heritage, but by heading toward the future, and this advancement toward the future is imposed upon us by our ingenuity and by our past. In our history we have been the link transmitting knowledge from the East

to the West, and from the West to Europe, thanks to our links with the entire world, our presence at the meeting of the two seas, and our geographical position. This obliges us to play our role for the good of our continent, to preserve these characteristics and assets. This can only work if we search for foreign languages that will enable us to live with the 20th century, and which will allow us to become men of whom the Arabs, the Muslims and the Africans can be proud.[2]

King Hassan's statement was perhaps the first political reaction to the Summer University, dealing with the subject of the Amazigh issue, which he had previously declared did not exist in Morocco. Following his statement, however, some opponents of the Amazigh cause who had monitored the session started calling us the "royalist youth," on the grounds that the king had shown bias toward us by employing the concepts of "heritage, authenticity and Berberism."

However, we all ignored these accusations, as everyone who had attended the event and engaged in the communication between the organizers, the audience, and the lecturers had seen the truth: that we were independent from both the government and the political parties, that what we were defending was our deep intellectual and political convictions, and that we were only expressing the historical, linguistic, and civilizational reality of Morocco.

That said, this official response from the highest authority in the country was not reflected on the ground. The local authorities saw the success of the project and the king's speech as gains for which we must pay a price, as if these gains came at the expense of their failures, as they had been unable to prevent the university taking place. The first reaction to this was that they tried to assassinate me on the last night of the event, considering me the key element joining everything together. They had become convinced of this through my activity and responsibilities in the organization, from conception to realization.

This failed attempt to eliminate me came after a series of attempts to silence us and bury our voice, targeting certain founders of AMREC. The authorities focused on the founding members of the association, considering them the root of the problem that must be eradicated at its base. Therefore, we cannot rule out that the possibility that the authorities were behind the kidnapping in 1980 of Boujoumaa El-Habbaz, whose fate is still unknown. This was followed by the trial of Ali Sidqi Azaykou, who in 1982 was sentenced to a year in prison for publishing an article, in Arabic, in the magazine *Amazigh*, expressing his views on the history of Morocco. This article had been released in the in the *El-Kalima* journal of the Souss Association of Religious Scholars, without causing any problems at the time, so this was an empty accusation. The real intention was to silence the voice of truth in addressing Moroccan history from a national perspective. The authorities in Fes also threatened and intimidated Ahmed Akouaou, accusing him of extremism over his writings and his relationship with Algerian activists in Tizi Ouzou, among other baseless charges.

All of this came immediately after the first Summer University, which had bewildered the authorities, meaning they now moved to silence the founders of the association. However, the matter did not end there. The authorities in Rabat also refused to renew the passport of Ahmed Boukous, and we were only able to secure its release when I intervened by contacting a sympathizer with our association who worked at the Associations Section of the Security Directorate in Rabat, Abdelkader Al-Omrani. He was able to intervene with the police to have the passport released. The authority's accusations against Boukous were all related to his activities in the leftist movement, in which he was active at Dar Al-Maghrib in Paris while he was preparing his PhD.

These are some of the pressures, then, that were manifestations of the official reactions to our association organizing the first session of the Summer University. Although they varied in time and intensity, they all had the same aim: to silence these voices expressing the aspirations of the Amazigh—that is, the Moroccan people—to restore the status of their language, culture, and civilization, and to finally rid themselves of the dependency and intellectual and political alienation that were afflicting the country.

The authorities' punitive political reactions lasted for several years, because they knew very well that this promising beginning of expressions of Amazigh identity, by a significant elite, would extend to the public, not only at the university, cultural, intellectual, and ideological levels but also at the party political level. Therefore the authorities saw it as an open challenge, and they dealt with events according to their perceptions of these developments, which were in any case inevitable.

Reactions on the Cultural Level

The participation of Professor Mohammed Chafik, who was then director of the Royal College (a school dedicated to educating the princes and princess of the Alaouite dynasty) and had held several senior education positions, was a strong message from the authorities that the Amazigh cause was a national responsibility from which nobody should be excluded, regardless of their administrative position or their intellectual or ideological orientation. Furthermore, speech of the late King Hassan II in Ifrane, mentioned above, was for us a signal that he had received this message. King Hassan later made the move of appointing Mohammed Chafik to the Royal Academy of the Kingdom of Morocco. This was seen as a message to Amazigh activists that their message and protest against the marginalization of everything Amazigh had been heard, and that Chafik was considered the representative of their aspirations within one of the state's most prestigious academic institutions.

As for other cultural reactions, and those related to the political parties, the Summer University marked the start of discussions of the Amazigh issue within several political organizations, especially those considered left-wing: the Progress and Socialism Party (PPS), the Socialist Union of Popular Forces (USFP), and the Organization for Democratic and Popular Action (OADP). Reactions varied from one party to another, but the common feature was that their youth wings demanded a dialogue on the subject, in light of these parties' lack of literature or positions on the Amazigh issue. The Socialist Youth, a wing of the PPS, organized meetings with Amazigh activists to clarify and understand all dimensions of the Amazigh issue, while the others limited themselves to encouraging their activists to engage in analyses and express personal positions in their newspapers: *El-Anoual*, the *Socialist Union*, and *El-Alam*. These were based on their personal perceptions and were mostly emotive treatises built on Arab nationalist perspectives, far removed from the Amazigh linguistic, cultural, and civilizational reality of Morocco. Yet despite the negativity and backwardness of these arguments, the Amazigh issue had become the topic of the moment and imposed itself culturally and politically.

In response to the trend reflected in these reactions, Arab nationalists in Morocco turned to their allies in the Middle East, seeking material and moral support to strengthen Arab nationalism in Morocco, in a bid to counter the modern nationalist trend reflected by Amazigh discourse. This was a trend that had surprised them, because they believed that their Arab nationalist ideology had taken root in the Moroccan mind and become a reality in society, thanks to the vast amounts of money spent on achieving this goal. Accordingly, these entities in Morocco intensified their contacts with the Arab East to drum up support in the media and by organizing cultural activities to support the Arab nationalist camp in Morocco. This campaign reached the point of an orchestrated attack on the Amazigh cause, both in Morocco and more broadly in North Africa. A dossier of articles published by *Anoual* to this effect is just one example, and the creation of the "Forum for Thought and Dialogue" association is another, to which I shall return.

These activities also included an increase in the number of trips, sponsored by the Arab nationalist regimes, particularly to Iraq and Syria.

This political onslaught was accompanied by a media campaign to the same effect and for the same purpose. Many articles were published on topics connected to the Amazigh cause, with the aim of misrepresenting it and defaming it. They included:

- An article in Arab and international newspaper *Annahar*, "The Berber in the Arab Maghreb: The Secret of Sudden Consciousness," by Siraj Mohammed Mounir (May 5, 1980)
- An editorial in French-language newspaper *Maroc Soir* titled "Defending and Illustrating Berber Culture," by Ahmad Al-Alawi (March 28, 1980)
- An article in *El-Alam* cultural newspaper, "The Sociology of Amazigh Dialects of Morocco," by Ahmad Boudhan (July 9, 1982)
- A report in *El-Alam* on the symposium "The National Culture: Between Elite Culture and Popular Culture," by Rashid Banani (March 25, 1981)
- Notes on the "Anoual" symposium on the topic "Culture, the Educated and the Problems of Change," in *Al-Ahdath* newspaper (January 30, 1981)
- "Donatism: The First Spontaneous Socialist Experiment in the Maghreb, Before Islam," in *Al Muharrir*, by Mohammed al-Habib al-Fourkani (May 27, 1981)

These are just some of the articles published during this period following the first session Summer University in August 1980, during which Algeria and Morocco witnessed a series of events related to the Amazigh issue.

POLITICAL AND INTELLECTUAL TRANSFORMATIONS IN NORTH AFRICA

I believe that the organization of the Summer University in Agadir in August 1980, and the reactions it provoked, as well as the events in Tizi Ouzou, Algeria, in the spring of the same year, were the start of a fundamental change in this region of the world. These two events were the first indications that this change had arrived. However, they were also an inevitable result of the major struggle intellectuals and activists had waged to confront an unacceptable reality, imposed by the ruling political and cultural elites, that obscured and concealed the historical and cultural realities of North Africa. It was clear that the authorities were beginning to understand this message, and both Algeria and Morocco were beginning to witness this cultural revolution in its true form, which rejects any imposed reality that is out of harmony with the civilizational, linguistic, and cultural reality of the Amazigh people in North Africa.

In Morocco, both authorities and political parties believed that what had been aired and expressed at the Summer University would go unheeded, or at least that its impact would be limited to those who had been present. However, when the session's proceedings were published, it became obvious that things were now serious, and that the project would have an impact both for intellectuals and for society at large. After they were published, these notes became a key reference point for Amazigh discourse more generally.

Our work did not stop after the first session of the Summer University in Agadir. We pressed forward with our creative struggle to spread awareness, now based at the association's headquarters, which we opened in the Hassan district of Rabat in 1981. This became a meeting point and a space for disseminating our message. It soon transformed into an Amazigh cultural center that attracted students, academics, and the general public to listen to lectures by university professors who were active within the Amazigh movement, as well as those interested in history, social sciences, and popular culture in general.

This headquarters was officially opened at a ceremony attended by activists of the association from Rabat, Casablanca, Kénitra, and Mohammedia. I delivered the opening speech in written Amazigh, the first of its kind in this period of our association's history. I would like to mention to just a few of the presentations that were given at this headquarters, all of which were aimed at deepening our understanding of our language and our Amazigh identity, which is at the core of our heritage:

- "Linguistic Studies on Amazigh," by Dr. El Houssaïn El Moujahid, February 26, 1982
- A presentation on the proposed National Institute for Art and Folk Expressions, by Dr. Ahmed El-Ghazali, on March 5, 1982
- A presentation on language and the self among the Amazigh, by Dr. Ahmed Boukous, on April 17, 1982
- A semiotic reading of photographic images during the protectorate, by Dr. Moustafa El Chazli, on May 14, 1982
- A discussion on a research paper on *aḥwāsh* dance, by Professor Ahmed Bouzid and Ahmed Assid February 20, 1982

- A joint session with the Association of Comparative Literature, on May 21, 1982
- A psychological reading of "Hamou Onamir," by Dr. Lhoucine Ait Bahcine, on April 2, 1982

I would like to note here that Ahmed Assid, who was then a student, joined us in the early months of 1982. We were introduced by Mohamed Moustaoui, during a visit to a friend who was sick at Ibn Sina Hospital. I proposed to Assid, who was studying at the Faculty of Arts in Rabat at the time, that he join the association, which he did. He arrived at the association as Ahmed Bouzid was working on his research paper on *aḥwāsh*, a collective dance and performance style practiced by Amazigh tribes in the Atlas Mountains. I suggested to Assid that he conduct a critical reading of it alongside Omar Amarir, as they were both interested in this aspect of Amazigh heritage.

I was impressed by Assid's intervention. I mentioned to some senior members of the association that this student would go on to play a significant role in Amazigh culture, and that we should guide and take care of him to help him achieve his full potential.

That is indeed what happened. I began assigning him various literary and academic tasks the same year as he joined the association. Yet for reasons unknown to me, by the end of the same year, he had suddenly stopped attending the association. However, in the early 1990s, we were surprised to see some of his writings in the *Socialist Union* newspaper. In 1992, Abdelaziz Bourass and I met him at a seminar about musician Lhaj Belaid in Tiznit. After some considerable effort, we managed to convince him to return to Amazigh activism and to dedicate his intellectual efforts to the cause. He accepted and was tasked with leading the Taroudant branch of AMREC and joining the Summer University in Agadir. Finally we made an effort to bring him from Taroudant to Rabat, and he joined the central office of the association.

PREPARATIONS FOR THE SECOND SESSION OF THE SUMMER UNIVERSITY

As soon as we managed to publish the proceedings of the first session of the Summer University, given our insistence within the association on continuing our struggle for our cause, we began preparing and thinking about organizing a second session in the summer of 1982, as a parallel to our daily work both at the association's headquarters and nationally. We paid no attention to the articles that were being published to attack or defame

Amazigh culture, nor to the harassment and potential reactions the authorities were preparing to prevent us from continuing our work as activists. As
soon as the authorities became aware that we planned to organize a second
session of the Summer University, and realized the stage we had reached in
our academic and material preparations, they gave us a nasty shock: They
arrested Ali Sidqi Azaykou. This sent us a clear message that we should stop,
but it also reflected the dilemma the authorities were in, due to the intellectual and political convulsion caused by Amazigh activism in the political
and intellectual milieu both locally and regionally. They opted therefore to
arrest Azaykou, put him on trial and imprison him on charges of spreading
tendentious ideas regarding the history of Morocco. These were of course
baseless charges, because what he published in *Amazigh* magazine, in Arabic, had already been published in the *El-Kalima* magazine affiliated with the
Association of Scholars of Souss, and it did not contain attacks on anything
considered sacrosanct. Rather, it expressed his point of view on the history
of Morocco: simply a perspective, which gave no reason for the writer to be
punished. It bears repeating that Azaykou was also a member of the Amazigh
Association, which had organized a lecture by Senegalese President Léopold
Sédar Senghor on "Authenticity and Modernity in Amazigh Culture." For
the authorities, these events showed the extent of the influence of Amazigh
activism, which they felt had to be stamped out, for the political and cultural
reasons mentioned above. The trial of Ali Sidqi Azaykou was, in reality, a
threat to all Amazigh activists.

THE TRIAL OF ALI SIDQI AZAYKOU DURING PREPARATIONS FOR THE SUMMER UNIVERSITY

The arrest of Ali Sidqi Azaykou was not a random move by the authorities. They were very aware of his dedication and sincerity in his intellectual
choices, and the extent of his dedication to the Amazigh cause, convictions
he would not abandon. The authorities also paralyzed the work of the "Amazigh" association, in which Azaykou was a key figure. Yet not only did we
overcome their attempts to stop us preparing for the second session of the
Summer University but we also turned Azaykou's arrest and trial into a significant political event, in which freedom of expression itself was on trial.
Many ideas about history, civilization, and rights were discussed in court, to
which national public opinion would not have been exposed were it not for
this opportunity provided to the Amazigh movement to express them, and
to expose the harassment threatening Amazigh activism in our country.

The first person to inform me of Azaykou's arrest was Abdelaziz Bourass, who called me from Casablanca. A meeting had been planned at his house on the weekend, as part of preparations for the Summer University. Ahmed Boukous also met me and confirmed the news. I called Azaykou's home for more information. The meeting had been set to take place in Casablanca on Saturday, but Boukous suggested that we should not attend it until the situation became clearer. Therefore, I delegated Ahmed El-Ghazali to represent us at this preparatory meeting, which was attended by many of our brothers in Casablanca.

After some investigating, I learned that the lawyer Abderrahman Ben Amrou had been hired by the Amazigh association to defend Azaykou. I did not have a close relationship with Ben Amrou, despite knowing his political beliefs, and he, for his part, knew neither me nor my beliefs to the point where he could reassure me, or give the matter the care and attention it deserved. Therefore, I went to Kénitra to visit Dr. Omar El-Khattabi, whom I know and trust. I informed him of the arrest and the importance Ali held for us in the Amazigh movement. I explained to him the seriousness of this arrest and the possibility that the authorities were planning a wider escalation against the movement. We agreed to keep in contact to manage the matter and to prepare for any emergency. Then he picked up the phone and called Ben Amrou, asking him to receive me immediately and to take my statements seriously. He said I would explain to him the case of Azaykou, whom Ben Amrou had seen merely as an element of the youth movement, and had paid little attention to the affair. I then went to meet Ben Amrou at his office. We talked for more than an hour and a half, during which I briefed him on the Amazigh cause and the struggle since the creation of AMREC in 1967. I told him that our detained brother was one of its founding members, with no relation to the popular movement, as the lawyer had thought, and that the arrest was part of the authorities' strategy to intimidate us, in keeping with their political agenda. I also presented the lawyer with some of the association's literature, including a book on the proceedings of the first session of the Summer University. He responded by telling me that it was the first cultural trial to happen in Morocco, and that he was acting as defense counsel on a subject he had never thought about before, totally unlike the political subjects and pleas to which he was accustomed. Therefore, we agreed that he would supervise the procedural aspect of the trial and would welcome in his office the volunteer lawyers to agree on what steps to take during the trial. These lawyers would handle the defense side, being well-versed in the academic aspects of the Amazigh issue. After agreeing to this, Ben Amrou immediately set out to visit Azaykou in prison, to inform him of all these details and to reassure him that a team was preparing his defense. I also began contacting a group of lawyers in Rabat, notably Hassan Id Balkassam, who was a member of our association. Throughout the trial, I remained the link between them and Azaykou.

During his first session in court, I was surprised by something that greatly pained me. His friends, whom I had expected to be at the court to attend the trial and support him—even morally—during this monumental day for the Amazigh Association, stayed away. Ali looked at me as he was getting out of the police car and shook his head. I understood what was going through his mind at that moment, noting this painful truth.

AMREC however mobilized dozens of lawyers from various Moroccan cities to defend him, and indeed, the hearings were rich in intellectual debate. Much was said about linguistic and cultural rights and the distortion and defamation that had long harmed readings of our history. We also discussed the systematic exclusion of Amazigh language and culture from all areas of public life, from education to the media and the judiciary.

The authorities, however, were plotting another conspiracy against Azaykou. During the trial, he was informed by a female lawyer that certain parties were ready to release him if he retracted the ideas he had expressed in his article. Upon learning of this proposal, we told him through Id Balkassam that we rejected the idea and that Azaykou should not retract his ideas, as this was a conspiracy to damage his credibility and would eventually harm our cause. He agreed, rejected this proposal, and remained steadfast and unwavering. He was sentenced to a year in prison, while retaining his full dignity and strength of character. In the association, we did what was necessary to support his family during this crisis, which affected him and the work of Amazigh activism in general.

Thus, Azaykou's trial and the intellectual and political arguments for which it became a platform increased public awareness of the depth of the Amazigh discourse, its legitimacy, and its determination. The authorities failed in their plan to scare us into halting preparations for the second session of the Summer University in August 1982. Instead, the work continued, the program was set, and the theme of the session was chosen: "Popular culture and change."

We prepared for the second session and convinced many cultural figures and activists, as well as a number of intellectuals associated with political parties, to participate, as we had done in the first session. Before going to Agadir, through my contacts with administrative officials in Rabat and with leading activists who had direct connections with authorities in the south, we learned that they had decided not to authorize us to hold the session.

They kept on stalling, without disclosing why. Just a day before the session was due to start, Ibrahim Akdime and I paid a visit to the governor of Agadir at the time, Mohammed Motia, at his office. He flatly told us: "Here: My phone is at your disposal. If you can obtain authorization from officials in Rabat, you are welcome. If you go to the hall without this authorization, I will lock you all up." These were the governor's words, and indeed, I tried several times to contact officials at the interior ministry, as well as other ministers. Not a single one responded. In other words, they had been instructed not to issue us a permit, and they preferred not to talk to me, because they had not one single objective reason to justify this ban.

It was clear that the authorities had initiated this harassment as another way to stop the spread of the Amazigh cause and to prevent us from raising awareness of Amazigh identity among Moroccans. However, as usual, we did not stop. We welcomed the scholars as they arrived in Agadir from other cities, and we held meetings so they could present their ideas and lectures at the homes of certain activists, without the authorities knowing about it. Some of these meetings took place in cafés within or outside the city, or in Aourir, just up the coast from Agadir. It was tangible that the authorities had become extremely irritated by the activism of the Amazigh movement; this was why they had fabricated Azaykou's trial and banned us from organizing a second Summer University. They seemed to think that this would be enough to stop Amazigh activism.

After Azaykou's trial, I carried on with the dialogue I had started with Ben Amrou regarding the Amazigh cause, of which he had admitted his total ignorance. He was a leading figure in the Socialist Union party at that time. I suggested we open a dialogue on the subject after the Summer University in August 1982. He approved of the idea, especially after I explained to him how the Amazigh movement had started as an associative activist movement from the womb of civil society, raising the issue of linguistic and cultural rights in Morocco—rights that are fundamental to human rights as a whole, as stated in the Universal Declaration of Human Rights.

On my return from Agadir, after we had been prevented from holding the second session of the Summer University, I invited Ben Amrou to dinner at my house, along with the late Dr. Omar El-Khattabi, who had introduced us when we were organizing Azaykou's defense. The three of us met over a meal at my home in mid-October 1982.

Through our conversation with Ben Amrou, who was not a rank-and-file party member but a leader, we began to realize the extent of the intellectual vacuum afflicting many party leaders on particularly sensitive issues like the Amazigh issue (i.e., the issue of identity in Morocco). He also clarified the extent of the dominance of such monolithic thinking on their thoughts and behavior. This was undoubtedly a result of them being influenced by Arab nationalist thought, which does not believe in cultural diversity or political difference. After I refuted all the theses he cited based on this monolithic view, he told me, "The overwhelming majority of Socialist Union members are Amazigh, and there is no reason the majority could not decide to change the party's current position." I told him that this was the epitome of opportunism: A leader should not follow where the majority is heading then change his direction to maintain his position, but should rather have a vision for the future, to educate and enlighten the base on intellectual and political issues of which they are unaware. Otherwise, what is the point of leadership?

The events that I have recounted from between 1980 and 1982, including trials, bans, and harassment, resulted from the dynamics of Amazigh activism and the growing public awareness of the Amazigh cause. These developments confused many intellectual and political entities, and, although their reactions varied, most of them agreed on the need to confront this Amazigh cultural tide, which they considered a revolution against the ideology and thinking they promoted. Despite the intensity of the attacks and opposition to Amazigh activism, they only increased the activists' determination, pushing them further to develop and disseminate Amazigh discourse. Here, I will narrate a series of events that resulted from the shake-up caused by the Amazigh movement, which had declared itself with such force during this period, as we have seen. I consider the decade from 1980 to 1990 a period of testing. The authorities used any means to test our determination and willingness to make sacrifices for our just cause. We were also subjected to another type of test, by political parties and some of their theorists, who tried to distort our message and confront it with all kinds of intellectual terrorism, or by organizing cultural and intellectual events hostile to our intellectual current. They used every material means and media they could find to achieve this, while we were deprived of all those means except for that provided by our determination and the sincerity and depth of our discourse. These entities' attacks on the Amazigh movement and its message were another kind of test we had to pass during this period.

NEW POLITICAL AND CULTURAL DEVELOPMENTS AFTER THE AGADIR SESSIONS

I have already alluded to the political and cultural efforts that had been waged to confront the growing Amazigh movement since the late 1970s, with the first Summer University session in the summer of 1980, the banning of the second session in 1982, and the events that happened in between. Here, I will talk about some reactions toward Amazigh activism, starting with the "Forum for Thought and Dialogue," which held its first event in April 1979 by organizing a seminar on "Arab Unity: Between Theory and Practice." The forum had an Arab nationalist leaning and was supported by Arab nationalist states, especially Iraq and Syria. This orientation was reflected by the arrival of large numbers of delegates from the Arab Middle East, who dominated the forum. The seminar, which lasted several days, was held at the Samiya Hall in Agdal in April 1979. As it was taking place, the president of the Al-Intilaqa cultural association, Marzouq El Ouariachi, happened to be in Rabat. I informed him about the seminar and said we should be there. He agreed with my suggestion. I had already attended the opening session with two other members from the association. The Arab nationalists were out in force, including most leaders of parties considered to be progressive and nationalist, such as the communist leader Dr. Ali Yata, the socialist figure Abdelrahim Bouabid, and the political commentator Abdelkrim Ghallab, as well as the ambassador of Palestine to Morocco and major cultural figures in these party currents. The first speaker was a Palestinian from the Center for Palestinian Studies, who spoke about Arab unity, neglecting to mention any role for the region's peoples in this unity because it was all to be achieved by the will of the military leaders ruling in the Middle East. He also ignored the fate of other ethnic and cultural entities in these states within this unity he envisioned. At the end of his presentation, there was a noticeable lack of applause in the hall, except for a few leaders in the front row. During the discussion, El Ouariachi spoke up. He asked why this unity was to be created by force, disregarding the opinions of the people, and inquired about the fate of other non-Arab entities within them. The speaker responded by dodging the question, as he was not in a position to criticize military regimes that were supposedly going to unify the Arabs. He said that given that union was the goal, the use of violence was legitimate, because, for him, the end justified the means. Regarding the fate of other entities, the speaker said that unity would require the melting of these minorities into the majority, in order to achieve a single state with a single language, a formula that fit the vision of Arab unity. Here, El Ouariachi asked again for clarification on the fate of the Amazigh in such a union. As soon as the audience heard the word "Amazigh," the hall erupted in applause, and all the Middle Eastern attendees in the front row turned around to see what had happened and why the audience was clapping with such enthusiasm. From that moment, whenever the audience reacted to discussion of the fate of Amazigh identity in this supposed unity project, opponents of Amazigh identity in the seminar claimed that we were engaged in a conspiracy to sabotage the seminar and to convey to the attendees our rejection of any such unity project that did not take into consideration the Amazigh character of North Africa. They also claimed that I had coordinated with a member of the forum, Dr. Zaki Moubarak, whom they consider to be associated with the Amazigh.

After this incident at the opening session, I carried on attending the forum alone, to observe and record, especially the comments of Moroccan thinkers and politicians, to document their positions and perspectives on matters following the rise of the Amazigh cause, and to find out whether they were taking this reality into consideration or not. I noticed that most people were using the term "Berber" when talking about Amazigh identity, except for the late lawyer Al-Faruqi, a member of the bar association in Rabat, who spoke positively and used the term "Amazigh." I registered myself to speak on the last day, in order to refute both the claims of speakers from the Mashreq and those of Moroccans. I knew this final session would be attended by politicians and journalists from pan-Arab newspapers based in London and Paris, as well as from the Middle East. I started my intervention by explaining that the Amazigh people's solidarity with the Palestinain people was not out of Arab ethnic identification or religious accusation, but because the Amazigh are a free people who love freedom and struggle for the freedom and liberation of all peoples. Indeed, the word "Amazigh" means "free" or "noble." Our support for the Palestinian cause is thus part of our support for the rights of all peoples, without discrimination on the basis of ethnicity, language, or religion. I also expressed regret that some Moroccans were using the term "Berber." There are no "barbarians" in Morocco; rather, there is an Amazigh people that has been there for thousands of years. I concluded with the fundamental observation that the Arabs were still framing their identity project through the mentality of the Umayyad empire, which I said was regressive. A durable unity project would be one in which peoples define their own distinct identity first, in complete autonomy, then choose with whom to unite. What kind of unity were the Arab military leaders dreaming of in which the peoples had no freedom to choose their own destiny? We were already witnessing with our own eyes a complete lack of democracy and human rights, the persecution of cultural and religious minorities, and other practices that totally disregard human rights. So what kind of unity were the Arabs speaking of in this painful reality? Unfortunately, the session chair was Omar Fassi-Fihri from the Progress and Socialism Party. He kept interrupting me and did not want me to finish my comments. He repeatedly said, "If you have a question for the brothers, ask it. Do not insult the brothers." However,

I followed through with my critique and delivered my message. After that, a sense of dissatisfaction pervaded among the Middle Eastern attendees, because I had said things they did not want to hear. Upon leaving the hall, dozens of students gathered around me and expressed their own concerns about what they had been hearing from speakers, all of it aimed at attacking Amazigh identity or distorting their own history right before their eyes, and they had not been able to do anything about it.

This was, to my knowledge, the first cultural and intellectual event organized by this forum. It was clear that it had summoned substantial material resources, inviting supporters from the Arab Middle East, to misrepresent and attack our Amazigh message, which was simply aimed at raising rational and objective awareness of Amazigh identity among all Moroccans.

There followed another seminar that was no less important and was entirely aimed at framing intellectual and political transformations through the lens of the Arab nationalist agenda, by any means. This forum in July 1982 was on the topic of "Political Action and Heritage." I wish to record, however, that this seminar saw a shift, albeit limited, in the positions of some political organizations in our country, after all the events since the late 1970s. This change was noticeable in a text produced by the political bureau of the Socialist Union on the same topic as the seminar, "Political Action and Heritage." It was a comprehensive presentation of the Socialist Union's views on the relationship between politics and heritage, spanning sixteen full pages. The following are key excerpts:

> Heritage, as conceived by scholarship and activism, extends through-out our entire historical path, from the time our society was found on this specific patch of earth. It is not confined to a specific temporal, spatial, intellectual, spiritual, civilizational, urban or cultural domain. Our heritage is one of temporal and historical-temporal action, whose roots strike down through thousands of years, on every inch of our soil, in the mountains, on the plains, coasts and seas. It does not belong to any social class, region, or city over another; rather, it is a histori-cal whole and a civilizational heritage that is indivisible and does not accept racial, confessional or temporal exploitation, as it is a product of our presence and our shared historical and civilizational action.
>
> As much as we act and struggle politically, we also act and strug-gle in terms of heritage, because just as we carry the concerns of the present and the aspirations of the future, we also carry in our souls and beings the characteristics of the past and its illuminations,

embodying the factors of momentum, movement, and the civilizational representation that are active in our heritage, our historical memory in the present and our spiritual and cultural starting point toward the future . . .

The social and political advances achieved by "Donatism" in the Roman era, when a Moroccan monk initiated a movement and a revolution that temporarily prevailed, was based on a social doctrine that bore strong the features of socialist organization in community life, production, and wealth distribution.

The Moroccan people carried out this religious-political transformation when they withdrew from Christianity and abandoned it in one fell swoop, as Christianity had become a tool of oppression and persecution at the hands of Roman rulers after the third century AD, when Emperor Constantine elevated Christianity to become the official religion of the Roman state.

The alliance of the Masaesyli tribes, in a coalition of resistance and liberation, the ancient Maghreb people's 17 revolutions against Roman colonization, their traditional, steadfast rejection of foreign domination by any power, and their resistance to integration in any form into its culture or civilization: all this helps explain our society's steadfastness and resistance against contemporary campaigns brought to bear against it, with the aim of distracting it, dividing it, westernizing it and diverting it from its true identity and existence.

This presentation demonstrated something of an improvement in the stance of the Socialist Union during that period. However, while it acknowledged Moroccans' historical roots, stretching back for thousands of years, the history mentioned in this presentation was unfortunately not yet accompanied by any intellectual or political development within the party to formulate a positive stance toward Amazigh language and culture, as a civilizational heritage and a cultural and social reality for all Moroccans, nor a recognition of their linguistic and cultural diversity.

This position paper represented the moderate stance of the Socialist Union at that time. Members of the Organization for Popular Democratic Action (OPDA), led by the activist Mohamed Bensaid Ait Idder, were more nationalist and more committed to Arab nationalism. They had little time for the Socialist Union's stance or that of the Istiqlal Party, some of whose thinkers expressed, without explicitly declaring it, enmity and hostility toward the Amazigh cause. The OPDA members saw themselves as bolder and more able to repress and silence Amazigh activists, using all forms of intellectual terrorism and making use of a number of progressive nationalist theorists. They believed all these assets would be enough to suppress the Amazigh tide and silence the advocates of Amazigh consciousness. Their membership mobilized for this task, both by writing articles on the subject and by producing works to counter our theses and defend Arab nationalist perspectives on issues of culture and identity in Morocco. Their goal was to Arabize Morocco entirely and to definitively eliminate any cultural diversity in our country. Here, it is worth citing the prominent Moroccan nationalist philosopher Mohammed Abed Al-Jabri, a well-known theorist of Arab nationalist thought. In his book *Lights on the Problematic of Education in Morocco*,[3] he wrote that "the comprehensive process of Arabization should target not only the elimination of the French language as a language of civilization, culture, communication and transaction, but also—and this is of great importance—make efforts to kill local dialects, both Berber and Arabic." Allal El-Fassi, a leader and theorist within the OPDA, also wrote a book in much the same vein, categorically rejecting all cultural diversity or difference of opinion. In "The National Question, the Amazigh Tendency, and the Building of the Arab Maghreb,"[4] he poured out all his rage against the Amazigh cause and its proponents, as well as expressing his rejection of any language or culture other than Arabic and his refusal to recognize any national or cultural identity in Morocco other than that of the Arabs. He saw calls for awareness of the Amazigh identity in Morocco as a trend in North Africa, which he considered indisputably Arab land, at the stroke of a pen wiping out thousands of years of history, civilization, and culture.

These people did not stop there. Their next step was to publish a dossier in the party newspaper *Anoual* about this "Berber tendency," in the words of Al-Fassi. It was full of malice and intellectual deceit, taking comments by Amazigh intellectuals out of context and citing them in a way designed to harm them so that readers would understand them in the way desired by those who prepared the dossier, not as the original authors had expressed them. The dossier was edited by Abdessamad Belkebir—a leading figure in the OPDA and a major opponent of the Amazigh cause—and Allal Al-Azhar. They used it to attack Ahmed Boukous, Abdellah Bounfour, and Ahmed Akouaou, who were angered both by the newspaper's intimidation of the Amazigh cause and by its attack on freedom of opinion and the right to differ. Boukous and Ahmed El-Ghazali were compelled to respond with their own article in the Moroccan newspaper *Al Balagh Al Maghribi*, titled "On Democracy, Unity, and Pluralism" (January 11, 1986). The late Mohamed

Baniyahya Soussi, who was the newspaper's director and editor-in-chief, quickly entered into the fray, with an article on "The Limits of Nationalism and the Boundaries of Amazighity" (Issue 118, January 20, 1985). Yet the beautiful thing was that while the Arab nationalists of the OADP had been convinced that they alone were capable of halting and eradicating the rising tide of Amazigh intellectual awareness, and would succeed where the Unionists and Istiqlal had failed, the publication of the dossier sparked exactly the opposite reaction. It unleashed a flood of letters and articles to the newspaper, too many to publish, all of them criticizing its accusations against the Amazigh movement and our intellectuals. Moreover, the newspaper and its management were subject to a barrage of insults, which ultimately forced them to contact us, appealing for articles by Amazigh activists in order to lighten these attacks. They also repeatedly claimed that they had intended no offense toward Amazigh activists.

From 1982 onward, a slew of articles were published on various aspects of the Amazigh issue, often dealing with it violently and emotionally. These Arab nationalists could not stomach the emergence of Amazigh identity, which some of them saw as a deviation that must be stopped.

Here are some of the articles in question:

- "Culture and Awareness of Unity in the Arab Maghreb," *Al Ittihad Al Ichtiraki*, July 16, 1985
- Dr. Mohammed Abed Al-Jabri, "The Arab Consciousness in Morocco: A Contribution to the Critique of Colonial Sociology," *Al Ittihad Al Ichtiraki*, May 19, 1986
- Dr. Abdelkrim Ghallab, "Explaining the Weakness of Arab National Consciousness in the Arab Maghreb (Wednesday Discussion)," *El-Alam*, May 28, 1986

ENLIGHTENED MOROCCAN INTELLECTUALS FROM OUTSIDE THE AMAZIGH MOVEMENT BEGIN CALLING FOR PLURALISM AND RESPECT FOR DIFFERENCE

Despite the strenuous efforts of Arab nationalists seeking to halt the rising tide of Amazigh discourse and rejecting its calls for cultural diversity and the right to be different, between the late 1970s and the mid-1980s, a number of prominent thinkers emerged who shared such principles with the Amazigh movement. They included Abdelkebir Khatibi, with his books *La blessure*

du nom propre (1974) and *Maghreb Pluriel* (1984), and Chraïbi Driss with
La Civilisation, ma mère!... (1972) and *La mère du printemps* (1982), which
he dedicated to the Amazigh and all the country's minorities. It should be
noted that all these authors were Francophone Moroccans, and thus further removed than others from the influence of Arab nationalism. So they
expressed their opinions, advocating for diversity and acceptance of difference as a framework for culture and intellectual development, without any
complexes.

One outcome was that in 1982, for the first time, an invitation was
extended to an activist from the Amazigh movement to participate in a project by progressive forces, as they called themselves. Up until then, the Amazigh movement had been excluded, and indeed was not even recognized
as being part of the progressive camp. That year, the Palestinian leadership
was forced to leave Lebanon in the face of the Israeli invasion. In solidarity
with the Palestinian struggle and with Lebanon, *Al-Thaqafa Al-Jadida* magazine invited a number of thinkers, other publications, and organizations to
a meeting to be held at the Union of Moroccan Writers, to discuss ways to
support the Palestinian struggle in its crisis. I was invited to this meeting,
on the nomination of Ali Oumlil, who was part of the Moroccan Association for Human Rights. It took place on September 13, 1982. I suggested we
name the project "The Group for Cultural Support for Palestine" instead of
"The Working Group for Palestine" to indicate the project's cultural character and avoid it being dragged into political labyrinths. At the meeting, I met
the progressive Moroccan writer Abdellatif Laâbi and commended him for
mentioning the Amazigh issue during his presentation at the event, in which
he had said that Moroccan thought was still captive to its wounds from colonialism, and that the Amazigh problem, if not addressed, would also become
a wound that would be difficult to heal. He also addressed other issues, such
as women's rights and the problems of Arab thought in general.[5]

This meeting represented the first recognition of the Amazigh movement by the main elements of civil society associated with the Left. It also
showed that the movement was becoming a force to be reckoned with. Such
recognition from these intellectual and activist forces also helped to refute
accusations by some that the movement was dependent on the Moroccan
regime. The initiative to support Palestine, meanwhile, did not succeed. It
quickly ceased to operate and did not achieve anything of note for the Palestinian cause.

A new phenomenon now emerged in the debate among Moroccan
intellectuals, particularly those from well-known ideological orientations.
While everyone now acknowledged the existence of the Amazigh current

in the Moroccan intellectual arena, a trend arose that recognized this fact but also sought to belittle it by considering it a minority cause in human, cultural, and civilizational terms. This trend saw the Amazigh as one component floating among many in Moroccan society. These people started talking about the Andalusians and Moriscos, which had not previously been discussed as components of the national identity. They also added the "African component"—as if the Amazigh were not Africans—and the Mediterranean dimension. By adding to this list of dimensions, they were attempting to dilute the fundamental, primary Amazigh component at the heart of our national identity by cramming in other dimensions, striving to portray the Amazigh as just one of several minorities forming the national identity. The best expression of this new trend, which was now strongly manifesting itself in the writings of Moroccan intellectuals, was Larbi Messari's speech titled "Morocco: An Identity Card," which he delivered at the Arab Youth Forum for representatives of youth associations from various Arab countries, as part of the sixth Arab Games in Bouznika on August 12, 1985. The following is an excerpt from Messari's speech, in which he introduced Morocco to his Arab brothers taking part in the forum:

> Morocco is fundamentally a western country, but its sympathies and the origin of its identity lie in the Mashreq, the East, despite it having several distinctions within the Arab Islamic family. In Arabic, as you know, the Maghreb is in the west. The Arabs considered it the farthest point in the west, and named it *Al-Maghrib Al-Aqṣā* (the Farthest West). The west, and this is why I say it is fundamentally a western country, is where Morocco's vital interests lie. By this I mean its neighbours to the north, its neighbors to the south, and in the region of the Arab Maghreb.
>
> The first thing that can be said is that this multi-dimensional Morocco is, in fact, several Moroccos. We are almost a confederation of minorities. Every one of us in Morocco belongs to a minority. We could be called a mosaic of peoples. And for a mosaic to be what it is, it must be composed of multiple colors and shapes. Moreover, for a mosaic to be what it is, its pieces must be bonded with an adhesive material. For harmony to prevail, the assembly must be balanced, otherwise, the pieces of the mosaic will become scattered shapes. This mosaic was bonded by the religion of Islam, and by a culture, which is Arabic. Here lies the secret.
>
> In this confederation of minorities, consisting of Arabs, Berbers, Jews, Moriscos, and Blacks, none feels marginalized, or less or more

Moroccan, than the other. I always like to cite the example of Moroccan Jews living abroad. Despite the complex factors that pushed them to migrate, they have maintained a strong link to their origins.

To ensure coexistence, Moroccans have invented suitable formulas for themselves so that all this diversity can live in balance. Therefore, Moroccans are open-minded, moderate in a Cartesian way, and have a natural sense of proportion: they know how to measure their own particularity and their place in the community of nations, without arrogance or complexes.

There is another thing about Moroccans: We are all refugees. The founder of our independent state, Moulay Idris, came to Morocco as a refugee fleeing Abbasid persecution by the descendants of Ali bin Abi Talib. The country's inhabitants welcomed him and honored him out of respect for his lineage, as he belonged to *Ahl al-Bayt* (the descendants of the Prophet Mohammed). Furthermore, they crowned him as their king, as they saw that he could be the material that would unite their tribal mosaic.

So we see that despite Messari's broad erudition, significant media experience, and good manners, he too fell under the influence of all-pervasive Arab nationalist thought and fell, sadly, into their trap. He adopted the method of historical and social sophistry that flows through this school of thought, rendering us a hybrid people with no authentic origins, a society without flavor or scent.

This new school of thought voiced by Messari emerged from the mid-1980s onward, after the Amazigh movement had strongly emerged on the Moroccan cultural scene. It had become impossible to ignore the Amazigh identity of Morocco and its people, so this current sought to define Moroccan identity as a diverse mix of Arab, Amazigh, Andalusian, African, and Mediterranean. In doing so, it blurred the lines—intentionally of course—between the national identity and the cultural identity of the Moroccan people. However, the former is Amazigh and cannot be considered diverse, because it is based on the fundamental components that set it apart: land, people, language, and civilization, all of which are Amazigh. The latter is indeed diverse, in terms of religion, language, and culture.

In this connection, in 1984 we published a book by the AMREC activist Abdellah Jachtimi. It was a collection of religious rulings and jurisprudential analyses by the religious scholars of Souss, an echo of a similar work by a group of scholars from Fes, on purely religious matters. Jachtimi's approach was to compare the Abrahamic religions (Judaism, Christianity, and Islam) in his commentary on parts of the book. This raised the ire of the scholar Makki al-Nasiri, who was then the head of the Council of Scholars in Rabat and Salé. He set about contacting officials, asking them to ban the book, even demanding that it be burned and its author prosecuted. This put the project's funder, the owner of the Al-Maarif press, in a difficult situation, and threatened to cost him huge losses. Al-Nasiri also accused us over the ideas in the book, which displeased him due to their incompatibility with his Arabist, traditional intellectual orientation. We, for our part, defended ourselves by making contacts as high up as General Moulay Hafid Alaoui, the chief of staff of the royal court, who resolved the issue after confirming that the book, to his knowledge, did not desecrate any sanctities. Instead, he ruled that the Council of Scholars should respond in writing to the ideas within it, if there were indeed any truth to these claims.

I should note that the association did not at this time publish books in its name, as it does today, but rather in the names of their authors. These included *The Basin* by Jachtimi, *Moroccan Amazigh Poetry* by Omar Amarir, *Langage et culture populaire au Maroc* by Ahmed Boukous, and the poetry collection *Iskraf* by Mohamed Moustaoui.

I have recounted this incident from 1984 to highlight the harassment we faced at the time, both from the authorities and their acolytes and from the political parties' media outlets, which gave us no opportunity to defend ourselves or express our opinions.

SEARCHING FOR WAYS TO PURSUE AMAZIGH ACTIVISM AFTER THE PUBLIC HIATUS IN 1983

As we have seen, we faced suspicion from the state in how it dealt with the Amazigh issue, including punishing activists, as previously mentioned, or banning our cultural activities, such as the second Summer University in 1982, as well as threats of worse if we continued to do anything at all. We also faced a media onslaught from the party newspapers, in the form of articles defaming our work and deliberately distorting the history of our people, as well as books calling for the imposition of Arab nationalism at the expense of our identity, language, culture, and civilization. Faced with all this, all we had was our determination to defend our Amazigh identity, and we continued to call loudly for engagement in this quiet Amazigh cultural revolution, aimed at breaking with the mistakes of our ancestors, which is what had led us to this state of cultural and political subjugation. We called for cooperative efforts to achieve our intellectual and political independence, and to restore the dignity of our distinct language, culture, and civilization. This was not a call for racism or the exclusion of the other, but rather a call for the country's cultural variety to be recognized and taken into account, and for respect for the right to difference and for deeper awareness of the Amazigh identity of all Moroccans. These were the principles and focal points of our struggle. This was a battle in which we had scant material resources to deploy, apart from the firm desire of our activists and those who believed in the justness of our cause.

Given our situation, we decided not to engage in confrontations with unpredictable outcomes, and opted to focus on internal action, rather than external activities that might provoke these entities. In late 1983, we were forced to give up the headquarters we had been using at Rue Al-Qasr Al-Kebir in the Rabat neighborhood of Hassan. We suspended our public activities and lectures and moved to working inside homes and thinking about other methods suitable for the current reality, in secrecy and steadiness. Despite all this, we did not abandon our activism, which we considered a national duty that required us to exercise patience, caution, and thought. We also worked to deepen our discourse and prepare for the future, waiting for the right conditions so we could reemerge into the public sphere and engage in an intellectual confrontation and serious activism to achieve our goals.

After we gave up AMREC's headquarters at the end of 1983, we were forced to work in semi-secrecy, using our homes as meeting places for the association. Given the situation at the time, we had to think of new ideas and projects that would enable us to continue conveying our message to the public and to counter the organized attacks by opponents of the Amazigh narrative. As the president of the association, I proposed to my fellow activists[6] that we confront this campaign against Amazigh identity by publishing a white paper responding to the various hostile ideas disseminated by Arab nationalists and others against our own. We particularly had in mind Allal El-Fassi's aforementioned book, *The National Message*, which was an example of the distortion, fallacies, and every other tool they deployed against us, including intellectual terrorism. The brothers liked this idea, so we decided on the main axes of the book and distributed the topics according to each of our specialties and specific interests. The history axis was assigned to Azaykou, who was now out of prison, although he was not present at our meetings. The religious aspect and its relationship to Amazigh identity was allocated to Mohammed Chafik. I was tasked with contacting him, and I conveyed to him our vision of the project. He asked me to clarify the approach required in drafting the text. I suggested that he formulate it as if he were having a dialogue, or as if it were a letter addressed to the Islamists, to explain that there is no contradiction between our defense of the Amazigh identity of Moroccans and the principles of the religion. Our reality is like those of all non-Arab nations in the Islamic world, including Persians, Turks, Pakistanis, and others. The Amazigh cause is simply about protecting our language, culture, and everything that distinguishes our people from other peoples. El Houssain Ouazi was tasked with drafting his text with the same approach but as a correspondence or a dialogue with our comrades on the left. These two currents were our main interlocuters during this period, and we needed to formulate a discourse to enable them to share our ideas and clarify any confusion about our intellectual direction, in order to counter those with preconceived notions against our identity and history. The other chapters were to cover scholarly subjects, including history, linguistics, literature, and philosophy, presented within a cognitive framework that would help clarify aspects of the issue from the cultural and civilizational perspectives. I was tasked with the topic of "Amazigh Identity and Cultural and Civilizational Responsibility"; Ahmed El-Ghazali was to write on "Teaching the Amazigh Language"; Hassan Id Balkassam on "Amazigh Linguistic and Cultural Rights"; Mohammed Alhyan on "Amazigh Culture"; Ahmed Boukous on "The Amazigh Language"; and El Houssain Ouazi would prepare a "Critique of the Prevailing Political and Ideological Position on Amazigh Language and Culture," in addition to Mohammed Chafik's chapter topic on "Islam and Amazigh Culture." Essafi Moumen Ali was engrossed during this period with composing the first work of Amazigh prose, the play *Wassan Samidnin*, which he published in 1983.

Something that should be highlighted about the mid-1980s is the emergence of rights-based discourse around the Amazigh issue. The lawyer Hassan Id Balkassam, after being tasked with writing part of our white paper on the Amazigh issue, became a specialist in the rights framework of Amazigh demands. This was something that we had not previously employed in our arguments. It was new to the Amazigh struggle, and Id Balkassam represented added value in this regard, linking our struggle with the realization of linguistic and cultural rights for all peoples, legitimate demands under the Universal Declaration of Human Rights. This aspect would be central to the work of "The New Association for Culture and Popular Arts" after he left AMREC in the early 1990s.

I should mention that Chafik's chapter on the topic of "Islam and Amazigh Culture" later evolved and was developed as a correspondence between Chafik and Sheikh Abdesslam Yassine, the leader of the Islamist Al-Adl w-Al-Ihssane (Justice and Benevolence) movement. This exchange eventually turned into the book *Dialogue with an Amazigh Friend*.

We met regularly in the homes of our fellow activists, dedicating each session to discussion of one of these papers. We would offer our observations and suggestions, and the author would be tasked with rewriting it, cutting it down, and highlighting the main ideas as much as possible. We continued our work like this for several months before shifting from thinking about the book to another project. Our new idea was to publish a magazine as the voice of our association and a platform for communication between activist intellectuals and the general public, instead of the white paper. The preparation of this magazine lasted throughout 1985. We held meetings to discuss it between February 1985 and January 1986, and Ahmed Boukous was appointed as director of the magazine, which was named *Tawusna*. We then decided to expand the editorial team to include Marzouq El Ouariachi and Qadi Qaddour in Fes, instead of limiting the magazine to our association's activists. Therefore, I went to Fes with El Houssaïn El Moujahid and Hassan Id Balkassam to discuss the matter with them and invite them to join the project. We met at Marzouq El Ouariachi's house and explained in detail the stages the project had gone through, saying we would like them to join the team without preconditions. We tentatively agreed to hold another meeting, and on March 20, 1986, we met again and discussed the political and cultural situation in the country. However, the project never came to light, partly for lack of funds and partly due to the reservations on the part of some activists such as Qaddour and El Ouariachi, albeit indirectly. After this, we feared that publishing the magazine would make it seem like a regional affair, and we in the association were keen on unity among the Amazigh both in Morocco and the wider Maghreb region, in order to achieve our legitimate demands. We therefore decided not to embark on such a project, despite the time, energy, and thought we had put into it. Rather, we sought to protect this unity, which we believed must be the basis for our struggle.

We were now in a prevailing atmosphere of instability around Amazigh activism, resulting from the behavior of the authorities and the maneuvering of the political parties alike, meaning there was a lot of uncertainty around treatment of the issue. Yet this did not prevent activists from working on their own individual cultural projects for the benefit of the Amazigh language, culture, and identity. Each of us selected a project to work on while waiting for matters to settle so we could return to public activism. Omar Amarir wrote a book about Amazigh poetry attributed to the eighteenth-century Tashelhit poet Sidi Hemmu Ettaleb, which was published in 1987. Mohammed Chafik produced a brief history of the Amazigh, titled *An Overview of 33 Centuries of Amazigh History*, published in 1988. Hassan Id Balkassam released his poetry collection *Taslit w'Unzar* in 1986, and Mohamed Moustaoui published his series *Tifaouin*, with the issues published in 1985, 1986, 1989, 1990, and 1991. I published a collection of my own poetry called *Tabrat* in 1989, and the late Ali Sidqi Azaykou released his own collection, *Timitar*, in 1988. As I have mentioned, Essafi Moumen Ali released his play *Ousan Samadnin* in 1983.

Thus, we continued our Amazigh struggle without interruption, according to the political circumstances, never wavering from our tasks in the struggle for the sake of our legitimate cause.

MY EXPERIENCE WITH THE ALIGH ASSOCIATION FOR DEVELOPMENT AND COOPERATION

I have already spoken of various events in the mid-1980s that had negative impacts on our work, which was hit by a malaise, particularly when it came to public-facing activism. We attempted to overcome this through our individual intellectual work. The general political atmosphere was also characterized by a certain tension between the political parties and the authorities. This led to the emergence of regional associations run by the state, labeled as the associations of the mountains and plains. In this context, the housing minister Abderrahman Bouftas was tasked with establishing an association for development and cooperation, named by the late King Hassan II as the Aligh Association for Development and Cooperation. The real purpose for establishing these associations was to counter the political parties by involving citizens and the affluent classes in directing the communal and legislative elections in the direction determined by the state—namely the interior ministry.

I had been friends with Bouftas since the early 1970s, when he was managing an agricultural supplies company called Promagri. I had also kept him informed about our association's activities from when we started publishing the *Arraten* journal, around the same time, followed by the *Cultural Exchange* periodical. As soon as he was tasked with setting up the new association, he summoned me to his house, along with other figures in the cultural field such as Lhoceine Ouajaj, Abdellah El-Krasifi, and certain senior officials and company directors such as Mohammed Bijaadh, Hassan Abu Ayoub, and Mohamed Hassad. At this first meeting, I was asked to help establish this association, along with a team that was to join us.

I thought long and hard about the proposal, taking into account the circumstances and the situation facing our activism, which we had temporarily suspended until the situation changed. I thought of taking advantage of this opportunity to make contact with various sectors, personalities, and events, while working on deepening awareness of the Amazigh cause and achieving some advancements for Amazigh language and culture as much as possible within this framework.

After all, I had some knowledge of such projects, despite the limited chances of achieving my cultural and intellectual goals. However, despite the difficulties, I did not rule out the possibility of the project making some basic gains for the southern region, which I had been nominated to oversee.

Therefore, I agreed to help Bouftas achieve his desire, and that of the state. Many high-ranking officials with ties to the southern region joined the association, and we set about drafting its statutes. Since I knew these people's capabilities, which were unrelated to the work of associations, I was able to bring on board many others who were sympathetic to AMREC and convinced by our intellectual orientations. This allowed me to create the necessary balance so that my voice and my work would not be lost amid the administrative structures of the state and the private sector. I brought twenty-two members onto the administrative council of "Aligh," and we worked with others to establish the association's statutes and the general program, which was an ambitious agenda touching all sectors of society, culture, and development. We held our meetings at a factory in Casablanca owned by Bouftas. I worked with Hassan Abu Ayoub and Mohamed Hassad, the current governor of Tangiers, as well as many other state officials and individuals in the private sector.[7]

As we were starting work on the association, Minister Bouftas asked me to put forward two individuals to join his office at the Ministry of Housing, to work for the association and on communication and public relations. After some thought, I contacted Mohammed Ben Yehia El-Ouajani and Belkacem Aknaou and suggested the idea to them. I asked them to call the minister directly, and he promptly hired them.

During our work on drafting the association's statutes and preparing its cultural, social, and development program, some members of the team became nervous about my positions and actions, and about some of the other people associated with our current. They went as far as to contact Bouftas and tell him of their fears, accusing me of being political and saying that my ideas might hinder their own ambitions. Upon learning this and finding out who had approached him in this way, I did not hesitate. I went straight to Bouftas at his office in the ministry and clearly stated my position, emphasizing that I had no ambitions in the association, neither to manage it nor to use it as a springboard to reach higher positions. I told him I was not competing with anyone who wished to attain such a position of any kind, and that my sole concern was to serve the public interest and to do what satisfied my conscience for the benefit of this region, deprived for decades, seeing this as an opportunity that might enable me to do so.

FROM PREPARATIONS FOR THE THIRD SESSION OF THE SUMMER UNIVERSITY IN 1987 TO THE AGADIR CHARTER IN 1991

Conditions of Preparations for the Third Summer University

This episode had barely passed when the situation that had driven me to join the Aligh association changed. Attention to human rights suddenly took on a notable international aspect. The fall of the Berlin Wall in 1989 prompted organizations for defending human rights and promoting openness globally to call for more democracy in various parts of the world. Many countries now shed their totalitarian regimes and dictatorial empires to reclaim their freedom and identity, whether in Asia, Latin America, or Africa. In this new international climate, which inevitably had an impact on our country, we at the association began to think about how to leverage these circumstances to relaunch our Amazigh activism and end the period of dormancy it had undergone due to the dangers associated with our work. In 1987, we had already decided to reorganize our association as part of a comprehensive program, starting by holding a general assembly and restructuring its organs, which had been halted for about five years, since late 1983. After that, preparations began anew for the third session of the Summer University, set for the summer of 1988. We wanted to draw a line under the banning of the second session, to unite the Amazigh movement, and ensure a wide range of intellectual activities and activism. We also chose to hold the third session in order to gauge the position of the state, to see if there had been any change in its stance toward Amazigh activism. We also wanted to see to what extent the political parties had developed their perspectives toward the Amazigh issue after all the intellectual work we had done to communicate our discourse to them through our intellectual engagements since the first session in 1980. We also decided to organize in ways that would respond to the demands of that period, and of the third Summer University, supporting certain associations and helping them to resume their activities so that we could move forward in a unified and harmonious way, to amplify our voice and deepen awareness of our cause through all available means, to achieve our legitimate demands.

The work of revamping and restructuring AMREC lasted throughout 1987, during which the general assembly was held and the national
office and national council were elected. We reorganized the association's
branches, focusing on those in Rabat and Casablanca, and revived mechanisms of communication among all members of the association in different regions, both old and new, to mobilize everyone for what was to come.
We knew it would be difficult, as the full array of our opponents would be
more prepared to engage us in battle with all their intellectual and material
resources. Knowing this, we focused on mobilizing all our human resources
first, paying attention to every detail in our work strategy as we prepared for
this relaunch.

From early 1988 onward, the association had made contact with Amazigh cultural activists in various regions of Morocco, especially those
responsible for the Summer University Association in Agadir, Rabat, and
Casablanca, with the aim of defining the association's structure and deciding
on the theme of the third Summer University so that we could set about
preparing to hold the event in the summer of 1988. The general assembly
was held at the house of Lahcen Kahmou, the president of the association
in Agadir. It was agreed that the theme of the session would be "Popular
Culture, Between the Local and the National." Our association was responsible for the preparations, both by securing a sufficient number of lecturers
with diverse intellectual orientations (as was the case in the first and second
sessions, despite the challenges we faced) and by providing the necessary
material resources for the session. I was elected to head the organizational
committee, which included most members of the office of the Summer University Association, with Kahmou as president and Mohamed Abzika as first
deputy, Jamaa Jeghaymi as second deputy, Mohamed Handayen as general
secretary, Hassan Al-Marjou as treasurer, Ibrahim Charkaoui as deputy treasurer, and Ahmed Bouzid as advisor.[8]

For all the reasons mentioned above, and in this context, we took it upon
ourselves to put everything we had into making this third session a success:
a new, fertile beginning for an enthusiastic form of Amazigh activism involving all kinds of cultural and associative activities.

In terms of intellectual participation, we were able to persuade a large
number of speakers to get involved in order to achieve our desired goal.[9] The
program also included many parallel cultural activities, such as readings by
a group of prominent poets,[10] and we also organized a trip to the old school
in Tanalt, Aït Souab.

A glance at the number of participants and their academic and political
acumen demonstrates the scale of the responsibility on our shoulders, as

organizers, to provide the necessary material and logistical support in terms of accommodation, food, and transport. Yet our huge enthusiasm and desire to make it a success, in the face of these challenges, pushed us to provide all that was needed without hesitation.

The top priority was to find accommodation. I decided to contact hotel owners in Agadir again, the first of them being Najem Abaakil, as I already had a good relationship with him and knew from my many conversations with him that he supported our ideas. He had even used Tarzazit jewelry, the symbol of our association, as the symbol of his hotel firm, Anezi. I had consistently kept him informed of AMREC's activities and various publications, right from the early 1970s. I promptly called on him at his house in Casablanca, accompanied by Abdelaziz Bourass, the association's head in the city, and Essafi Moumen Ali. As usual, he welcomed us warmly, and after we had chatted and discussed the political situation in the country, I opened the subject of organizing another session of the Summer University in Agadir. I explained to him the scale of the project and the resources that would be required, especially as concerned accommodation and food, and told him about the challenges we would have to overcome to make a success of it, for the sake of the Amazigh cause. I made him aware of our situation, given that the city council had not given us any support worth mentioning during the previous round, despite the importance of the event to the city's residents, and added that the Summer University would be the first of its kind in the country, meaning that Agadir would gain cultural and intellectual standing internationally too. Abaakil understood me well and, without hesitation, provided us with twenty rooms and food for their residents for the entire duration of the session. This made me immensely happy and reassured me that we would be able to make a success of the project, given this promising beginning. However, I told him that we were only asking for accommodation without food, to emphasize that our demands were not excessive. He appreciated and understood that, and thanked us.

As we continued our quest for financial backing, for the first time, I visited the minister of culture, Mohamed Benaissa, accompanied by Lahcen Kahmou. At this ad hoc meeting, I opened the subject of the Summer University and the possibility of supporting us to hold this session. After we explained its history and the intellectual stature of its contributors, he understood how important it was and promised to try to help us. After a while, I returned to him alone to stress how urgently we needed the financial support. We discussed a possible package, and he personally agreed to provide up to forty thousand dirhams. However, when I contacted the ministry's secretary-general, he informed me that the ministry could not possibly provide a single dirham from the year's budget and that the minister's promise could not be fulfilled. The secretary-general had already informed the minister that this was the case. After contacting the minister again to find a solution to this deadlock, he confirmed that regretfully, he was unable to help us. However, I proposed a solution whereby we would agree on a grant of not more than forty thousand dirhams, which would go to restaurants we would deal with in Agadir. Given his reputation among them, they would be able to give us credit until the end of the year, when the ministry would pay the bill in full. The minister liked this idea. After we had agreed, he told me, "Keep this a secret between us: As the saying goes, you didn't see me and I didn't see you! There are brothers who would take from me with their right hand and stab me with their left, and they would not appreciate me helping you." Indeed, I followed our agreement to the letter. I contacted the "Tafoukt" restaurant in Agadir, whose owner was a great man and agreed to what I proposed, accepting that he would not be paid until late December of the same year. I kept in touch with the minister and his assistants until the restaurant received its dues, right on time.

As I have explained, the primary goal of organizing this session was to gauge the pulse of all parties, particularly to feel out the authorities' stance on our activities. We also wanted to sound out the level to which the political parties and other actors wanted to engage in deepening awareness of Amazigh identity in Moroccan society at large. The experience brought me to the following conclusions.

Firstly, throughout the organization and implementation of the program, we noticed that the authorities stayed neutral. They did not interfere with our activities, refrained from causing any disruptions, and did not hinder the natural course of our work. This in itself was a positive indicator that the session would be a success.

Secondly, after several conversations with Dr. Mohammed Jesous, in which I told him at length about Amazigh activism, the achievements of the first session of the Summer University and about our Amazigh motto, "Unity in Diversity," he finally agreed to take part. So too did Dr. Ali Oumlil, along with Mohammed al-Habib al-Fourkani, who had recently been freed from prison and elected to parliament to represent the city of Agadir. They were all leading figures within the Socialist Union. We were also joined by Mohamed Soussi, who was a senior member of the Istiqlal Party. Securing the participation of such leaders and thinkers from these political organizations, along with others holding different intellectual convictions, such as Moukhtar El-Farouqi and the late Abdelaziz El-Farouqi from the Progress and Socialism party, gave this session an intellectual richness and brought new impetus to Amazigh activism in our country. The result was a Summer University that was enthusiastic and filled with intellectual debates that gave it a special flavor not found at similar cultural meetings.

Thirdly, I noted that for the first time, Ibrahim Al-Radi, the mayor of Agadir, attended the opening session, along with a union representative and al-Fourkani. All these individuals delivered speeches, a move that must be recorded as a political move by the local authorities to support the Amazigh cause, in contrast to previous occasions. The late Najem Abaakil also attended to show his support.

Fourthly, we regretfully noted that our brothers from the Intliqa Cultural Association in Nador were unable to attend. Their absence had a significant impact, given their weight as scholars and activists. This applies both to Ahmed El-Chami and Marzouq El Ouariachi, as well as the late Qadi Qaddour. We particularly missed them given their enthusiastic participation in the first session of the Summer University in August 1980.

Having made these observations, I would like to describe some of the cultural events, which were not void of aspects relating to politics and identity. Some talks by our friends affiliated with the Socialist Union party provoked reactions from the audience that were critical of their failure to take a clear stance on the Amazigh cause, language, culture, and identity, accusing them of a kind of evasion bordering on deceit. Some of the party's leaders in the city considered this type of criticism unacceptable and intervened with al-Fourkani to ask him to refrain from delivering his talk on the evening of Wednesday, August 3, 1988. This was a lecture, not a panel, meaning he was to be the sole speaker. Their goal was to sabotage the entire session and create gaps in our program. Indeed, I was surprised to receive an apology from Fourkani, and I had not been able to find time to rectify the situation. When his lecture was due, many audience members gathered at the hall. So I asked several experts to volunteer to form a panel on the same topic as had been scheduled, to counter this kind of practice by those who could not accept criticism from the audience or freedom of opinion and difference, and to prove to them that we were cohesive and that their attempts to shut us down would be futile, both now and in the future. Indeed, a group of experts took to the stage, some of whom I no longer remember, although Hassan Id Balkassam was among them.

In another incident, Mohammed Kessous faced similar criticism, as his presentation had been quite vague on the theoretical level. He had misjudged the atmosphere in the hall and the audience's level of knowledge of the Amazigh identity. He expressed certain opinions that displeased the audience and clashed with their convictions, and he faced harsh criticism in response. He was thus forced to respond in the form of another lecture with a different position to the first, and concluded by saying, "Whoever doesn't believe in Amazigh identity is like he who doesn't believe in Islam. A Moroccan is someone who walks on two legs, so he must have both his languages: Tamazight and Arabic." In the middle of this heated academic discussion, Lhoucine Jouhadi made a critical observation to Kessous: "Professor, do you not know that 'Kessous' comes from Tamazight 'ka-souss,' meaning you are from Souss?" Kessous replied, "My brother, we are in an academic session, there is no need for lies or evasion. I am Kessous, which is from 'Khsous' in Hebrew, because I come from an Andalusian Jewish family." Everyone in the audience laughed.

As was the case with Kessous's presentation, Dr. Ali Oumlil came under significant criticism from the audience for being too theoretical in his scholarly efforts and failing to connect his topic to cultural diversity or to differences in our social and cultural realities.

Prior to our trip to the old *madrassa* (religious school) in Tanalt, Hajj Ouain—a friend of mine from the Aït Ouain oasis on our way to the school—agreed to prepare breakfast for us at his home. I told him that we would be around forty people, and he happily agreed. We took a series of photos as souvenirs. Kessous, Fourkani, and Oumlil all came on the trip, along with a group of activists, lecturers, and journalists from the *Anoual* newspaper. Dr. Jouhadi provided us with a geographical and historical commentary on the area through the bus's loudspeaker throughout the trip. At the entrance to the picturesque school, we found the leader of the tribe, the school's religious instructor, and the students all waiting for us. We had lunch with everyone, listened to a lesson delivered in Amazigh by the school's supervisor, and Jouhadi gave us a presentation about the late scholar El-Hajj Lahbib, who was a great scholar of Souss and contributed to Ahmed El-Hiba's famous campaign against French colonial forces in Marrakech. Commenting on the trip, Kessous told me, "Brother, these people live in a wonderful balance of thought; they use Amazigh and Arabic, and are Muslims. The contradiction lies within us. We live with contradictions for no reason."

These are just some of the highlights of the Summer University, which saw many intellectual disputes amid this diversity and difference. The behavior of both lecturers and audience members also reflected their political leanings. This in itself was positive, because without this kind of intellectual friction and interaction, our ideas would not evolve or converge to reflect the shared principles that express our intellectual and civilizational identity.

The session drew to a close. It had been a great success on both the intellectual and political levels. Most importantly, it rejuvenated our enthusiasm to continue with our struggle, with renewed determination and persistence. We now put our efforts into preparing the proceedings of the session in text form, so that these important interventions could be documented and made accessible to everyone. Indeed, they were published by Okaz press in 1990.

As I have mentioned before, holding the third session of the Summer University was a means for us to gauge the stance of various parties on the Amazigh issue. The session was a success in this regard, and we immediately started implementing our strategy of putting Amazigh associations into action, by encouraging and assisting those that already existed at the time to carry out awareness-raising activities, creating a new environment of activism that would cover as much of Morocco as possible, mobilizing as many Amazigh activists and researchers as we could to make up for the years we had lost.

Our first step in this program was to support the Cultural Association of Souss, located in Casablanca, in organizing its first festival of Amazigh music on May 19 and 20, 1989. Our association helped organize this festival, mobilizing all its members in the city to help the organizers make it a success, contributing to organizing it, presenting lectures, or participating in performances. My daughter Touf Itri performed there for the first time, playing musical pieces by Lhaj Belaid and Boubker Anchad on the piano at the opening session, which was attended by Minister Abderrahman Bouftas, along with many figures from the worlds of business and culture.

The association was also quick to assist the municipal council of the city of Tiznit in organizing study days on the late artist Lhaj Belaid, in August 1990. Many members of AMREC contributed by hosting or preparing sessions, in partnership with the organizing committee from the municipal council. We always tried to support any project that aimed to strengthen Amazigh activism so it could regain its momentum and its impact on the national cultural scene. As the reader will see, most of these activities focused on artistic aspects at first, to mobilize the public, before moving on to other theoretical and political aspects that stir controversy for some and are provocative for others.

With the success of the Tiznit festival around this great artist, who hails from the region, we began engaging more deeply with the public. Our presentations appealed to audiences, who found something of themselves within them and discovered something about the importance of their culture and the stature of Amazigh literary and artistic figures.

With the growing success of our involvement in, and practical support for, various cultural projects at the national level, that same year we came up with the idea of publishing an Amazigh intellectual periodical as a tool for communication among the educated and a platform for Amazigh thinkers in all fields. It would be the first of its kind in the history of the Amazigh movement, as until then, all magazines and bulletins had been in other languages, and writing in Tamzight occupied only a limited space. We named the periodical *Amoud*, "the seeds," and indeed it contained the seeds of various harvests in the field of Amazigh thought, which grew under the care of different creative minds, in publishing, translation, short stories, language, and other areas of Amazigh culture. We published the first issue in April 1990, with a team consisting of me as the director and an editorial board consisting of Lhoucine Ouaizi, Hassan Id Balkassam, El Houssaïn El Moujahid, and Lhoucine Ait Bahcine. Four issues were published, and despite this low number, they have aged little.

We were working quickly, as we were convinced that the success of our cultural revolution required major work, given the scale of the intellectual and cultural takeover that had afflicted our society, including its educated and political classes. We believed time was not on our side, as we were deprived of audiovisual media tools or an education system in the Amazigh language. Moreover, the print media was monopolized by nationalist parties, and we were deprived of a platform that would allow us to express our ideas and call for a deepening awareness of the Amazigh identity of all Moroccans. Thus, almost as soon as we had published the Proceedings of the Third Session of the Summer University, we began preparing for the fourth.

However, before embarking on this, AMREC conducted an analysis of the situation and the achievements we had made so that we could set our priorities for the future by creating a new atmosphere that would further motivate activists and add value to the achievements we had made for the movement so far.

In this evaluation, we observed the following:

Firstly, we noted the establishment of an Amazigh association in Goulmima, named "Ghris" and headed by the activist Ali Harsh El-Rass. The "New Association for Culture and Folk Arts" headed by activist Lhoucine Akhiate, had also launched Amazigh activities, after operating only as a leftist organization generally concerned with folk culture. This year also saw the suspension of some Amazigh activities by the Intilaqa association in Nador.

Secondly, we noted Mohammed Chafik's publication of an Arabic-Amazigh dictionary, an achievement that had taken several years of work and made a major impact the cultural and intellectual scene. Considering these developments, positive and negative, and whether at the level of individual achievements or the development of Amazigh activism by associations, we realized there was a need to break away from using the term "folk culture," which we had been employing as a guise for Amazigh work during a transitional phase. Now, we needed to declare openly the Amazigh nature of our work and cultural activities, shedding the cover of "folk culture" that we had been using in our slogans, such as "Folk Culture: Unity in Diversity," "Folk Culture and Change," and finally "Folk Culture Between Diversity and Uniformity."

This decision was agreed upon at a meeting of AMREC, which resolved to present and defend it at the general assembly of the Summer University in mid-1990. Indeed, the proposal was discussed at the general assembly of the university, where we were able, albeit with difficulty, to reach an agreement to transition away from "popular culture" and adopt the term "Amazigh culture." Some of our brothers believed we should continue to use the term "popular culture" for a period, until the public was ready to accept Amazigh discourse and the accompanying terminology without controversy. However, we managed to convince them to accept the proposal. This decision was a historic one for our movement, as it definitively resolved the issue of terminology. Now, Amazigh culture was able to express itself linguistically and culturally in our society.

To reassure those who were still afraid to use the term Amazigh, AMREC decided to organize a festival titled "Amazigh Culture Days" in Rabat from January 16 to 23, 1990, under the slogan "Amazigh Culture: A National Responsibility," to expose those of us in the capital to any reaction from the authorities prior to the next Summer University. This carefully chosen slogan would have a significant impact on advancing the Amazigh cause, given its depth and the sense of responsibility toward the national heritage represented by Amazigh culture. During this event, we honored Mohammed Chafik as an Amazigh thinker, as he had published the first part of his Arabic-Amazigh dictionary, and we celebrated his intellectual work on behalf of Amazigh language, culture, and civilization. We also honored a prominent figure in Amazigh music, Ahmed Amentag. We held seminars dedicated to the works of both personalities and a unique book exhibition at the Ministry of Culture, along with a musical evening. The festival made significant cultural and political contributions. In recognition of his scholarly stature, the tribute to Professor Mohamed Chafik was chaired by the well-known Moroccan writer Abdelkebir Khatibi, known for his open-mindedness and advocacy for cultural coexistence and recognition of the right to differ. A cultural event of such prominence on Amazigh culture, in the capital of the kingdom, received substantial official attention, especially as Chafik is a scholarly figure, a member of l'Académie du Royaume du Maroc (Academy of the Kingdom of Morocco), and the director of the Royal College.

This created confusion among opponents of the Amazigh culture. It even surprised some activists within the Amazigh movement, who asked about our real motives for honoring such a scholar seen as so close to the state. I did not hesitate to respond to such critiques, arguing that Amazigh culture is a national responsibility, and that we at the association did not exclude anyone from serving their language and national culture, regardless of their administrative position, party affiliation, or religious creed. This choice and our initiative in holding the event were a message to state officials affirming this conviction.

Our initiative to honor Professor Mohammed Chafik, and its positive impact on a wide audience of intellectuals and Amazigh activists, prompted the "Association of Former Azrou High School Students," of which the professor had been president when Morocco won its independence, to organize a dinner party at the Hilton in the capital to honor him again. The professor invited me on behalf of the organizers as an honorary guest, and I accepted the invitation to join the honorary invitees, who were allocated a special table. As well as Professor Chafik, at the table were the late philosopher Mohammed Aziz Lahbabi and his wife, the late Abdulhamid El-Zammouri, the economist Mahdi Elmandjra, and Mahjoubi Aherdane.

I had not been told that there would be interventions from some attendees at the banquet. We listened to a speech by the organizers, followed by Professor Chafik talking about how he had completed his Arabic-Amazigh Dictionary after receiving permission from His Majesty King Hassan II. He had originally been asked to compile a dictionary of Amazigh words in the Moroccan dialect of Arabic, a project under the auspices of the Royal Academy. After this intervention, the floor was given successively to Elmandjra, who spoke about Chafik's work at the Royal Academy, and then to Dr. Lahbabi, who discussed his work for the Amazigh culture as dean of the Faculty of Arts. I was then given the floor. After praising Professor Chafik's work, I spoke about our duty as citizens and as parents to preserve Amazigh culture, emphasizing that we should not only cast the responsibility on others to escape from our responsibilities. I also spoke of the role of women in this regard and what they had done throughout history to preserve the Amazigh language.

The second major impact of the Amazigh Culture Days in Rabat was the decision of the Moroccan Writers' Union to organize a seminar on the topic of "Writing in Amazigh." This had been scheduled to be held immediately after our seminar but was postponed to April 1991. The goal of their seminar was to send us a strong response. During the initial preparations for the seminar, they contacted all the major figures in the Arab nationalist current, such as the philosopher Mohammed Abed Al-Jabri, Allal Al-Azhar, the journalist Abdelkrim Ghallab, Mohammed Kessous, and Abdessamad Belkebir. Some of these individuals refused to participate, which is why the date of the meeting was postponed to April 1991. Some of our colleagues from the Amazigh movement were also invited to participate, such as Ahmed Boukous, Dr. Chafik, Mohammed El-Chami, and El Houssaïn El Moujahid. Knowing that we were to address the Moroccan Writers' Union, and being aware of the Arab nationalist names that were to participate, we did not leave things to chance. I personally contacted Professor Chafik and coordinated with him on the subject. As he was to be one of the first speakers, alongside Kessous and Ghallab, at the first session, we agreed that his intervention should be clear, straightforward, and devoid of pleasantries; it should express firmness, self-confidence, and insistence on our positions. I confirmed that we would have a strong presence in the hall.

Indeed, we mobilized many members of the association, in addition to other activists, who would contribute with their interventions. The first session took place at the House of Culture in Rabat, with Ghallab, Kessous, and Chafik on the panel. We were surprised that Ghallab attended along with a number of leading members of the Istiqlal Party, such as M'hamed Boucetta, Aboubakr El-Kadiri, and Mohammed El Soussi.

Ghallab was the first speaker. His intervention was written, and he elaborately discussed the concept of a single language and the necessity of imposing it as the one language and culture of the Moroccan people, along with other unconnected observations. He did not say a single word on the topic of the seminar. Everyone was surprised by Ghallab's intellectual arrogance. He had appeared to believe that Kessous would share his opinion, given that they were both from the same bloc of the USFP. Mohammed Chafik spoke second. His presentation was objective, well-argued, and logical, in complete contrast to Ghallab's. Now, for the first time, the speaker was interrupted by applause, something that not happened once during Ghallab's intervention. Now we knew the hall was with us. After Professor Chafik had finished his presentation, Ghallab appeared to be hoping that the next talk by Kessous would take off some of the pressure. But he was to be disappointed. Kessous began his talk by praising Chafik, saying that he shared his opinion. He then simply suggested that there should be a national Amazigh charter to enshrine the national consensus on the issue of cultural and linguistic diversity in our country. He repeated what he had declared at the third session of the Summer University in 1988, that Morocco walks on two legs, Amazigh and Arabic, and it is not permissible to ignore either of them. By now, Ghallab was in an awkward, isolated position, as nobody else on the panel shared his opinion. When audience members responded, they sharply attacked him. These were not members of the Amazigh movement, but other audience members, who pointed out that he had not respected the topic of the seminar, and that his talk appeared to have been written ten years ago, as it failed to take into account the current cultural and political reality. In the face of this onslaught, most of Ghallab's supporters now abandoned him. I had briefly spoken to Kessous before going into the hall, and jokingly asked him, "What will you tell us, Doctor?" I had already been familiar with his opinions since the Summer University, where he had formulated his independent stance on the Amazigh issue. He jokingly replied, "I will say what I think, and as you know, whoever supports it will support it." Kessous was a true scholar who would express his opinions regardless of his political alliances and the positions of others. The following day, the seminar continued with talks by university activists on topics related to scholarship on literature, language, and culture. We had thus achieved another victory in the intellectual and political arena, which increased our enthusiasm, our confidence, and our determination to carry on with our hard work.

I have written about this seminar because it was held as a reaction by the Moroccan Writers' Union, immediately after the Amazigh cultural forum in Rabat. However, prior to this seminar, another event had taken place that was specifically related to Amazigh activism and that followed all the developments that I have mentioned—the first, second, and third Summer University sessions and our organization of cultural fora to mobilize public opinion around the Amazigh issue. In July 1990, Dr. Abdelmalek Ousaden and Dr. Chafik invited me for dinner at Ousaden's house in Imouzzer, without informing me of the topic of the meeting. I arrived, accompanied by my wife and my daughter Touf Itri. As soon as we had settled at our hotel, I went out and met some brothers from the Intilaqa association: Saïd Moussaoui, Mira Mohammed, Abdelwahab El-Hamouti, and Hassan Douhou. Moussaoui's first question was to ascertain the topic of the meeting I was to attend, to which I answered that I suspected it was a repeat of the previous initiative by Ousaden and Chafik in 1979. In any case, I told him, they had not informed me of the topic of the meeting.

Upon our arrival at Dr. Ousaden's house, we found Dr. Chafik along with Dr. El-Akkouri and El-Kabiri, who is a university professor, as well as Mohammed Ajaajaa. I did not know the latter two, as I had never met them at any seminar or association gathering. After dinner, Ousaden started to speak. He analyzed the country's political situation and the status of the Amazigh cause. He concluded that we needed to do something more than simply cultural activities, as the state would never take us seriously until we were a political force and engaged in politics. Chafik made comments to the same effect, speaking very briefly. Now, Ajaajaa came to speak, concluding that we were agreed; we should establish an association or a framework through which to engage in political work, because our cultural work alone would not lead us to any results. After they had spoken, clarifying their goals and what they were proposing to us, I recalled our meeting in 1979 at Dr. Ousaden's, on the same topic. He had invited us all to a meeting after the intense activities of the 1970s, involving movements at the universities and on the popular cultural scene. Now here he was again, inviting us to a similar meeting, after all that had been accomplished by Amazigh activists and associations, from intellectual works and awareness-raising to cultural and political activity on a national level. I was surprised that the doctor had not initiated such a project then, in circumstances that would have allowed us to pave the way for the Amazigh cause and normalize such activities. Instead, these initiatives were absent in the more challenging times, when Amazigh activities were suspended.

After contemplating the situation, I spoke, indicating that I was present at this meeting in my personal capacity and not as the secretary-general of the association. However, I acknowledged the profound significance of what our Amazigh activism had achieved, both on the cultural and intellectual levels, to deepen Moroccans' awareness of their Amazigh identity. It was a political act of the utmost importance, because it sought to change ideas and deepen awareness among Moroccans so they could rid themselves of their intellectual and political dependency. This could not be achieved through the practice of traditional politics, as it had thus far been practiced by the majority of the political parties and most politicians, whose only interest was in material and personal gain and their ambitions of reaching leadership positions in the administration or their parties.

I concluded that what was needed under our current circumstances was a militant campaign of intellectual and cultural activity that would raise a conscious generation of activists who would be up to a task of the level and magnitude of the Amazigh cause, which is our primary cause. I added that this work should encompass the entire national territory. This opinion did not sit well with the brothers who had proposed their project to us. Professor Mohammed Ajaajaa took the initiative and suggested that I join their group in my personal capacity while continuing my work for the association. I explained to them again that I could not engage in a project unless I was convinced of its feasibility and necessity, and that this project itself was not clear in its objectives. Ajaajaa again invited me to join the group, saying that those present would form its leadership and that he would work to find members who to join it after its launch. Our friends from Nador observed this discussion without intervening, and the meeting concluded without us reaching any consensus. However the project went ahead. It came to be known as Akraou Amazigh, an association made up of some founding elements of the Amazigh Association and some others.

Before the end of the eventful year of 1990, which was marked by major cultural and political activity for the Amazigh movement, I met with some brothers from the Intilaqa association in Imouzzer, again hosted by Dr. Ousaden. I discussed with them the situation facing activism in Nador, where their group had played a significant role in Amazigh cultural life. I told them of my hope that Amazigh cultural activity could be revived in the city, and proposed to visit them there to help find a solution to this unacceptable situation which had frozen the Amazigh movement. I pointed out that we were in dire need of stimulating intellectual activities in the region, to complement our efforts in other areas of Morocco.

They agreed, and we set a date for this visit, before the end of 1990. We held meetings at the home of Saïd Moussaoui, a well-known poet, and Mohammed Mira. They were attended by all the previously mentioned activists, many of whom had been involved in the Intilaqa association, which they said had been suspended by certain members of the Socialism and Progress Party who had taken over the association's office. During our meeting, I sensed their enthusiasm to do something, and their readiness for a new start. I made three suggestions to them. The first was to work on reviving and relaunching the Intilaqa association and to convince those who had closed it down to return to reason and reactivate it. However, I added that I was skeptical that this could be achieved and that, even if it were possible, it would take a long time. The second possibility was that they create a new association on their own initiative to start work immediately. The third possibility was that if they were unable to revive the Intilaqa association or create a new framework, we would put our association at their disposal and create a branch in the city of Nador, to enable activists to conduct their activities there legally, under the association's umbrella. I told them I would approve the opening of a branch without reservations, as I was personally acquainted with each of the Intilaqa activists. Thus, with these meetings in the city of Nador, I was able to contribute to the revival of the Amazigh movement in the region. After those meetings, I left them to consult among themselves and make an appropriate decision on what I had proposed. Saïd Moussaoui later hosted me at his home, where I met Mohammed El-Fadhili, the local MP who was also the deputy chairman of the Chamber of Counselors, and Saïd's brother Ahmed Moussaoui, also an MP, who became the minister of environment and sports. This was not the only time I visited the city of Nador, with which I formed a strong connection through my many friends and activists I knew there. First among them were Mohammed El-Chami and Saïd Moussaoui, who was the city's most distinguished poet and, incidentally, did not hesitate to participate in all cultural events wherever they were organized in Morocco, to exhibit his Rifian literary creativity. Moussaoui played a significant role in launching the Elmas Cultural Association and organizing many cultural events. He never hesitated to take the courageous stands necessary to defend Amazigh demands at meetings of the National Council for Coordination between Amazigh Associations, when I was the national coordinator for these associations, and he always sided with the most rational and objective positions.

All this activity, which lasted about a year, resulted in the establishment of the Ilmas Cultural Association, chaired by activist Mohammed El-Chami, which first announced its existence by signing the Agadir Charter in the summer of 1991.

NOTES

1. The Organization Committee consisted of Ibrahim Akdime, Afa Lhacine, Achifi Moulay El-Hassan, Ahmed Bouzid, and Lahcen Kahmou. The Research and Studies Committee included me, Abdellah Akhbar, Ahmed Akouaou, Lachine Amnakhraz, Ahmed Boukous, Mohammed Ben Yehia, and Ahmed El Aouani. The Editorial Committee comprised Lhoucine Ait Bahcine, Ounouch Hamdi, Lhoucine Jouhadi, Darqaoui Abdellah, Mestour Ahmed, El Houssaïn El Moujahid, and Ahmed El-Ghazali.
2. King Hassan II, *Inbi'āth umma*, section 25, 1980, 369–370.
3. Mohammed Abed Al-Jabri, *Aḍwā' 'alā ashkāliyyat al-ta'līm bi-al-Maghrib* (Casablanca, Dār al-Nashr al-Maghribiyya, 1974).
4. Allal El-Fassi, *Al-mas'alah al-qawmiyyah wa-al-naz'ah al-amāzīghīyah wa-binā' al-Maghrib al-'Arabī* (Dar El-Khattabi, 1984).
5. The meeting was attended by Mohamed Bennis representing the *New Culture* magazine, activist Abdelhamid Akkar from Al-Jusoor, writer Bensalem Himmich from Al Badil, politician Abderrahim Al-Bouazaoui from Al Muqaddima, Amhammed Krayen for Al Mabadi', Mohamed Barada, M'Barek Rabi from the Union of Moroccan Writers, Abdeljabar Al Sahimi, Abdellatif Laâbi, Ali Oumlil, me representing AMREC, Mohamed Al-Qasimi, and Lahbib Al-Talibi.
6. Ahmed Boukous, El Houssaïn El Moujahid, Hassan Id Balkassam, Ahmed Ghazali, El Houssain Ouazi, Lhoucine Ait Bahcine, and Mohammed Alhyan.
7. The association's Amazigh team members and those sympathetic to the cause included Hammad Al-Hadiki, Mohammed Oukouk, Ibrahim Akdime, Ibrahim Boulahroud, Ibrahim El-Charkaoui, Ibrahim Al-Lahiani, Ahmed El-Mrabet, Belkacem Aknaou, Hassan Boufous, Abdellah Aqchouch, Abderahman Fahim, Mohammed Benyahia, Mohammed Oudad, Mohammed Bensaïd, and Mohammed El-Mehdi Darqaoui.

8. The committee also included Lhoucine Ait Bahcine, Abdelaziz Bourass, Ibrahim El-Charkaoui, Hassan El-Marjou, El Houssaïn El Moujahid, Lahcen Kahmou, Mohammed Handayen, Hassan Id Balkassam, Jamaa Jeghaymi, and Mohamed Moustaoui.

9. Participants included: Mohammed El-Mehdi Darqaoui, Mohammed Raqibi, Jamaa Warzman, Mohamed Soussi, Id El-Faqih Ahmed, Ahmed Bouzid, Jamaa Bayadha, Mohammed Mohammed Alhyan, Ali Amhan, Moukhtar El-Farouqi, Abbas El-Charkaoui, Ahmed Boukous, Ahmed Dghirni, Ahmed Saber, Miloud El-Taifi, Amer Mouftaha, Mohammed Jesous, Lhoucine Ait Bahcine, El Houssein Kahmo, Mohamed Moustaoui, Mohammed Kaddah, Mohammed Abadrine, Hassan Id Balkassam, Mohammed al-Habib al-Fourkani, Mohammed Chafik, El Houssaïn El Moujahid, Ali Oumlil, Mohammed Ait El Haj, Lhoucine Jouhadi, Moustafa Naimi, Fatima Boukhriss, El-Farouqi Abdelaziz, and Mohammed Khaïr-Eddine.

10. They included: Hassan Id Balkassam, Moubarak Boulgid, Mohammed Adiouan, Mohammed Moustaoui, Ahmed Bouzid, Lhoucine Ouaizi, Ahmed Raghib, Lhoucine Jouhadi, Abdelkader Ababou, Ali Yakin, Mohammed Aknadh, Lhoucine El-Chaabi, and me.

CHAPTER 4

The Beginnings of Change and the Phase of Intellectual Confrontations, 1991–2000

THE BACKGROUND TO THE CHARTER ON AMAZIGH LANGUAGE AND CULTURE IN MOROCCO

The success of the third session of the Summer University in Agadir, in the summer of 1988, had a significant impact on Amazigh activism, both organizationally and in terms of its cultural impact. This was manifested in confirmation that the authorities were neutral on the issue, or at least did not hinder the session, and that an understanding had been reached with the political parties, some of whose thinkers took part in our activities, not to mention the intensive participation by activists in the Amazigh movement itself. All this encouraged us to move forward with the creation of cultural and organizational projects to make the most of our time and widen the circle of Amazigh cultural activities, such as with publications on Amazigh language and culture, as well as organizing bigger cultural events. In 1991, Mohamed Moustaoui published the fifth part of the *Tifawin* series, and Professor Hassan Id Balkassam released his Amazigh treatise *Isaqsi*. The association organized the first festival of Amazigh literature on May 17 and 18, 1991, at our Casablanca offices, under the slogan "Amazigh Literature: Reality and Prospects." This was the first conference organized within the framework of our awareness-raising activities to showcase Amazigh literature. The association published the proceedings of the event, under the title "An Introduction to Amazigh Literature: *'Taskla n Tamazight.'*"

This mobilization and these cultural activities were all part of the association's strategy of enhancing public enthusiasm for Amazigh activism, by encouraging associations and individuals to cooperate and participate in these activities to encourage communication and strengthen relationships between all these activities at the national level. To achieve this goal, AMREC took pains to invite comrades from the Ghris association in Goulmima, the Souss Cultural Association, the New Association for Culture and Folk Arts, and the association of the Summer University in Agadir, as well as independent Amazigh activists. They attended and participated in all our events and nurtured the communication we hoped for, especially our friends from the Ghris association, which had been renamed the Tilelli Cultural Association, which was, at the time, mostly concerned with developments in Tizi Ouzou, in Algeria, considering it the best model of struggle for the Amazigh cause. After these great efforts and communication, we were able to reach our goals. Their activism became integrated into the framework of national cultural activity, through their effective participation in all the Amazigh movement's projects on the national level, from the signing of the Agadir Charter to participation in the Coordination Council and all the resulting statements and stances adopted by our country's Amazigh movement. This major effort on our part was not a matter of coincidence. Rather, it was integral to our preparations for a significant and fundamental historical act, namely the issuing of a national charter on the Amazigh language and culture in Morocco. From the start of the preparations for this historical project, we in the association were convinced that it would only have the positive outcome we hoped it would for the political and intellectual arena if it were issued by all the Amazigh cultural associations in our country, without exception. Indeed, this was a fundamental condition for this charter to have the desired political and cultural impact; on the one hand, it would be issued by many components of civil society, and on the other, it would have the necessary national character.

From late 1990 onward, we started considering holding a fourth session of the Summer University, along with our other cultural and educational activities across the country. We held a general assembly of the Summer University Association at the beginning of 1991, at which we agreed to hold another session of the University in August that year. We also agreed on the following:

Firstly, that starting from 1991, we would employ the term "Amazigh" in our activism, where we had been using the framework of "popular culture." After all, it was our association that had called for this when we held the "Days of Amazigh Culture in Rabat." This was a subtle but important shift for our cause, as it explicitly stated the Amazigh identity of our language and culture, distinguishing them from other cultural components in our country.

The second element on which we agreed was the theme of this Summer University: "Amazigh Culture, Between Tradition and Modernity." These two decisions played a historical role in the future of Amazigh life in Morocco and for the work of Amazigh associations at this critical stage.

As we were preparing for the fourth session of the Summer University, the Casablanca branch of the association organized the First Forum for Amazigh Literature on May 17–18, 1991, under the slogan "Amazigh Literature: Reality and Prospects." This conference served as a preparatory process for the fourth session. It mobilized and brought together literary and intellectual energies from various regions of Morocco, and it fit with the association's strategy of bringing in our brothers from the Ghris association in Goulmima, to integrate them and get them actively involved in Amazigh activism in Morocco, as their main work had been on Tizi Ouzou in Algeria. Indeed, every Amazigh association in Morocco attended the gathering, as well as the cultural exchange it involved. I delivered the opening speech in their name, and the branch was represented by Abdelaziz Bourass. The Tamaynut Association was represented by its president Hassan Id Balkassam, the Ighris cultural association by its president Ali Harsh El-Rass, the Souss Cultural Association by Hamza Abdellah, and the Summer University Association and its president Lahcen Kahmou. They all delivered their associations' speeches at an opening session chaired by Mohammed El-Chami from Nador, as the Elmas Cultural Association had not yet been created. Thus, as can be observed from the unanimous desire of Amazigh associations to take part in such events, our strategy was to create solidarity and mutual support among these associations to accomplish their cultural work, on the one hand, and also to consult among us to unify our visions, in order to achieve the noble goals of the movement. The conference was distinguished by a high quality of research and abundant creativity.[1]

The attendance of researchers and advocates from every part of Morocco, along with all of the country's Amazigh associations, reflects the importance of this meeting, which gave the activists present a great boost of enthusiasm to double their efforts. Shortly after concluding it, we embarked on the preparations for the fourth session of the Summer University, which was scheduled for August 1991.

Given this level of enthusiasm, in order to avoid the fourth session being, like its predecessors, limited to theoretical, intellectual, and creative presentations, we decided to add value to our activist work, taking into account the gains we had made throughout our struggle, especially the increase in the number of Amazigh associations that had started to pop up across the country. This was an important phenomenon, as it reflected Moroccan society's growing awareness of the need to nurture the development of the Amazigh language and culture. However, we realized that unless we controlled this increase and established a theoretical and intellectual framework and vision for our work, we risked falling into a kind of intellectual chaos that could actually weaken our position in the face of rival ideologies and discourses.

During this discussion, and our search for the added value we hoped would result from this session, we had the idea of establishing a charter that would define the intellectual framework of our activism and lay out the broad lines of Amazigh aspirations, taking into account the country's linguistic, cultural, and civilizational realities and presenting objective, democratic proposals to resolve the question of cultural diversity in Morocco.

Ahmed Boukous had mentioned the idea of a charter during his talk at the first Summer University. El Houssaïn El Moujahid had later reminded us of this, praising the idea of a charter that would give a framework to Amazigh activism. Both of them had recently been involved in establishing a charter at the French language department at the Faculty of Letters in Rabat. Moreover, after we had been prevented from holding the third session of the Summer University in 1982, our work at the association had evolved and crystallized into several of the above-mentioned projects that we had been unable to carry out, such as the white paper and *Tawsna* magazine, as well as the cultural and intellectual activities we had managed to accomplish. Through all this intellectual effort, we prepared a draft of the charter. At a meeting on June 20, 1991, we adopted the papers we had prepared under previous projects, related to various aspects of the Amazigh issue. We agreed to rewrite them and abbreviate them into what would eventually form the basis of a charter. This meeting, which launched the drafting of the charter, was attended by Ahmed El-Ghazali, Lhoucine Ouaizi, Mohammed Alhyan, Ahmed Boukous, Hassan Id Balkassam, and me. The papers covered the following topics: Islam and Amazighity, Amazigh culture, the Tamazight language, prevailing ideologies, cultural and civilizational responsibility, teaching Tamazight and Amazigh culture, and Amazigh linguistic and cultural rights.

In the absence of a headquarters for the association, several meetings were held at these activists' homes, where these papers were discussed and enriched with ideas. Finally, El Houssaïn El Moujahid was tasked with drafting the final document. Ahmed Boukous was also asked, in the interests of transparency, to clarify the framework in which we were operating. Were we acting as independent individuals, or within the framework of an association, meaning our work would have a particular identity within a defined frame-work? I told everyone that the framework unifying us was the Moroccan Association for Research and Cultural Exchange (AMREC), which we had all joined and within which we were working. We could inform our com-rades at other cultural associations once the draft had been completed and the fourth session of the Summer University was approaching. Then they could bring their comments and suggestions to the meetings that would be held in parallel with the session, and we would sign the charter at the end. Everyone agreed to this plan, and work began on both the intellectual and organizational fronts. We all gathered at the Hotel School in Agadir when the Summer University was set to begin, as many of the workshops were set to take place there, and it was where everybody would eat.

THE EXCELLENT FOURTH SESSION OF THE AGADIR SUMMER UNIVERSITY: AUGUST 1991

Having introduced the fourth session of the Summer University as a his-torical milestone, along with the discussions that took place there and the resulting social and cultural achievements—primarily the establish-ment of a charter on the Amazigh language and culture, which defined the goals of Amazigh activism and the movement's stance on issues related to linguistic and cultural rights—I am obliged to make the following observations:

Firstly, this may be considered the first Amazigh summit in the history of the modern Maghreb, where a great consensus was achieved on all levels. The meeting of all six of the Amazigh associations present in Morocco at the time symbolized the unity of the Amazigh across the country, from north to south and from east to west, something that is unique to the Amazigh move-ment in Morocco compared to other Amazigh movements in North Africa.

Secondly, the event produced a historic charter, a collective achievement by the finest Amazigh intellectuals in Morocco, which was signed by the Amazigh associations as representatives of a civil society that struggles for the realization of a modern democratic state, guaranteeing human rights in their entirety and granting genuine citizenship to its citizens.

Thirdly, and for the first time in its history, the Amazigh movement and the Amazigh people arrived at an intellectual framework for Amazigh lan-guage and culture, in the form of this charter, through which the broad lines of the people's demands were crystallized to achieve its goals, and which could ensure the affirmation of its Amazigh national identity, an identity threatened by intellectual, cultural, and political assimilation, which it faced due to nationalist ideologies that were competing for dominance over it.

Fourthly, in parallel to the Summer University, there was a social summit that acted as a witness to the validity of this historical document. It was a summit of the women and children of the activists taking part in this historic gathering. Everyone was thus experiencing the event in all its details and developments. This had never happened in any of the cultural events we had staged in our struggle. It made this event an intimate family gathering, where everybody came together to achieve this historic accomplishment in the life of the Amazigh people.

Fifthly, this session for the first time featured specialized workshops, the first and most important of which concerned the matter of writing in Tamazight. It gathered the best teachers of the Amazigh language to discuss a project prepared by Essafi Moumen Ali on how to standardize Amazigh writing or its script. This was the first time experts had gathered in this way to find the best ways to standardize Tifinagh and determine the sounds and methods for drawing each letter, overcoming the differences and problems this posed.

Indeed, the participants made important observations on the subject, and the project's leader was tasked with taking them into account and discussing the project again later. AMREC later organized a meeting on the subject, dubbed "the National Committee for the Unification of Writing and the Dictionary," in Maamoura, in May 1992. Thus, the Summer University became a starting point for the unification of Amazigh writing.

THE SIGNING OF A CHARTER ON AMAZIGH LANGUAGE AND CULTURE IN MOROCCO

As I have shown, meticulous preparations were made for the Agadir Charter, by a group of educated activists involved in our associations. It was then presented to the representatives of other associations during the Summer University so that it could be scrutinized. A committee was formed for this purpose.[2]

After the charter had reached its final formulation, an extra paragraph was added on the constitutional status of Amazigh. However, it was not attached to the text until after Ahmed Abadrin, a lawyer, had made a presentation on the subject at the Summer University to gauge the audience's reactions. The main reason for the hesitation was that many politicians and activists were afraid to discuss or mention Morocco's constitution, as the document is under the purview of the king. Most politicians describe Morocco's constitutions as "granted" (drafted by a committee appointed by the king). However, we were happily surprised, as the audience was enthusiastic about the idea of giving Amazigh constitutional status, and agreed with the proposal. Therefore, the paragraph dedicated to the constitution was added to the final text, which was titled "A Charter on the Amazigh Language and Culture." This action, through which the Amazigh movement demanded a change to the constitution to ensure constitutional recognition and protection of the Amazigh language, was a major step that reflected our courage to clearly state our legitimate demands. This was something few political parties had done at the time and deserves to be noted and appreciated as a positive moment in the Amazigh struggle.

The charter was signed by the following dedicated individuals:

- me, for AMREC
- Mohammed El-Chami, on behalf of the Elmas Cultural Association
- Ali Harsh El-Rass, for the Ighris Cultural Association
- Lhoucine Akhiate, for the New Association for Culture and Folk Arts
- Lahcen Kahmou, for the Summer University Association

Following the signing, an accompanying record was drafted that chronicles this major step for the Amazigh movement. I am honored to publish it here in full, noting its historical importance:

Parallel to the activities that took place in the city of Agadir on the occasion of the Fourth Session of the Agadir Summer University from July 29 to August 5, 1991, two meetings were held on August 4 and 5 to discuss a charter on the Amazigh language and culture in Morocco, drafted and proposed by the Moroccan Association for Research and Cultural Exchange.

Participants in these meetings included:

- The Summer University Association in Agadir, represented by its President, Professor Lahcen Kahmo;
- The Moroccan Association for Research and Cultural Exchange, represented by the secretary-general of the Central Office, Brahim Akhiate, his deputy, El Houssaïn El Moujahid and association member, Ahmed Boukous;

- The New Association for Culture and Folk Arts, represented by its president Lhoucine Akhiate, and its secretary, Arhamoush Ahmed;
- The Elmas Cultural Association, represented by its president, Mohammed El-Chami;
- The Ghris Cultural Association, represented by its president, Ali Harsh El-Rass;
- The Cultural Association of Souss sent its apologies for not attending the meetings, after giving its written agreement on the final version of the charter.

After a fruitful discussion on all the amendments and proposals submitted by the presidents and secretaries-general of the above associations, the final version of this charter on the Amazigh language and culture in Morocco was approved and signed by all these associations on August 5, 1991, at the Hotel School in Agadir.

They also agreed to publish this charter and promote it widely.

- Ali Harsh El-Rass
- Brahim Akhiate
- Mohammed El-Chami
- Lhoucine Akhiate
- Lahcen Kahmou.

An important observation to make here is that had it not been for the secrecy that surrounded this project, from conception to completion, and the fact that everybody lived up to their responsibility to maintain this secrecy, the project would not have seen the light of day, for the simple fact that the opponents of the Amazigh struggle did not wish to see the Amazigh movement achieving such significant steps in its struggle.

A commemorative photo of the signatories was taken at the Hôtel Aferni, and the Charter was read at the closing session of the Summer University by Mohammed El-Chami, who had been deeply involved in the event both as an activist and in his capacity as president of the new Elmas association in Nador.

This session faced problems and difficulties that had not arisen in the previous sessions, both as concerned its organizational and intellectual aspects. As I have mentioned, it was a large event that included conference attendees and their spouses and children, in addition to artists and creatives. This required that we make tremendous efforts to provide all their material and logistical needs as well as creating the necessary atmosphere for the success of the session. Yet we overcame all these difficulties, tensions, psychological pressures, and intellectual challenges. Our success was consummated when El Houssaïn El Moujahid read out the final report and Mohammed El-Chami read the announcement of the Charter on Amazigh language and culture.

This session, the successes we achieved, and the value we added to our struggle by establishing this document, did not pass without leaving an impact on me. It had imposed great burdens on me, starting from the moment we began preparations for the session several months previously. It required a huge physical and intellectual effort to solve all the material and organizational problems, intellectual disagreements, and miscellaneous challenges. I had to be present at every location, day and night, dashing between all the organizing committees and the one drafting the charter, and even the kitchen, to head off anything that could negatively affect the progress of the session and the realization of its goals. All this stress weighed heavily on me and even left its mark on my body, in the form of a small rash that appeared on my forehead. This quickly expanded into a white patch that would have spread across my face if not for divine grace and my efforts to treat it with every kind of traditional and modern remedy people recommended.

I must also mention that after this major achievement by the six Amazigh associations, a document of endorsement was signed by prominent Amazigh activists, notably Mohammed Chafik and Abdelmalek Ousaden.[3]

As usual, a trip was organized to an old school in the area, this year to the Sidi Ouagag school where Abdullah Ibn Yasin, the founder of the Almoravid dynasty, had studied. This trip was led by Benider Jamea and Lhoucine Jouhadi. The session concluded with an evening of literature and art at the open-air theater, featuring *aḥwāsh* and *rwais* bands as well as modern groups from various regions of Morocco. Among the artists was Fatima Tabaamrant, whom I had visited at her home in Dcheira with Essafi Moumen Ali to convince her to participate in the closing ceremony, after discovering her artistic talent and the strength of her character. Fatima was to remain in constant contact with AMREC for her own intellectual training so she could rise to her responsibilities, as an artist, to deepen the awareness of the Amazigh identity among her wide, admiring audience. This had a significant impact on her work from that meeting in 1991 onward, and she never missed an opportunity to participate in our cultural events.

With the issuance of this charter, I can say that the period from 1980 to 1990 was for us a phase of testing, by various entities, whether the authorities, political parties, or intellectual circles. They tried our endurance and determination to continue, as well as our intellectual capacity to challenge ideologies and the prevailing ideas opposing the Amazigh cause, which grew and strengthened in the cultural and political arena. With the issuance of this charter, which crowned an intellectual and activist struggle that had begun in 1967, we entered another phase, the stage of real confrontation with these parties. The Amazigh associations now had a true intellectual reference point and clear demands addressed to the state, the political parties, and society at large. Thus, it became a true movement, born from the womb of civil society. What is also important to note is that these demands were made in the format of a dialogue, focused on the constitution, education, the media, and public life, meaning they were capable of evolving and reformulating their expressions, to keep pace with developments, as they were open files for this purpose.

1991–2000: THE PHASE OF CONFRONTATION

After the issuance of the Agadir Charter, as it came to be known, we had it translated into French, by Ahmed Boukous, and into English by the activist Jalali El-Sayeb. We now tasked ourselves with promoting and disseminating it in various circles. To illustrate the precision of the document, suffice it to say that no one in the national press or intellectual circles could find a loophole in it that could be exploited politically or ideologically to trivialize it or play down its value. The document was balanced, objective, and clear: all these entities simply opted to remain silent and ignore the topic in order to avoid helping to spread the ideas in the document, which laid out the legitimate demands of the Amazigh movement.

After this significant achievement, we started developing an outreach and communication program covering the whole of Morocco, launched from the association's branches in Marrakech, Kénitra, Casablanca, and Rabat. The association initiated these activities by organizing a meeting in Maâmora, of the National Committee for the Unification of Writing and the Dictionary on May 15 and 16, 1992. The aim here was to continue discussing the foundations discussed at the Fourth Session of the Summer University on the subject of standardizing Tamazight writing and the lexicon created by Essafi Moumen Ali, on which several observations and suggestions were made. The association invited as many experts and Amazigh creators as possible to this meeting.[4]

Those who spoke at this meeting made important observations on the process of standardization, without selfishness or sensitivity. Everybody rose above regional affiliations, focusing only on the interests of the Amazigh language as they examined the approaches of all the world's schools of linguistics and the experiences of others, as applied to the process of standardizing the Amazigh language. Thus, the meeting was the first truly scholarly initiative to create a basis for the process of developing and enriching the Amazigh language, with the participation of an elite group who were themselves Amazigh. For example, the meeting determined the number of phonemes (perceptibly distinct units of sound) to be adopted when standardizing the Tamazight spoken in Morocco.

That same year, for the first time, the association was allowed to participate in the International Book and Publishing Fair, through which it was able to publicize the existence of Amazigh books and writing. The association's pavilion was a place for dialogue and robust discussion between activists and visitors, who were surprised or even shocked by the presence of Amazigh books, and especially the strong presence of the Tifinagh script. These heated debates, among small groups of people in front of the association's pavilion, were attributable to the fact that it was next to pavilions belonging to Islamic associations and the *Al-Furqan* magazine, as well as associations belonging to the Moroccan Left. All these civil society associations were together on a marginalized side corridor leading to the toilet area of the exhibition hall, which was jokingly dubbed "the street of those who have incurred (God's) wrath." Despite all this discrimination we faced, we made efforts to display panels presenting our cultural activities and featuring pictures of our publications. Through these exhibits and discussions, the student audience, in particular, got to know the fundamentals of our cause and the demands of the Amazigh movement, as documented in the Agadir Charter, of which we distributed many copies to promote its contents and make it more widely known. Our participation in the International Book and Publishing Fair for the first time, in 1992, was thus an important occasion and gave us a new platform to showcase our achievements in the field of Amazigh language and culture. This made it a significant milestone for Amazigh cultural activity, which had begun to make its presence known and assert itself on the Moroccan intellectual and political scene.

As part of the association's role in spreading and deepening awareness of the Amazigh identity among all Moroccans, it set up intensive programs in many parts of Morocco, concerning various components of Moroccan culture. From the summer 1991 signing of the Agadir Charter onward, the association made an effort to invite activists from Amazigh associations to participate in and attend cultural activities we organized in various Moroccan cities. The purpose of this was to nurture continuous communication and dialogue between all these actors. We intensified these activities, organizing a study day in Marrakech on May 30, 1992, under the slogan "For the sake of Comprehensive and Purposeful Cultural Work," concluding with an artistic evening. I took part alongside Mohammed Farah, Hassan Id Balkassam, and Ahmed Asarmouh. We also organized Amazigh Culture Days in Casablanca between March 19–21, 1992, under the slogan "Amazigh Culture as a Component of National Culture." Through these activities, we began to implement and spread awareness about the contents of the Agadir Charter and the demands of the Amazigh movement.

OUR BATTLE AT THE NATIONAL COUNCIL FOR CULTURE

At the beginning of 1993, Mohammed Chafik, Ali Khedaoui, and I received invitations to take part in the fourth session of the National Council for Culture. After informing my comrades at the association about the invitation, we set out to prepare a memorandum to be addressed to the members of the council, to ensure our presence was strong and beneficial. I suggested to Chafik and Khedaoui that we present this memorandum in all three of our names, and they agreed. The session was held on January 18 and 19, 1993, at the Ministry of Public Works' headquarters in Rabat.

The three of us took part in the Cultural Heritage Committee under the banner of the association. This produced our association's first ever memorandum addressed to official bodies, as the National Council for Culture was established by the Ministry of Culture to discuss cultural issues at the national level.

The memorandum included several ideas, so I will cite some paragraphs from it here:

> Honorable members of the committee,
>
> It is no secret to any of you that a significant part of our cultural heritage risks vanishing, is not given the slightest official attention, for particular reasons which need not be mentioned in this memorandum.
>
> This marginalized space, left vulnerable to neglect, is the realm of Amazigh culture: its prose and poetry, its proverbs and sayings, and its arts, manifested in the creations of various artisanal crafts and architecture.
>
> As a result of this aberrant, unreasonable situation, opinions have converged on the need to draw attention to it, with a collective declaration known as the "Agadir Charter," signed by six cultural

associations representing different regions of the Kingdom, on August 5, 1991. Here is its full text, with a request for you to contemplate its contents. . . .

Thus, we urge the members of the Cultural Heritage Committee to issue a recommendation for the creation of a body tasked with considering and planning for the integration of the Amazigh language into the national educational and cultural system.

This was the first occasion that the Agadir Charter had been deployed at this level. The council comprised senior cultural and intellectual figures in our country, in addition to cultural associations with their various interests, and issued recommendations concerning cultural and intellectual issues as well as serving as an arena for theoretical debates in the field of cultural policy.

It was decided that the three of us would join the council's Cultural Heritage Committee, which consisted of more than thirty members and was chaired by the dean of the Faculty of Letters in Casablanca, assisted by Dr. Ahmed Toufiq, who was then the director of the Public Treasury, and Dr. Abdelaziz Touri, the secretary-general of the Ministry of Culture. I sat near the chairman, opposite Mohammed Chafik. The memorandum, accompanied by the Agadir Charter, was distributed to all those present. During the discussion, I tried to persuade the chairman to read the memorandum, which he refused, on the grounds that everyone had received it along with the accompanying documents. Nevertheless, we intervened whenever necessary by discussing the ideas contained in the draft prepared by the ministry. We made a number of proposals, all related to preserving Amazigh heritage, both symbolic and material. We also countered ideas that portrayed Amazigh heritage solely through its material aspects, like archaeology and folklore, neglecting its intellectual and civilizational depth and the relationship of Moroccan heritage with the Amazigh language, as a bearer of this intellectual heritage. The discussion was lengthy, and we kept our composure in the face of many provocative comments. As we awaited the report drafted by the drafting committee, we hoped it would take into consideration some of our suggestions and our observations on the ministry's draft, but we were to be disappointed. There was not a reference to Amazigh language or culture apart from a single, isolated sentence about linguistic diversity, with Tamazight at the end of the list of languages. Chafik looked at me and said, "Let's gather our papers, we can't work here. We're wasting our time." I replied, "Don't worry, now we can start using a different tactic."

I then requested to speak and went on the attack. As I was speaking, Dr. Kandiri, the former minister of education, interrupted without the chairman's permission. He addressed me imperiously, saying, "Enough, enough, you have spoken a lot and taken up a lot of time." At this, Chafik intervened and asked to speak. He supported me, saying, "Gentlemen, we have listened to many interventions, some deserving attention and others not, yet we listened silently." He added, "Let brother Akhiate complete his speech, as we have listened to others and will listen to more." The chairman then allowed me to complete my intervention. Seizing the opportunity, I made a plea, criticizing the officials responsible for the report that had not taken into account any of our suggestions:

> We believed that by inviting us to attend and participate as actors in the Amazigh movement, the Ministry, and through it the state, had changed its stance toward the Amazigh issue. I felt that the time had come where it would reconcile with itself, and that it was convinced of the need to deal positively and patriotically with the linguistic and cultural diversity in our country. I thought it had done away with the old behavior of marginalizing a fundamental pillar of our national identity, the Amazigh. Instead, here, we are seeing this negative behavior at this committee, by excluding our proposals, observations, and the documents we brought to contribute to the success of this meeting.

I continued: "I call on you to bear your responsibilities. From now on, we are not concerned with the recommendations you have presented to us. We will fulfill our national duty toward our country and our national Amazigh culture." I then gathered my papers and asked Chafik to leave the room with me. However, he preferred to stay to follow the session, along with Ali Khedaoui, to see what happened next. The room was filled with attendees from other committees, who had joined us to watch the final minutes of the committee session. They included Ouzzin Aherdan, Omar Louzi, and others.

After I had walked out to the outer lobby, the room turned against the chairman. The first person to talk after me was Ali Khedaoui, who accused the chairmanship of bias and discrimination against me. Everyone started demanding the floor, insisting that our proposals be included in the committee's recommendations. The chairman became besieged by these requests. Given the embarrassment my plea had caused, Chafik now approached me to ask for my assistance in drafting some of those recommendations.

I refused: "All the proposals are already in the committee's hands, and they know better than me how to draft them, as that's their task."

Thus, thanks to this offensive, five of our proposals were accepted into the committee's final recommendations. Many of those present came to speak to me, expressing their support for what I had said. Many of them told me they too were Amazigh, although this information came after this achievement, not before.

Here are the most important recommendations that we successfully fought to include in the committee's final report:

- Special committees should be established within the National Council for Culture concerned with various national cultures and languages of expression, including Tamazight, colloquial Arabic and Hassaniya.
- Efforts should be made to integrate our heritage into the educational system, in coordination with the Ministry of Education.
- Relevant authorities should work toward establishing an Institute for Amazigh Studies and Research.
- A comprehensive concept of heritage should be adopted that includes all forms of cultural and spatial assets, encompassing all the material and symbolic creations of Moroccan civilization in its various cultural components and means of expression, linguistically, kinetically and artistically, in its oral and written forms, whether in Standard Arabic, Moroccan Arabic, Tamazight, Hassaniya, or Moroccan Jewish dialects.
- A national body for cultural strategy should be established, with an advisory and referential status in the field of culture and heritage, to ensure continuity and oversight of plans and projects, and to provide the conditions under which experience may be accumulated toward a general philosophy aimed at preserving, introducing, and developing heritage.

This last recommendation was a summary of Professor Chafik's intervention on the cultural strategy in the committee.

What is noteworthy in these recommendations is that we managed to change the committee members' conception of heritage, which previously had not extended beyond the term's material aspects, such as buildings, rocks, and pottery. Now, they would promote it as a comprehensive concept that includes all human heritage: material, symbolic, linguistic, and intellectual. This was something that could contribute to the preservation and development of the Amazigh language and culture.

Another point worth noting is our insistence on mentioning the Institute for Amazigh Studies. This move transformed it from a demand of the Amazigh movement, mentioned in the Agadir Charter, to a national demand by the National Council for Culture.

These achievements were not as insignificant as one might think, considering the political and cultural situation under which they were achieved. As evidence of this, when I confronted the council, my friend Ahmed Toufiq, who had just finished drafting those recommendations with his group, told me, "That's the kind of strength and enthusiasm that will achieve your demands." I immediately responded, "Your position as an administrative official isn't the same as mine as an activist for a cause. Each of us has his way of engaging in activism, depending on his position." Understanding my meaning, he went back into the committee to finish the drafting process.

The year 1993 was full of achievements by the association, driven by our great ambition to accelerate the spread of awareness of our Amazigh cause across the entire country, by organizing the largest possible number of cultural meetings, and to bring the subject closer to the general public. We also hoped that these meetings would serve as a space and a forum for Amazigh activists and associations to communicate and exchange knowledge and experience to serve the Amazigh cause, especially as we had now developed an intellectual foundation that obliged us to hold these consultations and communications continuously. To achieve this communication, the association did not hold any event without inviting the largest possible number of these entities to attend.

In the year 1993, we organized:

- Amazigh Culture Days in Kénitra, under the title "Amazighity is a Fundamental Component of National Culture" (May 11–13).
- Amazigh Culture Days in Casablanca, under the title "The Amazigh Book and its Role in Developing National Culture" (May 16–18), with the participation of Lhoucine Jouhadi, Ali Belqadi, Abdellah Derqaoui, Mohanned Ait El Haj, Lhoucine Ouaizi, Mohammed Moustaghfar, Lhoucine Jouhadi, Lhoucine Ait Bahcine, Hassan Riyadh, Ibrahim Ait Hamou, and El-Akouzi Moubarak.
- Amazigh Culture Days in Marrakech, under the title "Amazigh Culture is a National Responsibility" (April 23–24), with El-Ardhi Moubarak, Ardi, Ali Khedaoui, Oubla Ibrahim, Ahmed Assid, Essafi Moumen Ali, Abdelaziz Bourass, Rachid Lhoucine, Ouaizi Lhoucine, El-Maaoui Abdellah, and Mohammed Bin Aliat.

That year, we made several public statements regarding rights. Firstly, the association took part in a national debate on the media, communication, and the right to information, organized by the Ministry of the Interior and the Media on May 29–31, 1993. Another was a statement we issued on Amazigh linguistic rights in Morocco, which was delivered to all participants in the World Conference on Human Rights that took place in Vienna on June 14–25, 1993.

Besides this, 1993 was notable for an initiative by the Amazigh associations in the form of a call to political bodies, national authorities, and the public, regarding Amazigh language and culture, dated May 29, 1993.

OUR BATTLE AT THE NATIONAL DEBATE
ON MEDIA AND COMMUNICATION

The Ministry of the Interior and the Media organized its first public debate on media and communication from May 25–31, 1993. Our association was invited to participate the day before it started—perhaps so we wouldn't have adequate time to prepare. However, we understood this and reacted with determination. The association quickly drafted a memo, which we distributed at the conference, expressing our view on the national media and the marginalization of the Amazigh media, which had long been prevented from performing its role in development, culture, and even informing the public, meaning that Amazigh-speaking Moroccans do not enjoy their right to information in the way that they should.

It should be noted that we did this at a time when Interior Minister Driss Basri had far-reaching influence across the whole of government. Indeed, he dominated and intervened in all aspects of Morocco's economic, political, and social life, allowing him to monopolize power in the country. Therefore, we risked a harsh reaction from the authorities, after our widespread distribution of that memo even before the committee had convened, and without obtaining permission.

Abdelaziz Bourass and I distributed the largest possible number of copies of the memorandum to the debate's participants before they entered the meeting rooms. The memorandum was written in the form of a protest, calling for democracy and defending the right to information as a fundamental human right. This dissenting, democratic style was met with rejection and a repressive reaction from the Ministry of the Interior, which encompassed the Ministry of Information and was nicknamed the "Mother of Ministries."

Given the importance of the memorandum, only the second of its type that the association had addressed to an official body and at a debate at this level, I would like to publish it in full, for posterity:

Memorandum on Amazighity and the National Media, to the Honorable Participants in the National Debate on Media and Communications (Rabat 29–31 March 1993)

Debate Attendees: You gather today to discuss the issues and the situation facing the media in our country, and to contribute to a democratic debate, in order to formulate general guidelines to inspire decision-makers and politicians as they draw up and implement national media policy in the short, medium, and long term.

The Moroccan Association for Research and Cultural Exchange, an organization that has, since the mid-1960s, shouldered itself with the responsibility of contributing, with its modest capabilities, to developing the Amazigh language and culture, sees it as its right and duty to draw your attention to the reality of discrimination against Tamazight, a national language, in our country's media, as well as suggesting some solutions that could alleviate the effects of this perverse situation:

1. Tamazight in the National Media: Between Exclusion and Marginalization

In our era, access to information is considered a human right. Language is the fundamental means through which this this right is practiced and enjoyed. Unless use is made of the language people understand and use to communicate in their daily lives and to understand the mass media, this right is devoid of meaning.

Seen in this light, the reality of the Amazigh language in our national media is pitiful.

As concerns audible media, we note that the post-independence (Moroccan) state inherited the "radio of the dialects" from the (French) protectorate. The officials responsible for this radio made no effort to develop it. Even its physical equipment was left to deteriorate and was not replaced. Thus, listening to this station has become very difficult, even in Rabat itself, and it is completely absent from many areas of our country. The broadcasting staff has not been strengthened with competent personnel, and only those who reach retirement age are replaced. The station's library of recordings and music records, dating back to the protectorate and shortly after independence, has not been updated, and is now prone to becoming and obsolete and unusable. The situation of neglect and marginalization afflicting the Amazigh section of national radio does not allow for any development of its programs—rather, it prevents it from fulfilling its duty of educating citizens and raising their intellectual, cultural, and educational level in a way that conforms to the principle of democracy in media.

As for the national television channel, once again, Tamazight is simply excluded and marginalized, apart from occasional broadcasts of a few Amazigh songs late at night, drawing on recordings made in the provinces. Amazigh culture is also marginalized in state-owned print media and the newspapers of the political parties, with the exception of a few weekly or monthly cultural pages in a handful of newspapers.

We believe that this undemocratic marginalization and exclusion of Amazigh culture and language, by both government and non-government mass media, constitute a severe injustice against the Moroccan citizen, who is the foundation of all the country's economic, social, and cultural development.

This deficiency can only be overcome with concerted efforts by the bodies responsible for the media in our country, by translating the recommendations of this debate into practical, democratic solutions, and by ensuring equality among all the country's linguistic and cultural components in terms of the right to mass media.

2. Proposed Solutions

We therefore present some solutions that will undoubtedly be enriched by your suggestions and proposals:

1. Consolidating the radio stations of the various Tamazight dialects into a single station, under the name "Amazigh Radio," which would broadcast programs collectively and be considered the second channel of national radio. It would be provided with the necessary means and competent and sufficient staff to fully perform its role, akin to the first channel, its counterpart.
2. Working to equip the national Amazigh Radio station with broadcasting and transmission equipment that enable it to cover

the national territory and also reach parts of Western Europe where diaspora, Amazigh-speaking workers reside.

3. Allocating slots for Amazigh programming at all regional radio stations, similar to those currently in place in Agadir and Tetouan, while working to increase the daily quotas of these Amazigh programs by adding morning broadcasting slots.

4. Allocating sufficient time for Amazigh shows on the national television channel, including segments for news, culture and entertainment, to be expanded and developed in the future.

5. Opening a regular slot for Amazigh culture, in the Tamazight language, in various national newspapers, regardless of their intellectual and political orientations.

6. Establishing a national fund for Amazigh music to preserve and develop the Amazigh musical heritage.

The opening session of the debate was held at the Hilton Hotel in Rabat, in front of a large audience, and presided over by Minister Basri himself. The late Ali Baata, who was noted for his support of government media, was to chair the debate. Abdelaziz Bourass and I, as representatives of AMREC, chose to take part in the committee on "Communication Institutions, their Surroundings and Audience." This was chaired by Professor Abdullah Chaqroun, who was known for his integrity and understanding, and tried as much as possible to manage the committee's proceedings democratically. He allowed me to read our memorandum and table it for discussion by the committee members, who numbered more than forty. We laid out the issues facing Amazigh radio and audiovisual media, as well as print media, in detail. This was useful to the other members, because most of them were unaware of the poor state of Amazigh media, and this debate was an opportunity to show them this regrettable reality.

Two incidents took place that had a significant impact on the committee. The first was when I described the poor state of Amazigh radio, the challenges it faces, and the poor quality and limited reach of its broadcast signal, which barely covers 30 percent of the national territory, among other facts of which the attendees were unaware. Chaqroun was surprised by this particular point, suspecting that I was exaggerating, and he said, "Some technicians must be brought in to confirm or refute this." In reply, I suggested they should bring in a radio with them in the afternoon, and we should all try to listen to the Amazigh radio station, which broadcasts from only two kilometers away from the Hilton Hotel. Then they would believe what I was telling them, without the need to bring in engineers and specialists. However, a radio engineer was brought in who confirmed to everyone that I was telling the truth. This surprised Chaqroun, and thereafter he was unable to refuse any request from me or Bourass, as we had shown ourselves to be credible, even if we had many demands.

The second incident was on the afternoon of the second day of the debate. I was surprised to see that Mohammed Bouanani, who had produced many television programs for Channel 1 and was a poet in classical Arabic, was present. Chaqroun introduced him to us in an exaggerated manner, as a great poet and media personality, among other grandiose descriptions, during a session on television programs and their contents. This gave me an opportunity to put this racist, arrogant person in his place. I had met him many times in the street but had not wished to offer him my observations or protest the misguided view of Morocco's history that he presented on television, or his disdain for the Amazigh people, culture, and civilization in his programs.

After Chaqroun's grand introduction, Bouanani began talking about television, claiming that officials were not giving enough opportunities to screen important cultural programs. He spoke of the importance of the Union of Moroccan Writers and the intellectuals involved in it, as well as the need to bring leading intellectuals from the Middle East to Morocco, among other things he deemed beneficial for our television. As he had appointed himself as a critic, qualified to present how things should be done, I requested to speak. Without mentioning the person concerned, I said,

> Morocco has enough of its own great intellectuals. Morocco has always been a source of thinkers and creators, for thousands of years. I don't need to mention them here, as I don't have a lot of time for my intervention. The main problem with our television lies in its language complexes: the Amazigh complex, the Arabic complex, the foreign languages complex. It lives in fear of dealing with these languages. The second problem is that respectable intellectuals want nothing to do with television, because it uses its authority to censor opinions, and edits in a way that removes any value from their contributions. These behaviors mean that no intellectual dares to go near television, which therefore ends up only showing a few trivial programs. I can give an example of this type of program. One presenter was talking about the city of Essaouira, narrating its history in detail. He came to the origin of its name, deducing that the city was called "Essaouira" because it was the first city to be "photographed" or appear on a postcard ("Essouira" is close to the word for "the picture" in Arabic). He completely omitted any mention of the city's Amazigh name and its history, throughout his entire talk. All those

familiar with the city's history know that the Europeans preserved its original name, "Mogador," which comes from the Amazigh "Mou-gadir," meaning "the place with a wall." This translated into Arabic as Essouira, which also sounds like a diminutive of "the wall." Thus, the presenter of this program was able tell these fairytales on television, with total disrespect for the audience. How is it conceivable that the city had no name until a picture was taken of it? This is a form of mis-information and disdain for the intelligence of the audience.

Bouanani understood that he was the presenter in question, as it was his program. He immediately stood up to defend himself, stating that he was not against the Amazigh but had mentioned many names in Amazigh. He began to stutter nervously because I had exposed his stance on the Amazigh issue and the triviality of his knowledge. He couldn't bear to stay in the hall after this and left without completing his presentation. This was just one of our confrontations during this national debate, all in defense of Amazigh language, culture, and identity. It was an opportune moment to expose some of the detractors from our cause, who hide behind the media. Many attend-ees had been unaware of the facts we mentioned, while others tried in vain to misrepresent our demands and the ideas presented in the document we had given to the participants in the debate. Despite all this, we were able to impose ourselves and obtain several recommendations that would serve Amazigh audiovisual media, including the following:

From the Committee on Legal Issues and Ethics of the Profession:

- To elevate all laws and regulatory procedures in the field of media and communications to fit with the spirit and provisions of the Moroccan Constitution, which enshrines in its clauses the structures of the state of law, the balance between institutions and the separation of powers, drawing inspiration from the values of Morocco ingenuity and its civ-ilizational values based on dialogue, tolerance, and pluralism (p. 41).
- In support of the decentralization policy pursued by Morocco, the committee discussed the situation of regional and Amazigh-language media, and emphasized the need to encourage this media in a way that responds to local and regional specificities (p. 43).

Regarding the communications institution, its environment and the audience, with which we were working, we can highlight the follow-ing paragraphs:

- The committee's deliberations resulted in a set of proposals that took into account the ideas we had presented and the contributions of all parties on the committee, which were related to the sectors mentioned above. These proposals aimed to enhance the work of the media and extend its influence and interaction with the geopolitical environment and with the audience, in order to consolidate the rule of law and democratize the right to information and communication, as well as putting the media to work to serve its civilizational and developmental message, which requires continuous material support for the human element, developing the mechanisms of communications in accordance with the themes mentioned in the royal message accompanying the discussion (p. 55).
- The audiovisual media should open up to civil society, engaging it in production to consolidate the path of democratization in establishing local decentralization (p. 60).
- Paying attention to national culture, popular heritage and the Amazigh language in radio and television, and improving the broadcast of radio programs, on a channel dedicated to this purpose (p. 60).

What should be noted in these recommendations is that we were able to employ expressions and terms with activist overtones, reflecting our approach and vision for the future as activists for the Amazigh cause, such as mentioning the need to establish support for the rule of law and democratization of the right to information and communication. These are important things that had been absent from our country's media. We were also able to recommend that attention be paid to the Amazigh language and culture, but for the first time not as a type of folklore. In so doing, we leaned on the theoretical reference points laid down in the Agadir Charter. This was an important gain for the movement at that time.

THE WORLD CONFERENCE ON HUMAN RIGHTS

I have previously mentioned the value that our learned activist friend Hassan Id Balkassam brought to Amazigh activism. This added value was represented in the human rights dimension as a new strategy, added to the Amazigh, cultural, and linguistic references that had underpinned our work until the Agadir Charter was established in August 1991. Thus, Id Balkassam, who was active within the New Association for Culture and Folk Arts, was noted for his rights-based approach, linking linguistic and cultural rights in Morocco to international human rights treaties. In this context, he proposed to AMREC that we draft a statement addressed to all participants in the World Conference on Human Rights, to be held in Vienna, Austria, from June 14–25, 1993. Indeed, we invited him for a meeting at the association's headquarters, where we discussed all aspects of the subject. We agreed that he and Ahmed Boukous would lead on the issue, and that each of them would prepare a draft statement so that we could agree on a final version at the following meeting. When that time came around, Boukous read his draft, which was very comprehensive and precise—so much so that Id Balkassam withdrew his own proposal. He promised Boukous that he would present the document at the conference, which he was to attend. We titled it "A Statement on Linguistic and Cultural Rights in Morocco, Addressed to All Participants in the World Conference on Human Rights."

What I want to draw attention to here is that after the signing of the Agadir Charter in 1991, the association, as I previously mentioned, would invite other Amazigh activists and associations to attend the cultural events we organized. Indeed, we did this at all our events both in the years preceding and following the signing of the Charter. Later, we started thinking about the importance of these associations joining us in signing statements upon whose contents they agreed, when they wished to do so, so that we could give the Charter itself real meaning by practicing consultation and solidarity, and so that these associations, located in different regions of Morocco, could follow national developments closely and feel that they had a role in directing the course of events.

This led us, for the first time, to invite other Amazigh associations who were not present with us in Rabat to sign this statement, after we had informed them of its content and purpose. This initiative, and subsequent ones like it, had a positive impact on Amazigh associations, both advancing the Amazigh cause and urging us to think more about new and effective mechanisms for our activism.

The second point I want to mention about this document is our use of the term "Indigenous peoples," which had never previously been part of AMREC's vocabulary. We used this term in our statement without being aware of its political content at that time. We believed it was innocent, reasoning that since all ancient peoples in history were original and authentic (*aṣliyya* and *aṣīla*), we did not consider distinguishing between the two terms in the statement, despite the vast differences between them. However, it later became clear to us that the term "Indigenous peoples" had been coined to refer to peoples whose lands had been usurped, who had faced genocide and had their lands colonized by other peoples, while those small populations who remained became unintegrated minorities in their own lands. The concept of Indigenous peoples was formulated to assist, empower, and help restore the dignity of these peoples, such as Native Americans, the inhabitants of Australia, and some Latin American peoples. We therefore realized that placing the Amazigh people in this category of "Indigenous peoples" was inaccurate. Indeed, it was an insult to us, as there are no Indigenous and non-Indigenous people in Morocco. Everyone is deeply rooted in this land and has been for thousands of years. Therefore, we changed our view on the issue of Indigenous peoples. The Amazigh question is not an ethnic, regional, or religious issue, but rather an issue of Amazigh self-awareness among all Moroccans. The difference over this point between our association and the New Association for Culture and Folk Arts, which adopted the idea of "Indigenous peoples," was a facet of the intellectual disagreement between the two associations.

THE CALL TO POLITICAL BODIES, NATIONAL ACTORS, AND PUBLIC OPINION ON THE AMAZIGH LANGUAGE AND CULTURE, MAY 29, 1993

This call represented the first direct appeal from the eight Amazigh associations that existed at that time in Morocco:

- The Moroccan Association for Research and Cultural Exchange (national)
- The Summer University Association (Agadir)
- New Association for Culture and Folk Arts (national)
- The Elmas Cultural Association (Nador)
- The Souss Cultural Association (Casablanca)
- The Tilelli Cultural Association (Goulmima)
- Asnfloul Association (Meknes)
- The Massinissa Cultural Association (Tangier)

This call was addressed to political bodies, national actors, and the Moroccan public, urging them all to live up to their responsibilities regarding the exclusion and marginalization being practiced against everything Amazigh, as well as calling on political parties to remedy the deficiency in their programs toward Amazigh language, culture, and civilization, and to commit explicitly to working on their development. The call reflected the association's tendencies toward dialogue and interaction with all the country's political components and associations, without exclusion or discrimination.

Moreover, this call, which came after the establishment of the Agadir Charter that had outlined Amazigh demands, showed that although Amazigh activism appeared to be cultural, given that its demands centered around the revitalization of the Amazigh language and culture and their integration into education, media, and public life as well as deepening Amazigh self-awareness among all citizens, it is, at heart, deeply political, because it aspires to change at all levels—intellectual, ideological, and political—as well as becoming a fundamental party in the desired process of change. Therefore, this call to these parties and organizations was fundamentally a political operation designed to emphasize our presence and announce our participation in politics, without presenting ourselves as an alternative to these parties and organizations. The signing of this call was conducted in the same manner as the previous statement: The association prepared it and communicated with other associations to request their approval so that the final result would represent the opinion of all these associations once it was signed.

Therefore, we must conclude that this period, from 1991—the year of the signing of the Agadir Charter—to the end of 1993, was truly one of change, a phase of Amazigh innovation on the theoretical level, and of the movement practicing effective pressure in the cultural, institutional, and political fields. It was also a stage of intellectual production, when various works were published, such as the *Tabrat* (The Message) anthology, the publication of *Taskla n Tamazight* (the proceedings of the symposium), alongside books about Dr. Mohammed Chafik and the musician Ahmed Amentag, part of an AMREC series on Amazigh personalities. There were also Chafik's "Forty Lessons in the Amazigh Language" and the book *Tigri Natbrat* by Essafi Moumen Ali. These creative, intellectual productions represented a solid foundation and launchpad for Amazigh cultural work. We took care to strike a balance between practical and communicative activism, and foundational intellectual work.

THE LAUNCH OF THE COORDINATION PROCESS BETWEEN AMAZIGH ASSOCIATIONS (THE PERIOD OF CONFRONTATION): 1994–2000

All these cultural activities, from the signing of the Agadir Charter until 1993, with the participation of Amazigh associations in organizing them, as well as official calls to various parties, on the initiative of AMREC, brought these associations to the realization that they must coordinate in order to give the Amazigh movement real momentum in the cultural and political arena. We also expected this from other associations, without forcing them in any way, so that the initiative would come from the associations themselves, acknowledging that there was a need to create a new mechanism to organize their work as activists. I remember that it was the activist Belaid Boudriss from the Asnfloul Association in Meknes who suggested moving forward in this way, by inviting Amazigh associations to discuss the possibility of creating a coordination mechanism among them, to enable them to contribute to the discussions on the issues at hand, and to take the necessary actions and initiatives that could serve the associations involved.

We welcomed this idea, especially since it stemmed from the associations' conviction of the need to take this step, an important one in the history of the Amazigh cause, to become a cohesive and harmonious force in their work, in line with their aspirations as expressed in the Agadir Charter.

To achieve this goal, I invited all the Amazigh associations to meet on January 26, 1993, at our headquarters.[5] We first reviewed the general situation of the Amazigh cause and recent developments, as well as what needed to be done to improve the associations' performance in the political and cultural space. At the end of the meeting, a preparatory committee was formed to prepare a foundation and a project for coordination among Amazigh associations. This consisted of me, El Houssain Ouazi, and Lhoucine Ait Bahcine (from the Moroccan Association for Research and Cultural Exchange), El-Baazati Benasser (from the Elmas Cultural Association in Nador), and Ahmed Arhamouch (New Association for Culture and Folk Arts).

The next meeting for the Coordination Council was scheduled for February 19, 1994, at 10:00 a.m. at the Cultural Exchange Association's headquarters. In the coordination meeting on February 19, we agreed on a coordination protocol, and I was elected as the first national coordinator for the Amazigh associations in Morocco.

THE COORDINATION PROTOCOL

It became clear at our meeting on December 26, 1993, that the general growth of Amazigh cultural activism necessitated a more advanced method of coordination, by rationalizing our collective efforts and making them more productive. There had been growing convergence among the leaders of the associations at various cultural occasions in the lead-up to the Agadir Charter in August 1991, which was followed by a series of joint projects, the most important of which was the meeting of the National Committee for Amazigh Writing and the Dictionary in Maâmora on May 15 and 16, 1992, where we issued a statement directed to political and cultural actors and the Moroccan public, and finally the memorandum to the World Conference on Human Rights on the situation of linguistic and cultural rights in our country, in May 1993.

To develop and build on this experience, we needed to define the principles, areas, and general rules of our coordination, which we agreed upon as follows:

1.   Principles of Coordination

The associations working in the Amazigh cultural field are united by the Agadir Charter. In order to effectively contribute to achieving the goals of this charter, coordination between them should focus on what unites them, starting from a holistic view of the Amazigh linguistic, cultural, and historical component of Moroccan society and its long-held special status, and on diversifying and developing the forms in which it develops, based on the values of cooperation, integration, solidarity, democracy, flexibility, and gradual progress, while motivating everyone to participate and contribute. These are the general principles guiding our coordination.

2.   Areas of Coordination

The areas of coordination are defined as follows, and the mechanisms it adopts vary according to these areas.

In the Organizational Field

We propose to exchange basic documents such as statutes, internal regulations, bulletins, and a list of planned programs, to be carried out periodically, so that each association can be aware of what other associations have done or are planning. In order to exchange this news at a reasonable speed, we all associations should obtain a fax machine as soon as possible.

In the Domain of Outreach

Each association is free to select the general topics it addresses and ways in which it promotes Amazigh culture, based on its capabilities and the conditions within which it operates. However, it is useful to inform other the associations of this in due time, so they can assist in finding speakers or contribute materially to such outreach events, whenever possible. It is also advisable that associations occasionally consider organizing activities of a national character, and determine their locations based on the capabilities, readiness, and initiatives of the other associations.

In the Media Domain

It is useful for coordination meetings to consider how to contribute to the development and enhancement of existing or future Amazigh cultural and media channels. It is also advisable that they discuss how to deal with other media platforms, such as newspapers, cultural magazines, television, and radio.

In the Cultural Accumulation Domain

This includes the publication of foundational scholarly studies on the Amazigh language, culture, and civilization, as well as distributing and making public written, audio and audiovisual Amazigh publications. We believe that the time has come for bold initiatives such as the creation of a printing and publishing body, in which the associations participate according to their capabilities, and the consideration of other methods of funding a series of joint works, such as the efforts of the National Committee for the Unification of Amazigh Writing and a Dictionary.

In the Field of National Cultural Policy

The voice of the associations must be constantly present, through letters, statements and collective declarations directed to the public and to the political class, especially the legislative and executive authorities, as well as to certain specialized bodies in ministries such as those of culture, education and Information. It is also necessary to consider how all these bodies might transform their commitments in this field into tangible achievements.

In the Field of Foreign Relations

Efforts should be made to disseminate information about the associations involved in Amazigh culture to the rest of the Maghreb and to other countries, especially those with a large Moroccan community, to facilitate communication between them and the associations. Thought should also be given to ways of establishing relationships with scholarly institutes interested in Amazigh culture or cultures in similar situations, in order to benefit from their capabilities and experiences, as well as relationships with certain international organizations.

3.   Rules for Coordination

Based on the above, we propose the following:

1.   A Coordination Council should be established, consisting of representatives from each association and an observer delegate from each branch.
2.   The Council should meet for two ordinary sessions per year and for extraordinary sessions as necessary.
3.   The admission of new associations to the council should be considered after they have declared their interest in the Amazigh language and culture in their basic statutes, and signed the Agadir Charter.
4.   The Council should pass decisions by a two-thirds majority vote.
5.   The Council may invite actors to attend its proceedings in an advisory capacity.
6.   The Council shall establish its internal regulations, and the Moroccan Association for Research and Cultural Exchange is entrusted with attending to the organization and management of its meetings until its structure is finalized.

Ratified and signed in Rabat on Saturday, March 19, 1994.

THE PHASE OF MEMORANDA AND STATEMENTS TO STATE BODIES IN THE NAME OF THE NATIONAL COORDINATION

During the coordination meeting on February 19, 1994, two memoranda were also agreed upon and signed in the name of the Amazigh associations. The first, regarding Amazigh cultural issues, was addressed to the prime minister, while the second was addressed to the House of Representatives, explaining our demands based on the Agadir Charter, and signed by ten associations. These two memoranda were accompanied by all the other declarations previously directed to official bodies, including the Agadir Charter.

The reason for the urgency was that I had learned from a contact that then-King Hassan II might be planning to deliver a speech including references to Amazigh issues, on the occasion of Throne Day, in March 1994. According to the same source, senior politician Mahjoubi Aherdane had been asked to submit a report on the Amazigh issue. I believed that we now had an opportunity to inform the authorities that there was an organized and active Amazigh movement on the political and cultural scene, with its own perspective on addressing the issues of cultural diversity in our country, and that the state should start addressing the Amazigh issue immediately. The letter to the prime minister was delivered to his office a few days before the Throne Day speech, on March 3, 1994. I remember that this happened to coincide with the visit of the Pakistani prime minister (Benazir Bhutto) to Morocco. I met her and her delegation in the lobby of the office and was struck by her strong personality. She walked with firm and confident steps.

Writing and delivering this letter was the associations' first move in the framework of the Coordination Council, and, as we see, it was significant because now we were forcefully knocking on official doors to express our demands. This letter was also the first announcement of the establishment of this organization for the Amazigh associations in our country. In the same spirit and context, we directed a memorandum with the same content to the House of Representatives, in its capacity as the legislative authority.

Since the Coordination Council was not a legal entity—that is, it had no status as an association or recognized organization—all the statements and memoranda it issued were signed with the names of all the associations that signed them, not the name of the council itself.

ARRESTS IN GOULMIMA AND THEIR CONSEQUENCES

Arrests and Trials

Throughout the mid-1990s, there were tensions pitting the authorities and the political parties against cultural organizations and the Amazigh movement. These tensions continued until King Hassan II issued a political pardon for detainees, and preparations were made for the constitutional amendment to be enacted in 1996, which aimed to appease opposition parties and bring them into the government.

As already mentioned, the Amazigh movement had submitted a memorandum to the prime minister and the House of Representatives including the demands of the Amazigh movement and signed by all the Amazigh associations existing at the time. On May 1, during Labor Day celebrations in Errachidia, participants chanted slogans demanding linguistic and cultural rights for all components of the Moroccan people. Some branches of the Tilelli Cultural Association in Goulmima took part in these celebrations to promote the Amazigh demands contained in the Agadir Charter, which were the same as those included in the letters to the prime minister and the House of Representatives. On the morning of Tuesday, May 3, 1994, seven participants in these celebrations from Goulmima and Errachidia were arrested.[6]

A glance at the names and professions of the detainees showed that they were all members of the Tilelli association. Ali Iken and Ali Harsh El-Rass, the head, were sentenced to two years in prison and a fine of ten thousand dirhams each, while Moubarak Taous was sentenced to one year and the same fine.

What can be deduced from this trial is that as the authorities had been officially informed of our demands, following the establishment of the Coordination Council; the state wanted first to intimidate us, but also to test us, to see if the council could survive. It also wanted to gauge the degree of civil society's solidarity with us, by observing its reaction to these unjustified arrests.

Indeed, strong responses came from all sides, condemning the developments from within the region. On May 5, 1994, all the political and cultural forces and associations in Errachidia convened and issued a statement condemning the prosecutions.[7] These organizations also decided to organize a solidarity and protest gathering on Sunday, May 8, 1994.

The local authorities therefore faced a strong show of solidarity and realized that the situation was not as they had suspected. As national coordinator for the Amazigh associations within the Coordination Council, I set out to confront the authorities' illegal attack on freedom of expression and opinion. The Council issued a statement on May 14, 1994, informing the public both nationally and internationally, and condemning the arrests of the Amazigh movement activists and their unionist comrades in Goulmima and Errachidia. I personally signed this statement, as the national coordinator, on behalf of eleven Amazigh associations.

A monitoring cell was also formed within the council to follow the developments of the trial and to do what we could to address the situation. International human rights organizations, including Amnesty International, condemned these unjustified and illegal arrests, as the detainees had not broken any law, but were merely expressing their cultural demands within the framework of the right to expression and opinion. These international organizations wrote directly to the royal court on the matter.

The authorities now found themselves in an awkward position due to these arrests, which had been intended to intimidate and threaten the Amazigh movement associated with the Coordination Council. After all, they could have arrested me personally, as national coordinator, as I had submitted the Amazigh movement's demands to the prime minister's office and the House of Representatives. However, the authorities preferred to strike at the margins, far from Rabat, the capital and the Morocco headquarters of international bodies and organizations.

My office at AMREC headquarters was bustling with activity. I organized regular meetings to follow developments in the case, to help organize the defense of the detainees. We managed to provide dozens of volunteer lawyers from various cities across Morocco, providing transport for them so they could be present at court sessions, and we helped the detainees communicate with their families to raise their morale during this ordeal.

The lawyers Hassan Id Balkassam, Ahmed Arhamouch, and Ahmed Dghirni were organizing the detainees' defense. Ady Bouarfa, a prominent trade union figure from Errachidia, coordinated with me in communicating with the detainees' families, working out of my office at the association.

During that period, I was interrogated at my office by a representative of Interior Minister Driss Basri himself, named Ibn Allal, who visited my office twice for this purpose. He asked about my life story, from childhood onward, my education, my political orientations, the objectives of my work with the association, and my relationships in Morocco and outside. During one of these interrogations, several leaders of the Amazigh movement were present in my office, including Mouloud Lounass from Algeria, Hassan Id Balkassam, Mohammed El-Chami, and Adi Bouarfa. When the official arrived, I accompanied him to another room, closing the door of my office on those present without them noticing. Only after he had left did I tell them what had happened.

As we used the media to fight this battle, which had been imposed on us, and through which the authorities were trying to thwart the Coordination Council from the start, we considered this a test, which we intended to overcome capably and competently, to guarantee that we would be able to continue striving toward our goals. Therefore, our association decided to organize the National Media and Amazigh Seminar on May 27 and 28, 1994. The country's media at that time was under the management of the Ministry of the Interior. By holding a seminar, we wanted to express our solidarity and to challenge the ministry so that it would not think that we were afraid of its illegal behavior toward the Amazigh cause, and to affirm that we were steadfast in our struggle.

We managed to attract a large number of journalists from various national media outlets, of various political affiliations, as well as all the Amazigh associations. We organized an exhibition in Casablanca displaying photos of the detainees, along with a significant number of articles that had been published against the Amazigh cause and its activists since the sixties, to make the authorities understand that our struggle and sacrifices were not new and would not end with this incident.[8]

The seminar was an opportunity for the speakers and associations present to express their condemnation of the arrests in Errachidia and the state's arbitrary practices against the Amazigh movement and its activists. They also voiced their commitment to the Coordination Council and their determination to continue the struggle until their demands, outlined in the Agadir Charter and the memoranda submitted to the prime minister and the House of Representatives, were met. A press release by the seminar also denounced the harsh sentences handed down by the Errachidia Court of First Instance, related above.

In the midst of this battle with the authorities, I reached out to Abderrahman Bouftas, a friend of mine who was minister of housing at the time. I have previously mentioned him with reference to the Aligh Association for Development and Cooperation. During these difficult days, I visited him at his house, along with Adi Bouarfa, who at that time had a separate issue with the minister of health, Abderrahim Harouchi. We had breakfast with the minister, and I asked him to convey to Driss Basri that the authorities' campaigns of harassment against our activists and the Amazigh movement in general were unjustified and unwarranted, as ours was a peaceful and democratic movement whose demands were related to linguistic and cultural rights. I said such practices would not benefit Morocco but could only harm it both nationally and internationally. Therefore, Basri should stop these provocative behaviors and refrain from escalating the conflict with the movement. Adi Bouarfa also presented his problem with the minister of health in order to resolve them through dialogue and mutual understanding, as he was a union representative at the ministry.

After these rulings against our brothers at the Tilelli Cultural Association, which came amid the initiatives I was taking as head of the Coordination

Council, along with our various allies, to press for the release of our brothers and a halt to the authorities' arbitrary actions against the Amazigh movement, I requested an appointment with the minister of human rights, Omar Azziman, through the head of his office, Ahmed El-Ghazali, who is a veteran of our association, as mentioned above. Indeed, a meeting was scheduled for May 17, 1994, and I was accompanied in this visit by Ahmed Arhamouch of the New Association for Culture and Folk Art, Belaid Boudriss from the Asnfloul Association in Meknes, and Naser Baazati from the Elmas Cultural Association in Nador. During our meeting, we explained to the minister the story behind these unlawful arrests, arguing that detainees from the Amazigh movement were merely expressing their legitimate demands, which are fundamentally aligned with universally recognized principles of human rights. The minister understood the situation and promised to do whatever he could in his capacity as minister of human rights. We provided a detailed report of this meeting to the Coordination Council.

While I was engaged in these ongoing and multidirectional efforts, Professor Mohammed Chafik invited me for lunch at his home, with Dr. Abdelmalek Ousaden, which I accepted. Our conversation focused on our struggle with the authorities following the arrests of our activist brothers. Chafik was keen to know everything about our plans and what the Coordination Council intended to do to address the situation. I was frank in my discussion, sharing all the details about our progress, actions, and plans. As I was preparing to leave, Chafik expressed his willingness to contribute to supporting our detained brothers, and said he had a check for five hundred dirhams as a contribution if we were collecting donations. I informed him that we indeed had formed a committee to gather support, but this process would only begin after the court of appeal's verdict on their cases. The committee that was responsible consisted of me, Belaid Boudriss, and Ahmed Dghirni. Therefore, I asked him to hold onto the check until the time was right.

At the association, we continued our efforts to defend the detainees, by dedicating pages in the *Tamounte* newspaper to articles about them and analyses of the verdicts and their illegitimacy, severity, and political implications.

AMREC, as coordinator among the associations, and I as the national coordinator, were in direct confrontation with the authorities due to these bold moves on several fronts. This raised concerns among some activists, who feared that the association itself might come to harm, given that it was considered the main hub for the Amazigh movement and the National Coordination. However, as AMREC's general secretary, I paid no attention to these fears. The association had taken upon its shoulders the responsibility of running the National Coordination and could under no circumstances shy away from its duty of solidarity in the face of developments, regardless of the cost.

THE SPEECH OF KING HASSAN II ON AUGUST 20, 1994

Indeed, all our efforts and struggle did not go in vain. King Hassan II decided to resolve the political deadlock at the time by announcing a pardon for all political detainees and prisoners of conscience, including the activists from the Amazigh movement detained in Errachidia. With this, the Coordination Council had courageously passed the test, asserting its existence and importance by securing the release of our detained brothers. This allowed us to start considering new initiatives related to developing the work of Amazigh associations, enabling them to play an active role in Moroccan civil society and to achieve the goals of the movement, as outlined in the Agadir Charter.

As we battled on, seeking to inspire activists and foster cohesion and solidarity among them, we at the association decided to organize the first meeting of creative Amazigh authors writing in Tamazight, in Agadir from July 29 to 31, 1994. I decided to honor the great writer Mohammed Khaïr-Eddine, along with an Amazigh author writing in French and the esteemed poet Mohamed Moustaoui. We had initially planned to hold this literary and intellectual event at the municipal hall, but the authorities suddenly prevented us from doing so, even after we had obtained a permit from the city's Pasha. I believe he had issued the permit without coordinating with the governor. He was later suspended, possibly over this incident. The authorities then cobbled together their own parallel event, rapidly organizing a meeting of the scholars and clerics of Souss in the same hall and at the same time, clearly with the undeclared aim of creating a conflict between us and them. However, we acted responsibly and did not fall into their trap. A case in point is that some of these clerics, led by cleric Abdellah El Guercifi, used their speeches to direct baseless accusations against our Amazigh movement. However, El Guercifi's outbursts, meant to please the authorities, did not resonate with the audience, and were seen as a cry in the wilderness. We faced this situation responsibly and held our meetings in various places like the Agrini hotel and cafés in Aourir (near Agadir), making this meeting unique. For the first time, it brought together the best Amazigh authors to discuss the future and development of Amazigh culture. It also gathered many activists from various regions of Morocco and from various associations, along with some of our brothers from Algeria. We took a commemorative photo of all these participants after the event held at the Aferni hotel. The meeting was attended by more than forty-five Amazigh writers.[9]

At the same event, in the name of AMREC and at the Aferni Hotel, I presented a splendid gift of juniper wood engraved with lemon wood, as a token to the brothers from the Tilelli Association who had been released. One of them, Ali Ikken, accepted it on their behalf. This was our first gesture of appreciation to these individuals, immediately after their release.

Following this major meeting, we issued a statement on the fact we had been banned from holding the symposium. Notably, it included this passage:

> The Moroccan Association for Research and Cultural Exchange had announced in the national press that it was organizing the Moroccan Symposium of Creative Amazigh Writers on July 29–31, 1994, in Agadir. This symposium aimed to foster communication among these creators from various literary genres and to discuss numerous issues related to both oral and written literature. The program also included a tribute session two major Moroccan writers known for their cultural creativity on the national cultural scene: Mohammed Khaïr-Eddine and Mohamed Moustaoui.

The meeting was thus memorable both for the fact that it was blocked by the authorities and that everyone else was determined to make it a success. Shortly afterward, on August 20, King Hassan II gave a speech commemorating the anniversary of Revolution of the King and the People (the national movement to end French and Spanish colonial rule). During the address, he said it was necessary to teach "Moroccan dialects" in the country's schools, at least at the primary level.

We in the Amazigh movement saw this unexpected comment as an official recognition of the legitimacy of our demands, and the crowning of our struggle and activism, even though the Amazigh language was not mentioned by name. The content and timing of the speech implied that he was referring to the Amazigh language and culture. Although this came in the context of an easing of years of political tensions, and an amnesty for political detainees and prisoners of conscience, we saw it as a necessary milestone toward breaking the psychological barrier that some people had faced when dealing with the Amazigh issue, as if it were taboo as long as the state was fighting it or had an unclear stance toward it. Almost as soon as he had delivered this speech on August 20, 1994, the authorities changed the way they interacted with Amazigh associations and Amazigh discourse in general.

PERSONAL AND COLLECTIVE PUBLIC POSITIONS
ON THE AUGUST 20 SPEECH

A Meeting at the House of Professor Mohammed Chafik

The day after the king's speech, a week-long film festival took place in Douarnenez, France, on the theme of Amazigh movies. It was attended by several activists of the Amazigh movement from Morocco, including Hassan Id Balkassam, Lhacene Oulzate, and Mohammed Mounib. During meetings there with activists from Algeria, they discussed the idea of creating a "World Amazigh Congress." Discussion of the idea continued throughout the following year. Participants at the cinema festival unanimously commended the Moroccan King's speech, seeing it as a positive step toward achieving the linguistic and cultural rights of the Amazigh people across North Africa, and in Morocco in particular.

On the day of the king's speech, I was in Agadir, where I had stayed for a few days following the event mentioned above. On my return to Rabat, on the morning of August 3, I went to the headquarters of the association. The first person who approached me there claimed to be from the interior ministry. He had spent several days waiting for my return, to inquire about a meeting to be held at Mohammed Chafik's house. I was surprised by this and informed him that I was the national coordinator, that I had not been invited to any such meeting, and that Mohammed Chafik had no relation to the Coordination Council. I asked if he knew him personally, to which he said no. I informed him that Chafik was a state official, the director of the Royal College (where members of the royal family are educated), and a former secretary of education. Therefore, I assumed that some of Chafik's friends might have wanted to gather some information and inquire about how Tamazight could be integrated into Moroccan education as per the king's speech of August 20. The man appeared to believe I was evading his questions with these responses. So he interrupted me, insisting that the meeting was of the Coordination Council, called by Chafik, and that the Amazigh associations would attend. This news surprised me, and I began to wonder why Chafik was involved in the coordination. I told him that I would find out what was going on immediately. Naively, he asked me to tell him about the details of the upcoming meeting. I retorted, "If you're the one informing me about the meeting and who is attending, how could you not know what the agenda is? Whoever informed you about it will also tell you the rest." The man left and never returned.

I immediately went to Professor Mohammed Chafik's house to find out what was happening. He confirmed that he had invited the Amazigh associations and had attempted to call me many times, but to no avail. He said the meetings would discuss the speech of August 20, and that he had prepared two statements for this purpose to present to the attendees. He showed me these statements and asked for my help in convincing the associations, as I was the national coordinator. However, I asked him not to present them to the associations, because their content did not align with the goals of the Amazigh movement.

Here are the texts in question:

The First Declaration

If it were not for the urgent necessity imposed by the circumstances, there would be no need to recall that Amazigh is one of the two fundamental dimensions of Moroccan identity, while Arabism embodies the second dimension, as the linguistic vessel for the Islamic creed and as a sociological reality. This is a self-evident truth that imposes itself in every objective and fair analysis of Moroccan historical evolution, and imposes itself brightly whenever our national entity needs to assert itself against foreign aggression or defend its territorial integrity. However, this self-evident truth has, over the past 10 decades, been subject to attempts to obliterate it, inspired by an irresponsible ideology or blind partisan zeal, by political actors whose minds were clouded by their longing for power.

Therefore, the cultural associations whose signatures are below see it as their essential duty to commend, with deference, the clear political vision with which His Majesty King Hassan II—may God bring him victory—has incessantly guided the affairs of state, as well as His Majesty's high ambition in establishing what is right and eradicating what is false. These associations have thus welcomed, with great delight and pleasure, His Majesty's decision regarding the teaching of the Amazigh language to all Moroccans, and they registered with full satisfaction and great joy our diligent King's resounding call to the nation to cherish all components of our identity, like for like.

Indeed, in his historic speech on August 20, 1994, His Majesty laid the cornerstone for an educational system that suits our distinctive Moroccan identity. It is to be hoped that this royal initiative will be a lantern to guide the National Committee charged with educational reform, constantly enlightening it, as it undoubtedly heralds a new cultural era in which we continue our journey toward a brighter future, dominated by tranquility and perpetual brotherhood.

The Second Declaration

The cultural associations listed below extend their greetings to Prime Minister Abdellatif Filali, encouraging him to continue on the path of rectifying the grave mistakes made, knowingly or . . . in the fields of educational, cultural and media policy, by the successive governments that have ruled Morocco since independence. They hope and expect that every official will take a lesson, in this regard, from the enlightened instructions included by His Majesty King Hassan II in his noble speech to the nation on Saturday August 20, 1994, corresponding to the anniversary of the Revolution of the King and the People.

These associations call on political parties that have repudiated Amazigh culture, despite its vitality, strength and continuity, and despite its authentic place in Moroccan civilization, to examine themselves and to work toward a true understanding of our Moroccan identity. They urge these parties to shed their reductive view of the dynamics that shape our destiny, and to let up with their tendentious propaganda, which is aimed at distorting our history and risking our future by alienating our rising generation from their identity, which they inherited from their ancestors.

Finally, they appeal to the supporters of tradition, urging them to look with reason rather than with passion at our vast Islamic cultural heritage, and to put the controversies it has produced to innovative and renewing work. In particular, they urge them to reflect on the notable causal relationships between the backwardness a civilization may experience, and its self-isolation during a period of its history. How wonderful it would be if the proponents of traditionalism would contribute to the renewal whose signs are now apparent, by helping Moroccan society first to open up to itself, and then to be open to the world, without dissolving into it.

The Coordination Council's Position on the Speech

Immediately after this visit to Mohammed Chafik, I contacted brothers from the associations in Rabat, such as Hassan Id Balkassam, who assured me that he would attend the meeting to see, hear, and discuss the subject, but that this would not be within the framework of the Coordination Council. When I met the brothers from the Tilelli Association at Café Balima, they confirmed the same thing, that they had accepted the invitation but would not commit to anything, because the Coordination Council had its own institutions and its system. Given that many representatives of the associations had come to Rabat, and that the Coordination Council's meeting was scheduled to be held in October, I invited everyone to meet at the association's headquarters after the meeting at Chafik's house. I had decided not to attend that meeting, due to Chafik's interference in the coordination, which was nothing to do with him; as national coordinator, I saw it as my duty to maintain the independence of the movement and its positions. My stance was also due to the speed of his invitation to these associations after the speech of August 20th, bypassing the official and organizational channels of coordination, as well as his invitations to many people who had not bothered themselves with keeping track of our news and our fate throughout our struggle with the authorities, and who only showed interest after the August 20 speech, when the battle was already over.

These questions and others like them dominated the meeting, from which I chose to abstain due to the lack of clarity about its purpose. Accordingly, the discussion there was intense and the meeting did not yield any results.

After that meeting concluded, everyone met at the association's headquarters to study the king's speech. The discussions were lengthy and went into the early hours of September 4, 1994. We concluded by issuing a statement regarding the content of the speech, as follows:

The Amazigh cultural associations gathered in Rabat within the framework of the Coordination Council on September 3 and 4, 1994.

After deliberating the situation of Amazigh linguistic and cultural rights following the royal speech of August 20, 1994, and listening to reports from the associations' representatives about the positive impact of this speech, which affirmed our country's linguistic, cultural, and civilizational diversity, they hereby express their satisfaction with the historic and visionary decision, announced in this speech, to order the teaching of the Amazigh language at educational institutions.

On this occasion, they call on the House of Representatives, the government and all state institutions to take all necessary measures, both legislative and administrative, to allocate a sufficient budget and to prepare qualified personnel and material and scholarly resources provided to implement the royal decision on the ground.

As concerns the media, they believe that the allocation of an Amazigh language news segment on television is a positive initiative that must be developed in both quantity and quality, and emphasize the need to add educational, cultural, and arts programs.

The Amazigh cultural associations, recalling their continuous cultural struggle aimed at establishing a democratic linguistic and cultural policy, adhere to their demands announced in the Agadir Charter of 1991 regarding the Amazigh language and culture, presented in memoranda to the government and the House of Representatives early this year, and insist on their right to be involved in everything related to the preparation of programs for linguistic, cultural, and educational policy, especially the national committee dedicated to studying educational issues. (Rabat, September 4, 1994)

The following day, after we had composed our statement, we (Mohammed El-Chami from the Elmas Cultural Association, Lahcen Kahmou from the Summer University Association, and me as head of AMREC and as national coordinator) decided to visit Mohammed Chafik to clarify any misunderstandings over developments during the previous days. Indeed, we visited him at home; present with him were Mohammed Ajaajaa, Lahcen Oulhadj, and Oudades Mohammed. We spoke at length on the subject. Dr. Chafik understood my position, and we informed him of the statement from the council. He expressed a wish to overcome the incident and said that the important thing was that a statement had been issued and that we continue working toward the future. We shook hands and put the issue to rest.

This incident was just one of the repercussions of the royal speech of August 20, 1994, around which opinions varied. There were those who took it as a starting point for engaging in Amazigh activism, as doing so was no longer dangerous. There were others who saw it as an opportunity to exploit the Amazigh movement's history of struggle to serve their personal ambitions and interests. Then there was the stance of the Amazigh movement itself, represented in the Coordination Council's statement, emphasizing the need to see how things would be implemented on the ground. As we have seen, the speech itself did not go beyond recognizing the legitimacy of Amazigh demands. Achieving these demands would require great effort and sacrifice from activists, actors, and Amazigh associations alike. Thus, the associations understood the general framework of the speech and its political context, and dealt with it cautiously, as it was for the time being only a speech, intended to ease the atmosphere at that time, and its contents had yet to be put into practice through tangible measures.

How the Associations Acted After the Speech

Before the end of 1994, the council put together a document entitled "Rules of Coordination," which was adopted at a council meeting on November 19, 1994, in Casablanca. From then onward, the council's activities became stronger and more regular. As national coordinator, I developed an ambitious program for the council's work and put together specialized committees concerning education, relations and communication, and the media, as well as an oversight committee to ensure the normal functioning of these committees. This latter committee consisted of me, as national coordinator, Belaid Boudriss, Hassan Id Balkassam, Amer El Hocine, Ahmed Dghirni, and Lhoucine Ait Bahcine.

At a meeting called for by the follow-up committee on May 4, 1995, the Coordination Council decided to make May 19 an Amazigh national day (*As Anamur n Tamazight*), celebrated annually with cultural activities. This date was chosen because it was the day the coordination protocol had been signed by the Amazigh associations. There were several proposals on the subject, including the date the Agadir Charter was signed (August 5), the date the Tilelli activists were arrested (May 3), and the date of the outbreak of the "Berber Spring" uprising in Tizi Ouzou, Algeria.

The matter was settled by setting the date when the national Amazigh associations in Morocco had met and laid the foundations of their organization, which is the date this protocol was established, to satisfy all parties that had proposed these dates. However, this decision was not implemented, and remained little more than ink on paper due to divisions in the council, for various reasons.

AMAZIGH ACTIVISM IN MOROCCO AND THE ESTABLISHMENT OF THE WORLD AMAZIGH CONGRESS

In 1995, the number of new Amazigh associations grew from seven to ten, and then fourteen. On July 1, 1995, they all signed a statement by Amazigh cultural associations in Morocco regarding participation in a preparatory conference for the World Amazigh Congress, to be held December 1–3, 1995.

I would like to point out something important—indeed, fundamental— related to this organization's goals. As the national coordinator for the Coordination Council, I had received from the preparatory committee for the Congress a draft of the proposed goals, and I noticed that some of these goals did not align with those of our association, which believes in preserving the independence of the Amazigh movement and refuses to dive into political quagmires. Therefore, I believed these points, which could entangle the organization, should be dropped, and that the congress should limit itself to cultural work that would serve Amazigh language and culture, and to coordinating between associations and organizations in various countries, in order to unify Amazigh activism and promote the Amazigh cause internationally. After all, our association had always focused on what unites the Amazigh and avoided that which divides them. The association did everything in its power to convince the members of the Coordination Council, at the meeting on July 5, 1995, which issued the statement on the preparation for the Congress, that it should rephrase that proposed draft. Following this discussion, the statement was ratified as follows:

1. The associations unanimously decided to participate in the preparatory work for the World Amazigh Congress.
2. The associations proposed that the body to be established should be a cultural, international, independent, non-governmental body, and that it be called the World Amazigh Cultural Congress.
3. The associations proposed that the aforementioned Amazigh Congress aims to develop Amazigh culture, language, and civilization in all regions where they are found, and to nurture communication and dialogue with other cultures.
4. The associations resolved to propose holding the founding conference of the World Amazigh Cultural Congress in Morocco.

This was signed by fourteen associations, including four that were new: the Izouran N Tamont Cultural Association in Souk Al-Arbaa, the Izouran Cultural Association in Ouarzazate, the Fazaz Association for Cultural and Social Development in Fes, and the Nakour Association for Culture and Arts in Al-Hoceima.

Regularizing the Status of the Tilelli Activists After the Royal Pardon

At the beginning of 1995, as national coordinator, I became concerned about the unresolved situation of our brother activists who had been released, despite the royal pardon. All of them were secondary school teachers. One day early in the year, the activist Ali Ikken visited me at the association's office. When I asked him about the issue, he informed me that he had registered the file at the office of Hassan Id Balkassam and that he didn't know why there had been a delay in resolving their situation. I asked him for a copy of the file, so he brought me the documents and their correspondence with the Ministry of Education. It turned out that the issue was related to the absence of a document from the Ministry of Justice proving the validity of their royal pardon.

I went straight to the minister for the Moroccan community abroad, Lahcen Kaboun, who is a friend of mine and the brother of Mohammed Kaboun, whom I have mentioned before and who was detained with Dr. Omar El-Khattabi. The minister welcomed me warmly, and I laid out the issue faced by the released activists, whose statuses had still not been resolved. He immediately called the minister of human rights, Mohammed Zayan, who asked me to visit him. As it was late, I called the secretary of the minister's office and asked her to schedule another appointment in the next two days. Indeed, she quickly set an appointment for the very next day. When the minister for human rights received me, all the directors of the ministry and the secretary were present in his office. When we began talking, he asked me a peculiar question: "What do you mean by Tamazight and how should it be taught?" I answered him that Tamazight was like any other language in the world, and should be taught like any other language. But he interrupted me, saying, "How will you teach the child a language other than the one he learns at home, and teach him the language you say is shared Tamazight? This is Nazism, it has nothing to do with human rights." He was speaking very emotionally. After he finished his speech, I replied, "Thank you, Your Excellency, you're in the government and you admit that what children are taught at Moroccan schools is Nazism and contradicts human rights. The languages children are taught at school right now are all new to the children; not one of them is taught by their mothers, whether it be Classical Arabic or French. Thank God Tamazight is not yet among these languages, which you accuse of being Nazi." The minister immediately fell silent because he realized he had made a mistake in his position of responsibility in the government. His outburst had also sparked derision among the directors, as I could see from the expressions on their faces.

After this strange introduction, the minister asked me to explain the activists' situation. He quickly understood, asking me to follow up the file with one of his assistants and committing to solving the problem as soon as possible by obtaining a document from the Ministry of Justice proving that these individuals had received a royal pardon. I did not have to wait long. The man in charge of the matter was a fine civil servant. He used a meeting of the Advisory Council for Human Rights to mention the issue to the minister of justice, who was present, and the problem was solved in less than two

weeks. After obtaining these documents, I informed the activists. I also contacted Mohammed Chafik and asked him to request a meeting for me with
the secretary-general of the Ministry of Education, a friend of his, so I could
expedite the procedures for the activists to go back to work. The secretary-
general received me and accepted copies of the relevant documents, pending
receipt of the original copies. He also assured me that he was preparing the
documents they needed and carrying out the necessary procedures, pending receipt of administrative correspondence from the high schools where
the activists had worked before they were arrested. Indeed, the secretary-
general did what was necessary, the problem was solved, and the activists
finally went back to their jobs.

AMAZIGH ACTIVISM INTENSIFIES AFTER THE AUGUST 20 SPEECH

In a new bid to support Amazigh activism, and in order to communicate
with the public on issues related to Amazigh culture in education, media, and
public life, the association in Casablanca organized a seminar in March 1995
on the subject of "Amazigh Language in Education: Concepts and Method-
ologies," presented by Essafi Moumen Ali, Lhoucine Jouhadi, Abderrahman
Bellouch, Belaid Boudriss, Ali Khedaoui, and me.

We also organized two study days for the various branches of the association, on the topic "For the Constitutionalization of Amazighity in the Next
Constitution." This was held April 4–5, 1995, in Marrakech, which I produced along with Abdelaziz Bourass, Ahmed Assid, Lhoucine Ait Bahcine,
and Essafi Moumen Ali.

That year, we also for the first time marked International Women's Day
with an important conference on the topic "Amazigh Women and Their
Role in Preserving the Amazigh Dimension of the National Identity" on
March 10, 1995, at the Bahnini Hall in the Ministry of Culture. Participants
included Fatima Tabaamrant, Lhoucine Jouhadi, Lhoucine Ait Bahcine, and
Lhoucine Ibn Ihya.

On April 22, 1995, we issued a statement about the situation of linguistic
and cultural rights in Morocco following the king's speech. As national coordinator, I prepared a report about the meeting on May 4, 1995. The report
included an agreement to form specialized committees on education, rights,
and media issues so we could prepare files on these issues, to be deployed in
our communications with relevant parties. We then formed two communications teams.[10]

What I am trying to point out here is that since AMREC had been tasked with managing the Coordination Council and I had been appointed as coordinator, I had put all the ideas and programs of the association to the service of the coordination. We no longer had programs as an association, but rather, whenever we thought of doing something, we put it to the council so it could be achieved within that broader framework. Thus, we placed our loyalty to the coordination above our loyalty to the association, at considerable material and organizational cost to the association. However, we placed the general interest of the Amazigh cause above that of the association.

SIGNS THE COORDINATION COUNCIL WOULD TERMINATE ITS WORK

After we had issued a statement about participation in the preliminary conference for the proposed World Amazigh Cultural Congress, reflecting our intention to create this entity, many associations within the coordination, as they implemented the plan laid out by the authorities, began to focus their work on the organizational aspect. This resulted in tensions between the associations and a dynamic that saw rival alliances emerge, as if the problem lay in the questions of organization: who is the president and who is subordinate, and who is more senior or junior within each association. The movement thus began to neglect to think about laying out a strategy to support programs of activity that would achieve its lofty goals, as set out by the Agadir Charter since 1991. After the coordination protocol had been agreed on in February 1994, the rules of coordination were put in place on November 19, 1994, and concluded with the establishment of a draft basic system for coordination between Morocco's Amazigh cultural associations, which was signed at the Coordination Council meeting on October 28 and 29, 1995. This final version additionally created a joint coordination committee. Thus, the council plunged into an organizational quagmire, sparking a war over positions. This was exactly what the authorities had planned: to blow up the council or weaken the coordination pending its final closure, even as the Amazigh movement neglected to come up with a strategy that could have achieved its goals. As the authorities succeeded in dismantling the ranks of the movement via the Coordination Council, they also worked on implementing the same plan in order to thwart the World Amazigh Congress at its meeting in the Canary Islands in the summer of 1996.

Following the Coordination Council meeting on October 28 and 29, 1995, at which the so-called "Coordination Council System Between

Amazigh Cultural Associations in Morocco" was established, a group of Ama-zigh associations was elected as a collective coordination committee, and Ahmed Dghirni was chosen as its coordinator. I found out through activists at other associations that the matter had already been settled at the Terminus Hotel prior to the meeting. The day after he was elected, he came to apologize to me, saying that he had been under pressure from certain associations, who had said that unless he ran against me, they would boycott him. I assured him that it was for the best, and that I had not taken on the direction of the coordi-nation for my personal interests but out of obligation toward a cause in which I believe. I promised him that I would help him in whatever he needed, and that there was no problem. The same day, Lahcen Kahmou, president of the Summer University Association, also came to me to express his regret over what happened. He was moved to the point of tears. He confirmed to me the role of the aforementioned people in what had happened. I was moved by his crying and I cried too, but I cried for the future of the coordination, that would inevitably become lost in those vain quandaries, and for the fact that the activist associations had fallen into the trap of those who had conspired against the coordination. Thus, that chapter was closed.

OUR STRATEGY IN FACING THE SETBACK TO THE COORDINATION AND THE LAUNCH OF THE ASSOCIATION'S COMMUNICATIONS WORK

As I have related, the Coordination Council now became dominated by behaviors that distanced it from its primary duties in formulating a strat-egy for effective, serious Amazigh action. Rather, it got trapped in rivalries between factions. This led our association, from early 1996, to suspend its activities within the council, after exhausting every means to push it in the right direction. This was done in order to keep the Amazigh movement out of this conflict, and to focus on strategic projects that could benefit the Ama-zigh cause without opposing or confronting those factions that had come to dominate the functioning of the council.

In order to prevent the Amazigh cause from becoming a victim of this conspiracy, the association quickly developed a comprehensive program of activities to resume its pioneering role, both politically and culturally, and to overcome the plan aimed at degrading or destroying Amazigh activism. Thus, we regained our freedom to act.

Politically, 1996 was the year of the constitutional amendment, which had been one of the main conditions demanded by political parties following the crisis of 1994, and which had led the late King Hassan II to pardon political detainees and prisoners of conscience. The association then decided to engage in dialogue with various political parties and components of society, including human rights and political organizations as well as independent national figures. This series of dialogues aimed to inform these entities about the demands of the Amazigh movement, especially constitutional recognition of Amazigh culture and language and acknowledgment of the Amazigh dimension as a fundamental aspect of Morocco's national identity. These meetings would also allow us to understand the obstacles preventing these entities from positively advancing their positions in favor of the Amazigh cause. This national dialogue on the Amazigh issue would aim to break down barriers and misunderstandings that had prevented some people from understanding Amazigh demands. This initiative was pioneering and left a significant impact on the organizations because the transparent and frank dialogues benefited both sides. Some of these dialogues took place at our association's headquarters and others at the headquarters of the political parties.[11]

This successful diplomatic campaign of communication and dialogue enabled us to bring the Amazigh issue closer to actors in the political sphere and civil society more clearly and objectively, without exaggerations and slogans, but rather through the power of argument and persuasion. Our hope was that this initiative, rather than changing reality and attitudes through a single meeting, would open a process of ongoing communication between all sides, and bridge gaps so that positions on the issues presented could evolve through persuasion and understanding. The association's team, which I led, consisted of the following colleagues from the national secretariat: Abdelaziz Bourass, Essafi Moumen Ali, Lhoucine Ait Bahcine, Lhoucine Ouaizi, and Ahmed Assid.

I recall that during our meeting with M'hamed Boucetta, the secretary general of the Istiqlal Party, he told us that more than 80 percent of the members of the National Council of the Istiqlal Party were Amazigh. He said his party had no problems with Amazigh identity and the Amazigh language. "If everyone on the council agrees to declare our Amazigh identity, I have no objection," he said. He also said that he supported the unification of the Amazigh language, as he would accept dealing with a single language. Finally, when Abdelaziz Bourass expressed annoyance at the party's stance toward the Amazigh issue and suggested that this obstinacy might lead to the creation of an Amazigh party, Boucetta responded, "That's fine, let it be founded by a member of the party, and I will deal with it as a party and there will be no problem." He went on: "What you are doing as an association is the real deal. You're the ones doing real politics, because you're changing the mentality of society as a whole, whereas we as party members are only concerned with our position in the hierarchy." Boucetta's response confirmed that he understood the subtleties of our Amazigh activism, which is aimed at deepening awareness of Amazigh identity among all Moroccans and liberating our society from political and intellectual dependency. This was the true cultural revolution that we were driving.

In our meeting with Ahmed Osman, a former prime minister and head of the National Rally of Independents, I made a presentation about the Amazigh issue and the exclusion and marginalization it had faced under successive governments. Afterward, he commented that he was among those who understood this issue and that, during his term, the government had decided to establish the Institute of Amazigh Studies, but severe disputes around the subject had prevented its realization.

The second thing that drew Osman's attention was our list of demands, which was the basis for these meetings. He commented that they should be rearranged by placing what is achievable, such as in education and the media, at the top of the list, and placing longer-term demands further down. In his view, if the initial demands were met and public opinion and officials started to deal with them in a national spirit, without fear of the consequences, the constitutional amendment would inevitably be achieved anyway. However, I explained to him that as a movement, we organized our demands according to their importance, and it was up to the government and to officials to deal with them, according to their awareness of the social, cultural, and political importance of these demands.

By relating these examples of the positions and views we heard, I want to illustrate the importance of these dialogues for uncovering truths we would not otherwise have discovered. Through them, we were also able to understand the perspectives of all sides involved in the issue we were addressing. After all, it is a shared issue that concerns us all, as citizens of the same nation.

At the end of these dialogues, the association organized a press conference at our headquarters on May 22, 1996. It was attended by many journalists who were seeing the association's headquarters for the first time.[12] This press conference gave a new momentum and a breath of fresh air to the Amazigh movement, extracting it from its narrow constituency and taking it to Moroccan society as a whole. It demonstrated that the Amazigh issue is a national responsibility, not limited to any individual or party. To mark the occasion, the association also issued a summary of the conclusions we had drawn from these meetings, which read:

Based on these initiatives and following rounds of dialogue, the association presented our interlocutors with a document containing the three core points that were the focus of the discussion, inspired by the Agadir Charter, and various memos directed to the government, political parties, and legal and political entities, primarily concerning the integration of the Tamazight language into the constitution, education, and the media. Their content is as follows:

- The dialogue, in general, showed that all parties were ready in principle to understand the issues raised by the demands of the Amazigh cultural movement, and to cooperate with the association to raise national public awareness of the importance and true dimensions of the issue, while continuing the dialogue in order to develop a comprehensive national vision toward it. These parties also expressed their feelings of having falling short on this issue, which could face various negative implications unless it is integrated into the national fabric, along with other fundamental and vital issues.

- Concerning the political parties, while some have showed interest in the subject and incorporated it into their overall programs, others attribute the lack of a clear stance on the issue to the existence of various factions within them that view the Amazigh issue from contrary perspectives. Therefore, they have come to consider the Amazigh matter as marginal and not urgent. While some parties have expressed the importance of including the Amazigh language in the constitution, others believe this could be achieved through accomplishing the demands of greater Amazigh presence in education and the media. The association urged the political parties to incorporate the Amazigh language into their programs and their media platforms, as well as in their political, social, and cultural activities. Some of them consider Amazigh demands an integral part of their program of democratic struggle, while others indicated that this issue was not currently among their priorities.

- As for human rights organizations, they expressed their understanding of the Amazigh movement's demands, which align with internationally recognized human rights conventions, and affirmed that cultural and linguistic rights could not be separated from Moroccans' other political, economic, and social rights. They said they could intervene most effectively in cases of violations of these rights. The association drew these organizations' attention to the need to emphasize Amazigh linguistic and cultural rights in their statements, whose neglect by officials constitutes a violation of Moroccan human rights.

- In the meeting between the association and representatives of the Islamic movement in Morocco, the latter noted that the principles of Islam do not conflict with the specific linguistic characteristics of peoples, and that the Amazigh language is not subject to any fundamental objection as a language, provided that its intellectual content is Islamic. The association affirmed that the Amazigh language, as a collective responsibility of all Moroccans, regardless of their intellectual and cultural orientations, can be utilized in all areas of development and awareness, including the religious field. Everyone noted the lack of use of the Amazigh language in religious guidance, whether in the press, in Friday sermons, or in writing and translation, especially the interpretation of the Quran, in contrast to the languages of other Muslim-majority peoples.

- In the meeting with certain components of the new Left, we discussed the efforts made by this political trend in favor of Amazigh linguistic and cultural rights, both through their media outlets and among students. We also presented the association's activities in this regard, and everyone voiced a desire to develop our cooperation and coordination to contribute to building a national democratic perspective on cultural issues.

- In the association's dialogue with cultural bodies, the latter showed an increasing interest in Amazigh cultural discourse and its various dimensions. They called for a quantitative accumulation in Amazigh artistic creations that would allow them to be included alongside Arabic creations in any cultural activity organized by these bodies. They also called for consideration of joint work between various cultural organizations in order to renew Moroccan culture in all its components.

- The meeting with certain party youth organizations raised many fundamental questions related to various aspects of the Amazigh issue. We also discussed the possibilities for joint action to develop the Amazigh language and culture, especially among the youth, as a central issue for democracy and human rights.

All parties agreed that the association's initiative to call for these meetings was positive, and that it should continue, as it was civilized behavior and could contribute to shedding light on all aspects of the Amazigh cause.

The association, as part of its cultural program, was now also working to expand its presence at the international book exhibition, hoping this could be a powerful signal declaring the existence of Amazigh culture and Amazigh literature, which deserves a distinguished place in the national library. We believed that the Amazigh books at the international book exhibition represented African literature, given that the Amazigh language and its script are both Amazigh and African. Therefore, the association organized its pavilion at the international exhibition in 1996, and it was visited by the ministerial delegation led by Minister Abdellah Azmani. The importance of the association's organization of the Amazigh pavilion lies in the fact that it provided an occasion for discussion circles among students, visitors, and activists of the Amazigh movement alike about the Amazigh language, culture, and identity. The pavilion also played an important role in communication and networking among all those who were interested, both Moroccans and foreigners.

In the organizational framework of the association, the national office also organized training days for the benefit of the association's branches to discuss and understand its strategy, so that activists could be equipped with intellectual mechanisms for action, relying on the strength of argument. This meeting was organized in the city of Marrakech.

THE ESTABLISHMENT OF THE PRINCE MOHAMMED ABDELKRIM EL-KHATTABI FOUNDATION FOR STUDIES AND RESEARCH

The year 1995 marked the return to Morocco of Mohammed Basri, widely known as Fqih Basri, a prominent resistance and opposition figure and a leading official in the National Union of Popular Forces. He had been included in the royal pardon of 1994, which extended to political figures, both at home and in exile, as well as prisoners of opinion. Just days before his return, a magazine published an interview with him, I believe it was *Al-Zaman*. In this interview, he touched on the Amazigh issue, saying he considered it a vestige of colonialism in Morocco, suggesting that colonialism had planted the seeds of this cause and that, therefore, those who advocate for Amazigh linguistic and cultural rights, remnants of that colonial era, should be opposed. This stance revealed Fqih Basri's complete ignorance of the issue and of the struggles the Amazigh movement had undergone for the sake of linguistic and cultural demands in our country.

After reading the interview, I asked the late Dr. Omar Al-Khattabi to organize a meeting to which we would invite Fqih and some of his trade unionist comrades to discuss his views on the Amazigh issue. Indeed, Khat-tabi organized this meeting at his home, attended by Fqih Basri, Moham-med Al-Taheri, Ahmed Bengalilou, Al Amide Tanouti, the unionist activist "Damouh" from Kénitra, and Larbi Azroual. I brought along a collection of our association's publications to present to the Fqih. The primary topic was the Amazigh issue. I reminded my interlocutors of the interview with the magazine and of Fqih Basri's misguided opinions on the Amazigh issue in Morocco. I spoke at length about the struggles of the Amazigh movement and the objective reasons for calling for linguistic and cultural rights in our country. I argued that the Amazigh identity is not a product of colonialism, as he well knows, pointing out that his mother, who nurtured him with Ama-zigh breastmilk, was not created by colonialism. I said that peoples around the world took pride in their languages and their cultural and civilizational heritage, so how could he deny this reality in Morocco and ignore the right of Moroccans to preserve and develop their national Amazigh language? I said that as a member of the resistance and as an activist, he should be at the forefront of defending these linguistic and cultural rights of our people. He appeared surprised by this presentation and the presence of all these attend-ees. I then presented him with our publications on the Amazigh issue.

After my presentation, he acknowledged that he had been unaware of all these matters and developments within Morocco. He assured me that he would review all the publications I had given him, and that we would stay in contact in order to continue the discussion and exchange opinions. Indeed, we contacted each other several times after this meeting, and he evolved and clarified his stance through various student meetings and in his television interviews, in which he acknowledged the linguistic and cultural diversity of our country and the necessity of caring for and supporting Tamazight along-side Arabic.

Several months after that meeting, and after his stance toward the Ama-zigh issue had developed, we began to think about creating a framework through which we could engage in cultural activities that would serve our national culture and rewrite our history from a national perspective, hon-oring the sacrifices of our people and its political and intellectual sym-bols throughout history. We reached an agreement to establish the Prince Mohammed Abdelkrim El-Khattabi[13] Foundation for Studies and Research. We would meet in Rabat at the home of Mohammed Tahiri, a prominent opposition activist who had spent time in exile in Algeria and was now the owner of the Tahiri bookshop in the Agdal district of Rabat. We dedicated ourselves to drafting the basic laws of the institute and defining its goals, and we contacted several intellectual and political figures to join the initiative. While we were making these contacts, the news reached Abdelkrim Al Khatib, who told us he was angry that we had not contacted him from the beginning. He also protested because we had omitted to use the title "Prince" (Emir) as that was the title granted to Mohammed Abdelkrim El-Khattabi by his fighters. Indeed, we added this title to the name of the institute. The late Dr. Omar El-Khattabi emphasized that the institute should include all the intellectual currents in our country. I and Mohammed Chafik were among the Amazigh activists.[14]

After this office was constituted, it was agreed that the documents would be taken to Hoceima to be lodged at the prefecture, on March 5, 1996. I was personally tasked with preparing the file and accompanied Omar Al-Khattabi and Dr. Jeridi from Kénitra in the latter's car. We set an appointment in Guercif with the other brothers, Khatib, Ramid, and Taheri, and had lunch with MP Filali. We spent the night at Khattabi's house in Ajdir, where we held a meeting with many activists from associations in Al Hoceima. We were warmly welcomed by the governor of Al Hoceima, whom we visited in his office: I, Omar Al-Khattabi, Mohammed Al-Taheri, and Sleiman Mrabit as well as Abdelmedjid El-Fakiri, who lives in Al Hoceima, were present. The governor praised the initiative and voiced hopes that the institution would be fitting of the national personality it was to honor. He informed us that we could obtain the deposit receipt from the office of the district president in Ajdir after noon. However, we had decided to leave Al Hoceima after noon, and we arranged that Fakiri could collect the deposit receipt. After visiting the martyrs' cemetery and the landmarks of Ajdir, we left the city. When he welcomed us, the governor was not aware of the composition of the team, which included such a number of former opposition figures and members of various political and cultural currents. He informed the authorities in Rabat, and their immediate response was to hold up delivery of the receipt. Our friend in Al Hoceima informed us that he had not received it. The authorities made the excuse that the file was incomplete, and started procrastinating in delivering the receipt, until everyone was convinced that the local authorities had received an order not to recognize the institution.

That year coincided with the seventy-fifth anniversary of the Battle of Anoual,[15] so the institution decided to commemorate this anniversary in Ajdir from July 19 to 21, 1996. However, we received a letter from the district commissioner of Beni Ouriaghel (Ait Youssef Ouali section) informing us that we were not authorized to commemorate this anniversary, on the pretext that we had not obtained a deposit receipt for the institution. The associations and party branches in Al Hoceima all strongly condemned this decision to deny us permission to commemorate the seventy-fifth anniversary of the Battle of Anoual.[16]

In the context of this dispute, we held a press conference on July 22, 1996, at the National Bar Association headquarters in Rabat, chaired by Dr. Omar El-Khattabi, who welcomed those present. Mohammed El-Taheri introduced the subject, and as vice secretary-general of the institution, I discussed developments from the founding of the institute to that day.

But the authorities had already found a way to counter the deadlock. They founded a similar institution in Casablanca, under the name "Fondation Mohammed Abdelkrim Al Khattabi," run by some of the fighter's descendants, granting it the status of public utility at the time, circumventing our project and preventing us from achieving our goals.

ON THE LETTER TO THE ROYAL PALACE IN JUNE 1996

As I have previously mentioned, political actors in the opposition had impressed upon the late King Hassan II the need for a constitutional amendment as a condition for their participation in the management of public affairs. The King had agreed to this condition and asked the parties to submit their proposals on the subject. We in the Amazigh movement were aware that despite our dialogues with them, the political parties had neglected our demands for constitutional recognition of the Amazigh language, which would ensure its legal protection, allow it to benefit from state advantages, and guarantee it equal opportunities with other languages. This being the case, we decided to submit our proposals on the subject directly to His Majesty. The task of drafting the proposal was assigned to the brothers Hassan Id Balkassam, Mohammed El-Chami, Ahmed Dghirni, Essafi Moumen Ali, El Houssain Ouazi, and me, in coordination with Abdelmalek Ousaden. When we had finalized the text of the letter and informed the associations of its content, Ahmed Dghirni, the joint steering committee coordinator, tried to exclude me from signing it. However, El Houssain Ouazi informed me of Dghirni's intentions, so I rushed to his office along with the others, where the five of us agreed to sign it: me, Hassan Id Balkassam, Mohammed El-Chami, Ahmed Dghirni, and Abdulmalek Ousaden, whose signature was made on his behalf by Ahmed Dghirni. I insisted to Dghirni that the order of signatures be as follows: me, Hassan Id Balkassam, Mohammed El-Chami,

Abdelmalek Ousaden, Ahmed Dghirni. It was agreed that this letter would be delivered to the king's senior advisor, André Azoulay. I was tasked with contacting Azoulay's office, and we scheduled an appointment at the royal court the following morning. When he received us, I explained the subject and motivations of the letter, and some of the brothers intervened to provide further clarifications. To make this meeting cordial, I said to the advisor, "As you are Amazigh like us, which your name indicates, you're also concerned with the subject, so you have the authority to add whatever details we have missed in our letter to His Majesty." This caused the advisor to laugh, but he also appreciated our respect for him.

He continued, "I promise you that I will convey the message to His Majesty this afternoon. However, I cannot promise you the date of the response, or even whether there will be a response." Then we left the office. As we were leaving, Mohammed El-Chami told Dghirni, "If it weren't for our brother Brahim Akhiate, we wouldn't have made it this far, Mr Ahmed." As the advisor had warned us, we did not receive a response. Furthermore, our demands were not considered in the constitutional amendment, which was put to referendum and approved on September 13, 1996. On the first of that month, twenty-two Amazigh associations issued a statement regarding this marginalization, which said:

The Amazigh cultural associations in Morocco, which gathered in Rabat on Sunday, September 1, 1996, announce to the Moroccan public and citizens around the world of the following:

- They take note that the draft constitution of September 13, 1996, does not reflect the aspiration of the Amazigh cultural associations in Morocco to overcome the marginalization and exclusion afflicting the Amazigh identity and language in Morocco.
- They recall and reaffirm the legitimate demands they have previously expressed on various occasions, and via the messages they have sent to various state institutions, political parties, and rights organizations, as well as the contents of the petition signed by a large number of citizens.
- They confirm their determination to continue the struggle until their legitimate demands are met, and call on everyone to shoulder their responsibilities regarding the exclusion of the Amazigh language and identity from the country's constitution.

To summarize these years of Amazigh activism, which were rich in political and intellectual developments, I am obliged to note that this period witnessed significant intellectual developments among the membership of the association, which supported the framework of Amazigh discourse and evolved to dig further into the Amazigh issue, giving it a real civilizational and intellectual dimension and highlighting its unique status on the national cultural scene. This was evident in the association's publication, in 1995, of the book *Tagrast n Wargas n Rabbi*, which was an autobiography of the Prophet Mohammed (peace be upon him) in Tamazight, by Lhoucine Jouhadi. Through this book, we wanted to show that the Amazigh question transcends political and religious divisions among individuals. Rather, it is a national issue that concerns all Moroccans. The association also made efforts to translate Islamic literature into Tamazight, in harmony with Morocco's Amazigh identity.

I sent a copy of this book to Abdesslam Yassine, the leader of the Islamist organization Al-Adl w-Al-Ihssane, with a dedication in Tamazight. He replied by gifting me his book on economics, and thanking me twice, in his words: once for the gift of the book, and once for the beautiful Amazigh words in the dedication.

The year 1996 also saw the publication of the book *The Awareness of Our Amazigh Identity*, by Essafi Moumen Ali. This book was the fruit of major efforts, and came after a wide-ranging, deep discussion about national identity within the association. I would like to note that its author played a significant role in deepening those discussions and in crystallizing the association's ideas and concepts of the Amazigh identity of Morocco. All his writings, regardless of the topic, focused on shaping and defining our view of the national identity, breaking with the prevailing, alienating, and divisive concepts of identity. Following the publication of his novel *Awsan Samidnin* (The Cold Days), all his subsequent writings were dedicated to this important topic, which amounts to the core of the Amazigh issue. They included *Awareness of Our Amazigh Identity*, *An Amazigh Conversation with the Prime Minister*, and *Letters to the Amazigh People*, which crowned this project of deepening Amazigh self-awareness among all Moroccans. Therefore, he is owed much credit for formulating these concepts within the association and subsequently generalizing this discourse and the literature of the Amazigh movement.

The year 1997 saw three significant events in the field of Amazigh associative work: the first forum on the coordination strategy, known as the Maâmoura Forum; the first World Amazigh Congress in the Canary Islands; and the thirtieth anniversary of the founding of the Moroccan Association for Research and Cultural Exchange.

THE MAÂMOURA FORUM TO SAVE THE COORDINATION

As I have previously indicated, the national Coordination Council deteriorated throughout 1996, and everyone became convinced that it was impossible to make any progress in coordinating our activism in such a situation. Some of us began to realize that we needed to overcome this crisis and look for initiatives to get the body out of this pitiful situation. Our association had suspended cooperation with it, after running out of patience and having tried all the available means to resume coordination seriously and with mutual respect for the choices of member associations.

It was in this context that the Elmas Cultural Association took the initiative, inviting Amazigh associations to meet in Nador on December 28, 1996. Our association was invited to attend, which we accepted, due to the close relationship between our two associations and the respect and appreciation we held for its founders and activists. At the meeting, everyone welcomed the attendance of our association after its long absence from coordination gatherings. We were represented by Essafi Moumen Ali, Abdelaziz Bourass, and me. The associations in attendance refused to read a report drafted unilaterally by one of the members of the preparatory committee, who claimed that it was the committee's report. We discussed all the problems of the coordination, and we agreed upon the need to relaunch the entity on a new foundation in order to overcome the crisis. To achieve this, we agreed to organize a national seminar on coordination strategy among the Amazigh associations. Our association was put forward, and I was proposed as its chair, to head the organizing committee of this debate. I suggested that I be joined by four representatives of Amazigh associations close to Rabat, and the following were chosen: the Cultural Association of Souss (Casablanca), the Tamesna Association (Casablanca), Izoran (Souk El Arbaa), and the Tamaynut Association (Rabat).

Thus, the meeting in Nador took place in a fraternal atmosphere, full of hope that this conference would be a new beginning and would produce a clear strategy around which the Amazigh movement would gather in order to achieve its noble goals. This meeting was named *Tawamat* (Brotherhood), and we all listened to the "Amazigh Brotherhood" anthem sung by Essafi Moumen Ali, which we all echoed with him, underlining the amicable atmosphere that prevailed at the meeting.

This committee met several times, and a number of associations prepared their concepts for the coordination and visions of the future work of the associations. As head of the organizing committee, I booked the

Maâmoura Institute at which to hold the conference. I contacted the local authorities and obtained approval to hold it there on March 29–30, 1997. The organizing committee, which I chaired, the Collective Management Committee coordinated by Ahmed Dghirni, and the preparatory committee chaired by Mohammed El-Chami met on February 23, 1997, at the Tamaynut Association's headquarters, to put the final touches on all arrangements. We agreed to invite representatives of political parties and civil society organizations, and to appoint reception, financial, and media committees, as well as agreeing on the individuals who would represent the associations on the stage, and that Mohammed Chafik would deliver a lecture. After these meetings, documents were prepared about the strategy for coordination among the Amazigh cultural associations, the basic system for coordination between them, and a proposal for a "Maâmoura Declaration." All this was carefully prepared in marathon meetings held at our association's headquarters. At the end of the meeting on February 25, 1997, we agreed to hold another meeting at the same place on March 15, which was held as scheduled.

However, during this period of preparation and leading up to it—that is, after the coordination fell into intellectual and organizational chaos—Hassan Id Balkassam had been promoting the idea of a coordination system with two wings: political and cultural. He argued that the associations were only involved in cultural work, while he and some of his friends in Tamaynut were preparing a political project in the form of a party or organization that he aimed to link with Amazigh activism. Therefore, he had prepared a draft that he wished to announce at this seminar, along with any associations and individuals who would adopt it. We did not express any reaction to this tendency at the time, feeling that everyone had the freedom to choose their own stance. We were also convinced that the associations were aware and able to distinguish what was beneficial for their Amazigh activism and what was not.

In this regard, our stance at the Cultural Exchange Association was that through our Amazigh activism, we were already fulfilling our political role correctly and in all its manifestations, as we had our demands for which we were striving and a strategy for achieving them. We believed that the Amazigh issue was a larger political issue than any hypothetical political party. Thus, we distinguished between our political activity and the politicization of the Amazigh issue, which we opposed, as this would require an economic, social, and cultural program agreed upon by a particular group. We believed that the Amazigh issue was a cause for all Moroccans, regardless of their social class and political convictions. This required us to resist the politicization of the Amazigh cause, which would divide people. Rather, we were working to unite all forces for the benefit of our cause. This was our stance at the association, and we did not accept the politicization of the Amazigh issue. We sought to achieve our demands through various means of legitimate activism and within the framework of dialogue with all Morocco's political components and associations, with their various ideological perspectives.

Therefore, despite this behavior, which had the intention of exploiting the seminar to raise a topic far removed from the meeting's purpose, we did not pay any attention to it, in order to avoid it distracting us from what we were about to undertake.

However, as we were finalizing the program and less than half an hour before the end of our meeting on March 15, 1997, some members of Tamaynut surprised us by presenting us with copies of the new issue of the association's *Tasafout* newspaper. Mohammed El-Maakchaoui, the president of the Izoran N Tamount association in Souk El Arbaa, and Mohammed El-Taheri, from the Massinissa association in Tangiers, noticed that the issue contained news items that slandered their organizations. I also noticed that the issue included an article with an attack on our association, regarding our relationship with our late activist Boujoumaa El-Habbaz, which was nothing but a string of fabrications from the imagination of its author, totally removed from reality. I did not express any reaction as I was managing the meeting, as head of the organizing committee. El-Maakchaoui and El-Taheri, however, confronted Hassan Id Balkassam, saying such behavior was not befitting someone aware of his responsibilities toward what we were about to undertake.

In this tense atmosphere, I was forced to suspend the meeting, due to the lack of a conducive environment or willingness to continue preparing for the conference, and the impossibility of working with this kind of behavior going on. Thus, the preparations for the Maâmoura conference ended, after everything had been agreed at the meeting on February 23, including the suggestions from the committees that would operate during the conference, including the media committee.[17]

After the regretful incident at the March 15, 1997, meeting, I and Mohammed El-Chami, in our respective capacities as chairs of the organizing committee and the preparatory committee, sent a message, signed by us both, to each of the associations to inform them and explain the state of preparations for the conference. Here is the text of the letter:

Azul filawn (Peace be upon you),
   Noting the responsibility the National Council for Coordination has bestowed upon the Organizing and Preparatory Committees

to prepare for a national conference on the coordination strategy, scheduled to be held on March 29–30, 1997;

Noting the obstacles they have faced, and which hindered their ability to complete their tasks during the last meeting, on March 15, 1997, in Rabat;

The two committees find themselves embarrassed to communicate to all the Amazigh associations that honored them with this responsibility a summary of what happened, in order to avoid all misinterpretations. They further intend to present the details of what occurred at the next session of the council.

The two committees had fully prepared for the conference in all its moral and practical aspects. Their last meeting was on March 15, 1997, in Rabat. While they were busy completing their tasks, they were asked to meet with the Collective Management Committee of the Coordination Council, which was summoned by its chairman. The Collective Management Committee then requested that the two committees report on their work, which they had not yet completed. However, the committees presented what had been accomplished.

After the Collective Management Committee had thanked the two committees for their major efforts over the previous several months, some issues were put to discussion that could have been resolved amicably. Among them were objections to journalists being present within the media cell. During the discussion between those who insisted on their presence and those who objected, the head of the Fazaz Association withdrew from the meeting, announcing that his association would not take part in the conference.

Next, the chair of the Collective Management Committee announced that the conference would not take place. This prompted the president of the Tamaynut Association to remind them that the conference had been decided by the council in its previous sessions, and that if it continued to in its stance against the conference, this would force the president of the Tamaynut Association to summon its board in order to dismiss him from his role as representative of the coordinating association.

Even as the resulting tension made work impossible and some of those present tried to calm the atmosphere, one of those present began distributing copies of the latest issue of the *Tasafout* newspaper, which, according to some of the associations, contained blatant defamations against them, even as they were preparing for the conference. This enflamed tensions even more, and the meeting broke up.

Thus, the committees see no way to inform the Amazigh cultural associations about this unfortunate event other than through transparency and honesty, so all the associations can shoulder their responsibilities to overcome the difficulties that the joint coordination now faces.

To give the reader an idea of the stage of preparations for the seminar, many important documents had been prepared, including a draft of the proposed "Maâmoura Declaration." Our association had prepared two important drafts that were to be presented to the conference attendees. The first related to the strategy of coordination between the Amazigh cultural associations, and the second concerned the basic system of coordination. Both took into account the experiences of the Amazigh movement throughout its activist work, and would contribute to shaping new horizons and a vision for the national coordination.

THE FIRST CONFERENCE OF THE WORLD AMAZIGH CONGRESS IN THE CANARY ISLANDS IN 1997

Preparations for the first conference of the World Amazigh Congress took place, then, amid internal conflicts, particularly in Morocco, within the Coordination Council, resulting from its infiltration by associations loyal to the authorities, whose goal was to dominate the coordination or to disband it, in accordance with the authorities' wishes. The coordination suffered as a consequence, ceasing to carry out any serious or impactful initiatives in the cultural and political arenas. Thus, I can say that these people indeed succeeded in neutralizing the coordination and bringing it to the point of total paralysis. Having succeeded in their plan, they now set out to cause the failure of the World Amazigh Congress at its inaugural conference, in the Canary Islands in August 1997. Were the Congress to fail, this would benefit the Moroccan and Algerian authorities equally, as neither of them wished to see an international organization emerge that might play a role on the global stage to expose the authorities' human rights abuses and their refusal to recognize linguistic and cultural rights in their respective states.

Everyone prepared to attend this gathering in the Canary Islands, from European countries and North Africa—Libya, Tunisia, Algeria, Niger, Mali, and the Tuaregs in the Sahara Desert—as well as Amazigh associations in the Canaries and the Moroccan associations, divided among themselves due to the unnatural situation imposed on them by the disharmony that plagued the coordination.

In this sorry situation, delegations from the associations traveled from Morocco, according to their alliances, to attend this meeting, each association with its own agenda. Everyone gathered in the city of Agadir to depart from there to the islands. Representing our association were: Abdelaziz Bourass, M'barak Al-Ardi, and Mohammed Bouchdouk. The association's goal in participating was to work to find common ground between the factions without entering into conflicts with any side, because we were painfully aware that the timing of the conference, given the situation facing the Moroccan coordination, would not help or play any role in changing the course of events. Therefore, I decided not to attend the conference. When everyone gathered at the Aferni Hotel in Agadir, and after I had confirmed that I would not attend the conference despite being with them at the hotel, Dr. Ousaden quickly asked me, "Are you sure that you're doing the right thing by not traveling with us?" I told him that he would know the answer to this question after they returned from the islands. I stayed alone in Agadir waiting for what would result from the conference in these difficult circumstances.

The outcome was exactly as I had feared. Associations loyal to the authorities attended, along with a large number of the wealthy and of activists from remote and impoverished areas, who were helpless due to their poor living conditions. Their poor financial situation meant they were exploited to implement the authorities' agenda, as had happened in the coordination. Throughout the conference, these loyalist associations opposed everything presented by the nonloyalist ones, and proposed alternatives that contradicted anything that could lead to unity and solidarity among the Amazigh associations in Morocco. The result was that there was no Moroccan representation on the Federal Council of the Congress, and everyone left the conference disappointed. Its president, from the Canary Islands, was elected without any input from Morocco, the country with the highest percentage of Amazigh speakers in North Africa. This tragic situation was a new victory for the authority's associations, whose goal was to dominate or cripple the congress, as they had with the Coordination Council. However, while this was a bitter reality, it was only a temporary victory. The situation was corrected at the second conference in 1999. This outcome was natural because it was merely a reflection of the reality of the coordination itself, which was the answer to Dr. Ousaden's question about why I did not accompany them to the conference.

The Canarian president of the congress decided to visit Morocco with a group of members of the executive office in a bid to mend the disputes between factions the country. I invited them to a dinner on behalf of our association, and also invited Hassan Aourid, who was in the process of preparing his university research on the Amazigh and Islamic movements; we often visited each other's offices. The meeting was also attended by brothers from the association's board: Abdelaziz Bourass, Ahmed Assid, Lhoucine Ait Bahcine, and El Houssaïn El Moujahid. We clearly informed the president about situation of Amazigh activism in Morocco, especially the penetration of the movement, and told him that this would take time to resolve. The delegation left Morocco without being able to do anything. All this led the president to resign from the role around a year into his tenure.

Following this unfortunate incident, the Moroccan press addressed the topic with surprise and regret over the divisions in the Moroccan ranks in front of the other delegations, something that was a source of shame for Moroccans generally, those who speak Amazigh and those who do not.

THE ASSOCIATION'S INITIATIVES TO OVERCOME OUR FRUSTRATION FOLLOWING THE CONGRESS

Faced with this situation, the association decided to organize a national symposium on the topic of "Amazighity Now" to commemorate the thirtieth anniversary of its founding, and as part of a cultural program we created to commemorate this anniversary.

The topic was carefully chosen by the national committee so that the association could play its role in the struggle, healing the wounds and the frustrations of this setback and restoring their determination to continue their path of activism rather than giving up. The association worked to ensure that the conference included many activists from the Amazigh movement, members of political organizations, and independent actors, to give everyone the opportunity to evaluate the results and clarify their visions and positions objectively and with a sense of responsibility and patriotism. The symposium was held on December 12 and 13, 1997, at the hall of the Ministry of Culture in Rabat, in two sessions. The first was titled "Amazighity: The Cause and the Movement (or the Politics of the Amazigh Struggle)," with participants: El Houssaïn El Moujahid, Khalid Alioua of the Socialist Union of Popular Forces party, Mohammed Chafik, Khalid Jamai, a journalist at the Istiqlal party's *L'Opinion* newspaper, and Lhoucine Ouaizi. The second session was on "Amazighity: Cultural Discourse, References, Principles and Slogans" and included Ahmed Boukous, Ahmed Assid, Mohammed El-Chami,

Ezzeddine Bennis from Bada'il, Omar Amkasou from Al-Adl w-Al-Ihssane, and Abdelhay El-Mouden, a university researcher.

We as an association were able to publish the proceedings of this important conference, as part of our 1998 collection. The gathering was an event that managed to breathe life back into the Amazigh movement. We managed to persuade all significant cultural entities to participate on the scholarly side, or to be present at our activities, ensuring the communication needed to bring about a fresh start. The conference had a significant impact on both activists and associations, as everyone began to seriously think about overcoming the shameful situation in which the movement found itself following the incident at Tafira (in the Canary Islands) and started to consider freely how to correct its course. Everyone realized the risks posed by the infiltration of the coordination, as I have explained. To overcome the situation, groups of associations started to distance themselves from the compromised coordination body and began forming coordination groups and regional federations in order to overcome the situation and demolish the obstacles and the distracting problems facing the coordination, which were hindering strong and effective Amazigh activism. Our association's strategy, which was to distance itself and avoid engaging in the struggle over the Coordination Council in order to avoid falling into the trap of those trying to drag us into such conflicts, helped maintain the Amazigh movement's trust in our work. This was also thanks to our continuous presence on the national scene, through our writings and publications, as well as our intellectual and political dialogue. Eventually, everyone could see through the conspiracies that were targeting the Amazigh movement, both on the Coordination Council and at the congress. Through its strategy, our association deprived those actors of the opportunity to shut down Amazigh activism and neuter it on the intellectual and political scene. Contrary to their plans, our work continued actively and effectively, something that would become clear in the course of future events.

As a result of the infiltration of both the Coordination Council and the congress, coordination groups were formed in various regions of Morocco: a federation of associations in the north, coordination bodies in the center and the southeast, and Tamount Nifous in the south, as well as the national associations AMREC and Tamaynut. Thus, the associations managed largely to free themselves and began to manage their affairs and set out their own programs, outside the framework of the compromised coordination. These groups were formed over the years 1998 and 1999. After organizing that seminar, the association pushed forward, organizing a communicative training meeting for its teams from various branches, on the topic "Amazighity and the Future," on July 12–13 in Anza, near Agadir. This was followed by the commemoration of the late Nait Abdelhamid Oulhaj Said in his birthplace of Ahermoumou, forty days after his death, as per his will. He passed away on August 26, 1998, in Kénitra. I carried out this duty on behalf of the association, in respect for the great sacrifices he had made for Amazigh language, culture, and identity. He was an activist within the association and contributed with his writings to our *Arraten* and "Cultural Exchange" periodicals, by collecting Amazigh proverbs and poetry as well as his own historical writings. He was also the one who guided Hassan Id Balkassam to our association, when the latter was searching for a framework in which to carry out his Amazigh activism, and when the late Abdelhamid was managing the Popular Movement's center on Avenue Patrice Lumumba in Rabat, in the late 1970s. I was accompanied to this commemoration by Dr. Abdelmalek Ousaden, a great friend of the deceased, as well as another of his friends, Yassine, who was the director of a primary school in Rabat. I spoke about the late Nait Abdelhamid as a man devoted to the Amazigh cause and to his homeland Morocco: He was a man of resistance, who was imprisoned and tortured, as I mentioned in my book *Amazigh Men of Action: The Deceased*.[18]

As usual, the association had a section at the International Book and Publishing Fair, where it displayed all its publications on the Amazigh cause and on Amazigh language, culture, and identity. This also served as a meeting point for activists, the curious, and the general public, both supporters and opponents, to discuss the issue. Occasionally, significant intellectual circles formed to bring the topic closer to the public.

Throughout 1998, the association focused on publishing books that addressed issues related to the Amazigh cause and supporting the Amazigh movement in the intellectual and political arena. It published a book containing the proceedings of the "Amazighity Now" seminar, comprising the talks of the various speakers there. We also published Essafi Moumen Ali's "Amazighity: Dialogues with the Prime Minister," an important work in which the author held an imaginary dialogue with the prime minister on the subject of the Amazigh issue. Its publication coincided with the start of Abderrahmane Youssoufi's term in the office as part of what was known as the "government of alternation." Essafi Moumen Ali's book addressed all the issues he envisaged the prime minister raising with his interlocutors, tackling them in a sophisticated and convincing manner. By the end of the conversation, the prime minister is convinced of the legitimacy of the Amazigh demands and the importance of Amazigh identity for Morocco and Moroccans.

As part of the same effort, the association published another book by Dr. Ahmed Assid, with the title *Al-Amazīghiyya fī Khiṭāb al-Islām al-Siyāsī* (Amazighity in the discourse of political Islam). This book emphasized the need to avoid the politicization of religion in dealing with the Amazigh issue. The Amazigh question is an intellectual and civilizational issue and a question of identity that implicates all Moroccans, regardless of their political affiliations and religious beliefs. The use of religion to oppose the discourse of the Amazigh movement is inappropriate and a misplaced form of political exploitation. The association organized several seminars on this topic as it launched the book, in order to clarify any confusion about the relationship between the Amazigh cause and Islam. We argued that under no circumstances should the Amazigh issue be linked to any religious or ideological school of thought, as it is a national issue that concerns all Moroccans, regardless of their political orientations and religious and ideological convictions. We organized these seminars in the cities of Rabat, Agadir, and Kénitra, with the participation of many intellectuals and interested parties. The most important was in Rabat on Saturday, January 23, 1999, at the hall of the Ministry of Culture, with the participation of: Mohammed Boudhan, Dr. Abdelghani Abou El Aazm, and Hassan Aourid, and moderated by Belaid Boudriss.

Before concluding this discussion on the events of 1997 and the unfortunate outcome of our attempt to address the situation of the national coordination, I must mention an important event. Abdesslam Yassine, the leader of the Islamist organization Al-Adl w-Al-Ihssane, released a tape in his own voice, in Tamazight. I have previously mentioned our dialogues with the political parties and civil society organizations in 1996. Among our interlocutors were several Islamic associations, among them Al-Adl w-Al-Ihssane. As a result of this dialogue, these associations agreed that the citizen had a right to be addressed in their Amazigh mother tongue by their preachers, as was the case in Friday sermons and religious guidance lessons historically, since the Amazigh embraced Islam. What, then, was the problem with religious scholars and preachers communicating in the language of the people today? Or was there an ideological stance against the Amazigh? These frank questions embarrassed our interlocutors from these associations, and they all acknowledged that our observations were valid. This prompted the group's supreme guide, Yassine, to issue a recording in Amazigh and in his own voice, so that the group would not be accused of having an ideological stance on the issue. Fatima Achaq wrote an article on the recording in *Al-Hayat Al-Youm*, a daily newspaper, on November 14, 1997, titled "An Amazigh Release from the Heart of the Siege."

THE AMAZIGH ISSUE UNDER THE "GOVERNMENT OF ALTERNATION"

Besides all these events surrounding the Amazigh issue, whether in terms of associative work or regarding intellectual activities such as publications, seminars, and activities, which was a major help in overcoming the frustration resulting from the Canary Islands debacle, this year was also a very particular one in Moroccan politics. Since the passing of the constitutional amendment, a necessary step to satisfy the opposition—as represented in the *Koutla*[19]—to the point where it was close to going into government, everyone had been hoping that such an event would bring new developments: more democratic gains, social equality, and linguistic and cultural rights. The Amazigh movement was particularly keen to see these developments take place. On March 14, 1998, King Hassan II charged Abderrahmane Youssoufi with forming the government, and, after more than a month of consultations, Youssoufi formed a political government out of the Koutla's majority. He presented his government's program to parliament in April 1998. However, it was a disappointment to the Amazigh movement, making no significant mention of our cause, in contrast with the hopes of those who had believed that the progressive opposition would be more open to, and understanding of, Amazigh demands, considering them legitimate, popular, and realistic. The parts of the declaration dealing with this subject did not live up to the required level and offered little hope for the future of the Amazigh language, culture, and identity. What it did say was the following:

In the section "the Educational and Cultural Sector":

We will be sure to alter training programs and educational curricula with the aim of enabling our youth to master the national language, Arabic, to revive Amazigh culture, and to open up to foreign languages.

In this paragraph, the government stated that Arabic was *the* national language, in contradiction with the constitution, and said it would work to revive Amazigh culture, without mentioning the Amazigh national language, its status, or what would happen to it in the realm of education and teaching. Mentioning culture alone while ignoring the language implied a focus solely on the folkloric aspects of Amazigh culture, as was the case with the Moroccan media.

Regarding Morocco's integration into the new world of communications, the statement read: "In the field of communications, the government will work on establishing a general framework that enables the strengthening and expansion of freedom of expression and information, based on respect for pluralism, independence, and community ties." It did not mention Amazigh speakers' right to information, leaving the paragraph vague as to what it meant by pluralism, and without mentioning Amazigh culture; pluralism, as understood by officials, was meant to encompass Arabic and foreign languages. Thus, through these paragraphs, we can see the continued exclusion and marginalization of the Amazigh language, which disappointed activists toward that government and showed that it in this regard, at least, it was no different from its predecessors. Therefore, with this frustrating government program, as 1998 began, a shadow was cast over our work. After analyzing the situation, we concluded that we needed to gather our energies and accelerate our activism, without waiting for this government to make any significant change, as it was no different from its predecessors in its perspective on the Amazigh issue.

In activating this new dynamic, AMREC wrote a letter to Prime Minister Youssoufi on April 30, 1998, to inform him of Amazigh demands and to highlight his responsibilities. The letter was published in the *Bayane Al Youm* newspaper on May 8, 1998, and included a set of demands in the fields of education, culture, the media, and human rights.

Following this correspondence, the association's activists focused on the press as a tool for applying pressure, publishing many articles defending the Amazigh cause. For example, Abdelaziz Bourass published an opinion piece in the *Al-Mustaqil* weekly newspaper, under the title "Awareness of the Amazigh Identity: The Amazigh Issue and the Government's Program." This media activism was met with a counter-campaign from factions supporting the government. The newspaper *El-Alam* published a provocative article on May 22 under the title "The Mentality of Amazigh Agitation and Separatism." *Al-Mustaqil* then published an interview with me, under the title "Amazighity Is Not an Ethnic or Separatist Cause, but a Cause for All Moroccans," dated June 4, 1998. *Taouiza* newspaper also published an article on July 15, 1998, under the title "Amazigh University Activities Send a Message to the Minister of National Education" and another news item about a letter from the Elmas Cultural Association to the Prime Minister. In its issue of July 17–23, *Al-Mustaqil* published an article under the title "The Issue of Amazigh Writing: Three Different Letters for Writing One Language." *Bayane Al Yaoume* published another interview with me on November 13, under the title "Brahim Akhiate Takes a Shot at the Minister of Culture." Indeed, this interview contained our first criticism directed at a minister in this so-called "government of alternation."

I have only mentioned some of what was written during this period immediately after the formation of that government and the sidelining of the Amazigh question on its agenda. This media campaign coincided with the deterioration of the situation in Algeria. A well-known Amazigh musician, Lounes Matoub, was assassinated. Our association issued a statement on this incident, which was cited by Al-Sharq Al-Awsat on July 26, 1998. On November 17, Istiqlal leader Abbas El Fassi provoked the Amazigh movement during a talk show on Channel One, speaking of the need for "Arabization and the spread of the Arabic language." "The Istiqlal party does not accept the integration of Tamazight into the national education system, in order to preserve the system's unity," he said. The association released a statement on December 17, 1998, fitting for this provocative and irresponsible declaration. It read:

Abbas El Fassi, the Secretary-General of the Istiqlal Party, stated in an episode of a debate program broadcast by the Morocco's Channel 1 on 11/17/1998, in the context of comments about the need for Arabization and the promotion of the Arabic language, that the party rejects the integration of Amazigh into the national education system, in order 'to preserve its unity', and that teaching of the language should remain optional for those who desire it, in certain regions, within a framework of regionalism.

At a meeting on 12/17/1998, the National Office of our association discussed this matter and concluded the following:

1. We see this position as excluding Amazigh from the education system across Morocco, something expressed publicly for the first time by a leader of a political party in Morocco, although it had previously been done more subtly. We also consider it contrary to the content of the royal speech of August 20, 1994, which spoke of the necessity of teaching Amazigh, at least in primary education, without discrimination between the children of Morocco or between its provinces.
2. The emphasis on the compulsory teaching of Arabic and foreign languages, and the view that the teaching of Amazigh is optional, cannot be justified within the democratic project in which the Istiqlal Party claims to be participating alongside other parties. Rather, it reflects a political stance driven by factors and orientations alien to the spirit of democracy, even after the party held its most recent conference under the slogan "Democracy First."
3. Raising the possibility of teaching Amazigh in certain regions implies a repressed political instinct among certain influential

elites, which divides Morocco into "worthy" urban areas and
others on the margins of development. Linking Amazigh culture
with specific regions means a refusal to recognize the national
dimension of this language, which is present throughout the
country, from Tangiers to La Güera. Those who speak it are
not fenced off in safari parks in the rural areas, or at the tops of
mountains. They are active in national production in all areas of
life.

4. We note that this strange position taken by the Istiqlal Party,
    through its Secretary General, is a new formulation of the colo-
    nial decree known as the "Berber Dahir," notwithstanding the
    difference between the goals of colonialism and the goals of the
    elite that has benefited since independence.

5. This publicly stated policy has deep roots in the texts and think-
    ing of the leaders and historical symbols of this party, who never
    forget to affirm that the Arabization they advocate does not
    mean a rejection of foreign languages, yet at the same time never
    address the fate of the national, Amazigh language under such a
    program. This is also evident in the bill submitted by members of
    the Party to the House of Councilors,[20] whose contents seek to
    eradicate the Amazigh language through the demand for Arabi-
    zation in public life, and even for penalties against "anyone who
    fails to use Arabic in transactions" amounting to a fine of 10,000
    dirhams, "to be doubled in case of recurrence"!

6. This demand to exclude the Amazigh language from the national
    system poses a deep threat to Moroccan unity, which can only
    be solidified by taking into account the multilingual reality of
    Morocco in the national education system.

We adhere to the democratic goals of the national struggle for
true, comprehensive, and just development, and for unity based on
the recognition of all the components of our existence in history, not
just some of them to the exclusion of others. We call on all vital forces
in the country to seriously consider the issues of Amazigh language,
culture, and identity, and to recognize it as a critical issue, without
which a united and advanced Morocco is unimaginable.

As I have mentioned, in light of the government's disappointing program, we decided to double our efforts, actions, and writings to confront
this unacceptable situation. I have already cited some of our media writings

in this battle. Alongside this media effort, we managed to produce a series of academic books to promote our efforts on both theoretical and intellectual levels, all of them published by AMREC:

1. *Taghlaghalt n Wadhan*: A collection of stories first published in Arabic but with Amazigh origins, by Libyan poet Saïd Sifaw, translated by Lahcen Ouazi into Tamazight.
2. *Amazighity: Dialogues with the Prime Minister*: An important work by Essafi Moumen Ali, in which the author holds an imaginary dialogue with the prime minister on the subject of the Amazigh issue.
3. *Amazighity in the Discourse of Political Islam*: In this book, Ahmed Assid explains the relationship between Amazighity and the position of Islamist discourse in Morocco on the Amazigh issue.
4. *Amazighity Now*: The proceedings of the 1997 conference that marked the thirtieth anniversary of the establishment of the association.

In 1999, Morocco witnessed a series of major political developments and cultural events. First and foremost were the death of King Hassan II on July 23 and the accession of King Mohammed VI to the throne of his ancestors. The year also saw the publication of the National Charter for Education and Training, by a Royal Commission chaired by royal advisor Abdelaziz Meziane Belfkih. The Second World Amazigh Congress also took place in August 1999, and there were significant actions and intensive initiatives related to Amazigh media, as well as the 11th National Congress of the Association, in October 1999.

OUR RESISTENCE TO THE NATIONAL CHARTER ON EDUCATION AND TRAINING

The field of education in our country had faced consecutive setbacks since independence, due to the fact that it fell under the control of opposing and nonnational ideologies, simultaneously. This situation has not yet stabilized or risen to a level that met the aspirations of Moroccan society. There are three types of education in Morocco: traditional education; education at schools run by the Ministry of National Education, which is manipulated by ideologues and planned by political party demagogues who exploit the illiteracy and emotions of the people to continue implementing these policies; and foreign-run schools, which cater to the children of those same elites who are manipulating the public education system. The goal of this elite is to prevent the children of the general public from competing with them for high-ranking economic, cultural, and political positions. Thus, our education system continues to lack a clear and stable linguistic policy, making it a victim of educational policies that are weak and non-nationalist, both in form and content. Moreover, the country suffers from a shortage of educational infrastructure in the cities, and a total absence thereof in the rural areas.

In this context, the late King Hassan II had asked parliament in September 1994 to form a National Commission on Education, tasked with reforming the educational system. His request coincided with the release of the political prisoners, on Throne Day (August 20). This commission comprised various political and union representatives, and lacked a single representative from the Amazigh cultural movement. It failed to provide anything positive to save our education system from this crisis, focusing again on Arabization and on an outdated vision of education and training. The king decided to dissolve this committee, due to its ineffectiveness and shortsightedness, and assigned his advisor, Abdelaziz Meziane Belfkih, to form a new team independently of parliament, encompassing all the country's political trends as well as civil society entities, unions, and teachers—but again, without the participation of the Amazigh movement. This approach, from the beginning, smacked of mismanagement, as it indicated that the government had already taken a position on a national project whose ostensible aim was to reach an agreement on education and training that would satisfy everyone.

As soon as the makeup of the committee had been announced, the Amazigh movement mobilized to confront this illogical and unacceptable situation. Our association sent a letter to Belfkih on "the status of Amazigh in the anticipated educational reform" dated April 2, 1999. In it, we reminded him of the content and significance of the king's speech of August 1994, and of the various memoranda that the Amazigh movement had sent to relevant authorities, parliament, and political parties on the subject of integrating Amazigh language into the education system. This reflected our conviction that the process of building a national identity and strengthening the resilience of the Moroccan nation would require the establishment of an integrated national education system, able to impart universal human values alongside values derived from the authentic traditions and historical experience of our people, through openness to the economic and social surroundings and all components of the national cultural environment. We also included in this message our proposals related to the integration of Amazigh into education, for all Moroccans.

Several months later, the association was called upon to discuss these topics with the advisor at the royal court. We again informed him of our ideas and opinions on the necessity of integrating Tamazight into the Moroccan school system, as it is a national language that all Moroccans have the right to learn, as well as being fundamental to every developmental, human, cultural, social, and economic process, as it is the language people use in their daily communication. We also sent messages to political parties on the same subject, urging them to bear their historical and national responsibilities by living up to their role to integrate Tamazight into the education system. Yet despite all these actions, our reception by the advisor, his receipt of our notes and proposals, and the fact that he listened to other groups from the Amazigh movement, the Charter on Education and Training disappointed the Amazigh movement. It took a humiliating stance toward Tamazight, giving it an inferior status compared to other languages. For example, in Section 2 it stated, "Fortifying the teaching of the Arabic language and its use, mastery of foreign languages and openness to Tamazight" (p. 51). Also, on the subject of "openness" to Tamazight, paragraph 115 stated, "The relevant educational authorities may choose to use Tamazight or any local dialect to familiarize (students) and facilitate the start of teaching the official language in primary education" (p. 52).

This is how the Charter on Education and Training expressed its view on Tamazight and the status it would grant this national language in the education system. The charter faced a barrage of criticism, especially from the Amazigh movement, associations and activists alike. Everyone considered this demeaning status as an expression of contempt and an insult to Moroccans in general, as Tamazight is their national language, and to Amazigh speakers in particular, because such a stance considered them second-class citizens. The issue prompted our association to publish a book titled *The Amazigh Language in the Charter of Education and Training, or the Policy of Linguistic Discrimination*. The behavior expressed in the charter was a form of linguistic discrimination, deliberately laid out by the document's creators. We saw this as a dangerous step that we could not simply accept, as it could cause the outbreak of a linguistic conflict that could turn into an ethnic conflict within Moroccan society. The book therefore gathered all the articles that analyzed the dangers represented by the charter, as well as all the correspondence mentioned above. The association held a press conference on Wednesday, November 3, 1999, on "The Amazigh Language in Government Action and in the National Charter for Education and Training." This was attended by a significant number of journalists, to whom we distributed copies of the book. The association also wrote to newly enthroned King

Mohammed VI on this topic on October 22, 1999. We concluded our let-
ter by saying, "While we look forward to the measures and decisions Your
Majesty will take to bring about the change we desire, we at the Moroccan
Association for Research and Cultural Exchange are honored to appeal to
Your Majesty to remedy the noticeable deficiency in the National Charter
on Education and Training regarding the teaching of the Amazigh language,
in order to preserve the uniqueness of the national character, of which the
Amazigh culture is the essence of its authenticity and heritage."

Our press conference on the issue was significant, as it clarified our
criticism of the government's actions and explained the risks of ignoring
Tamazight in the Charter of Education and Training, both politically and
culturally. In the same context, the association issued a statement denouncing
the neglect of the Amazigh language in government policy, dated November 3, 1999, which read:

> The authenticity and depth that Amazigh culture represents in our
> national civilizational heritage, with roots in the depths of history, is
> apparent to all Moroccans. Today, this is evidenced by the continued
> presence of the Amazigh language and culture in the social and cul-
> tural fabric from the north of Morocco to its south, in its cities and
> its countryside. This shows that despite the diversity of cultural influ-
> ences, the Amazigh aspect remains at the core of our cultural identity
> and is a factor that distinguishes it through the ages.
>
> However, this importance has not been clearly translated into
> official policy in education, culture, media and scholarly research,
> in which the Amazigh language and culture have been marginalized
> from independence to the present day, and systematically excluded,
> in an effort to erase their essence and eradicate their remains. The
> struggle between the ideological camps of Arabization and Franco-
> phonie, which placed Morocco between eastern and western forces,
> has led to the consolidation of its intellectual dependency and cul-
> tural alienation, as well as the weakening of its sense of national
> identity and the authentic civilizational values that characterize the
> Moroccan character, threatening the unique nature of our cultural
> entity with schizophrenia and extinction.
>
> As a direct response to this, and due to the conspiracy of silence
> adopted by some of the advocates of liberation, political and social
> democratization since independence, who excluded the Amazigh
> language and in some cases called for its eradication, the Amazigh
> cultural movement was launched more than four decades ago in

order to lobby for the integration and use of the Amazigh language in every comprehensive and democratic developmental project, to embody its national character and reinforce rights and the rule of law. The result of this struggle was the official recognition of the right to Amazigh language in education, expressed in the royal speech of August 20, 1994, which called for the teaching of the Amazigh language in primary education. Many democratic forces and actors in society also backed the Amazigh cultural movement's demands. This was followed by the current government's first declaration to parliament, which recognized the Amazigh language as a component of the national identity and need to 'revive' it, but without translating that into concrete decisions or measures in the sectors of education, media, culture, and other public services.

The Charter on Education and Training, which was produced by a commission on which the Amazigh movement was not represented, and which did not even take its views into account, only went as far as allowing teachers to resort to the Amazigh language or any other local dialect to ease the process of teaching the official language, i.e., Arabic. This demonstrates a total lack of desire to teach the Amazigh language, the national language of all Moroccans, in public education—unlike all other languages. Thus, the establishment of faculties at certain universities for research and for Amazigh linguistic and cultural development, as well as to train trainers and prepare related programs and educational curricula, has become pointless, due to the absence of any link to the teaching of Tamazight in public education.

The Charter came as Moroccans were hoping for democratic solutions for the various critical issues they face. Instead, they were surprised by references to measures that only serve to deepen linguistic preferentialism, normative comparison and narrow utilitarianism between our civilizational components. This prevents the achievement of national unity on democratic foundations, in keeping with the wishes of King Mohammed VI, may God give him victory, in his speech to inaugurate the current parliamentary session, in which he emphasized the need to "integrate education into its environment and making it open to the era, without denying its civilizational components and our Moroccan identity with all its tributaries."

We at the Moroccan Association for Research and Cultural Exchange condemn the government's procrastination and its failure to keep its promises toward the Amazigh issue, as required as part of its national responsibilities. We denounce the intentional absence of Tamazight teaching in primary and secondary education in the draft Charter on Education and Training. We call on all democratic forces, including Amazigh cultural associations and actors, to mobilize in order to achieve our legitimate demands, which are part of the broader demands of democracy. They include the acceleration of the teaching of Tamazight as the national language of all Moroccans, at all education levels, granting it the status it deserves in the audiovisual media landscape, guaranteeing the right to information in languages understood by citizens, and ensuring the preservation and development of Amazigh cultural heritage, through support for the publication of books, and for the arts and forms of aesthetic expression, as well as efforts to employ the Amazigh language in managing administrative and judicial affairs, to bring tangible substance to the slogan of decentralization and bringing the administration closer to the citizen. Such efforts could empower Amazigh language and culture to play its vital role in contributing to the nation's comprehensive development. All of this demands legal guarantees provided by declaring Tamazight a national and official language in the constitution.

The national press who attended this conference published a stream of articles. Here are some of their titles:

- On the comments of Abbas El Fassi: "The Independence Party Seeks to Abolish the Amazigh Language, and Its Secretary-General Divides Morocco into 'Useful' and 'Not Useful,'" *Al-Haraka*, January 22, 1998
- "The Amazigh Take Shots at the Istiqlal Party," *Al-Ousboue*, January 25, 1998
- "No to Excluding Amazigh from National Schools," *Bayane Al-Yaoum*, December 26, 1998
- "The Amazigh Movement Asks King Mohammed VI to Intervene to Activate Decisions Made by His Late Father Hassan II," *Al-Sharq Al-Awsat*, January 2, 1999
- "An Amazigh Letter to His Majesty the King," *Bayane Al-Yaoum*, November 1, 1999
- "No Talk About a National Charter for Education with the Exclusion of Amazigh," *Al-Ahdath al-Maghribiyya*, November 4, 1999
- "The Proposed Charter for Educational Reform Is Reminiscent of the Colonial Dahir," *Al-Haraka*, November 11, 1999
- "The Draft Charter on Education and Training: The Amazigh

Language Only for Familiarity and to Serve the Arabic Language," *Tamazight*, November 18, 1999
- "The Education and Training Committee: The Nationality of the Draft Charter in the Balance," *Akraou Amazigh*, December 1, 1999

These are just some examples of the articles that followed the press conference we held at the association. They reflect the extent to which their writers were aware of the dangers of excluding the Amazigh language from this charter.

This gives a sense of the strong reactions the proposed Charter on Education and Training sparked among the Amazigh movement, which confronted it with all possible means of protest throughout 1999. I will return to this topic later when I talk about the implementation of the charter and the resulting protests and positions from the Amazigh movement.

THE 11TH NATIONAL CONFERENCE OF AMREC AND THE ACCOMPANYING EVENTS

We began 1999 with the national conference of the association, in late January, under the slogan "Comprehensive Development is Contingent on Integrating and Employing Amazigh." As indicated by the slogan, this was the first time we had linked the Amazigh cause to development. No people can develop without employing their language in development programs, whether cultural, social, or economic. Amazigh and Moroccan *dārija* are the languages of communication in our country, and no culture can be built without linking it to the people's aspirations for growth and progress, and with the modernization and development of that same culture.

We held our eleventh conference in the city of Bouznika in an unusual and tense political situation, resulting from all social and political tensions of 1997 and 1998, which I have described above. These resulted from the formation of the government of alternation, which was set up to alleviate such tensions. The conference was the first to be held outside the headquarters of the association since its establishment. The opening session was distinguished by the presence of many political and human rights figures who had taken part in dialogues with us in 1996 as part of our campaign of diplomatic outreach to political parties, national figures, and youth and human rights organizations. Representatives of the Moroccan Organization for Human Rights (OMDH) attended the opening session, including its president Abdelaziz Bennani; Mohammed Moujahed, head of the Moroccan Press Association; the president of the Istiqlal Youth, Abdullah al-Bakkali; and Addi Sbai, president of the Popular Movement's youth wing; as well as representatives of Amazigh associations. The local authorities had a noticeable presence at this conference because it was the first event of this size held by an Amazigh association known for its decades-long struggle. The authorities were waiting to see what recommendations would emerge and what positions would be taken at the conference. They were also evaluating the association based on the presence of political actors and the extent of civil society's interaction with the Amazigh community, based on the speeches of the organizations and bodies present. One person at the conference was an English journalist from the BBC, who covered it from the start and conducted many interviews with the association's activists who were present. His segment was broadcast several times on BBC Arabic radio, allowing listeners to immerse themselves in the atmosphere of the conference. But the story went that the Amazigh in Morocco had held their conference in Bouznika and sang their national anthem, among other exaggerated statements intended to sensationalize the event, making the listener believe that a major political shift was underway in Morocco. Alongside this report, the journalist published an article in a British magazine about the Amazigh issue and the Moroccan throne, claiming that the Amazigh posed a threat to the Moroccan monarchy, given the scale of our coalition and our strong defense of our Amazigh identity. Moreover, he wrote that we were in the process of translating the Quran into Amazigh, with the intention of completely forgoing Arabic. The journalist had written this after meeting Lhoucine Jouhadi, who had informed him that he was in the process of translating the meanings of the holy book into Amazigh. The journalist had accompanied Jouhadi to his home, where he was shown some samples of the translated texts into Amazigh, a mundane fact on which the journalist based his reporting. No sooner had this article been published than the Arabic-language *Al-Majalla* magazine, issued in London, contacted me and asked me to answer several questions it would send me, so I could respond to the English journalist's report. The magazine dedicated a significant amount of space to the topic, across two issues.[21] In Issue 994 was an article titled "Berbers and Islamists in Morocco: Has the Battle Begun Because of a Project to Translate the Meanings of the Quran?" It began: "A high school history teacher in Casablanca does not seem like a potential threat to Islamic coexistence in North Africa. Yet Lhoucine Jouhadi is putting the final touches on a project that could shake the Moroccan establishment to its core." This introduction alone gives a sense of how these people perceived, in the simple act of translating the meanings of the Quran into Amazigh, a threat not only to Arabic but even to the Moroccan state. They also titled my responses: "Those aiming to annihilate our identity will not be comfortable with this project." I answered their questions as follows:

Translating the meanings of the Quran into Amazigh responds to three motivations:

1. Tamazight is an Islamic language, and one of the languages through which the Islam was promulgated for centuries. It is absurd that the Quran is translated into foreign languages like French, English, and Spanish, but not into Tamazight.
2. A Tamazight translation of the Quran had already existed in the Islamic history of Morocco, during the Almohad era (1121–1269), but it was lost; this necessitates its re-creation, to recall of the role of the Amazigh language in Islamic history.
3. Many of those who oppose the rights of the Amazigh language in education, media, and the constitution resort to tendentious arguments, such as the claim that Arabic alone deserves attention in these areas because it is the language of religion and the Quran, and thus that it is sacred.

In the same issue, the magazine published an opinion piece by the philosopher Mohammed Abed Al-Jabri, under the title "There Is No Harm in Translation If It Is Accurate." In it, Al Jabri also confirmed that the meanings of the Quran had been translated into Tamazight during the Almohad era, something he considered part of Morocco's history. He concluded that the translation did not pose a problem as such, but that as the Prophet Mohammed (PBUH) said, acts are judged by their intentions: If the intention behind the translation is to benefit a sector of people who do not know Arabic or cannot read it, then it is beneficial. However, if it is for political purposes, then this poses a problem. The publication of the translation would no doubt cause some problems, especially in the media, and care must be taken to avoid this.

In the following issue, *Al-Majalla* published another article under the title "Is Amazigh a Language or a Counter-Identity?" This article put forward two other positions on the subject. The first, by Ouzine Ahardhan, had the title "Morocco Is an Amazigh Country and This Is the Fundamental Basis of Its Identity." The second, by Abdelkrim Ghallab, was titled "Amazighity, A Matter Out of Place." In it, he argued (as do all those who oppose the

Amazigh identity of Morocco) that the Moroccan people are formed from various ancestries like other nations, and therefore it is illogical to claim that Morocco is ethnically Arab or Amazigh. The ethnic argument is thus irrelevant, leaving only the civilizational and cultural elements.

All this was triggered by the writing and radio reports of the English journalist, who took advantage of our conference to spread ideas and conclusions that were nothing but abstract assumptions, and had little to do with the truth. However, this did not pass without strong reactions from the authorities. Several members of the security apparatus contacted Lhoucine Jouhadi to ask about his translation of the meanings of the Qur'an. He was subjected to several bouts of harassment, aimed at intimidating him and preventing him from completing his work. He should not have told this to the journalist in the first place: We at the association had decided on the project as part of a program of transmitting Islamic thought in Amazigh—that is, translating some writings on Islam. Yet we had been cautious since the mid-1970s, when we had proposed the project to Imhammad El-Othmani, a graduate of Dar El-Hadith El-Hassania.[22] We had temporarily shelved the project due to the unfavorable political circumstances and the dangers it might pose us as individuals or an association. We had published the Al-Hawd investigation by Abdellah Al-Rahmani Al-Jachtimi, and an investigation he had produced on Soussi activism. After his death, we asked Lhoucine Jouhadi to write the biography of the Prophet Mohammed (peace be upon him) in Tamazight, which we also published. We then asked him to translate directly the meanings of the Qur'an, convinced that this would be a great challenge that would conclusively prove the ability of the Amazigh language to express deep intellectual ideas. We had surrounded the project with the necessary secrecy until it could be completed and until we could choose the appropriate circumstance to announce this historical and intellectual achievement.

MY POSITION BETWEEN AMAZIGH ACTIVISM AND THE ISLAMIC MOVEMENT

Despite the financial difficulties I was experiencing and the problems it caused, I did not give up my activism. Rather, I pressed on with the challenge, and we organized several cultural and educational activities. Among the most important were seminars in various cities dedicated to readings of the book *Amazighity in the Discourse of Political Islam* by Ahmed Assid, published by our association. The most important of these seminars was in Rabat on Saturday, February 23, 1999, in which Mohammed Boudhan,

Dr. Abdelghani Abou El Aazm, and Hassan Aourid took part, and which was chaired by Belaid Boudriss.

This activity received significant media coverage, which contributed to enriching the dialogue on the topic of Amazigh and its relationship with political Islam. One article was published in the *Tamazight* newspaper on February 4 under the title "Amazighity as a Social Project," and the same issue covered the aforementioned seminar on the topic of the book.

On a related topic, the student wing of the Al-Adl w-Al-Ihssane (Justice and Spirituality) Islamist movement organized a large cultural week in Rabat during this period of debate over the Amazigh identity, especially given the publication of our book and that of their leader Abdesslam Yassine, titled *Dialogue with an Amazigh Friend*. Moreover, this phase was marked by the formation of the government of alternation, in which the opposition took over the executive, an event that itself sparked debate in political circles and among association members alike about the political situation in Morocco. In light of all these developments, the Islamist movement's youth wing invited professors, researchers, and politicians to participate in these seminars throughout the week. Most invitees from the left, or from the various intellectual and political currents that had a stance on the movement, refrained from participating. For my part, I agreed to participate, based on my belief in the right to differ in opinion, and my respect for the brothers in the Justice and Spirituality movement, despite our differences on some of their opinions on Amazigh identity and their view on how the country's political system should be run. I was warmly received by the group's officials (Dr. Fathallah Arsalan and Dr. Abdellah al-Chibani, among others). The attendance was very large, including male and female students, and two members of the association were taking part in the seminar. It may be that those who had suggested that I take part wanted to embarrass me, given what had been presented in the book mentioned above, which the community considered to be directed against its ideological orientations. Some even considered some of the book's contents to be a form of atheism, among other opinions. Some also believed that I would be embarrassed by questions about Sheikh Yassine's book on the subject of the Amazigh language, as he considers the Arabic language sacred, simply because it was the language in which the Quran was revealed.

The spotlight was therefore on me and what I would say at this seminar, as the other speakers were from the movement, and their analyses chimed with its standpoint, which did not stir controversy or debate. Thus, I faced many questions regarding my stance on the government of alternation, the political situation in the country, and the content of the aforementioned book, considering our association had published it, as well as my opinion on Sheikh Yassine's book. I was able to pass this test wisely, maintaining their esteem for me by answering their questions objectively, without attacking the foundations of their ideology nor compromising my own principles. I explained to them the history of the Amazigh movement, showing them that it had emerged from the womb of society, just like their movement, and that our movement was independent of political parties or the state. I added that it was our duty, within the framework of freedom of expression and the right to hold differing opinions, not to fall into the trap of futile conflicts, because this is exactly what the authorities and some of the political parties wanted, so they could continue to monopolize and keep their grip on power. I had hardly finished making this point when the hall erupted with applause. Regarding the book and the ideas it proposed, I said they were like any other subject, open to debate, and that everyone had the right to refute them and present evidence against them. However, I stressed that the book did not contain a single idea or even a phrase calling for atheism or denigrating religion. I urged the students to read more and to broaden their horizons by reading all kinds of books instead of becoming intellectually isolated, and to be prepared to accept the opinions of others. On the topic of Sheikh Yassine's book, I told them that I had sent the sheikh a book we had published in Amazigh, *Tagrast n Warqas n Rbi* (The biography of the Prophet), and I wrote the dedication in Tamazight. The sheikh replied by dedicating his book on economics to me and thanked me twice in his dedication, firstly for giving him the book and secondly for the intricate Tamazight phrases I had written in this dedication. Moreover, I had continuously participated in events organized by this community when he was under house arrest. However, I told the students that I did not agree with the sheikh in considering the Arabic language as sacred. It is simply human creation like all other languages, and there is no Quranic text that defines it otherwise; if there were, this would in effect be succumbing to the idolatry that Islam had opposed from the start. What is sacred to me is the content of the divine message, not the language, which is merely a means to explain and spread the message. Indeed, this linguistic role is the task of all the world's languages, because the Quran was revealed for all peoples. However, I justified the sheikh's negative stance toward Tamazight by the fact that he was under house arrest and, until now, he had not had the opportunity to communicate with those who champion the Amazigh cause, a national campaign aimed at achieving the linguistic and cultural rights of the entire Moroccan people, something that transcends ideological and political differences. I also explained to them the episode with Fqih Basri, who had been in a similar position. He had made hostile comments toward the Amazigh issue just before returning to the country following decades in exile. Due to his long absence, he had not been aware of the intellectual and political developments that had taken place here. As soon as he entered the country, I had contacted him at the late Dr. Omar El-Khattabi's house in Kénitra, in a session with a group of his old friends, and I explained the matter to him. He eventually understood the subject and retracted his statements, no longer taking problematic positions on the Amazigh question.

This presentation lasted for hours, as the audience drowned me in questions of this type. When the meeting ended, the students began chanting slogans in Tamazight. The movement's leaders were astonished by this response. I jokingly said to Arsalan, "There you go, I've convinced them; will you ever invite me back?" My friends left, but I stayed with the students, who came from all regions of Morocco, and answered their many questions about the Amazigh issue and its future in the country.

AMAZIGH ACTIVISM AND THE STRATEGY OF CIVIL SOCIETY PARTNERSHIPS

In the context of this dynamic around the Amazigh issue, which was increasingly occupying the minds of political and civil society actors, the Socialist Union of Popular Forces organized a summer university in Bouznika from September 1 to 9, 1999, under the theme "Plurality in the Associations: What Is to Come?" I was invited to attend this summer university, and I lectured on September 5 on the topic "What Role for Amazigh Associations in Morocco?"

As we pressed forward with our awareness-raising work around the Amazigh issue, which covered all facets of life—political, intellectual, and organizational—we published a book on "The Amazigh Question in the Charter on Education and Training, or the Policy of Arabization." This comprised various documents including correspondence and pictures of articles that followed the publication of the charter, as well as articles about the danger of excluding Amazigh from the national curriculum, while the Charter on Education and Training considered it merely a tool for introducing children to the official language, Arabic. We also held a press conference on "The Amazigh question in the work of the government and in the draft National Charter on Education and Training." At this conference, at the association's headquarters on June 3, 1999, we laid out the risks of the charter and its likely consequences, making it clear that we held the government responsible for everything that would result from the exclusion of Amazigh from the nation's schools. The press conference itself was titled "No Democracy While Amazigh Is Marginalized." This generated strong reactions in the national press; to demonstrate this, it suffices to cite an article in *Al-Haraka* newspaper on June 11 under the title "For an Education That Does Not Deny Our Civilizational Components and Our Amazigh Identity: The Proposed Charter for Education Reform Is Reminiscent of the Colonial (Berber) Decree."

Also as part of this media campaign we waged throughout 1999 in order to create a momentum toward achieving our demands and making our cause known on all levels, the association organized a seminar in partnership with the National Union of the Moroccan Press (SNPM), on November 12 and 13, in the Mustapha El-Najjar hall of the Moroccan News Agency. The topic was "Amazighity and the National Media," and the event coincided with National Media Day. The lecturers included SNPM President Youness Moujahed, on "The Right to Information"; Ahmed Assid on the topic of "Amazighity in the Official Media and the Party Political Press"; Lhoucine Ait Bahcine on "Amazighity in the Media and Development"; El Houssine El-Chaabi on "An Initial Evaluation of the Position of Tamazight in the National Media"; Lhoucine Idrissi on "Evaluating Tamazight Print Media from 1982 until Today"; and Larbi Benterki and Abdullah El Hakim Karbouz on "The Place of Tamazight in Audiovisual Media." The seminar also included talks and testimonies about the experiences of those working in Amazigh media, and about the newspapers, with participation of the chief editors of *Tawiza*, *Tasafut*, *Tamakit*, *Agraw*, *Tamunt*, and *Tamazight*. The national press devoted extensive coverage to the event, most of it favorable to the Amazigh cause and in its relationship with both print and audiovisual media. This major media event ended with a final statement that read:

> A study conference was held at the headquarters of the Moroccan News Agency in Rabat on the topic of "Amazighity and National Media" on Friday and Saturday, November 12 and 13, 1999, on the initiative of the National Union of the Moroccan Press and the Moroccan Association for Research and Cultural Exchange, with the participation of a number of people working in the national media, of various audio-visual and print genres. This meeting was held in a new context, as Morocco experiences profound political changes. Our young king has renewed his trust in the current government of alternance, and made many clear signals to achieve the necessary change in all fields. This conference also coincided with the commemoration of the National Day of Media on November 15, contributing

to the development of the national debate on the media landscape, its obstacles, achievements, and the role expected from it in developing and bringing about the success of the democratic transition in our country.

This meeting produced the following recommendations:

1. The recommendations of the first national media conference, held on May 29–31, 1993, should be updated and implemented, as they have remained little more than ink on paper.
2. Efforts must be made to democratize public media by liberating it from any guardianship that might restrict its freedom of expression, creativity, spirit of initiative and professionalism. Efforts should be made to strengthen languages of mass communication, and to link the media to development, so it contributes to improving citizens' awareness of the values of citizenship, democracy and modernity, as well as integrating it into the process of social transformation.
3. Efforts must be made to guarantee a high degree of professionalism in the media and the provision of the material and technical capabilities needed to keep up with innovations in communications technology, while paying the necessary attention to the social, material and moral needs of those who work in the national media, granting them opportunities for further training and to deepen their expertise in their fields of work.
4. Media policy must be reconsidered, establishing a new strategy that respects the Moroccan identity, highlighting its distinctive elements, and deepens the values of diversity and cultural and linguistic difference, in a way that helps to strengthen national unity based on the principles of tolerance and mutual respect.
5. There is a need to address the injustice that has plagued Amazigh language and culture in the national media, especially in public media outlets, by putting an end to the policy of linguistic and cultural exclusion, and stopping the behavior of marginalization and belittlement of Amazigh media professionals, especially in the radio and television sector. They should be empowered with the necessary means and tools to perform their tasks in an environment of equality and equal opportunities. The top-down management style should be abandoned in order to open up the

possibilities for them to show their competencies and creative energies.

6. There is a need to strengthen the broadcasting capabilities of Amazigh radio to cover the entire national territory and other places areas where members of our Moroccan diaspora reside abroad, in a context of equality with other languages.

7. All elements of the national press should seriously engage with the Amazigh language, culture, and identity, and stop the practice of marginalization and exclusion, working toward opening channels of communication, dialogue, and discussion in this regard.

PREPARATIONS FOR THE SECOND WORLD AMAZIGH CONGRESS

I have previously written about the first conference of the World Amazigh Congress, held in the Canary Islands, and its negative outcomes for Morocco, especially as the country was not represented on the body's Federal Council due to disputes among the Moroccan participants.

As the second congress approached, set for August 1999, and the term of the executive office neared its end, different factions began to mobilize to win over the associations. During this period, two orientations emerged. The first called for the congress to be postponed, to allow for more careful preparation, without setting a specific date. This camp was led by Ouzzin Aherdan and "Fergal," who was leading the Congress on behalf of its elected leader. This argument faced some pushback, as it implied the risk that the conference would never be held at all, or that this camp would manage to dominate it, by controlling the preparations and dictating what kinds of associations would be invited. The second orientation held that the conference must take place on its scheduled date and that the problems should be dealt with, regardless of their nature, arguing that this was the only way to ensure that the organization itself could endure and to avoid it closing down for good. This camp was supported by Lounes, the main rival of Aherdan and Ouzzin.

As this struggle was playing out, AMREC studied the situation and prepared a statement on the matter, which we released at a seminar organized by the Elmas Cultural Association in Nador in late December 1999. This seminar, which was open to all, was focused on the teaching of Tamazight, so I attended in person as secretary general of the association, along with Abdelaziz Bourass and Essafi Moumen Ali, as well as many representatives of Amazigh associations and influential actors including Fergal, Loutas, and Ouzzin. During one of our private meetings at the conference in the hotel where we were staying, we listened to all these parties, and during this session, we distributed the statement we had prepared for this purpose, in which we announced our support for holding the conference in Lyon, France, on its scheduled date in August next year, thus preempting the proposal by Fergal, Lounes and Ouzzin, which posed a danger to the future of the World Amazigh Congress. In our statement, we called to mind what they had done at the Tafira conference. Our rational stance was appreciated and supported by the majority of the associations, with the exception of those who were in Ouzzin's orbit. As soon as we had made our position known, he and his companions left Nador, as we had stripped him of the opportunity to dominate the congress and control its fate, giving the associations a new chance to manage it instead and sparking hope that we could revive this organization and keep it going. From that night, preparations began for the second conference, to be held in Lyon in August 1999.

We as an association decided to attend the conference this time, to give it a new dynamic, after the obstacles it had faced previously. Moreover, our national office decided that I should attend in person, unlike the first conference, from which I had been absent for the reasons I have described previously in this memoir. The national office also decided that I should stand for election as president of the congress, in the hope of changing its course and mode of operation. We took this decision knowing that it could slow down our activities if we were to invest all our capacity into making the congress capable of the communication and impact we hoped it could have on the cultural and political levels, particularly in North Africa. Many of the other Moroccan associations also pledged to vote for a Moroccan to head the congress, and the Tanaynut association agreed to back AMREC if I were to lodge my candidacy for this position.

Despite the difficult financial situation I was facing due to having stopped working, with the impact this had on the association's activities, I decided to drive to Lyon with Abdelaziz Bourass, Ali Khedaoui, and Ibrahim Akdime. I was put forward to chair the conference, which of course was not attended by Ouzzin Ahardan, the Tilelli Cultural Association from Rachidia, or the Asnfloul Association. The majority of the Amazigh associations from Morocco, Algeria, Libya, the Tuaregs, and the Canary Islands attended. We overcame the organizational challenges with great enthusiasm. The Moroccan associations held meetings to unify their viewpoints and positions without problems. At the end of the conference, in the sessions dedicated to nominations,

I presented my candidacy for the presidency and presented my manifesto, which I vowed to implement if I won, as follows:

1.   To dedicate this term to developing a clear strategy for the World Amazigh Congress, answering the big questions that were hitherto unanswered, and to understanding what united us and what divided us, because it was not enough to set goals in the absence of a strategy. I felt it was necessary to develop such a strategy in cooperation and partnership with many of our thinkers and specialists in various fields related to the Amazigh issue.

2.   To work on empowering the administration and headquarters of the Congress to enter our national territory of North Africa, instead of remaining in exile.

3.   To open a dialogue with all parties concerned with the Amazigh issue in North African and European countries, from governments and political parties to social and cultural organizations, in order to bring the Congress closer to the people in the Amazigh homeland.

4.   To ensure that the World Congress serves Amazigh associations in their homelands, in order to achieve their goals on the ground, instead of these associations serving the objectives of the diaspora, which had so far dominated the thinking and organization of the World Congress.

During this period, I was surprised to find that most of the associations abroad supported the candidacy of Rachid Rakha, who belongs to the diaspora. They were not impressed by my manifesto, especially since these associations were Algerian or based in Europe, and had not yet warmed to the idea of dialogue with the bodies I had mentioned. They also wanted the diaspora to control the overall direction of the congress. But what really surprised and disappointed me was the stance of Hassan Id Balkassam, who made his support for my candidacy conditional on linking the Amazigh question with that of the Indigenous peoples. This was something the association opposed, because we believe that the Moroccan people and the inhabitants of North Africa as a whole are an Amazigh people, and no other people has a place in the region. The term "Indigenous peoples" refers to peoples who are subjugated by others who have colonized their lands and turned them into marginalized and oppressed minorities. They therefore employ the framework of Indigenous peoples' rights to win support and rights within their countries, in order to integrate and benefit from development to improve their dire living conditions. This applies to the Indigenous peoples of North and South America and to the Aborigines of Australia. However, we, as an Amazigh people, do not fit into this reality, because we live on our land and govern ourselves.

Therefore, I strongly rejected Id Balkassam's condition, which surprised me and those around me. Indeed, due to this stance, Meryem Demnati gave him a severe verbal reprimand in front of everyone, accusing him of being opportunistic and deceitful, and saying he could not be trusted.

I did not react. Rather, I thanked God that I had not won, for several reasons: firstly, my terrible financial situation, which would not have allowed me to perform my task optimally, and secondly, the fact that association was saved from having to halt or reduce its activities. Above all, I was convinced that those at the congress had not yet reached the level where they understood my argument in a way that would allow us to take the Amazigh World Congress beyond its current state and to gain the Amazigh popular support it deserves, both domestically and internationally. I left the session convinced that most associations, through their officials, were only concerned with organizational matters and the struggle for positions, instead of focusing on the strategies they would need to develop to achieve their goals. This lack of strategy was what would cause the congress to suffer successive crises in the following years.

Yet, all this aside, my brothers from the association shared my joy that we had been able to complete this second conference successfully, keeping the congress going and getting rid of those trying to sabotage it and its future, even if only temporarily.

NOTES

1. It included contributions from: Mohammed Adiouan, El Houssaïn El Moujahid, Mohammed al-Habib al-Fourkani, Handain Mohammed, Mohammed Ait El Haj, Ibrahim Oubila, Lhoussain Skanfal, Ahmed Assid, Lhoucine Ait Bahcine, Lhoucine Jouhadi, Lhoucine Ouaizi, and Rachid Lhoucine. The following also took part: Hassan Id Balkassam, Ali Beidni, Ahmed Dghirni, Ibrahim Oubila, Hassan Ourarouk, Brahou Lhoussain, Othman Bouftas, Hamza Abdellah, Ahmed Allouhmo, Omar Taous, Abdelaziz Bourass, and Essafi Moumen Ali.
2. The committee was made up of me, Lahcen Kahmou from the Summer University, El Houssaïn El Moujahid, Ahmed Boukous from AMREC, Lhoucine Akhiate and Ahmed Arhamouch from the New Association for Culture and Folk Arts, Mohammed El-Chami from the Elmas Association, and Ali Harsh El-Rass from the Agaras Cultural Association. The Cultural Association of Souss apologized as it was unable to attend these meetings but approved in writing to the contents of the charter.

3. The organizing committee for the event consisted of the following activists: me as president, and members Lahcen Kahmou, Jamaa Jaghaimi, Mohammed Hendayen, Mohammed Aknadh, Moubarak Id Mouloud, Ibrahim Oubla, Hassan El-Marjou, Abdelaziz Bourass, Lhoucine Ait Bahcine, El Houssaïn El Moujahid, Hassan Id Balkassam, Ahmed Abadrin, Lhoucine Ouaizi, and Lhoucine Ajkoun. The following researchers, activists, and intellectual and political personalities also took part: Abdelsalem Bin Mis, Qais Marzouq El Ouariachi, Bnasser El-Baazati, Ibrahim Aarab, Essafi Moumen Ali, Rahou Taounza, Lhoucine Ben Ihya, Brahim Oubla, Lhoucine Ouaizi, Said Hanine, Mohanned Aït El-Haj, Abdelkabir Al-Khatibi, Lhoucine Jouhadi, Qadi Qaddour, Hamdi Ounouch, Mohammed Hindayin, Moubarak Radouan, Abdelrahman Bellouch, Ahmed Arhmouch, Hassan Id Balkassam, Ahmed Abadrine, Jamaa Jighaimi, Mohammed Moustaghfar, Mohammed Abu Hmid, Belkacem Amzil, Abbas El-Charqawi, Lahcen Madi, Jamaa Beneider, Ahmed Boukioudh, Mohammed Moukhlass, El-Jilali El-Saib, and Rachid Ahmed Rakha.

4. They included Mohammed Chafik, Ahmed Boukous, Mohammed El-Chami, Jalali El-Sayeb, El Houssaïn El Moujahid, Mohammed Chtatou, Beleid Boudriss, Essafi Moumen Ali, Ali Khedaoui, Abdelaziz Bourass, Mohammed Aknadh, Mohamed Moustaoui, Lhoucine Bin Yahya, Hamza Abdellah, Bin Omar, Hassan Id Balkassam, and Lhoucine Jouhadi.

5. The following representatives from various associations attended this initial consultative meeting: From the Moroccan Association for Research and Cultural Exchange: me, Lhoucine Ait Bahcine, Abdelaziz Bourass, Ahmed Assid, and El Houssain Ouazi. From the New Association for Culture and Folk Arts: Ahmed Arhamouch and Aminah Ibn El-Cheikh. From the Summer University Association: Mohammed Handain and El-Zat Hassan. From the Ghris Cultural Association: Mouha Mokhlis. From the Elmas Cultural Association: Mohammed El-Chami and El-Baazati Benasser. From the Tanoukra Association in Nador: Moustafa Benomar. From the Souss Culture Association: Hamzah Abdellah and Amer Lhoucine. From the Tiwizi Association in Ait Melloul: Akil Brahim.

6. They were: Ali Harsh El Rass, a teacher and president of the Tilelli Cultural Association; Moubarak Taous, a teacher and general secretary of the same association; Ali Iken, a teacher and the archivist of the association; Omar Darwich, the treasurer of the association; Ahmed Kikich, a teacher and trade unionist; Ali Ouchen, a teacher and trade unionist; and Said Jaafar, a teacher and trade unionist.

7. This meeting included: the Socialist Union of Popular Forces, the Organization for Democratic and Popular Action, the Socialist Democratic Vanguard Party, the Democratic Confederation of Labour, the Moroccan Association for Human Rights, the National Association of Unemployed Graduates in Morocco, and the National Committee to Support Detainees, Abductees and Families of Detainees.

8. The following brothers took part in the seminar: Mohammed Al-Arabi Al-Masari, Ahmed Boukiyoudh, Abdelaziz Bourass, Mohammed El-Chami, Khalil El-Samlali, Lhoucine Ait Bahcine, Ahmed Adghirni, Lhoucine Ouaizi, Lhoucine Jouhadi, Lahcen Oulhaj, Ahmed Arhamouch, Mubarak Boulkid, Lhoucine Bizgaren, Hussein Barho, Mohammed Moustaoui, and Mohammed Salou. The following associations participated: The Summer University Association in Agadir; The New Association for Culture and Popular Arts of Souss, in Casablanca; the Asnfloul Association in Meknes; the Massinissa Association in Tangier; and the Tilelli Cultural Association from Errachidia.

9. They included Fatima Tabaamrant, the late Mohammed Ejoui, Lhoucine Jouhadi, Houssaïn El Moujahid, Mohammed Salou, Lhoucine Ouaizi, Mohamed Moustaoui, Ali Ikken, Amina Ben Sheikh, Lhoucine Ben Ihya, Mohammed Benamrou, Lhoucine Ait Bahcine, Essafi Moumen Ali, Mohammed Mounib, Mohammed Loufari, Lhoucine Amer, Mohammed Hendayin, Rachid Lhoucine, Abdellah Rachkilou, Brahim Ait Hemmou, and Darwich Omar.

10. The first was for parliament and government and was made up of AMREC, the Elmas Cultural Association, the Asnfloul Association, the Summer University Association, the Renaissance Cultural Association, and the Tiwizi Association). The other committee was focused on the political parties, and included the New Association, the Massinissa Association, the Souss Cultural Association, the Tilelli Association, the Nokour Association, and Fazaz.

11. They included: The Party of Progress and Socialism (at its headquarters), the Istiqlal Party (at the office of its secretary-general), the Socialist Union of Popular Forces (at the party's headquarters), the Popular Movement (at the movement's headquarters), the Democratic Labor Action Organization (at our association's headquarters), and the National Rally of Independents (at the residence of its president, Ahmed Osman). Our association's headquarters hosted meetings with the Moroccan Association for Human Rights, the Moroccan Association for Human Rights, the Istiqlal Youth, the Socialist Youth, and the Islamist-leaning associations: the Future Islamic League, Justice and Spirituality (Al-Adl w-Al-Ihssane), and Reform and Renewal.

12. Among them were the head of the press union, Larbi Messari, the editor-in-chief of Al-Alam, Abdeljabbar Al-Sahimi, Abdellah Baqqali from the Istiqlal Youth, Ahmed Boukiyoudh from Bayane Al Yaoum, and reporters from various newspapers and magazines belonging to the Amazigh movement, Agence France-Presse (AFP), and several individuals of various political and cultural shades. They included Mohammed Chafik, Lahcene Oulhaj, and Mohammed Ajaajaa from *Tifawt* magazine.

13. Translator's note: Better known as Abdelkrim, Khattabi was the leader of a 1921 Amazigh independence revolt against the Spanish protectorate in northern Morocco, and president of the resulting Republic of the Rif. The campaign provoked a brutal response from both Spain and France, including chemical attacks against civilians. By 1926, the better-equipped colonial powers had subdued the movement, and Abd el-Krim was deported to Réunion, a French outpost in the Indian Ocean. He died in Cairo in 1963.

14. The other founding members included: Dr. Omar Al-Khattabi, Ahmed El Mourabit, Abdelmedjid El-Fakiri, Mohammed Chafik, me, Abdelnabi El Filali, Dr. Ahmed Jeridi, El-Moustafa El-Ramid, El Mehdi El Manjra, El Mourabit Souleiman, Fqih Basri, Mohammed Eikbal, Mohammed Kharshish, Mohammed El-Taheri El-Jouti, Dr. Abdelkrim Al Khatib, and Mohammed El Haihi. The executive committee of the institution consisted of: Dr. Omar Al-Khattabi as president, activist Fqih Basri as vice president, Professor Mohammed Chafik as vice president, Mohammed El-Taheri El-Jouti as general secretary, me as assistant general secretary, Abdelnabi El Filali as treasurer, Abdelmedjid El-Fakiri as assistant treasurer, Souleiman El Mourabit as advisor, and Mohammed Kharshish as advisor.

15. Translator's note: The Battle of Anoual, in 1921, saw Abdelkrim's forces win a resounding victory against Spanish forces, described as the worst defeat in Spanish colonial history.

16. They included the Socialist Union Party, the Istiqlal Party, the Progress and Socialism Party, the Democratic Labor Action Organization, and the Vanguard Party. The Moroccan Labor Union, the General Union of Moroccan Workers and the Democratic Labor Confederation also condemned it, as did the Moroccan Association for Human Rights, the Nakour Association for Culture and Arts, the Numidia Cultural Association, the Chouala Association for Education and Culture, and the Badiss Association for Fine Arts.

17. This was to be formed by: Lahcen Oulhadj, Lhoucine Ait Bahcine, Abdellah Hattous, Imbarek Boulkid, Brahim Shaaban, Nadir Hassan, Ahmed Ouass, Mounir Kejji, and Bouya Azkazaou. A management and administration committee was also proposed, consisting of Amer El Houssein, me, Mohammed El-Maakchaoui, Mohammed Bouchdouk, Youssef Ouannan, Najib El-Bakroumi, and Ahmed Hassan. On the Reception and Accommodation Committee were Abdullah Hamza, Mohammed Bzeigh, Lahcene Basta, Ahmed Arhamouch, Mohammad Boulaaras, and Belaid Abouski.

18. Brahim Akhiate, *Rijālāt al-ʿamal al-amāzīghī, al-rāḥilūn minhum* (Rabat: AMREC, 2004).

19. Translator's note: a political coalition between the Istiqlal Party, the center-left Socialist Union of Popular Forces (USFP), and the left-wing Party of Progress and Socialism (PPS).

20. Translator's note: the upper house of Morocco's parliament.

21. Issue 994 of March 6–12, 1999; and issue 996 dated March 20–26, 1999.

22. Translator's note: an Islamic studies center established by King Hassan II.

CHAPTER 5

The Period of Fundamental Changes at the Institutional Level, 2001–2003

OUR BATTLE TO TAKE DOWN THE EDUCATION CHARTER

The year 2000 marked the start of the implementation of the Charter on Education and Training. Therefore, we began the year by sending a message to members of the Moroccan parliament (deputies and counselors) to ask them to ensure that forthcoming legal bills would contain provisions clarifying the principles and mechanisms for integrating Tamazight, as a national language, into all educational levels and for all Moroccans. As we mobilized against the poor status of Tamazight within the Charter, we sent another letter, this time to the heads of parliamentary blocs as they held a special session to discuss the document's legal framework. In order to step up the pressure on parliamentarians and the government in this regard, AMREC decided to organize a protest in front of parliament on March 14, 2000, in coordination with the Tamaynut Association. We asked the local authorities for permission to hold this peaceful protest. However, on March 13, we received a written response from the governor of Rabat prohibiting us from doing so. We ignored this reply, and a group of activists gathered in front of the parliament. They were dispersed, and our association's headquarters was surrounded by the Rapid Intervention Police. We could see that they were ready to intervene forcefully unless we backed down from our decision. In response, we gathered inside the association's headquarters, where we discussed the topic and proposed to counter the authorities by organizing a protest march to be prepared by all components of the Amazigh movement.

This was the birth of the "Tawada" march, which took shape later through meetings at our association's headquarters and the formation of a national committee to achieve this project, as I shall relate in due course.

ON OUR DIFFERENCES OVER MOHAMMED CHAFIK'S STATEMENT ON THE AMAZIGH NATURE OF MOROCCO

The passing of the late Hassan II, the accession of Mohammed VI to the throne of his ancestors, the publication of Sheikh Abdesslam Yassine's memorandum "To Whom It May Concern," and the unveiling of the Charter on Education and Training, which gave Amazigh the inferior status of a language merely "for instruction": All these developments, in my opinion, had put the institutions of the state on edge. Every force in the country was now working to assert itself by announcing its presence and seeking to place its issues on the political and cultural agenda. The royal establishment was therefore faced with the challenge of coming up with solutions that would please everyone. In Yassine's memoir, he criticized the rule of the late Hassan II, the monarchy, and the king's status as Commander of the Faithful. Seeing as the government was from the political bloc that included the socialists, Istiqlal and the Progress and Socialism Party, it was easy to conclude that as the only two factions outside of power were the Islamist movement and the Amazigh movement, a convergence of the two would inevitably pose risks to social and political peace, from the rulers' perspective. The solution to this was to create a conflict, or at least a distance, between them. It is not unlikely that this analysis set the context for Professor Mohammed Chafik's issuing of a statement on the Amazigh issue in Morocco, considering the political situation at the time. Chafik himself declared to me, in a conversation during that period, that a few days after the publication of Sheikh Yassine's memoir, Hassan Aourid visited him at his home and asked, "Where do the Amazigh stand on this memo?" Chafik's answer was: "In a month or a little more, you will see what the response is." I did not make up these words. I am very aware, from my knowledge of Professor Mohammed Chafik, that he is precise in his expression and does not speak whimsically, being a state official and a veteran in the corridors of power. I recalled this conversation with him after he had released his statement. One day, after he had drafted his statement, he sent for me, via Lhoucine Jouhadi. It was a Friday. We went to Chafik's house, and Hassan Oulhaj was also present. The three of us sat with Chafik in his office, and shortly after, Lehbib Fouad entered, carrying copies of the statement. It appeared that Fouad had been tasked with printing it.

After handing these papers to the professor, he left. Professor Chafik took a copy of the statement, gave it to me, and said, "Read this and give me your opinion." After I had read a few pages of it, I promptly said, "Professor, some of these ideas contradict with the principles of the Amazigh movement." He replied, "Continue reading, and you'll discover more." I finished reading the statement and made some initial observations, then we began to discuss how it would be signed, and to whom it would be sent. When we had concluded this discussion, he asked me to agree to the content of the statement as it was, and to prepare a list of activists in various Moroccan cities, so he could approach them and ask them to sign it. I told him I could not possibly accept it in that form and asked him to give me a copy to present to the association's board. Then we would then determine our position on it and make suggestions. He flatly refused, arguing that once the statement had left his house, it was as good as published, and it would no longer be confidential enough to send to the government. However, to continue the conversation, we scheduled a meeting at our association's headquarters the following Saturday morning with Lahcen Oulhadj, to discuss it and suggest who might sign it. That evening, I returned to Professor Chafik's house with a list of names, but I did not hand it to him. With us were Mohammed Ajaajaa, Mohammed Oudades, Lahcen Oulhadj, and Youssef Agouri. The professor extensively praised me and my spirit of struggle, telling them, "This is the person who will mobilize people, and will go to the south for the purpose of collecting signatures." Knowing that I was out of work and facing financial difficulties, he brought two thousand dirhams for this task, believing that he had now convinced me of the statement and that I would sign it and carry out this mission. I was making every effort to continue my contacts with him and gather more information about the motives behind the statement. I was also waiting to hold a meeting of the association's board, the following Tuesday, to inform them about the essence of the statement and to discuss our position on it. At that meeting, after we had dealt with the rest of the agenda, I informed the brothers about the statement and what had happened between me and Professor Chafik, about the content of the statement and my initial observations on our strategy. We then discussed all aspects of the subject, from the political circumstances and the contents of the statement to the question of whether it was the right moment to issue it, as well as what might lie behind it. Those present included Ahmed Assid, Ali Khedaoui, Abdelaziz Bourass, Lhoucine Ait Bahcine, Essafi Moumen Ali, and El Houssain Ouazi. Their main observations on the statement were as follows:

The statement was written in an emotive and sharp manner, criticizing every side without exception, from the royal establishment to political parties, whether from the nationalist, right wing, and Islamist camps. This could easily mean that we would sabotage ourselves, by being isolated and antagonistic toward everyone, in contrast to our strategy of dialogue, aimed at opening channels of communication to convincing every part of society of the justice of the Amazigh cause and persuading all these political currents and associations to become concerned with the issue too. Thus, it was in our interest to win them over to our side, rather than declaring them enemies.

The statement also acknowledged the existence of ethnicities in Morocco, including Amazigh and others, as well as claiming that Morocco has Amazigh and non-Amazigh regions.

It did not make a single mention of the Agadir Charter, a document that was one of the major references of the Amazigh movement and had been signed in 1991 by the six associations at the heart of the movement.

The statement also dismissed the work of Morocco's Amazigh associations as futile, failing to mention their achievements or their sacrifices within the framework of the national Coordination Council and their future role within the struggles of civil society, which is the womb that gave birth to both Amazigh associations and groups campaigning on other important national issues such as human rights, women's rights and so on.

Without going into the details of their other observations, suffice it to say that we settled on the most important among them and decided that the national board of the association would sign the statement—but only on the following conditions:

- That Professor Chafik accepted the creation of a small committee of Amazigh campaigners to redraft it, add what needed adding and delete certain things that did not need mentioning, in order to give the statement the formulation of a joint, collaborative document issued by the Amazigh associations, as a follow-up to the Agadir Charter.
- If he refused to accept these conditions, we suggested that Professor Chafik should issue the statement in his own name, as its owner and author, and allow it to be discussed in the media as a private statement on the Amazigh question.

In the end, the board tasked me with informing Professor Chafik of our decision. They placed me in a delicate position with this assignment, and I asked some of them to volunteer for it, but they refused and insisted that I undertake the task alone. After this had been decided, I waited two more days to prepare myself for the task. I knew Chafik very well and could predict how this would land with him. On the morning of the third day, I visited him at home and informed him of the office's decision. I told him that neither I nor the members of the board would sign the statement unless it was amended by a small committee of activists representing the Amazigh associations. Were he not to accept this, I also encouraged him to issue the statement in his own name, as its publication would spark a useful public debate. As I had expected, after listening to me, the professor stood up and refused to make any change to the statement. He said our observations on it were incorrect, and that there was no third party behind the statement. He became very emotional, as he had not expected this response, being convinced that I would go along with his project. After he had calmed down a little, he told me that he would consider how to deal with the matter in light of what I had said, and whether to issue the document as a pamphlet or in the form of an article, or to abandon it altogether. These were all the possibilities he mentioned at the time. Despite this difficult conversation between us, he got up and accompanied me to bid me farewell at the door of his house.

After this meeting, Professor Chafik decided to go ahead with his project, aiming to get as many Amazigh groups and activists as possible to sign the statement. Despite my explaining to him at length why I refused to sign, he still appeared to hope that I would eventually relent. Three days after I had visited him, he rang me and asked me to come and visit him, even for a quarter of an hour. I went back to his house, supposing that there were new developments on the issue. When we were in his office, he quickly said to me, "I'm asking you to sign. There are four signatures on the list, I want you to be the fifth." I was embarrassed again, and I reiterated my position: I did not represent myself alone, and this was not about me personally. It was the decision of the national office of the association. I could not simply break with its decision, nor could I sign a text whose contents I did not support, and which contradicted my principles. Therefore, I asked him to forgive me, as once again I could not fulfill his request. Of course, he was upset that this meeting had not succeeded. When he accompanied me to the door of his house, I asked him to smile before I left. I insisted on it, even kissing his head as I insisted that he smile. Finally, he did, and we parted amicably. I had insisted like this because I knew that this incident was transient and would pass. What remained constant was our brotherhood and friendship, which spanned decades, and our zeal for our Amazigh identity, even if we disagreed over how best to defend it.

After I had left and refused to sign, Professor Chafik began to collect signatures, appealing to various people to help him gather as many as possible. He did everything in his power to persuade members of our association's board to sign, contacting them personally. However, he only managed to persuade Ahmed Assid, our secretary-general, and Ali Khedaoui, who was an advisor to the association. After this, there was much discussion of the statement, its content, and the reasons why we had refused to sign it. In order to avoid subjective interpretations of our position, Abdelaziz Bourass from the association's branch in Casablanca managed to obtain a copy of the statement, enabling the weekly newspaper *Al Mustaqil* to publish it in full in order to inform the public of its contents. The press now discussed the statement, and both supporters and critics voiced their views.

Having publicly made clear our position on Professor Chafik's statement, we at the association went back to work implementing our national program, steering clear of the conflicts that came in the wake of the statement. My relationship with Professor Chafik cooled during that period, so we would not irk one another in our decisions, but our relationship eventually returned to normal.

OUR RETURN TO AMAZIGH INTELLECTUAL AND POLITICAL ACTIVISM

As we continue to wage our battle for the integration of the Amazigh language in education, in response to the Charter on Education and Training, Abdelkrim Al Khatib and Mahjoubi Aherdane issued a statement, in their personal capacities, in which they demanded that Tamazight be recognized as an official language. The association contacted them both, expressing appreciation for their stance but urging them to formulate their positions within their organizations rather than taking public positions in their individual capacities.

The association also organized its second "Conference of Moroccan Amazigh Creative Writers" from March 1 to April 2, 2000, in Marrakech, a follow-up to the first meeting in Agadir back in August 1994. Many Amazigh writers took part. Such meetings are important because they nurture communication and interaction between Amazigh creators. More significantly, they encourage Amazigh writing, whether in terms of theater, cinema, music, or novels and stories—that is to say, the realm of publishing, a realm into which Amazigh writing had yet to make its entry.

This event coincided with the death of my mother, may God have mercy on her. I received the news by phone during the opening session of the meeting, so I left to head straight to my town of Ait Souab to attend her funeral.

Continuing with the association's strategy of making connections with political bodies and organizations working on social, human rights, youth, and women's issues, we initiated a new dialogue on the Amazigh issue, involving all these groups, as we had done in 1996. Through this, we reaffirmed our belief that the Amazigh question is a national responsibility and in the interest of everyone. To this end, we held meetings with these entities to inform them of their responsibility to support the Amazigh cause and to support the Amazigh movement in achieving its legitimate demands, which are in the interests of the entire Moroccan people, Amazigh-speaking or otherwise. We tried to make them feel that achieving these demands was at the heart of realizing and consolidating a distinct national identity. We also focused on dialogue with parliamentary blocs, both in the House of Representatives and the House of Councillors, to urge them to live up to their role of holding the government to account on the Amazigh issue, whether regarding education, media, or public life. The association had gained significant experience through these dialogues with political parties of various inclinations: socialist, Leftist, Islamist, or moderate. The association's political role is no less important than its cultural and organizational roles. We operate on all fronts, seeing them as integrated and interrelated. This direct, pluralistic engagement with all components, and the rational discourse for which the association is known, is appreciated by all its interlocutors, regardless of their differences in opinion or in their priorities, even including over the timing of when demands must be achieved. What is more, many political parties started inviting the association to lead seminars and organize study days for their constituencies on the Amazigh issue, with the aim of bringing this issue closer to their activists. This was a major achievement that benefited the Amazigh cause.

THE ESTABLISHMENT OF THE AMAZIGH BOOK PRIZE AND THE AMAZIGH FILM FESTIVAL

The association stayed active in the realms of creativity and publishing, running a stand at the annual International Publishing and Book Fair organized by the Ministry of Culture in Casablanca, this time in February 2000. Every year, the association had consistently presented works published on the Amazigh question or in Tamazight, making the stand a meeting point for creators and writers and presenting the state of the Amazigh arts. This year the association did something different, creating an award for Amazigh books, as such works were still excluded from the book awards organized by the Ministry of Culture. Therefore, we allocated several awards for this purpose, in different fields. These awards were presented at the International Book Fair. The winners included Ahmed Ziani (for poetry), Mohammed Achiban (for short stories), Essafi Moumen Ali (for theater), Lhacen Ouazi (for translation), Mohammmed Akounadh (for children's books), Abdelaziz Bourass (for mythology), and Lhoucine Jouhadi (for translation).

The awards ceremony was attended by representatives of the press and the Moroccan Writers' Union. *El Alam* newspaper published two photos, on the same page as its report on the king presenting the book award in Marrakech, allowing readers to comment. That year, we also organized the first Amazigh Film Festival in Morocco, on July 13–15 at the Sidi Belyout Cultural Complex in Casablanca. This event marked the start of a new era for Amazigh culture, being the first time such creative work was introduced to the public. Many prominent figures from theater and cinema in Tamazight and Moroccan *dārija* (colloquial Arabic) attended. The event sparked discussions on the current reality and the future of Amazigh cinema, and awards were presented to actors and directors to encourage them, as well as honorary awards. The event had a major impact on those concerned.

THE LAUNCH OF THE "TAWADA" PROJECT

As we sought to implement the proposal by our activist brothers at the association's headquarters, after they had been prevented from protesting in front of Parliament against the Charter on Education and Training, we and the Tamaynut association wrote to the other Amazigh associations on October 4, 2000, inviting them to a meeting to discuss effective ways of achieving our demands. We suggested a meeting at AMREC's headquarters at 3:00 p.m. on October 14. Hassan Id Balkassam and I signed the letter.[1]

The concluding statement of this meeting read as follows:

> After evaluating all the activist initiatives by the various elements of the Amazigh cultural movement, the participants agreed to do the following:
>
> - Organize a march under the title "Tawada" ("March") in support of the Amazigh cause;
> - Set up a national oversight committee to ensure the initiative's success, in collaboration with local committees, open to all Amazigh groups and associations, and forces supporting the democratic struggle of the Amazigh cultural movement;
> - Invite various Amazigh associations, groups and activists and all civil society organizations to recruit and mobilize to make the march a success, with the same spirit and enthusiasm as that with which they recruit to support all just national and international causes.
>
> Note: the precise date of the march remains to be determined.[2]

The national committee for Tawada was then established on February 13 and 14, 2001, at the headquarters of our association, in the presence of the Tamaynut association (which was represented by Abdellah Hitous and Mohammed Idouch); the Coordination of the Southeast (represented by Moustapha El Barhouch); and the Coordination of Development Associations in Tafraout (represented by Ibrahim Akdime).

The new committee consisted of:

- AMREC
- Tamaynut
- The Confederation of Amazigh Associations in the North
- Tamount Ifous
- The Coordination of Development Associations in Tafraout

The meeting also resulted in the creation of a communication cell, composed of: Tamount Ifous, AMREC, and the Coordination of Development Associations in Tafraout, as they were located in the Rabat-Casablanca axis. Abdellah Hitous wrote the minutes of this meeting.

The National Committee for Tawada continued to mobilize for the march, which we hoped would be a historic event by any measure. We held another meeting for this purpose on April 21, 2001, at AMREC headquarters, and issued an important and historic statement in this situation, which included the following:

In the framework of preparations and arrangements for "Tawada," the National Committee held its regular meeting on April 21, 2001. After discussing the points on its agenda and the state of Amazigh linguistic and cultural rights, as well as updates on the current situation, and after evaluating what has been accomplished and what remains to be completed to make "Tawada" a reality, it announces to the national and international public the following demands:

1. The provision of legal guarantees for the Amazigh language by enshrining it in the constitution as a national and official language of the country. The National Committee also denounces the government's position on the Amazigh issue in its first manifesto, and its neglect of the question in its second.
2. Amazigh language and culture enjoying their full and legitimate rights in the media, through the drafting of a national, democratic media policy. The committee denounces all forms

of opportunism over the Amazigh issue, as well as the frenzied campaigning by certain media outlets.

3. The integration of unified Amazigh culture and language at all levels of the educational system; the committee denounces the provisions of the National Charter on Education and Training, which is a manifestation of linguistic and cultural discrimination.

4. The adoption of the Amazigh language at all national institutions.

5. The adoption of the Amazigh language in the workings of all national institutions, to ensure the dignity of the Moroccan Amazigh on his land.

6. An end to the systematic ban on Amazigh personal names and to the distortion and Arabization of place names and flags.

7. A total rewriting of Moroccan history from the beginning, with an objective, national reading, to restore the Moroccan personality through all its historical, intellectual, political, and artistic symbols.

Based on the above, the national committee for "Tawada" announces that the march will take place at the end of October 2001, and calls on all components of the Amazigh cultural movement, activities, regulatory bodies, and every democratic individual who cares about the nation to contribute to this historic event, to achieve the legitimate demands of the Amazigh cultural movement through which the Moroccan personality can be fulfilled and national unity achieved.

What is notable in this statement is the involvement of the Confederation of Amazigh Associations, of the Tadla-Azilal region, which joined the national associations and coordination committees making up the committee organizing the march.

The national committee confirmed the date following a meeting on June 22, 2001, when it issued a statement in solidarity with the uprising for identity, dignity, and social justice in Algeria. It included the following:

The national committee for "Tawada," which gathered in Rabat on June 22, 2001 for its last meeting, considered the measures and organizational steps needed to mobilize for the national "Tawada" march scheduled for October 2001. It also discussed developments in the Kabylie region and all parts of the Algerian homeland, where a popular uprising is ongoing, for the sake of Amazigh identity, human

dignity, and social justice, and against exclusion, economic marginalization and a policy of linguistic and cultural discrimination against
Amazigh language, culture, and identity.

We announce the following to the national, Maghreb, and international
public:

1. We condemn the criminal acts committed by Algerian forces of
    repression against the Amazigh popular uprising, as well as the
    intransigence and procrastination of Algerian officials vis-à-vis the
    legitimate demands of the Amazigh.
2. We stand in full solidarity with the families, martyrs, detainees, and
    activists of the Amazigh popular uprising in Algeria, as well as with
    Algerian democratic forces, in their legitimate struggle to build a
    state of law and to ensure that the citizen can enjoy dignity in all its
    dimensions: cultural, economic, social, and political.
3. We condemn the deliberate media blackout practiced by many
    Moroccan media outlets, as they attempt to play down this popular
    uprising and obscure the Amazigh identity aspect of it, which has
    implications across the Maghreb region.
4. We call on all democratic political forces and civil society organiza-
    tions to support the demands of the Amazigh social movement in
    Algeria and in all Maghreb countries.

The National Committee for Tawada held its last meeting on October 13,
2001, and issued the following statement:

Representatives of the Amazigh associations forming the National
Committee for Tawada met in Rabat on Saturday, October 13, 2001.
After examining the situation of the Amazigh linguistic and cultural
rights, in light of national and international developments, they
decided the following:

•   To call on all Amazigh cultural associations and Amazigh activists
    at university campuses to intensify their mobilization and form
    more local committees in preparation for the "Tawada" march;
•   To recall the just demands of the Amazigh cultural movement,
    including the constitutional recognition of Amazigh as a national
    and official language; the democratization of education and the
    media; and to consider the Amazigh demand as an indivisible whole;

- To call for a broader meeting including the national committee and representatives of the local committees for "Tawada" on December 23, 2001, to set a date for the "Tawada" march.

After this meeting, at which the next meeting had been set for December 23, 2001, as per the statement above, the Tamaynut and Tamount Ifous associations decided to hold the meeting in Tarrast, Agadir, without consulting the national committee overseeing preparations for the Tawada march or informing me personally, except for a note placed in the association's mailbox the day before the meeting by Abdellah Hitous, inviting me to attend. He did not even call me to explain the reasons for this last-minute invitation. The same happened to the other coordination bodies and federations in the north and the southeast. When I called officials at these bodies, they expressed their disapproval at this conduct and the two associations' lack of consultation and approval from the other federations over the location of the meeting. The federations asked me to issue a statement of condemnation over this undemocratic behavior, but I suggested that we pause until we understood their motives. Indeed, we did not issue any statement on the matter, nor did we or the coordination committees or federations attend the meeting in Agadir. A handful of local associations participated. Following that, on February 9, 2002, another meeting was convened at the headquarters of Tamaynut in Casablanca, gathering the remaining associations.

I have narrated events as they took place, in their chronological sequence, on the subject of preparations for the Tawada march, since the inception of the idea at our association's headquarters, after the ban on our gathering in front of parliament on March 14, 2000, and up until the final, by-the-book meeting of the National Committee for Tawada on October 13, 2001. All these events are related in the minutes of our various meetings. However, these events and the preparations for Tawada cannot be understood in isolation from their historical context and the political circumstances at the time. The year 2000 was the first year of King Mohammed VI's reign. Given the state of crisis, the new monarch sought to calm the situation by recognizing the legitimacy of the Amazigh demands. Indeed, he addressed this topic in detail in his Throne Day speech in July 2001, as part of a preemptive strategy prior to the date set for the Tawada march in October 2001. This event in itself was historic, and its importance should not be understated. It amounted to a message to the Amazigh movement that he had heard our message, carefully considered our decision to take to the streets, and understood its content, and therefore that now we should be patient and cautious in making further decisions. This is why we decided to suspend the march set for October 2001, to wait and see what concrete actions would follow the royal speech. Our association issued a statement to the Moroccan public, expressing appreciation for the contents of the royal speech regarding the Amazigh cause:

> The National Committee of the Moroccan Association for Research and Cultural Exchange met in Rabat on Tuesday, July 31, 2001, and discussed the contents of the royal speech on the occasion of the second anniversary of His Majesty King Mohammed VI ascending the throne of his blessed ancestors. It thus informs the nation of the following:
>
> - It highly values His Majesty's tendencies toward major reforms, which aim to complete the foundations of a modern democratic society, based on the objective facts of our identity and civilization, which aspires to establish a state of law and justice, citizenship, and the realization of comprehensive development.
> - It considers the decision to establish the Royal Institute of Amazigh Culture, alongside His Majesty and under his supreme patronage, with far-reaching prerogatives, a historical decision and a courageous step toward restoring the dignity of the Amazigh language, culture, and identity.
> - It calls on all components of the Amazigh cultural movement and all democratic forces to support, fully and effectively, the success of this comprehensive, democratic reform project and to stand firmly against its opponents, first and foremost the anti-Amazigh lobby.
> - It hopes that the creation of the Royal Institute will be the first step toward providing constitutional protection to the Amazigh language as a national, official language, alongside the Arabic language.

We issued this statement to praise the speech and its content, but we also stressed our demands and the need for their swift realization, so that the speech would not remain simply an attempt to calm the situation, devoid of any real follow-up to implement its contents.

2001: THE YEAR OF MAJOR TRANSFORMATIONS

The events of 2001 were a natural consequence of developments the previous year, which I have related—notably reactions to Mohammed Chafik's declaration and our preparations for the Tawada march to express our demands for the Amazigh cause. The national press continually covered these issues, voicing support, opposition, or skepticism, but ultimately all this coverage worked in favor of the Amazigh national interest, which was now firmly on the state's agenda and urgently demanded measures and decisions, whether by the royal court or the government.

I consider 2001 a year of major transformations, in light of the political and procedural decisions that were taken in favor of the Amazigh cause. Among the most important were the royal decree of July 30, 2001, on the occasion of Throne Day, and the king's speech in Ajdir on October 17 of the same year, in which he announced a decree establishing the Royal Institute of Amazigh Culture. This step by His Majesty marked the beginning of a new political and cultural era in Morocco, which would have very important implications for the country's future as it reconciled with itself and consolidated its unique identity.

The media published extremely bold articles on all these topics, many of them written by activists from our association. Among the most important were:

- El Houssain Ouazi, "In Opposition to the Marginalization Afflicting the Amazigh Cause, We Call for an Amazigh Intellectual Movement Within the Socialist Union," *Al-Mustaqil*, February 2, 2001
- Abdelaziz Bourass, "For Full Citizenship," *Al-Mustaqil*, March 1–7
- Ahmed Assid, "History and Myth in the Discourse of the National Movement, or the Meaning of Nationalism," *Al-Ahdath al-Maghribiyya*, May 23, (in four parts)
- "The Unionists' Positions on the Amazigh Issue Are the Same as Those of the Independents," *Al-Haraka*, April 13
- Ismail Al-Alawi, "The Amazigh Issue Transcends Politics and Ideology, Because It Is the Issue of All Moroccans," *Al-Sharq Al-Awsat*, April 23
- "The Abolition of Demagogic Arabization, Between the Demands of Modernity and the History of the National Movement," *Al-Ahdath al-Maghribiyya*, February 9
- Abdelhak Mrini, "Harmonious Roles for Arabic and Amazigh in Morocco; The Former Is the Language of Doctrine and Islamic Culture, and the Latter Expresses Moroccan Authenticity," *Al-Sharq Al-Awsat*, November 29

These are just some examples of the discussion and analysis in the media related to the political and cultural events of the years 2000 and 2001.

THE BATTLE FOR RIGHTS AT THE FÉDÉRATION INTERNATIONALE POUR LES DROITS HUMAINS (FIDH)

At the end of December 2000, AMREC received an invitation from the Fédération internationale pour les droits humains (International Federation for Human Rights, or FIDH) to participate in the global body's 34th conference, to be held in Casablanca from January 10–14, 2001. We were the only Amazigh association invited to this conference. For this purpose, we prepared a working paper that laid out the injustices afflicting Amazigh language and culture in Morocco, as well as the manifestations of racial discrimination that the Amazigh face in the fields of education, culture, and human rights, in addition to the lack of constitutional protection for their language. The association's delegation consisted of me, Abdelaziz Bourass, Ahmed Assid, Mohammed Bouniss, Essafi Moumen Ali, and Ali Belkadi. We took part in the second committee, which dealt with discrimination, racism, and cultural pluralism, and the fourth, which was on justice and exclusion.

At the opening session of the conference, our delegation was stupefied to note the total silence and deliberate ignorance of the Amazigh issue reflected in the speeches delivered by the two main Moroccan rights groups at the conference, the Moroccan Organization for Human Rights and the Moroccan Association for Human Rights. We conveyed our protest to them regarding their hostile positions toward the principles of human rights.

During the proceedings of the second and fourth committees, we distributed to delegates the paper that we had prepared in three languages on the topic, along with a copy of our pamphlet, "The Charter on Education and Training, a Policy of Linguistic Discrimination," to explain the subject to conference attendees.

Over the following three days, the delegation clashed with opponents of linguistic and cultural rights from the two previously mentioned Moroccan organizations, on both committees. However, by the strength of our arguments, we were able, despite their objections, to convince attendees from all over the world that our viewpoint on Amazigh linguistic and cultural rights in Morocco was valid. This led those present to adopt the Amazigh cause as a human rights issue, leading both workshops to issue a historic recommendation on Amazigh language and culture in Morocco and across North Africa as a symbol of marginalized languages and cultures internationally in the context of globalization.

After this recommendation was read out and unanimously approved at the public session, where final reports from the four committees were presented, AMREC's delegation did everything in its power to present this recommendation to the special conference of FIDH, so it would be included among the draft resolutions to be considered by the conference, meaning its monitoring and implementation would become binding on the Federation. The delegation succeeded in convincing many of the organizations present to support this. Notably, these included African organizations—which saw Tamazight as an African language that they were obliged to protect and defend—as well as the Kurdish, Turkish, Cypriot, and Ecuadorian organizations. The Moroccan Organization for Human Rights also finally agreed to adopt the recommendation, after realizing that it would be the biggest loser if it were to equivocate even as the international consensus moved to adopt the recommendation. The only person who held out against this international consensus was the lawyer Abderrahman Ben Amrou of the Moroccan Association for Human Rights, who did everything in his power to prevent the recommendation from being adopted. However, he was unsuccessful in his efforts, in the face of the international consensus on recognizing the Amazigh linguistic and cultural rights in their homeland, Tamazgha. Thus, the Amazigh cause secured international legitimacy on the land of Tamazgha, coinciding with the Amazigh New Year 2951 (January 13, 2001).

The association thus succeeded in issuing its recommendation on the Amazigh language and culture at the fourth conference of the FIDH, from January 10–14, 2001, as follows:

> The model of the nation-state that appeared in Europe and later spread throughout the world has contributed to the marginalization and exclusion of languages and cultures that have been unable to obtain official or national status within those states. Linguistic and cultural discrimination has found its way into the very system of the modern state. Globalization has contributed more and more in our era to the spread and perpetuation of a monolithic culture. However, there are languages and cultures that have managed to defy this process of forced unification, and today, they have the right to persist, in a framework of mutual respect and equality.
>
> As human rights defenders, we have a duty to contribute to the preservation of these languages and cultures. Given that Morocco is the host country of the 34th conference of the International Federation for Human Rights (FIDH), we have decided to dedicate this recommendation symbolically to Amazigh culture, which we consider one culture, alongside many others, that is threatened in a world of creeping globalization. In this context, we demand recognition and

constitutional protection of the Amazigh language in Morocco and North African countries, to ensure its integration in the fields of public education, media, communication, public administration and justice. This recognition should contribute to guaranteeing the rights of Amazigh speakers, promoting their role in the development process, and supporting democracy.

This conference was thus a new opportunity for our association and the Amazigh movement in general to confront the opponents of our cause. This included Moroccan human rights organizations, which are selective about the rights they champion and do not pay attention to linguistic and cultural demands, thereby excluding a key element of the Universal Declaration of Human Rights. The recommendation issued by the conference also amounted to an international recognition of linguistic and cultural rights in our country. Having obtained this recommendation, we did not sit idly, but launched a media campaign about it, drawing attention to the two Moroccan human rights bodies' opposition to the recommendation—particularly Abderrahman Ben Amrou, who opposed airing the question of Amazigh linguistic and cultural rights, and was strongly against the recommendation being issued. Thus, *Al-Mustaqil* wrote on January 20, 2001, that "on the margins of the 34th congress of the International Federation for Human Rights, a strong presence of Amazigh linguistic and cultural rights in the recommendations and decisions of the conference." It also published the association's memo and the conference's recommendations. *Al-Haraka* also published an article on January 22, 2001, titled "Human Rights as Recognized in Morocco, Not Universally: Abderrahman Ben Amrou Does Not Deserve the Title of Human Rights Activist." The weekly newspaper *Al-Ousboue* ran an article in its January 19 edition titled "Facing the Human Rights Federation, Moroccan Amazigh Denounce the Ban on Amazigh names." As we exerted media pressure on Moroccan human rights bodies that had neglected our linguistic and cultural rights and opposed the international recommendation, the Moroccan Association for Human Rights finally issued a lengthy statement on January 24, defending its president, Ben Amrou. The association acknowledged his position, but said, "The reticence of the president of the association was due to his commitment to the decisions of the [association's] fifth national conference . . . the sub-bodies of the association are the bodies authorized to review or develop the conference's decisions."

However, the president's negative and bizarre position, in the name of his association, hurt his reputation among members of the association at many of its branches. This damaged his attempt to be reelected as president of the association, and he lost to Abdelhamid Amine.

Following this episode, AMREC sent a letter to the head of the Consultative Council on Human Rights, urging him to end discrimination against the Amazigh language and culture in the fields of education, media, administration, and the judiciary. *Al-Mustaqil* published the text of this letter on Wednesday, May 7, 2001, which read:

> In the context of the democratic transformation underway in our country, which has increased the aspirations of all national forces for the building of a state of law and human rights, in accordance with all the speeches of His Majesty King Mohammed VI, we urge your esteemed council to integrate Amazigh language and culture into the recommendations it raises to His Majesty, to end the injustice afflicting Amazigh language and culture in the field of education, by integrating them into public education at all levels, like other languages and cultures, as well as into the field of the media . . . and in the fields of public administration and justice. We also urge the same in the field of legislation, by abolishing the Ministry of the Interior's ruling that prohibits the registration of Amazigh names for newborns in the civil status register; by issuing a legislative text that prevents the distortion and Arabization of Amazigh names and places, which deprives them of their historical and geographical meanings; and by amending the constitution to affirm the Amazigh aspect of Morocco's national identity and enshrining the Amazigh language as a national and official language.

THE BATTLE OVER THE CONSTITUTION

We have seen how Moroccan rights organizations opposed cultural rights, reflecting the fact that they were more or less subordinate to political bodies, which, in turn, had not developed their own perspectives and analyses or updated them to reflect the social and cultural reality of the country. Thus, they were living in a kind of schizophrenia, between politics and human rights. Even as they claimed at human rights forums that they defended human rights, in practice they ignored linguistic and cultural rights, which are core elements of the Universal Declaration of Human Rights. This showed that their stance was based on political positions, not on defending human rights comprehensively.

In this context, and to highlight the importance and urgency of giving constitutional protection to the Amazigh language, we at the association decided to organize a seminar in Casablanca on the topic "Toward the Constitutional Recognition of the Amazigh Language." The aim was to promote this rights issue and to sensitize public opinion to its importance, as giving constitutional recognition to the Amazigh language would contribute to solving many problems and could put an end to the administrative and political barriers that obstruct human rights work in our country. It would also ensure the rights of Amazigh language and culture in education, the media, and public life. However, the seminar was banned by the local authorities. In response to this arbitrary ban, the association decided to publish the contributions of academics and human rights activists who had planned to participate, in a book bearing the same title as the seminar. Thus, we hoped to bring their ideas to as many readers as possible. Published in 2002, it also included a collection of other documents related to the topic. The contents were as follows:

- "Inclusive Demands That Cannot Be Postponed," by me
- "Is Constitutional Protection of the Amazigh Language a Gateway into the Amazigh Identity Struggle, or a Result of It?" by Dr. El Houssain Ouazi
- "Reflections on the Problem of Constitutionalizing Amazigh Language," by Dr. Abdelatif Aknouch
- "Excluding Amazighity from the Constitution Violates the Sovereignty of the Nation," by Essafi Moumen Ali
- "Amazighity and the Democratic Constitution," by Abdelaziz Bourass

As I said, the book brought together a significant collection of documents concerning the Amazigh issue, including the Agadir Charter and certain statements related to the subject.

Following the unjustified ban of the conference, the Casablanca branch of AMREC issued a press release, which concluded as follows:

The Casablanca branch of the Moroccan Association for Research and Cultural Exchange hereby announces, to the national and international public, that it strongly condemns and denounces this new act by the authorities, which can only be considered another form of linguistic, cultural, and ethnic discrimination against the fundamental and essential component of the Moroccan people and its national culture.

After the publication of the book, titled *For the Constitutional Recognition of Amazigh*, the association held a press conference at our headquarters in Rabat. Given the importance of the subject, it was attended by the national press, and we distributed copies of the book. The following mentions in various newspapers give an idea of the press coverage of this conference: "The demand for the constitutional recognition of the Amazigh language, and the freezing disagreements," Mustafa Hairan, *Al-Sahifah*, February 15, 2002; "The constitutional battle for constitutional recognition of Amazigh is an attempt to correct Moroccan identity: Brahim Akhiate confirms that constitutional recognition of Amazighity is essential to preserve linguistic and cultural peace," Asma Al-Amrani, *Al-Mustaqil*, February 14, 2002; "The Moroccan Association for Research and Cultural Exchange publishes a book renewing its demand the constitutional recognition of the Amazigh language" M.R., *Bayane Al Yaoume*, February 14, 2002; "Moroccan Amazigh activist Brahim Akhiate rejects politicization of the Amazigh issue because it transcends various ideologies," *Al-Sharq Al-Awsat*, February 14, 2002; "Calls for constitutional recognition of the Amazigh language as a national official language," *Al Ahdath Al Maghribiya*, February 2, 2002; "Brahim Akhiate at a seminar on the constitutional recognition of Taamzight: 'We are striving for a national consensus on constitutional recognition of the Amazigh language,'" *Al Tajdid*, February 15, 2002; "Brahim Akhiate: The Amazigh issue has become a cause," *Al Jumhour*, February 6, 2002; "Amazigh demands return to the forefront and 'constitutionalization' becomes more urgent," *Al Jumhour*, February 28, 2002. The news agency Agence France-Presse also attended the press conference, and the French newspaper *Libération* wrote about it, as did *Le Monde Amazigh*. Thus, the issue of the constitutional recognition of the Amazigh language became the topic of the hour at all political and public forums.

AMAZIGH ARTISTIC BREAKTHROUGHS

The year 2001 was notable for the fact that we began opening new cultural horizons to nurture and develop Amazigh culture through practice and writing. The association organized the first Amazigh Theater Festival from December 29–31 in Agadir, which became a stage for artistic competition and theatrical creativity, enabling Amazigh culture to grow through scriptwriting and the training of competent theater artists. This would also, in the future, provide the world of cinema with competent actors, just as the theater became a vibrant channel of communication between educated Amazighs—with their artistic creativity—and the audience. Theater could also contribute to deepening awareness of Amazigh identity of Moroccans in general.

For the same reasons and motives, the association organized the first Amazigh arts festival in the city of Beni-Mellal on November 9 and 10. These two days encompassed all manner of Amazigh arts, outside the realm of folklore with which these arts had long been presented, and which in the minds of many Moroccans were limited to dance and song. This program included an exhibition of paintings using Tifinagh script and a book exhibition, as well as seminars on Amazigh arts, covering architecture, architectural decoration, and traditional *zerbiyya* carpets. We also organized a night of theater and a literary/musical evening featuring the well-known musician Fatima Tabaamrant. The event was an opportunity to present the full range of Amazigh arts and their various schools, from the length and breadth of Morocco, and to correct the image imposed on these aspects of our national heritage.

TWO LANDMARK ROYAL SPEECHES, AND THE BIRTH OF THE ROYAL INSTITUTE OF AMAZIGH CULTURE

King Mohammed's Throne Speech in July 2001, marking the second anniversary of the young monarch's rule, was a momentous occasion not only for the Amazigh cause but for the future of Morocco and all Moroccans. Indeed, its ramifications stretched beyond Morocco's borders to the entire Amazigh homeland in North Africa. The parts of the speech dedicated to the Amazigh language, culture, and identity suggested that a quiet cultural revolution was underway in modern Morocco. The young king was the first monarch to talk about the Amazigh identity and the Amazigh people's legitimacy on its land in North Africa. Decades after most of the national territory had been liberated from foreign colonial occupation, I felt that this speech marked the start of the liberation of Morocco's national identity from dependency, enabling our national Amazigh language to enjoy sovereignty in its homeland at last, to grow and to develop with the will of the Amazigh people—that is, the people of Morocco and of the entire Amazigh nation. After the Amazigh people had fallen into a deep slumber over the sovereignty and official recognition of their national Amazigh language, and the dangers that threatened the Amazigh identity of the Amazigh people in their lands, this speech was like the announcement of the awakening of an entire people, both Amazigh speakers and nonspeakers, to revive Amazigh identity before it was too late, in contrast to the fate of many peoples who had lost their national languages in Egypt, Syria, Lebanon, and those of many peoples in Latin America. Thus, the Amazigh people in North Africa would become a leading example and a prototype for the liberation of a national identity from all forms of domination, provided the leadership has sincere intentions and a strong determination to achieve national awareness among the people about the importance of its true identity, which completes its independence and sovereignty.

The following is a key excerpt from His Majesty's Throne Day speech:

> Building on Our Majesty's belief that democracy is not only an embodiment of equality under a unified nation state of law, but must also enjoy cultural depth manifested in respect for the diversity of cultural and geographical specificities, and in giving them the appropriate space to endure, innovate and maintain their diversity in a way that weaves a harmonious national unity, we consider Throne Day, which embodies the unity of our people and the link between our past and our present, and which urges us to think about a better tomorrow for our nation, the prime occasion to candidly address you, our dear people, on a vital issue that concerns us all: namely, the issue of our distinctive national identity, which is characterized by diversity and pluralism, just as it is distinguished by cohesion, unity, and a unique character throughout history.
>
> Its pluralism stems from being constructed on diverse pillars: Amazigh, Arab, Sahrawi, African, and Andalusian, all of which contributed, through their openness and interaction with various cultures and civilizations, to honing and enriching our identity.

In another paragraph, His Majesty urged the Moroccan people, with courage and a firm and decisive will, to carry out vital reforms. He continued:

> At a time when we are undertaking decisive reforms in many important fields, armed in this struggle with a solid will, confident in the wisdom and courage of our people, draped in divine care that blesses every noble effort inspired by virtue, committed to strengthening the pillars of our ancient identity, and bearing in mind the necessity of giving a strong new impulse to our Amazigh culture, which constitutes our national wealth, to allow it to preserve, raise up and develop itself, we have decided, alongside our majesty and under our high patronage, to establish a Royal Institute of Amazigh Culture. We task this institute, as well as promoting Amazigh culture, to work alongside the relevant ministerial sectors to formulate, prepare and

monitor the process of integrating the Amazigh language into the education system.

We shall also task this institution, for which we shall soon oversee the preparation of the *ẓahīr* (royal decree) establishing it, with proposing appropriate policies to enhance the status of the Amazigh language in the social, cultural, and national media space, and in the local and regional affairs, thus embodying the cultural dimension of the new concept of authority that we insist on establishing and activating in an ongoing manner, so that all regions of the kingdom can manage their affairs within the framework of local democracy we are working to consolidate, within the scope of the nation's unity, in which we firmly believe.

The desire expressed in these paragraphs, and these decisive reforms, would find their interpretation and substance in the content of the decree establishing the Royal Institute of Amazigh Culture, whose mention alone was a revolutionary project for the benefit of the Amazigh cause, and a rational initiative to liberate our national identity and build a new Morocco, reconciled with itself, strong in its distinctive personality, glorious and ancient in its history. These, in my view, were the landmarks of a revolution that was coming to fruition in our country.

Given the importance of this event, the association did not hesitate to issue a statement praising the speech and the good news it represented for the Amazigh and for Morocco in general. We said it was a national cause and one for which we were all responsible, and that His Majesty had vindicated our stance, confirming that Amazigh was the responsibility of all Moroccans. We also expressed our appreciation of his speech and all that it contained. Our statement read:

> The National Office of the Moroccan Association for Research and Cultural Exchange met in Rabat on Tuesday, July 21, 2001, and discussed the content of the Throne Speech on the occasion of the second anniversary of His Majesty King Mohammed VI's ascension to the throne of his blessed ancestors. It announces to the Moroccan public the following:
>
> • The Association holds in high esteem His Majesty's great reformist steps, aimed at completing the construction of the foundations of a modern, social democratic project, based on the objective realities of our identity and civilization, and which aspires to

consolidate the state of law, rights and citizenship while achieving comprehensive development.

- It considers the decision to establish the Royal Institute of Amazigh Culture, under His Majesty's patronage and within his broad prerogatives, a historic move and a bold step toward restoring Amazigh language, culture, and identity.
- It calls on all components of the Amazigh cultural movement and all democratic forces to contribute fully and mobilize effectively to implement this comprehensive, modern democratic reform project, and to stand firmly against its opponents, notably the anti-Amazigh lobby.
- It hopes that the creation of this Institute will be a first step toward providing constitutional protection to Tamazight as a national and official language, alongside Arabic.

Thus, we clearly laid out our position on this bold and historical step by His Majesty King Mohammed VI toward liberating our national identity and construct a democratic Morocco reconciled with itself, with a strength borne of will, so it could build a future at the hands of all its children.

THE APPOINTMENT OF THE BOARD OF THE ROYAL INSTITUTE OF AMAZIGH CULTURE

In the last paragraph of our statement, we indirectly expressed our hope that the king's announcement of the creation of the Institute was not simply a kind of lip service aimed at calming the situation. This had been the case with the 1994 speech of the late Hassan II, who had promised to integrate the Amazigh language into education but whose promise was never implemented. However, His Majesty King Mohammed VI was as good as his word. He promptly issued instructions to prepare for the creation of the Royal Institute of Amazigh Culture, in fulfillment of his vow. On the morning of Friday, September 21, 2001, I received a call from royal advisor Abdelaziz Meziane Belfkih, who asked me urgently to meet him at his office. He insisted that I provide him with a list of the names of Amazigh linguists, writers, and activists whom I could suggest as members of the board of directors for the Institute announced by His Majesty.

This request came as a surprise to me, especially as I was asked to provide him with the list that same day, a Friday, by 5.30 p.m. I took great care in drawing it up, to be neutral and to avoid succumbing to the pressures of my affiliations to a region or to the association, or any other consideration, and to be fair and equitable to the people I know in the Amazigh movement, whether cultural and intellectual activists or those at the universities. I felt I carried a great responsibility on my shoulders: toward the state, on the one hand, and toward the Amazigh cause on the other. Therefore, I acted responsibly and knew I would bear the consequences of my choices. After I had drawn up an initial list, I presented it to Mr Belfkih, who received me in the afternoon of Friday, September 21, 2001, in his office at the head-quarters of the committee for the Charter on Education and Training. I had detailed this first list with the achievements of each person in their area of specialization or their intellectual interests or affiliations with associations, as well as their birthplaces and approximate ages. The advisor also asked me to give my opinion on some of the names he presented to me, and he explained to me why he had chosen me for these tasks, both of suggest-ing the list and giving an opinion on some of the names: In his opinion, I was a veteran of the Amazigh movement, and the association I head has gained a good reputation in its long struggle over four decades. Hence, he had decided that I should share this responsibility with him, and he would rely extensively on my help. As we were browsing some of the names, he showed me personal files on the candidates. I asked him about these clip-pings, saying, "Aren't these clippings prepared by 'The Information?'" He immediately understood that I meant the interior ministry, but he denied this and said that they were the work of his assistants, who had worked to collect this information through articles and writings they had found in newspapers and publications on the Amazigh issue—not from intelligence sources at the Ministry of the Interior.

Some of the files contained errors concerning people's specialisms, regional origins, and affiliations with associations or their history of activ-ism, which I corrected, to ensure that the information was correct and that the selection would be based on sound criteria. At this first meeting, I gave the advisor an initial list of fifteen proposed names of cultural activists and association figures. As he examined it, his eye caught the name of Ahmed Assid, whom I had included, despite Assid's criticism of me. The advisor jok-ingly said, "Here's your friend." I replied, "I always leave my answers to such people to history and to their consciences. But since you have entrusted me with the responsibility of proposing names, which is a national responsibil-ity on a scale I fully understand, I've made my proposals considering nothing but their abilities, their intellectual capacities and their role in the struggle, regardless of our personal disputes or differences in opinion." I also made sure that the advisor would consult others, particularly Mohammed Chafik, for more suggestions of names he might see as necessary and qualified for membership of the institute's board of directors.

The advisor also raised the issue of the title of the head of the institute and whether this person should be called the president, director or dean. We agreed on the title "dean" ('amīd), as the body was to be an academic institution, and the title of dean commands esteem and respect. As we were leaving his office, I asked about the roles and responsibilities of the board members concerning the management and direction of the institution, and whether they would receive financial compensation appropriate to the role they were taking on. The advisor did not have time to think about this question, as I had surprised him with it, but he said the work would be voluntary and without compensation. I did not discuss this spontaneous response with him further but left the discussion for our meeting the next day.

The following Saturday, at 4:00 p.m., I met Mr Belfkih again so I could provide him with another list of eight further suggestions for the board of directors, and so we could continue our conversation on the topic and everything related to it. We waited for a while in the department's garden before the guard came to open the office for us. As were waiting, we discussed some of the names on the list, underlining some names, double-underlining others, and not marking some names at all. Our conversation then turned to the question of Tifinagh script. I explained to him that the association supported the writing of Tamazight in its Tifinagh script because we saw the subject of identity in its entirety, and the Tifinagh script as a fundamental element in the Amazigh identity. He told me that he could not imagine street signs in public places written in Tifinagh. However, I told him that reactions to such a move would be like anything new in life, but it would become familiar over time. When we reached his office, our conversation continued on such important matters, alongside our discussion of the names. He asked me if I had any suggestions of names or ideas about who should head the institute. Before I answered, I asked him, "Would it be possible for a current advisor to the king to take on this task?" He quickly answered, "No, that would be impossible." I asked this in order to find out whether it was possible to put forward Hassan Aourid, or the advisor himself. Having ruled out this possibility, I told him I knew four people I believed were the most capable of taking on this responsibility, according to my knowledge of them. The first was Mohammed Chafik, who was a statesman and already knew His Majesty. The professor knew the workings of the state thanks to his experience in several administrative and educational positions, and he was an academic man. My second suggestion was Ahmed Toufiq. Belfkih interrupted me, asking, "Who is Ahmed Toufiq?" I said he was minister of endowments and

Islamic affairs, who had managed the Institute of African Studies and had done a great job as professor of history at the Faculty of Letters and Human Sciences in Rabat. He also knew Tamazight, Arabic, French, and English, all of which qualified him well for this task. The third name I suggested was El Houssaïn El Moujahid, who was an administrator of great caliber on whom Professor Toufiq relied in managing the Institute of African Studies, had gained experience in several institutions, and was able to communicate well and manage problems intelligently. I also proposed Ahmed Boukous, due to his scholarly abilities and his loyalty to the Amazigh struggle. He was a founding member of AMREC, which had set this struggle in motion. Here, the advisor interrupted me and said that if Moujahid were not chosen as the dean, he would be made general secretary. I asked if Professor Chafik had already been contacted regarding the selection of members of the administrative board. He replied that this would be done after other matters had been settled and his team had a clear vision of how the project would look. After we had finished discussing the questions of roles and who might fill them, I reminded him again of the question I had raised in our previous discussion: whether members of the board would be compensated. He had previously told me that their participation would be voluntary, so I cautioned him that many in the Amazigh movement would see this decision as having a political dimension, if Amazigh-related jobs were the only ones not paid by the state. Thus, we would see the state's refusal to pay members of the board as an insult to the activists, intellectuals, and cultural figures involved, as well as an insult to Amazigh culture itself, whose dignity we were working to restore. The advisor understood that such a policy could harm the project in everybody's eyes before a single step had been taken toward launching it. He told me that he would suggest that the institute's board be run on the same terms as the Royal Academy. For the record, in the first list I submitted to him, I included twenty-one names, along with a further eight on the second, making a total of twenty-nine people. When the composition of the board was announced, His Majesty appointed Mohammed Chafik as the institute's first dean. As they consulted, it emerged that nine of the people I had proposed had been chosen for the administrative board: Ahmed Boukous, Jilali al-Saib, Essafi Moumen Ali, Ali Khedaoui, Ahmed Assid, Hassan Banhakeia, Abdelsalam Khalfi, Mohammed El-Chami, and me.

I note here that since I had declined to sign Professor Chafik's statement, with the subsequent developments and the fate of the statement itself, I had not visited the professor. The situation had pushed me to cut off ties with him so that our relationship would not be misinterpreted, especially after he was appointed as dean of the institute, and as ever more activists called him and he was nominated for more positions. Indeed, I had no contact with him, except in Ajdir, where we were invited to listen to His Majesty's speech and to read the decree creating the Amazigh Language Institute, on October 17, 2001.

I also note that the authorities had invited most of the people I had put forward for the board, although I did not inform them, except those belonging to the association, whom I began contacting them by phone to find out whether they had been summoned to Ajdir or not, without telling them that I had submitted a list including their names. One of these was Ali Khedaoui, who accompanied me in the car to Ajdir along with Essafi Moumen Ali. Khedaoui wondered why he had been invited, and as he insisted, I told him that I had submitted a list to Royal advisor Abdelaziz Meziane Belfkih that included his name. I told him I had written the two lists by hand, and that Belfkih had kept the originals while I had kept copies as proof.

The local authorities in Rabat had contacted me by phone to confirm my attendance. They insisted that everyone gather at the prefecture of Khénifra in formal black suits. Indeed, upon our arrival at the prefecture, then-minister of interior Driss Jettou—whom I had known since 1975 when he was managing a footwear company in Casablanca—welcomed me and my companions. He was with Belfkih and Dr. Abbas El-Jirari.

A DIVISIVE "ANTI-RACISM" PETITION

During this period, politician Abdellatif Ouammou led an initiative by the Party of Progress and Socialism (PPS)'s "Renewal and Democratic Progress Team" in the House of Representatives, presenting a bill aimed at amending Article 1 of the Journalism Law, related to tackling racism (Chapters 39 bis. and 44 bis.). The bill, No. 86 of May 10, 2002, was cosigned by Ouammou, Masoudi Ayachi, and Aïssa Ouardighi.

In parallel with this bill, the French-language weekly *La Verité* published a petition calling for opposition to racism, in its Issue 68 of May 3–9, 2002. The petition carried a preamble stating that it "opposes practices against the Jews, on the part of extremist movements, and against the Arabs, on the part of certain Amazigh extremists." It became clear that those behind this petition, signed by many ministers in the government of alternation and by well-known intellectual and political figures, were the leaders of the PPS. The party's "Unity and Democratic Progress Team" in parliament had submitted a bill aiming both to supplement the Press Law and to complement the Penal Code on aspects related to combating racism. It stipulated punishment for any person, entity, or institution found guilty of practicing any form of racial discrimination against any person or group of persons. Ouammou, a Progress and Socialism MP, explained this in a statement under the title "Yes to a Law Against Racism, No to All Forms of Racial Discrimination."

However, this came after the launch of a campaign against the petition. What caused this storm of violent responses was that the magazine had published the petition alongside this paragraph linking the Amazigh cause with racism, and that this had been signed by a large number of state officials, political leaders, and thinkers. This made it impossible for us to remain silent about the incident and the support the petition had attracted. Therefore, in response to this unpatriotic behavior, aimed at distorting the noble aims of the Amazigh cultural movement, the Amazigh associations responded appropriately by rejecting it and calling for its perpetrators to be held accountable. Since the majority of the petition's signatories were from the PPS, a member of the party's political bureau, Nabil Benabdallah, tried to find a way out of this predicament, especially as the 2002 legislative elections were rapidly approaching. Benabdallah claimed that the magazine had contacted them asking to sign a petition against racism, without making them aware of the preamble. Thus, he explained, they had signed it on principle. Then, when the petition was published in the magazine, they considered it incomplete and incorrect, and asked the magazine's editors to correct the mistake. They had then added to the offending phrase in the preamble the phrase "acts of racial discrimination directed by some Arabs against the Amazigh." Benabdallah added that after this correction there was no longer an issue, as in his view the party rejected racism, and was working in the House of Representatives to propose a bill in this area.

But this attempt to absolve the party from the petition was unconvincing, as evidenced by the fact that most of the signatories were from this party, including its secretary-general himself, who was minister of agriculture in the government of alternation. However, the affair did not stop there. PPS activists began to object to their names being included on the list of signatories, including Mohammed Salou and Mohammed Boudra, members of the party's central committee. As Amazigh associations and activists continued to issue statements against the petition, signatories began issuing a trickle of their own statements announcing that they were withdrawing their names, claiming that they had been victims of the magazine. They said the journalists had called them to ask for their signatures, without informing them of the offending preamble. The press published a statement by Abdelkrim Benatiq, then-minister of foreign trade, who wrote that he did not know that the petition included a reference to the Amazigh question. Similarly, the minister of human rights Mohamed Aujjar said he had signed on principle, in opposition to racism, without being aware of the text. Thus, one by one, the signatories withdrew their names, claiming that they had agreed to sign the petition over the phone without reading its text. The only person who broke with this consensus was education minister Abdallah Saaf, who declared that he stood by his signature on the petition and clung to his Arab nationalism. The weekly magazine *Maghreb Al Yaoum* published an article to this effect, with a picture of the minister, in its edition of May 23–29, 2002.

The Amazigh associations made various statements against this racist petition. AMREC issued a statement on May 7, 2002, on the subject and on our view of the 2002 legislative elections. It noted, in particular:

- Our bafflement that defenders of Amazigh linguistic and cultural rights were being singled out and accused of racism, being described as "Amazigh extremists" who practice racism against Arabs.
- Our condemnation of this reversal of facts, by which victims demanding their rights were portrayed as the oppressor.
- We called on all Morocco's democratic forces, whether political parties, associations or human rights groups, to denounce this irresponsible, racist stance, which would only encourage extremism and intolerance, and to strongly oppose any similar attempts.
- We called on all components of the Amazigh movement to intensify and coordinate their efforts to achieve Amazigh demands, and to use the upcoming legislative elections as an opportunity to expose and punish the opponents of Amazigh linguistic and cultural rights as the enemies of progress, democracy, national unity, and social peace.

Human rights organizations also backed the Amazigh associations in their position against the petition. The Moroccan Center for Human Rights issued a statement saying that it did not consider the Amazigh movement nor the nationalist movement racist, as long as their goal was to promote coexistence within the framework of unity. It also called on all national forces and activists to remain vigilant to the danger of being dragged into issues of coordination of efforts of convergence, and to build reciprocal acceptance between all cultural and ideological groups seeking coexistence under the umbrella of the one nation.

The national press covered this backlash against the petition, raising doubts about the intentions of its writers. On May 17, *Al-Ousboue* weekly newspaper published an article in its "The First Step on a Slippery Slope" section titled "Ministers Sign an Anti-racism Petition—and the Amazigh

Decide to Punish Them." The article featured a picture of me and of Minister Abdallah Saaf, as the writer had misunderstood our association's statement as a call to use the elections to punish all those behind the petition. The *Amazigh World* newspaper also published an article titled "The Newspaper of Trust Against the Truth," while *Attajdid* published an article on May 22 under the title "An Anti-Racism Petition Casts Its Shadow over the Upcoming Elections," whose author Driss El Ganbouri highlighted my personal stance after this hail of responses against the petition. As I told him, we had two options: to vote punitively or boycott the elections entirely. This was indeed the angle of his article. *Al Haraka* newspaper published a front-page article on May 11: "Amazigh Activists Demand the Trial of Four Ministers."

Al-Mustaqil published an article titled "Interactions over the Case of the Anti-Racism Petition," analyzing the points we had made in our statement. It particularly noted our regret that the Arab nationalist extremists continued with their erroneous and systematic opposition to Amazigh linguistic and cultural rights—first and foremost, the minister of national education, who was a leading member of the Democratic Socialist Party, and who had been a leading signatory of the petition against the Amazigh. *Al Haraka* also published a piece on May 22, part of its coverage of our statement, under the title "The Anti-Amazigh Petition: A New Version of Linguistic Discrimination." In the same edition, it published another article titled "The Left's Petition Against Racism: The Amazigh Are Described as Racist for the First Time in Their History."

However, the most important article on the subject was by the journalist Mustapha Antara, *Al-Mustaqil*, on May 20, 2002, under the large title "The Petition of Sedition." It said that serving ministers, Arab nationalists, want to swim against the current of the royal will, and that activists from the Amazigh movement are in a showdown with the Arabist racist current, raising a strong prayer of condemnation.

Following this barrage of protest and articles in various media outlets, through which members of the Amazigh movement expressed their indignation, the magazine and those behind the petition attempted to alleviate the pressure on themselves by adding to the preamble the phrase: "Acts of racial discrimination directed by some Arabs against the Amazigh." However, this only confirmed the malevolence of its writers and changed nothing. One result of this campaign against them was that some of them were unable to run in the legislative elections, as they were certain that we would run a ferocious campaign against them. Many candidates from the Progress and Socialism Party also met with a chilly reception in their constituencies due to their party's involvement in this racist petition.

If we consider the magnitude and timing of this incident, it is impossible to conclude that it was accidental or a simple miscalculation by the magazine, which somehow inadvertently published this preamble accusing the Amazigh of racism, for the first time in their history. Rather, it was a calculated move by certain parties, and one that victimized others. In my opinion, the enemies of the Amazigh cause within Morocco's body politic could not stomach the intellectual and political developments underway in Moroccan society and the gains made by the Amazigh movement during that period. Nor could they comprehend the groundbreaking royal directives contained in the Throne Speech and the Ajdir Speech of 2001. They believed that these tendencies would diminish their own ideological and cultural influence in our country and, furthermore, would take Morocco further and further from Arab influence and from the Arab political and cultural system. Therefore, they had attempted—through this failed plot—to stir up tensions, in order to reshuffle the cards and put the Amazigh cause in the dock, urging state institutions to backtrack on the achievements we had made for the Amazigh language and Amazigh culture, pending the fulfilment of our other demands. Of course, all this was in opposition to the express directions of the king. The position of the education minister Abdallah Saaf was particularly clear. These people, it appeared, had not grasped the lessons of history but had adopted intellectual terrorism against us by evoking the so-called Berber Dahir to weaken our will and accuse us of being the descendants of the colonial Resident-General Hubert Lyautey who signed it. Some of their thinkers' writings attempted to erase, at the stroke of a pen, our history and identity. This was particularly true of the writings of Abdelkrim Ghallab. His February 1977 article for *Al-Doha* magazine, "The Arab Identity of This Morocco" is just one example. In it, he wrote, "It is a little-known fact that Morocco belongs to the Arab world due to genealogy." To summarize, the real question is this: Who are the real racists in this proud country, whose citizens have coexisted for thousands of years, without the issue of racism between them ever being raised, until we ourselves were ourselves accused of racism?

However, the exposure of this plot from the start, the firm response by the Amazigh movement, and the declarations by some signatories to the petition that they had been tricked and that there was something odd about the conspiratorial methods used to persuade them to sign it without first reading it, all helped thwart this conspiracy against the Amazigh cause. Another factor that helped was the timing. The petition's publication as the country was preparing for elections meant that reactions to it posed a threat to the interests and future of the political elite, which was seeking to win over the electorate. Statements by associations and declarations by various figures, threatening to boycott the elections in order to punish the signatories of the petition and their political parties, dealt the knockout blow.

This episode demonstrated to everyone that the Amazigh movement was alert and aware of the political situation in our country, day by day. It also showed us that the political awareness of Amazigh activists, as Moroccan citizens, had deepened, accumulating experiences that would provide us with immunity and strength to counter all the plots being hatched against our cause as we continued to struggle in order to achieve all our demands with awareness and responsibility.

OUR BATTLE WITHIN THE MOVEMENT FOR A DEMOCRATIC CONSTITUTION

Another aspect of the political shift in 2002 was that civil society, represented by political bodies, organizations, and cultural associations, began taking initiatives reflecting the concerns and aspirations of society, despite the marked absence of the traditional parties of the Koutla—Istiqlal, the USFP, and the PPS—after they had taken power as part of the government of alternation. King Mohammed VI's accession to the throne also fueled civil society's hopes for change, both in terms of how the country was governed and in terms of the source of power—that is to say, the constitution. This document had undergone some amendments in 1996 during the life of the late Hassan II. Now, everyone was hoping for further amendments to reflect popular aspirations for a more democratic life in the era of the new King.

This prompted a large group of civil society organizations to call for the establishment of a movement to demand a democratic constitution. From mid-2002 onward, several preparatory meetings were held to prepare for the launch of this movement. They were first convened by the youth associations of the parties making up the Koutla. AMREC soon joined, from the Amazigh movement, and the network started to broaden as we suggested that the Tamaynut association join. More invitations went out to political parties and organizations, depending on what was to be agreed, until some twenty-seven associations, civil society bodies, and political parties were involved. The initiative was launched from the headquarters of the Moroccan National Press Union (SNPM) on May 20, 2002, by the following organizations: the youth wings of the Socialist Union of Popular Forces, Socialist, Democratic and Istiqlal parties, the Moroccan Association for Human Rights, the Moroccan Writers' Union, the Movement of Moroccan Democratic Socialists, the

Civilizational Alternative Association, the Party of Progress and Socialism, the Loyalty to Democracy current, AMREC, the Tamaynut Association, the Truth and Justice Forum, the Moroccan Association for Progressive Women, and the Movement for the Nation and the Democratic Way.

Given the multifarious nature of this gathering, the first challenge it had to overcome was to establish a theoretical foundation for its work, representing the lowest common denominator on which all its members could agree. From the outset, it was clear that all the member organizations, from progressive to Islamic, were solely focused on constitutional amendments related to power, the division thereof, and reducing the powers of the monarch. None of these organizations addressed other issues related to development, culture, and national identity. This prompted us to place such matters at the top of our own priorities in these discussions, resulting in several heated discussions with some parties, including Abderrahman Ben Amrou, who urged us to avoid the issue of identity, claiming that the movement's members would not be able to agree on a formula on the subject. Moustafa Moatasim, from the Civilizational Alternative, argued that for his organization, the country's identity was Islam, and therefore there was no need to debate it further. In the face of this challenge, Lahcene Ouazi and I, as the sole representatives of the Amazigh movement amid this crowd of Arabist-Islamist organizations, threatened to withdraw from the project unless it was agreed that we discuss identity as a central topic. The questions of identity and linguistic and cultural rights were the main elements omitted from the existing constitution at the time, and we could certainly not take part if the founding document of the movement made no mention of Morocco's national identity or the question of cultural rights, which lay at the heart of our demands. As we insisted on these demands, everyone was forced to accept the consensual formula we contributed to drafting, expressing the desire on which we had insisted. Thus, we imposed the question of identity as a subject for a national conference of the movement.

At a meeting on June 24, 2002, we discussed the location for the press conference to announce the birth of this movement. At first, we selected the hall of the Moroccan Arab News Agency, but the agency's management refused to give us permission, due to the sensitivity of the subject. What is more, it banned its journalists from covering the press conference at all, which we decided to hold at the press association on July 6, 2002. I was elected by the participating organizations to preside over the press conference, which took place after the last meeting on June 24, 2002, at the headquarters of the Moroccan press association. This was, for me and for my brothers in the Amazigh movement, an honor for our movement and a recognition by everyone of the seriousness of our work and a sign of appreciation for our steadfast positions in defending our cause, long marginalized by these organizations.

In my introduction to the announcement of the "Movement to Demand a Democratic Constitution," I focused on the circumstances that had given rise to the initiative, some of which I have mentioned above. I also spoke of the timing of the press conference, just prior to the start of campaigning for the 2002 elections. I emphasized that the current constitution was no longer fit to bring about a state based on institutions and the rule of law, and noted that the political, social, and cultural developments Moroccan society had undergone also reflected the need to change the constitution. I also pointed out that this attempt to establish a movement demanding a democratic constitution was the first of its kind, rising from the various components of civil society rather than from initiatives by political parties. This initiative, then, broke the monopoly that the authorities and parties had held over politics, in the absence of civil society. The conference was attended by a large number of journalists and representatives of organizations active in the movement, as well as a distinguished presence of actors from the Amazigh movement.[3]

After they had spoken and had a chance to read the draft "Announcement of the Establishment of the Movement to Demand a Democratic Constitution," there was a lengthy discussion, particularly over the final two paragraphs, which stated:

- The framework to demand constitutional amendments is to be called the "Movement to Demand a Democratic Constitution."
- This body shall undertake the initiatives required by this task of struggle, which aims to allow our country to enjoy a democratic constitution, guarantee political, civil, economic, social, and cultural human rights, protecting our national identity and Morocco's unique character, and ensuring the sovereignty of the people as the source of all powers.

The audiovisual media covered this meeting, and in my statement to them, I reiterated what I had said at the start of the seminar, to further promote these ideas. The national press also covered the event, publishing several articles on the topic. Journalist Asma El Amrani wrote in the weekly newspaper *Al-Mustaqil* on July 10, 2002: "The creation of a movement demanding constitutional amendments has broken the political parties' monopoly on politics." *Casa* newspaper's Abderrahim Tafnout published an article on July 9, 2002, under the title "The 1908 Constitution, a

Missed Opportunity." *Al-Ahdath Al-Maghribiyya*'s Oussi Mouh Lahcene wrote an article called "The Announcement of the Founding of the Movement Demanding a Democratic Constitution," dated July 2002. *Casa* also published an extensive analytical article about the event on July 12, under the title "Consensus on an Issue . . . How Hard It Is to Reach." It said:

> What distinguishes this initiative, fundamentally, is the circumstances in which it was launched: Morocco's entry into the political whirlwind of discussion and preparation for the upcoming elections. We are nearing the end of the term of the consensus government, which many Moroccans had hoped would undertake much-needed reforms, including constitutional reform, even though the three parties of the *Koutla* had turned a blind eye to the constitutional demands despite having insisted on it previously. . . . This also demonstrates the growing strength of civil society, which has started gradually to assert itself, and here it is today, contributing—or rather, taking the initiative, for the first time in Morocco, to create an associative, intellectual and political framework to demand a true democratic constitution.

Al-Ousboue weekly newspaper wrote about the event on July 12, under the title "In an Attempt to Hold the Funeral of the Traditional Parties, Multiple Political Forces Demand a Constitutional Amendment." The following is an excerpt:

> The initial press conference to announce the demand for a constitutional amendment was chaired by the president of the Moroccan Association for Research and Cultural Exchange, Brahim Akhiate, who represents the Amazigh camp which demands that the Amazigh language be included in the constitution, although it does not differ from other political currents in its demands for a constitution that delineates the powers of each party in the state.

We at AMREC paid close attention to this episode, given our conviction of the need to contribute, along with other components of civil society, to the construction of Moroccan society and to nurture responsible dialogue with all its components to map out the future horizons of our country. Based on this principle, we made the headquarters of our association available for the movement's various meetings, and as I was the general coordinator of this movement, we set the program of the movement and decided to organize three national conferences to sensitize public opinion to the work of the movement and the need for constitutional amendments.

The first took place in Rabat, on the topic of "The Separation of Powers and Mechanisms of Democratic Government." The second was in Meknes, addressing "Constitutional Guarantees for Human Rights and National Identity," and the third was in Marrakech, on the topic of "The Constitution and Mechanisms of Popular Oversight." All these conferences went ahead at the scheduled time and place, and were attended by many prominent experts, researchers, and activists from the world of politics and associations. We took part in all of these meetings, but we particularly focused on the one about identity, in Meknes, where I personally delivered an intervention whose contents had been agreed by AMREC, Tamaynut, and Azetta, the Amazigh Network for Citizenship. Dr. Khalid Naciri and Mohamed Atarguine also took part, alongside a gentleman representing the Islamist current. The Amazigh movement had a significant presence in the hall at this meeting, which resulted in a large and enthusiastic discussion, given the political and cultural sensitivity of the topic of identity.

After these seminars, we had planned to prepare a report synthesizing all the ideas that had been aired there, to serve as the groundwork for a national gathering of the movement, set for May 24–25, 2003, in Bouznika. We sent a request for a booking to the conference center on March 12, 2003, in the name of four associations: ourselves, the Democratic Youth Movement, the Tamaynut Association, and the Istiqlal Youth. However, I had been busy organizing the Spring of Amazigh Culture in Rabat, which our association held in March. Our colleagues who had been tasked with drafting the report took advantage of my absence to prepare a document that excluded the issue of identity and the cultural dimension from every section. When I met them after the end of our cultural festival, still at the association's headquarters, they caught me by surprise with this paper, in which I noticed the systematic exclusion of questions of identity and the cultural dimension. Some of them began to justify this, on the pretext that we needed to avoid everything over which we differed, and other baseless excuses. This led me to reject the document in its entirety. I prepared my written notes on topics that had been excluded and presented them to the writers for discussion by their organizations, for acceptance or rejection. My categorical rejection of the paper in its initial form was shared by the Tamaynut Association. I informed Abdellah Hitous of my position and my reasons, and he confirmed his support for my stance. Thus, it became clear to me that our colleagues at these organizations were still unable to overcome their hostile attitudes toward the Amazigh question, or to understand the critical significance and status of the two points on which we were insisting: acknowledgment of the Amazigh dimension as a fundamental aspect of Morocco's national identity, and the status of Amazigh language, culture, and civilization in the democratic constitution to come. These principles could not be abandoned or overlooked for any reason.

Faced with our insistence and our steadfast position, and after they had consulted their political bodies, it became clear to me that they were incapable of transcending their selective view of the constitutional amendment. Thus, they had fallen into a terrible contradiction with globally accepted concepts of democracy and human rights in their entirety. Their view of democracy was narrow and far removed from the comprehensive concepts recognized internationally. After this, they stopped coming to the association's headquarters, indicating their inability to maintain a serious discussion about identity and linguistic and cultural rights—or to justify their negative positions toward the Amazigh question.

Activity within the movement demanding a democratic constitution drew to a halt, or became limited to a few organizations who leaned toward the same ideology, so we could no longer see any reason for this framework to exist, except to publish a book in the name of the movement, summarizing all the statements and positions of the various currents that had formed the movement since its inception but failed to formulate any unified stance on the constitutional amendment desired. After this book was published, those remaining in the movement made another attempt to build bridges with the Amazigh movement and formulate an agreed position on the status of the Amazigh question in the constitution. The movement organized a seminar on Sunday, December 19, 2004, at the Larbi Rodiyas venue in Rabat's Mellah district. It was attended by many speakers from the Arab nationalist current, opposed to the Amazigh, who came hoping to impose their ideas on the seminar. However, they failed to do so, in the face of the firmness and objectivity of our demands for the inclusion of the Amazigh dimension as a fundamental aspect of our national identity, and for the official recognition of Tamazight alongside Arabic. With this firm position, we insisted that there could be no democracy without the Amazigh language, culture, and civilization having a presence in democratic constitution we were demanding. The association was represented at this decisive seminar by brothers from its national office: Dr. Abdelaziz Bouras, Dr. Ali Belkadi, and Dr. Mubarak Al-Ardi. Our association's relationship with all components of the movement remained natural and consultative.

I have narrated this episode as an example of our relationship with some political groups and associations, primarily on the "progressive democratic" left to demonstrate the extent of the suffering we endured in our dialogues with them, because they were unable to deal objectively with the reality of Morocco's culture, civilization, and identity.

THE STRUGGLE WITHIN THE BOARD OF DIRECTORS OF THE ROYAL INSTITUTE OF AMAZIGH CULTURE

The formation of the institute's board of directors was finally announced and held its first meeting on July 25, 2002, in the hall of the Royal Academy. This meeting was attended by the appointments committee, which consisted of the kingdom's historian Abdelwahab Ben Mansour, royal advisor Abdelaziz Meziane Belfkih, palace spokesman Hassan Aourid, and Dr. Abdellatif Berbich, the secretary of the Royal Academy.

The board of directors comprised three groups: one representing organs of the state (the interior, education, and culture ministries, academies, and universities), a group of Amazigh activists, and a third group of intellectual and administrative actors.

After the departure of the appointments committee that had overseen this inauguration, we all returned to the meeting room to hold the first official meeting of the board, chaired by the dean, Professor Mohammed Chafik. He spoke of the contents of the royal decree establishing the institute, the body's role in promoting Amazigh culture, how the board would operate, and other ideas and suggestions relating to the council's work. When the discussion began, I was the first to speak. I began by congratulating all the members of the board on the trust placed in them by His Majesty when he selected them as its members and told them that the creation of this institute should be seen as just the first step toward achieving the other goals of the Amazigh movement. I also made an important point that Professor Chafik had neglected to mention in his remarks, which was that we must remember that this achievement was the fruit of the Amazigh movement's struggle over more than three decades. It was therefore not a gift or a grant, but rather a response to the Amazigh cultural movement and an official recognition of the legitimacy of its demands, as well as of the struggle of its heroes, some of whom we had lived alongside and others whom we did not know. Therefore, I said, we should remember and acknowledge them on this occasion, recalling those who had passed away, such as Abdellah El-Rahmani Jachtimi from Agadir, who was both a prominent activist and a researcher and investigator of manuscripts of Amazigh culture, as well as being a pioneer in Amazigh associations. Another was Mohammed Ait El Haj, from Ait Ouarayn,

Guercif, an educator and a graduate of the Qarawiyyin University (in Fes). Then there were Mohamed Mezouar, from northern Guercif, an exceptional educator and activist; Hassan Atbaji, from Azilane, a university professor and major researcher and activist; Qadi Qaddour from Nador, a university professor and activist; Mohammed Nait Abdelhmid from Ahermoumou, a hero of the resistance, notable activist, and writer; and Muhammad Albensir (widely known as Mohamed Demsiri), a musician and activist who was committed to his art and his cause. I added that we must not forget the missing activists of whose fate we still knew nothing, despite how much we, the associations, had asked the authorities—the Ministry of the Interior and the Advisory Council for Human Rights—to reveal what had happened to them. Here I specifically mentioned the activist and university researcher Boujoumaa El-Habbaz, one of the founders of AMREC in 1967, who had been missing since 1981. I continued:

> It is also our duty on such occasions to mention our appreciation for the struggle of our brothers who were arrested for the Amazigh cause, and were prisoners of conscience in our country. I recall our brother Ali Sidqi Azaykou, who was tried and imprisoned in the summer of 1982, and is present with us as a member of this council, and the brothers in the Tilelli Cultural Association in Errachidia, Ali Harsh El-Rass, Taous Omar, and Ali Yaken.
>
> Therefore, gentlemen, this occasion, and particularly this first session of the Institute's Board of Directors, should not pass without us expressing our appreciation and acknowledgment to them all for the sacrifices they made to achieve our legitimate goals, among which was the creation of such an institute responsible for standardizing and developing Amazigh language and culture.
>
> Thus, we must acknowledge that we are here thanks to the sacrifices of such activists, both the living and the deceased, as well those who continue to fight to achieve the remaining legitimate demands of the Amazigh movement. We did not arrive here without reason or by coincidence. This is the trust and the historical duty I felt from the first moment, and which I must fulfill toward all these people, at this moment in particular, so please forgive me if I have spoken too long.

My remarks were the first of a series of similar comments, by which the activists present distinguished themselves from the other groups on the board. I also noticed the embarrassment and annoyance felt by some members, who were not comfortable with being reminded of the Amazigh movement's struggle, despite the fact it had led to the creation of the institute and their presence at this very meeting.

Upon our exit from the hall, many of my activist brothers gathered around me and congratulated me, saying that it would have been unreasonable and unjust were this historic occasion to pass without mention of the struggle waged by the movement and its activists.

One issue that had been under discussion from the start was that the dean and some of the university professors on the council insisted that the institute was a purely academic, scholarly institution whose role was limited to the development of the Amazigh language and culture in a purely scientific manner, and that it had no political role. We as activists, by contrast, considered the board as an advisory institution, meaning that it did not operate in isolation from the political aspects of the subject in its formulation of strategies and its relationship with its surroundings. Our presence on the board, as activists, reflected the will of the royal court that we play an advisory role in managing Amazigh affairs, offering strategic proposals on current issues related to the management of the Amazigh question. The board of directors, as the political element of the institution, would thus take decisions, while the research centers would be responsible for executing the strategy decided by the board. As activists, this was our view of our role on the council.

Due to these contrasting perspectives, we were always in a state of quasi-confrontation in our discussions, and the other party appeared uncomfortable when we used political terms in our analyses. One early error by the institute was to appoint directors to the institute's research centers before the final list of board members was revealed. This resulted in a clash of roles, as a board member could end up also acting as director for one of the research centers, meaning that he would always take positions on the board that would serve his interests as a research center director. That is to say, he would take sides with the researchers and abandon his role as a member of the board, which had the final say on any decisions. This contradiction led to major problems until it was overcome through their substitution later on.

Another aspect of the disputes within the board during the early years of the institute arose from the residual tension over Professor Chafik's statement, which I have discussed above. The board included the people who had signed it, particularly those who were on the statement's committee, who had been brought onto the board by Dr. Chafik through his consultations with advisor Belfkih. This group considered itself a powerful lobby due to its relationship with the dean. There was also a group that had refrained from signing the statement and was mainly composed of members of the board of AMREC. Therefore, all our discussions on the issues at hand carried the marks of this history, despite the fact we had moved beyond the statement and its motivations and all the tensions it had created. Dr. Chafik himself indirectly referred to the affair in his opening statement, saying:

> Then came the Throne Speech of 2001, which settled the dispute and put an end to quarrels that had raised cries we now hope can be forgotten, along with the misunderstandings that characterized its verbal exchanges of blows. The Throne Speech was fair to all, and clearly laid out the fundamental elements of our cultural identity, placing each in the place appointed to it by history, thus responding to the demands of pure, academic logic.

OUR STRUGGLE FOR THE USE OF THE TIFINAGH SCRIPT

As soon as the Royal Institute's board of directors was inaugurated on July 27, 2002, a thorny and strategic task awaited it: resolving the question of the choice of script for writing the Amazigh language. I call this thorny and strategic because it is a political, civilizational, and historical matter. We as activists of the Amazigh movement at that time understood that the board was the political section of the institute, as it would discuss topics from all their aspects, political and cultural, and submit proposals to higher circles for approval or rejection before they were implemented by the research centers that constituted the academic side of the institute.

AMREC had had a clear stance on the issue of the script since the early 1990s. At the Maâmoura seminar on Amazigh writing and the alphabet in 1992, we had established that we would deal with the Amazigh question in a comprehensive way. Thus, the Amazigh language could not be separated from its Tifinagh script; we considered the Tifinagh alphabet a fundamental element in Amazigh cultural identity. Being written in Tifinagh characters would free our language from its dependency on other linguistic systems, whether Eastern or Western. Therefore, we held that Tifinagh was essential to our liberation, on a symbolic and civilizational level.

Before the issue of the script was brought to the board for discussion, AMREC quickly published a book titled "For the Adoption of the Tifinagh Alphabet in Teaching the Amazigh Language," as part of its Amazigh Studies series in 2002. This book contained a collection of articles all related to the Tifinagh question, laying out its history and the question of writing the Tamazight language. The book included contributions by Mustapha Aachi,

Dr. El Houssain Ouazi, Dr. Abdelaziz Bourass, Dr. Abdelrahman Ballouch, Dr. Moubarak Boulkid, and Dr. Ali Khedaoui. They all presented arguments calling for the official adoption of the Tifinagh alphabet for writing Tamazight, arguing that it was the most suitable alphabet for this purpose, especially given it had undergone significant moves toward standardization in order to keep pace with new discoveries and research.

The association's clear stance on the need to formalize the Tifinagh script did not come out of a vacuum, nor was it an emotional decision. Rather, it resulted from the association's experience with the Arabic and Latin scripts from the time it began documenting Amazigh heritage through its publications *Arraten* and "Cultural Exchange," as well as its *Amoud* periodical. All these were written in the Arabic script, while some articles appeared in Latin script. Finally, we had concluded that there could be no future for the Amazigh language unless it were taught and written in its own historical script, Tifinagh.

Therefore, at the board meeting on December 23, 2002, we agreed to meet on the following January 30 and 31 for a session dedicated to settling the matter. This announcement was like the launch of an election campaign between the three alphabets—Arabic, Tifinagh, and Latin—for the honor of being the script in which Tamazight was written and taught.

From the outset, our association declared itself in favor of the Tifinagh alphabet, in alignment with our steadfast principles toward the Amazigh language, culture, and identity. Some others chose to promote Latin script on principle, although they had no convincing justifications or national, religious, social, or civilizational references to support their choice.

A third group defended the Arabic script. This camp comprised members of the Islamist and Arab nationalist currents, who wanted Amazigh to remain subservient to Arabic in terms of language, culture, and civilization. They saw writing the Amazigh language with its own letters as a departure from the Arab system, and a declaration of intellectual and cultural independence on the part of the Amazigh and Moroccans at large. They used every available means to defend the Arabic script, particularly associating it with Islam, and attempting to sanctify it to achieve their goal of imposing the Arabic script on the writing of Tamazight.

In the context of this campaign, many articles were written by all sides, arguing in favor of this script or that. Each side also published articles attacking their rival camps. However, despite the fact that these writings were sometimes heated and aggressive, they helped demonstrate the depth of the issue, addressing all its political, religious, civilizational, and identity aspects. Ultimately, they allowed everyone to become convinced of the choice that was eventually made, meaning it was a truly national decision, not an individual or factional stance.

To illustrate this debate and the level of vehemence associated with it, it suffices here to mention a few of the articles in question.

On January 23, 2003, *Al-Mustaqil* dedicated a full page to an interview with me, regarding the Amazigh issue and current issues in Morocco. They titled the interview with my comment: "The Arabic language and *Francophonie* have benefited from hundreds of millions, unlike the Amazigh language, which has been imprisoned for 40 years." The newspaper's weekly edition for February 3–9, 2003, carried a response, by Ahmed Bouzelmadh, to those who believed the Amazigh language should be written in the Latin alphabet, stating that "claiming that the Latin alphabet is the universal alphabet is a colonization of Tamazight." *Ahdath al-Maghreb*'s Issue 1465, dated January 25, 2003, carried an article by Essafi Moumen Ali titled "Choosing the Official Script for Writing the Amazigh Language Is a Political Issue, Not an Academic One." Then on March 24, *Al-Jarida* carried an article by Ahmed Ballout who stated that "the Amazigh script . . . is an issue that concerns every Moroccan." On January 14, *Bayane Al Yaoume* carried a front-page article stating that "calls for Latin or Arabic script to be used to write the Amazigh language, are both wrong." The newspaper published this article based on a statement it had received from our association regarding its stance on the script. Journalist El-Hossein Idrissi wrote in *Al-Haraka* newspaper on February 6, 2003, that "the Tifinagh script has the right to enter schools in its homeland."

This discussion, which was sometimes close to a battle, revolved around three official positions. The first was summarized in a statement by the association on January 9, 2003, titled "A statement in favor of the official adoption of the Tifinagh alphabet for teaching Tamazight." This was the same name as the title of the previously published book to which I referred above. Our statement read:

> The national board of the Moroccan Association for Research and Cultural Exchange met on Thursday, January 9, 2003, at its national headquarters to discuss developments in the integration of Amazigh language into education.
>
> After reviewing the various political, ideological, technical, academic, pedagogical, and civilizational aspects associated with selecting the most appropriate script for teaching;
>
> In harmony with the principle of unity in diversity as the basis of a democratic state, and as a guarantor of linguistic and cultural peace,

based on linguistic and cultural equality in a framework of integration and solidarity;

Considering that the Tifinagh script, which has undergone development and standardization in terms of linguistic adaptation, poses fewer technical problems compared to the Arabic and Latin scripts, as well as enjoying a flexibility that makes it academically capable of keeping up with technological and computational development;

Seeking to avoid confusion and disruption when writing two different linguistic systems with the same letters, and the resulting psychological stress, frustration in communication, and waste of classroom time among school children, due to the lack of equal opportunities;

Underlining the need to preserve and value this symbolic and civilizational element with its deep roots in history, and which expresses the collective sentiment of all Moroccans, whether they speak Arabic or Tamazight, and one that is embodied in their collective heritage, from rock drawings to artistic productions, architecture, decoration, carving, embroidery, weaving and other arts, and culminating in tattoos on their bodies;

Following from all these political, ideological, technical, academic, pedagogical, psychological, and civilizational considerations, the Moroccan Association for Research and Cultural Exchange declares that the Tifinagh script is the most appropriate script for teaching the Amazigh language, and calls on authorities to formalize its status as such.

Some components of the Islamist movement also staked out positions. The first was in an open letter by Dr. Ahmed Raïssouni, the president of the Unity and Reform Movement, urging Professor Chafik to adopt the Arabic script for writing Amazigh, for five reasons:

1. It was the Amazigh themselves who voluntarily adopted the Arabic script, which they used for many centuries; their leaders, scholars, and writers wrote in it. Adopting the Latin script would deviate from that choice and deny that heritage.
2. Adopting the Arabic script would help spread the Amazigh language and attracting people to it, as it is the most widely understood script among Morocco's educated classes.
3. Writing Tamazight in Latin script was a colonial choice made in the context of attempts to break the Amazigh away from Islam and sow division between them and their Arab brothers in Morocco.

4. Adopting the Arabic script is an affirmation of the Islamic identity of the Amazigh people, similar to other Islamic nations that have adopted the Arabic script; even those that have been forced to drop it have made efforts to return to it and still use it unofficially.
5. Adopting the Latin script would create a division with Moroccans who speak Arabic, and a barrier to cultural commonality between them and their Amazigh brothers.

Support for these views came from the student wing of the Unity and Reform Movement.

Al-Tajdid newspaper published an article titled "We Reject Any Attempt to Impose the Latin Script, by French Diktat, for Writing Amazigh." The third and final group supporting the Arabic alphabet came from the Souss Scholars' Association, which in statement called on "all actors to pursue a path of civilized dialogue and scholarly discussion." The association's position differed from the previous two, as the statement recalled the history of the Tifinagh script as an ancient script for the Amazigh language; however, the association believed it would be better, today, to write Amazigh in Arabic script.

Al-Asr newspaper dedicated a whole section to Amazigh writing, under the title "The War on the Arabic Alphabet." It contained the following articles:

- Abuzid Al-Muqri' Al-Idrissi: "We demand that everyone carefully consider the terrible consequences of any decision that further divides the Moroccan people into two nations and two peoples."
- Ibrahim Rida: "This subject must be dealt with outside the framework of an ethnic, ideological approach."
- Ahmed Harzni: "Some Amazigh excessively oppose everything Arab, Islamic, and Eastern."
- Majdouline Al-Monabahi: "From a linguistic research perspective, Arabic is the most suitable (script) for teaching Amazigh."
- Ahmed Dghirni: "The choice of script should be based on the subject, for example: Latin for the science and technology, Arabic for religious studies, Tifinagh for the arts."
- Saïd Lahcene: "The question of writing scripts is an academic issue that should be resolved by specialists and scholars."
- Abdelaziz Al-Tahir: "In the realm of teaching Amazigh, Amazigh heritage and production are the best evidence of the suitability of Arabic letters."

Within the Amazigh cultural movement, given our association's clear choice in favor of the Tifinagh system, I reiterate that our brothers whom I mentioned earlier, who were members of the board of directors, were mostly on the committee of Mohammed Chafik's statement. Their fixation in this battle was to fight against our association's objective, patriotic choice of the Tifinagh script, and to oppose the Arab nationalist-Islamist camps in their choice of Arabic script. This led them to defend the Latin script, which has no connection to the civilizational, historical, and religious reality of Morocco. By doing so, they made a grave strategic mistake. They rushed to call for a meeting by the Assid Association in Meknes as part of a study day on October 5, 2002, by a group of Amazigh associations, and they issued a statement arguing that Latin script should be used to write Tamazight. In its first statement, it argued that "the script that currently enables the writing and teaching of Tamazight with ease and a lower degree of pedagogical and technical obstacles, and allows for greater economy in time, effort and expense, is the Latin alphabet." This statement was intended to exert pressure on the members of the board to dissuade them from adopting the Tifinagh script. Moreover, this camp even threatened to withdraw from the board if the Arabic script were adopted.

Yet what is striking when examining the stances of the Islamists and Arab nationalists, on the one hand, and advocates of the Latin script, on the other, is that neither side dared openly attack the Tifinagh script, as it is a national script. Instead, each side defended the script of a language from elsewhere. Moreover, they waged a smear campaign against us, promoting the claim that the association chose the Tifinagh script as a tactic to counter the Latin script, thereby paving the way for the adoption and approval of the Arabic script. This is clear from the weekly newspaper *Assahifa*, Issue 87 of January 15–21, 2002, which bore the title "The Conflict over the Script Continues Within the Royal Institute for Amazigh Culture." It read: "It is well known that the associations and community activists gathered in Meknes on October 5, 2002, unanimously decided to adopt the teaching of Amazigh with the Latin script, but a minority of the members of the institute's board of directors defend the ancient 'Tifinagh' script for identity and emotional reasons, in a bidding war aimed at indirectly promoting the Arabic script. This struggle over the script is likely to intensify in the coming days as the board of directors meeting approaches."

These were some aspects of the heated conflict that characterized the preparation and groundwork for the institute's decision on a script for writing Tamazight. The most important file on the subject was in *Assahifa* (issues 94 and 95, of January 2003), under the headline "Will There Be a War of

Identity in Morocco?" It was presented in the form of a seminar at the newspaper's offices, in which supporters for each of the aforementioned camps participated.

Among the defenders of Arabic were Saadeddine El-Othmani,[4] Abdallah Saaf, and El Yazid El Barka. Supporting the Latin script were Ahmed Assid, Meryem Demnati, Lehbib Fuad, Mounir Kaji, Abdellah Hitous, Mohammed Bahri, and Nour El-Arj. The advocates of Tifinagh were me and Abdelaziz Bourass. Ahmed Dghirni also took part, but simply attacked all sides throughout, without revealing his own position. The debate was chaired by Abdelaziz Koukass and Ahmed Bouz. The resulting articles became an important record for understanding the motivations of each side. In order to bring these arguments into the public realm, particularly to students, University City Souissi II held another symposium on February 26, 2003, on the subject "Which Script to Achieve the Amazigh Self?" I was invited to participate, and Mustafa Al-Khalfi from the Islamist current also attended. In the same context, and to clarify our position so that it would not be exploited as if it were an attack on the Arabic language, I gave a lengthy interview to *Al-Tajdid*, which is close to the Islamic current. This was published in its issue of January 13, 2003, and included my remark: "When we call for Tamazight to be taught in the Tifinagh script, we are not calling for people to stop writing in Arabic letters."

THE PROCEEDINGS OF THE BOARD MEETING IN JANUARY 2003 TO DECIDE ON THE SCRIPT FOR WRITING TAMAZIGHT

At the board of directors' meeting in late December 2002, it was decided that the body would meet in late January to determine the appropriate script for writing and teaching the Amazigh language. In preparation for this historic session, the Language Adaptation Center and the Didactics Center were tasked with preparing an academic report on the three alphabets, presenting the features of each and the problems related to its use in writing the Amazigh language, to explain the issues to the members of the council in isolation from the various pressures they might face in making their decisions. This report was duly prepared and distributed to members of the board.

On January 30 and 31, 2003, the board met at the Sofitel Hotel, overlooking the Oued Bou Regreg river, after weeks of heated debates over the issue of choosing the script and pressure that some had tried to apply on board members to adopt particular stances. All this meant that the meetings were a test of whether or not the board could make the most suitable choice, and of its capacity to rise above the wranglings and decide what script was the most appropriate for writing the Amazigh language, a historic and fateful decision.

The first session was dedicated to listening to the report, which did not advocate for any choice. Afterward, members were each given an opportunity in turn to express their positions and opinions, a preliminary stage in which each member presented his own view in his own way. While the opinions of some were already known due to debate in the media and through statements issued by the associations to which they belonged, others had not previously announced their opinions. What I discovered at this first meeting was that most of the old guard of the Amazigh movement were in favor of the Tifinagh script, as something inherent to the Amazigh language. These included Essafi Moumen Ali and Ali Khedaoui from AMREC—it had been their choice from the beginning. It turned out that it was also the choice of Abdelmalek Ousaden, who had not previously expressed his opinion. The Meknes group had tried to sway him, but he chose the correct and rational opinion by backing the Tifinagh script, as did the late Ali Sidqi Azaykou, Ali Amhan, Mohammed El-Chami, Ilyas El-Ammari, and Ahmed Boukous. While these individuals had now declared their support for Tifinagh, the representatives of the ministries said they did not yet back a particular script, pending the completion of presentations and consultations. The supporters of the Latin script had been well known since the Meknes statement on October 5, 2002. They were Ahmed Assid, Mohammed Ajaajaa, Aghraz Mimoun, Mahmoudi, Jilali al-Saib, Meryem Demnati, and Bougrine. These were clear in their choice of the Latin script, as was Hassan Id Balkassam, given that his association was among the signatories of the Meknes statement. The remaining members of the board had not taken a position until that moment.

After the meeting, I went up to my brother Ali Sidqi Azaykou and congratulated him on taking a clear stance from the beginning. He was surprised and asked me why I was saying this. I explained to him that I had no doubt of his dedication to Amazigh and its script, but I reminded him that at the beginning of our journey of activism in the mid-1960s, and when we had first met and established AMREC in 1967, he was the first to introduce us to the ancient Tifinagh script. Being a history teacher, he had informed us of the existence of an Amazigh alphabet. "Now sir, here we are voting for it, in such a forum, so it can become the official script for the writing and teaching of the Amazigh language," I said. That was why I had congratulated him, as well as myself and all those who had struggled for the future of Tamazight. Now he understood and smiled.

On the following day, January 31, we continued with the critical, political aspect of our discussion, during which we could respond to the interventions of others and to refute their claims, which were not based on any objective foundation. Dr. Chafik began the meeting with a detailed and ample presentation about the Tifinagh script's historical, civilizational, and educational aspects. The opponents of the script were shocked and caught by surprise by what they felt was a promotional presentation by Chafik. This left the Meknes faction on the board in disarray; they no longer understood what was happening. We, the script's supporters, continued with our arguments, like lawyers given one last chance to lay out a case. Essafi Moumen Ali spoke in his usual manner, convincing and providing irrefutable historical, intellectual, and political arguments, as did Ali Khedaoui in the same direction. I also spoke, elaborating on the political and identity dimension of the choice of script and its strategic importance across the Amazigh homeland. I explained that this decision would be a turning point in the history of the Amazigh people across North Africa, and that those hesitant to support Tifinagh were simply lacking the courage to make this historical decision, perhaps because they felt dispossessed and unable to break away from the attraction and domination of Francophonie and Arabism. I told them a well-known Amazigh fable of the fox and the pigeon, in which the hedgehog advised the pigeon to shed its fear of the saw with which the fox was threatening it and told them they should do likewise and no harm would come from it. Everyone laughed as they knew the story. I also presented them with another proof, drawing on educational pedagogy—a points system for evaluating pros and cons of a decision, which I laid out on the following table:

	Amazigh	National	Islamic	Points
Tifinagh	Yes	Yes	Yes	3 points
Arabic	No	No	Yes	1 point
Latin	No	No	No	0 points

When one responds to these questions objectively, detached from emotions and bias, one rapidly reaches the conclusion that Tifinagh is the most suitable script, as it is simultaneously Amazigh, national, and Islamic. Arabic meanwhile scores only one point, as it is Islamic but not national, having originated overseas, and Latin has no relation to the Amazigh homeland nor to the Amazigh language.

Thus, we defended the Tifinagh script with every means of argument, but in the end, I unveiled a document I had not mentioned previously. This was a statement from the Amazigh grassroots movement within the Moroccan National Union of Students, issued two weeks earlier on January 15, in Casablanca, where representatives of the Amazigh cultural movement from across Morocco had gathered. In the statement, they had expressed their positions on the discussions underway about the script and the constitutional issue, and they had told me and provided me with a copy of the statement so I could use it to defend the Tifinagh script.

I had kept this statement secret from everybody at the session, and from those who had appointed themselves as speaking in the name of the Amazigh movement, but were ignorant of—or were simply ignoring—even the prominent activists present with them on the board. I read them the demands of the Amazigh cultural movement, limiting myself to the first four requests in the statement, which were as follows:

- Constitutional recognition of Tamazight as an official, national language within a genuine democratic constitution;
- Teaching of Tamazight at all levels of education, in its original Tifinagh script;
- Its incorporation into all public services (administration, business, etc);
- A restoration of the stature of our true national symbols and a rewriting of the history of Morocco with national pens, to reveal the fate of all the disappeared, first and foremost Boujoumaa El-Habbaz.

After I had read this crucial statement, Hassan Id Balkassam got up from his seat and came over to look at the statement, of whose existence he had been unaware. He was among the supporters of the Latin script, and his association Tamaynut had been present at the Meknes meeting. As the council digested this new information, the matter was put to vote, and the results were as follows:

For Tifinagh: 14 votes
For Latin: 13 votes
For Arabic: 5 votes

Tifinagh had come out on top. However, it still needed to achieve a two-thirds majority of those present to be adopted. There were thirty-two people present, and one member of the council was absent. The competition had now come down to Tifinagh vs. Latin, and the session was paused for consultations. But with Arabic out of the running, some of those who had voted for Latin decided to give their votes to Tifinagh. This was natural, as they were not in fact originally against Tifinagh—rather, they had feared that Arabic script would be made the official script for Tamazight. In the second and decisive round of voting, Tifinagh received twenty-four votes, against eight for Latin. Thus, through this democratic process and two rounds of voting, Tifinagh was selected as the script for writing Amazigh, following a fierce battle in the media and scuffles elsewhere to influence the board's members in support of this or that script.

January 31, 2003, was thus a historic day marked by this great political and cultural achievement. The decision amounted to a declaration of the Amazigh language's liberation from foreign domination, its independence from other educational systems, and the construction of its own, unique intellectual and linguistic edifice. This applied not only in Morocco but would also have an impact on the Amazigh homeland across North Africa, from the Siwa Oasis in Egypt to the Canary Islands in the west.

This decision was also a strategic achievement by the institute's board of directors during Mohammed Chafik's term. The professor deserves great recognition for this realization, through his wise and insightful management of the debate and the disputes. I call this a strategic achievement to reaffirm once again that in our view as activists, the board's role was a strategic, political one, despite the opinions of some of its members, as I have said.

I must also mention something personal related to this historic battle. My children and, in particular, my wife lived through every moment of this period with me, with all its events and tensions. My wife knew that for me and my friends in the association, this was a life-and-death struggle, a once-in-a-lifetime battle for us and for the Amazigh cause. She would call me during sessions to find out the results, and as soon as she learned that Tifinagh had won, she rushed to buy a bouquet of flowers to present as a gift to Essafi Moumen Ali, Ali Khedaoui, and me. The three of us had borne the burden of defending our association's argument on the board of directors. Indeed, these comrades accompanied me back home, and we shared these moving moments in our lives.

In another touching moment, the painter "Al-Zayani" from Tinghir presented me with a large, signed portrait of me, with old Tifinagh letters in the background, in appreciation of my personal efforts to support the script. Such moments, with their historical significance, cannot be easily forgotten.

Hardly a week had passed since the board of the Royal Institute of Amazigh Culture submitted a request to King Mohammed VI to approve the adoption of Tifinagh letters when His Majesty responded. On February 10, 2003, he officially supported the board's choice of Tifinagh as the official script for writing the Amazigh language. The reactions to this decision were mixed but were not as intense as when the project was just a proposal, as most parties accepted the decision. There were still, however, some who did not yet accept this reality. Dr. Ahmed Raïssouni, head of the Movement of Unity and Reform, wrote in *Al-Tajdid* newspaper on February 3, 2003, that "the decision to adopt the Tifinagh script is artificial, arbitrary, and undemocratic." Al-Muqri' Al-Idrissi also expressed his regret at the decision, because he had expected the Arabic script to be adopted and believed that the decision would erect an iron barrier between the two communities that he claimed comprise the Moroccan people, the Arab group and the Amazigh group. Unfortunately, these individuals still believed that there were two peoples, Arab and Amazigh, in Morocco, and the fulfillment of certain Amazigh demands angered them, due to their jealousy over this people and their fear for national unity. Then again, they would not lift a finger when policies were imposed in favor of the "other side" under their system of classification.

Many newspapers quickly wrote about the decision, a historic event with political and cultural implications for our country, trying to understand the viewpoints of the actors involved and to bring the topic closer to their readers' minds. *Al-Mustaqil* interviewed me at length for an article it published on January 23, 2003, under the title "Arabic and 'Francophonie' Benefited from Funds in the Billions, While Tamazight Was Marginalized for 40 Years." This interview covered several aspects, including the reasons why some members of our association had worked so tirelessly to defend the Tifinagh script, what the association would have done if a script other than Tifinagh had been adopted, and a question about the nature of the Amazigh identity of Morocco and its people. It also discussed whether the association, in existence now for more than three decades, might establish a political party. All these ideas had begun to be discussed in the wake of the decision to adopt Tifinagh as the script for writing Amazigh, owing, as I said, to its connection to the political and intellectual transformations Morocco was experiencing or was going to undergo. One major opponent of the decision was the writer Idriss Drif, who published an article in *Al-Ahdath Al-Maghribiya* on January 24, 2003, in which he poured out his anger at this decision and at the Tifinagh script itself, to the point of denying that the letters were even Amazigh. Drif was someone who would not accept a single concession to the Amazigh cause. The title of his article was "The Tifinagh Alphabet or Tifiniqt?" (an echo of the Arabic word *finiqī*, meaning Phoenician). This had nothing to do with the real meaning of tifinagh, "our discovery," or *tifinaq*, the writings of the Tuareg in the Sahara Desert. This article was a reminder of the writings I have previously mentioned, from the 1970s onward, whose authors used intellectual terrorism against the Amazigh cause. However, I do not want to dwell on the negative reactions to this decision, as they were weak and only represented the views of their writers. Most political organizations and associations took a neutral position on the decision, especially as it had received the royal blessing, and now the majority of articles, both in French and Arabic, looked to the future and what would follow the official recognition of the script. However, the event opened another subject regarding Morocco's linguistic policies. The researcher Mohammed Ghoneim published an article in the January 23–29, 2003, edition of the *Al-Ayyam* weekly, titled "Toward a National Dialogue on the Linguistic Situation in Morocco." In it, he wrote: "Building a culture accepting of difference necessitates the work of the 'self' and the 'other' . . . as well as much action, justice, democracy, human rights, positive tolerance, equality, solidarity, the philosophy of recognizing the other and the collective avoidance of violence, both physical and symbolic." In the same vein, on February 5, *Al-Mustaqil* published Mohamed Atarguine's view in the form of a question: "After the script, is constitutional recognition of Tamazight on the horizon?" I note too that Dr. Saadeddine El-Othmani, the secretary-general of the Justice and Development Party, called me by phone the day after the decision and asked me to meet him at the party's headquarters. During our meeting, he suggested that the association organize a study day for the party's activists on the question of constitutional recognition of the Amazigh language, as the party had received the message from the adoption of the script, and did not want to be taken by surprise on the constitutional question. They duly organized this event at the party's headquarters, which lasted a full day and was attended by activists and members from various branches. It was a significant and fruitful interaction with them. Three members of the association led the study day: Abdelaziz Bourass, Essafi Moumen Ali, and me. The association also provided participants with a collection of books it published on the topic of constitutional recognition of the Amazigh language the previous year.

OUR BATTLE ON THE BOARD FOR UNITY OF THE AMAZIGH LANGUAGE

On Monday, January 29, 2003, by order of His Majesty the King, Professor Mohammed Chafik was honored by the institute, at the Royal Academy, in the presence of many intellectuals and his friends—first and foremost Hassan Aourid, the official spokesman of the Royal Palace and the permanent secretary of the Royal Academy. The grand ceremony was opened with a speech by Ahmed Boukous. The speakers discussed the personal aspects of the honoree, and all praised his scholarly achievements and his impact on the field of education and training throughout his career as a statesman. In his speech, Aourid reminisced about an event fifteen years earlier:

It was the presentation of the first Amazigh dictionary, by Mohammed Chafik, commissioned by one of the oldest associations which had taken it upon itself to promote Amazigh culture, with openness, insight and wisdom: the Moroccan Association for Research and Cultural Exchange. The hope was to revive Amazigh culture and breathe life back into its language, which was a daunting task, if not completely fanciful. Those who kept this promise sacrificed much of their lives and their comfort, and their efforts were met with indifference, suspicion and doubt. During that period, Mohammed Chafik had composed a poem entitled "*Ider wayur*," expressing the despair of the period and the despondency of Amazigh-speaking intellectuals. Yet that meeting, convened by the Association for Research and Cultural Exchange, had instilled a new spirit and confidence.

After this honor, the first important session of the Royal Institute of Amazigh Culture's board of directors was scheduled for March 6–4, 2004. The top item on the agenda was the topic of teaching the Amazigh language and activating the partnership agreement between the institute and the Ministry of Education. On the first day of this session, we were surprised by the release of three pedagogical books for teaching Tamazight in the first year of primary school, each book dedicated to a dialect of the Amazigh language, and all under the title *Awal inou*, "My Language." In the first year of primary school, blue was designated for the Tarifit dialect, green for the Atlas dialect, and yellow for Tashelhit. As the council had not decided on these matters, this development took its members by surprise, especially those from our association. We believed in the unity of the Amazigh language, just as we believed in the unity of the Amazigh nation and the Amazigh people, something that could only be achieved through the unity of its language. The decline of the Amazigh language had been a result of the fact that it was not written down, the marginalization of its script, and the fact that it was kept as separate dialects throughout North Africa, in the absence of any initiative from officials, throughout history, to unify them. We also believed that teaching Tamazight in the form of dialects would subsequently lead to the creation of several languages nationally, which could undermine the unity of the nation and the Moroccan people. Therefore, it was essential right from the start to have a strategy to unify the Amazigh language as it exists, to arrive at a standard Amazigh language to be taught and written, in order to tackle the current complex situation of the dialects. By taking this stance, we did not intend to ignore the diversity and local specificities of the Amazigh language, which we believed would continue to survive in our daily lives as means of popular communication and creativity. But they would exist alongside a standardized Amazigh dialect for education and writing, which would act as a unifying thread joining all these linguistic branches, integrating the modern terms and concepts required to modernize it.

Taken by surprise, we began to ask officials from the two centers responsible, the Linguistic Adaptation Center and the Didactics Center, as well as the dean, what was going on. Their response was that unification could only happen over the long term, and that they were convinced of this and believed that the Amazigh language would be taught as separate dialects in this way until it was unified at some unspecified time in the future. This was meant to present us with a fait accompli.

After hearing these unconvincing responses from the researchers and the dean, we board members who were from AMREC sprang into action. That same night, as secretary-general of the association, I called for an immediate meeting of the national office so the three of us who were on the board of the institute could inform them of the situation. After extensively examining all aspects of the issue, the possibilities and speculations about the reasons behind this policy, we issued a statement firmly rejecting this approach to teaching the Amazigh language dialect by dialect. We, in agreement with the thrust of the King's Ajdir address and the decree establishing the institute, believed that Amazigh was the language and the property of all Moroccans, and that it would be taught to all their children, whether they speak it or not, which would necessitate its unification. The statement read:

> Following the publication by the Ministry of National Education and Youth, in collaboration with the Royal Institute for Amazigh Culture, of the three textbooks for teaching the Amazigh language to Grade 1 primary school pupils;
>
> Noting that the contents of these three books teaching various dialects of Tamazight instead of the standard unified Amazigh language, despite each of these books bearing the title "Amazigh Language";
>
> The National Office of the Moroccan Association for Research and Cultural Exchange met on March 4, 2004, and having discussed

the subject, it announces to national and international public the following:

- Based on the Agadir Charter, which makes the teaching of Standard Amazigh one of its basic demands;
- Recalling the consensus achieved by the various components of the Amazigh cultural movement on this fundamental demand;
- Affirming this movement's rejection of the Charter on Education and Training, which approved the teaching of Amazigh dialects and their harnessing to serve the official language, thereby consecrating linguistic discrimination in our country;
- Drawing on the historic speech of His Majesty the King, who said: "Amazighity, which has its roots deep in the history of the Moroccan people, belongs to all Moroccans without exception";
- Referring to the Royal Decree that established the Royal Institute of Amazigh Culture, in which His Majesty stipulated that 'the Institute participates, in cooperation with relevant governmental authorities and institutions, in implementing the policies adopted by our noble Majesty and helps integrate Amazigh into the educational system, ensuring its radiance in the social, cultural, and media space nationally, regionally, and locally.

The National Office declares the following:

First: It utterly rejects the adoption of the aforementioned books for use in public education, and demands their replacement with a single book that reflects the demands of the Amazigh movement and the royal desire, represented in the teaching of the Amazigh language to all Moroccans.

Second: It calls on all components of the Amazigh movement, civil society and politics to be alert to the danger that teaching dialects poses to national unity and the cohesion of the Moroccan people, and appeals to it to demand the teaching of Standard Amazigh, alongside the Arabic language.

The standardization of the Amazigh language is a strategic matter, similar to choosing the right moment for successful improvisation. The future of the Amazigh language lies in growth and development to achieve linguistic balance within society. Morocco respects the languages used, without one language dominating another. Instead, there must be equal opportunities among these languages.

This was the first problem faced by Ahmed Boukous after he became dean. Given that the issue of unifying the Amazigh language was a strategic one just as important as the selection of the script, we fought for it with the intensity and determination it deserved, to reach the most appropriate and beneficial solution for the future of the Amazight language so it could grow, develop, and create a linguistic balance between all the languages used in Moroccan society, rather than one dominating the others. They should enjoy equality of opportunity.

Our brothers on the board of the institute perceived our rejection of the publication of three separate textbooks as a revolt against them, or suspected that we had undeclared goals we aimed to achieve through this uprising, even though we were friends and activists with a shared concern for the future of the Amazigh language. Yet despite their reactions toward us, we did not see the issue as one of hostility. Rather, as we explained in the statement, we saw things from the perspective of principles from which we could not deviate: the defense of the unity of the Amazigh language and the unity of the Amazigh people. Once again, the national press also got involved, and each party defended its viewpoint through the media. The brothers at the institute each mobilized their teams to defend their perspective. We at the association used our tools as activists and as an association through seminars, interviews, and communications, doing everything we could to support our stance that the language must be unified. Thus, this battle for the unification of the Amazigh language was similar to the battle for the Tifinagh alphabet, and it led to tensions and misunderstandings between us and our old friends at the association who were now officials at the institute.

My approach to addressing these topics and achieving our desired goal was based on direct communication, to convince the relevant authorities overseeing these files, in parallel with the battles we waged in the media— and on the board itself—as an association. My goal was to provide them with all the necessary evidence, and to highlight for them the political and cultural aspects of the topic, as well as demonstrating to them the positions I defended on the issues discussed on the council were driven by a sincere national spirit, and that the solutions I proposed were not related to political horse-trading or selfish motives. I had engaged in these communications when the topic of the script was raised, and I did so again regarding the unity of the Amazigh language. Despite the difficulties I found in convincing these entities, objectively and politically, of the arguments mentioned above, my efforts did not go in vain. Rather, they helped these entities understand our point of view and furthered our arguments, which were based on a national spirit, as they were in the interests of the nation, and because defending the

Amazigh cause is out of love for the nation. These communications were not limited to one party, but rather, I spoke to many people, to pave the way for a decision based on objectivity and defined by courage.

The following are some of the newspaper articles published on this subject:

- *Al-Sabah*, February 12, 2004: "Pedagogical and Technical Obstacles Facing the Teaching of Amazigh," by Abdullah Nahari.
- *Al-Tajdid*, January 1, 2004, "The Royal Institute of Amazigh Culture, Between Internal Differences and External Accusations," by Ahmed Aamari.
- *Al-Ahdath Al-Maghribiya*, Issue 1922, April 30, 2004, "A Criticism of the Ministry of Education's Policy on Teaching Amazigh Dialects."
- *Al-Sahara*, October 2, 2004: "The Process of Teaching Amazigh in Its First Year Did Not Achieve Any Notable Educational Outcome." In this interview, Professor Abdelaziz Bourass said the Amazigh cultural movement had confronted this dialectical division, which fundamentally undermines the principle of the unity of the Amazigh language.
- *Al-Mustaqil*, March 10–16, 2004, "Aspects and Risks of Entrenching the Policy of Amazigh Dialects," by Mustafa Antara.
- *Al-Akhbar Al-Maghribiyya*, May 13–19, 2004, "The Amazigh Moulawy Elite and the School Textbook War: From the Script to the Book War," Mohamed Atarguine.

In an interview with *Al-Mustaqil*, published in its April 14–20, 2004, issue, Ahmed Boukous stated, "There is no divide, no abyss, and no contradiction between the Institute and the Amazigh movement."

From our side, after our statement on the teaching of Amazigh, the association organized a series of seminars nationally to explain our position on the issue of teaching Tamazight. The Casablanca branch organized a seminar on January 3, 2004, at Markab al-Maaref on the topic "Amazigh After the Agadir Charter." Participants included Aday Lihi, Essafi Moumen Ali, me, Ali Belqadi, Lahcene O El-Si Mouh, Mustapha Antara, and Hicham Madaacha. The Mohammedia branch also organized a seminar on the topic of "Teaching the Amazigh Language," and in February 2004, the association organized a series of awareness activities on "the teaching of Amazigh in Moroccan schools." On April 8–9, 2004, a seminar was held in Meknes on the teaching of the Amazigh language in public schools, with the participation of Hamani Aklaai, Ahmed Al-Awam Ashaaban, me, and Abdelaziz Bourass. The

Imintanoute branch on April 17 held a seminar titled "Teaching Amazigh in Public Schools, the Reality and the Prospects," as did the Mohammedia branch, with Khala Al-Saidi, Abdelaziz Bourass, and Abdelrahman Ballouch.

These were just some of the cultural activities AMREC organized to explain our position on the teaching of Amazigh and our rejection of the dialect-by-dialect approach to integrating it into the education system. The association did not limit itself to the media and public events. Rather, I made my own personal efforts, approaching senior officials to convince them of our viewpoint. I contacted His Majesty's Advisor Abdelaziz Meziane Belfkih at his office at the Education Committee on Thursday, April 1, 2004, after we had issued a statement on the subject. I briefed him about our viewpoint, the political dimension of the issue, and the dangers of this approach to teaching Amazigh, a position he understood. I also told him that there were no bad intentions regarding the institute and its staff, but that the issue stemmed from our firm conviction regarding the unity of the Amazigh language, which was the basis of the unity of the nation and that of its people. Similarly, I quickly arranged a meeting with Dr. Hassan Aourid at his residence in Harhoura, at 3:30 p.m. on Tuesday, March 23, asking him to convey our position and its national dimensions to His Majesty. He assured me that he would do so, and that the matter was understood and noted.

The press covered our activities through every stage of this movement, helping to bring our viewpoint to the national public. We also made some contacts with Moroccan political parties and associations with the aim of informing them on the subject of teaching Amazigh in Moroccan public schools, and the need to use a unified language so as not to contribute to the linguistic Balkanization of the country. We also held an official meeting with some members of the political bureau of the Socialist Union, chaired by the party's first secretary, Mohamed El Yazghi. This meeting was cited in the Political Bureau's weekly newsletter in the party newspaper of November 14–15, 2004, and reported by the *Akrawa* newspaper under the title "Amazighity Between El Yazghi and Akhiate," on November 2, 2004. *Al-Haraka* newspaper, the mouthpiece of the Popular Movement, wrote that "student textbooks enshrine the teaching of dialects instead of the language," and the National Popular Movement's *Al-Maaraka* newspaper March 12–18, 2004, wrote that "AMREC rejects student textbooks for teaching Amazigh."

Many members of the association's council took part in this campaign, contributing articles and interviews. *Al-Tajdid* newspaper contributed by holding a dialogue seminar between me and Belaid Boudriss, who was now director of the Didactics Center at the Royal Institute, under the title "Teaching Amazigh Between Experimentation and Fear of Failure," in its issue of

July 2–4, 2004. This campaign bore fruit. During board meetings following that of March 4–6, at which we were informed about the publication of the three textbooks, we perceived a change in tone among officials at the institute, who finally committed to the quest of unifying the Amazigh language. We were also informed that the publication of three separate textbooks would not be repeated in this manner, and that the unification of Amazigh would no longer be an open-ended process, but would be completed within a maximum of six years. This unification would be carefully executed, relying on all branches, with the integration of modern terms and the unification of Amazigh grammar and a dictionary. Indeed, this was the case when the second-level textbook was published. In a single book, the teacher could find everything needed for each lesson, presenting all the dialects of the language used in society, without exclusion. Both the student and the teacher would thus deal with a single Amazigh language, not three.

As a postscript to our experience throughout this battle for the Tifinagh script, and our second battle for a unified language, we proposed to the board of directors that well-thought-out strategies be put in place as a road map to deal with issues related to education, the media and communication with society at large, in order to explain our policies and choices in these sectors. The board acted on this after the end of 2004, something that was truly difficult and challenging for all the administrative officials and members of the board.

For us at AMREC, the years 2003 and 2004 had special historical significance, as they were a test of our ability to adhere to the principles for which we had fought and continued to fight, while acting within an official institution, taking into account that we were a minority compared to the other currents represented on the board of directors. Despite this status, we succeeded in making our voice heard and in reaching our goals—the goals of the Amazigh cultural movement—on many strategically important matters.

We ended the year 2004 by organizing a symposium in Casablanca on October 20, 2004, marking the third anniversary of the Ajdir speech, under the theme "The Royal Speech in Ajdir: Political, Cultural, and Symbolic Implications," with the participation of many intellectual figures, including Mustapha Antara, Essafi Moumen Ali, Abdelaziz Bourass, Ali Belkadi, and me.

THE 12TH NATIONAL CONFERENCE OF THE MOROCCAN ASSOCIATION FOR RESEARCH AND CULTURAL EXCHANGE

The opening session of AMREC's twelfth conference was held on January 24, 2004, in the hall of the Ministry of Culture, with representatives from all the political parties and national civil society bodies. The parties were represented by the Socialist Union, with two members from its political bureau, Istiqlal, with two representatives of the party's Secretariat-General, the head of the Justice and Development Party's parliamentary group, the secretary-general of the Fadhila party, and the secretary-general of the Covenant Party, Chaquir Achahbar. The opening session also included the president of the Moroccan National Press Union (SNPM), the national coordinator of the Movement to Demand a Democratic Constitution, as well as representatives from the Amazigh associations Tamaynut, Azta, and the Federation of Associations in the North and Tamount Ifous. This list suffices to demonstrate the size of the assembly and the seniority of the representation present. While our eleventh conference in Bouznika in 1999 had only seen representatives from youth organizations and rights groups, the twelfth was distinguished by a much greater presence, from all political leanings, as well as associations. This demonstrated these organizations' endorsement of our national approach to promoting the Amazigh cause, avoiding wrangling and provocation. None of this would have happened were it not for our clear strategy of communication, through our meetings with political leaders and heads of the associations, as well as the clarity of our statements issued by the national office on national issues, which were characterized by objectivity and placing the national interest above all else.

Some of these people addressed the gathering and praised the struggle of our association and its national and objective approach to the Amazigh issue. We surprised the attendees by opening the conference with Amazigh anthems performed by a group of children brought by the association from Tiznit, specifically for the event. We followed up the conference in Harhoura on January 25 and 26, 2004, where the delegates did an excellent job of updating and developing the association's strategy to match new developments on the ground. One of the main features of this strategy was its focus on calling for unity and solidarity among the components of the Amazigh movement, to overcome its fragmentation and to focus on communication and openness. This strategy also emphasized the need to give serious and targeted consideration to children and women, to open new horizons by educating children to connect them with their culture and helping them understand their Amazigh language, as well as organizing summer camps for children, with an element of teaching Amazigh, and recreational activities for them at youth centers. This new strategy also prioritized the training of youth leaders to take on this responsibility through theoretical and practical training sessions. This marked a new start for the association as it entered the field of training and practical, vocational work on Amazigh issues in the areas of education, theater, cinema, and the teaching of the Amazigh language, as well as continuing the theoretical role that the association had been performing for four decades by organizing political and academic seminars and by issuing publications serving the Amazigh cause in its relations to other national issues. The conference ended with the publication of a public statement affirming our constant positions on perennial issues and laying out our positions on the issues of the day.

The statement included the need for constitutional recognition of Amazigh and institutionalization of its use at state facilities and in public places, and to defend the unity of the Amazigh language in the fields of education, media, and state institutions, to correct misconceptions about the Moroccan identity and history, and to teach the Amazigh language and develop Amazigh media by improving radio broadcasts and establishing an Amazigh television channel.

EFFORTS TO MODERNIZE AMAZIGH CULTURE
BY LINKING IT TO DEVELOPMENT

I was reelected as the secretary-general of AMREC with the support of a majority of conference delegates, as an expression of their recognition of the role I had played and continued to play in furthering the Amazigh cause. The various organs of the association—the national council and the members of the national board—were also elected. The session was chaired by Zuhour Bandala, from the Fes branch of the association, marking the first time a woman had headed both a branch and the general conference of the association. This was a recognition of women's fundamental role in the development of the Amazigh language and culture, as in the development of society in general.

A WORD EVALUATING THE ACHIEVEMENTS OF
THE ROYAL INSTITUTE FOR AMAZIGH CULTURE,
ON JUNE 24, 2010, EIGHT YEARS AFTER ITS ESTABLISHMENT

The establishment of the Royal Institute for Amazigh Culture by His Majesty King Mohammed VI was a historical political event not only for Morocco but also for the North African region as a whole, given that the

Amazigh cause is common to all the countries that make up this region. The institute's creation therefore amounted to an announcement of the start of deep intellectual and political transformations in our country, aimed at reconciling it with itself, as well as a declaration of its political and intellectual independence.

The decree creating the institute constituted a road map for nurturing cultural pluralism in Morocco, and a declaration of our distinctive national identity, in which the Amazigh aspect is a fundamental element. Moreover, the decree laid out the practical measures that were needed to promote the Amazigh language and culture on a national level, in areas such as education, the media, and the public sector, to integrate it into public life, as the decree confirms and stipulates that the Amazigh language belongs to all Moroccans and that learning and speaking it is everyone's responsibility, without exception.

This initiative, and this new policy established by His Majesty through his decree, would be recorded in history as a pioneering Moroccan experiment in managing the issue of identity in relation to cultural diversity in our country, a courageous but rational experiment that can be cited as a successful example in its geographical context.

Given this awareness, on the part of the highest institution in the land, of the importance of the issue, as well the vast responsibility placed on the shoulders of this nascent institution in light of the political and cultural nature of the issue, the responsibility for managing the institution was assigned to a body comprising two integrated teams. The first was the board of directors, a strategic, advisory, political body comprising many stakeholders in the Amazigh cause or from the Amazigh movement. The second was composed of researchers and administrators representing relevant government sectors. It fell to all of these, as a cohesive team, to devise strategies, proposals, and recommendations concerning all aspects of managing this issue, and researchers specialized in various branches of the humanities were tasked with implementing these strategies on the ground, by putting in place tangible and effective mechanisms in order to reach the agreed goals.

Thus, the Royal Institute of Amazigh Culture, having been provided with the conditions and material resources it needed fully to perform its role and achieve the goals outlined in the decree, became, over time, a model for institutions in the same field across North Africa.

For these reasons, the board of directors found itself tasked with major strategic and intellectual responsibilities, and with finding realistic solutions that could be integrated into public education, media, and public life, with all the necessary academic efforts and political will from relevant parties in order to revive the language itself, ultimately putting an end to the marginalization and exclusion suffered by Amazigh language, culture, and civilization throughout centuries of our history in the face of languages and cultures coming from abroad.

In response to all these intellectual and strategic demands, the board of directors focused, from the outset, on developing strategies and a road map to serve as a reference framework for all the activities to be undertaken by the research centers. The board worked to place these strategies in an integrated framework to avoid any arbitrary elements in the institute's research and visions. This led the council to develop a clear strategy for the institute's work in the fields of education and audiovisual media; in the field of academic research on history, anthropology, and translation; as well as in printing and publishing, without neglecting to create committees at the board level to monitor these projects until they were completed, on time and according the visions the board set out on an annual basis. Strategies were also developed to organize the institute's relationship with civil society, including associations working on Amazigh issues as well as official and unofficial bodies, and establishing a dynamic strategy for communicative diplomacy with various components of the world of politics, as well as parliament and human rights and women's rights organizations, to enable the institute to impose itself as a key reference body in the cultural and intellectual sphere, and as an indispensable institution for managing cultural and media affairs in our country.

In the Field of Education

The board decisively and correctly selected the Tifinagh script for writing Amazigh, a choice that was not arbitrary or emotional but rather strategic and political, given the significant civilizational importance of the script and what it represents in terms of identity and the historical continuity of the Amazigh people in North Africa. This choice also had a political dimension, being a symbol of intellectual independence from the prevailing linguistic systems, which enabled the Amazigh identity to consolidate strongly despite all the attempts to obliterate it throughout our region, geographically and societally. This achievement alone would not have been possible were it not for the board members' deep awareness of the fundamental components of the Amazigh identity. This enabled them to overcome all the obstacles and political pressures exerted by various parties opposed to this vision. The board's adoption of the Tifinagh script, and the endorsement of this decision by His Majesty King Mohammed VI, restored sovereignty and intellectual and civilizational leadership to our people in North Africa, as this decision became a reference for these peoples—notably the Amazigh people of the Canary Islands, who chose the Tifinagh alphabet to write Amazigh, following Morocco's example. Furthermore, this choice of Tifinagh made the script a symbol of identity for artists and visual creators, and a symbol of struggle among activists from the Amazigh movement in all regions of Tamazgha, the Amazigh nation. This in itself was a clear indication that the institute was correct to choose Tifinagh as the script for writing Amazigh, and none of this would have happened were it not for this wise decision.

The institute was also able to overcome the challenges posed by the diversity of Amazigh dialects by moving beyond the idea of creating a textbook for each dialect and taking the decision to implement a process of standardization and regularization for the language, creating a single textbook that includes these dialects, with a view to gradually unify them by the sixth grade of primary school. It also made the linguistic and didactic efforts needed to implement this massive project, to enable the Amazigh language to be rationally integrated into the education system in our country and allow all Moroccans to learn Amazigh, a national language. Accordingly, it reconsidered the content of curricula to reflect this new intellectual orientation of our country, following these political transformations it had undergone and continued to experience under its leader His Majesty King Mohammed VI. It was imperative to rewrite official histories of Morocco to remove their shortcomings and impurities, and to restore the recognition owed to our people's intellectual and political symbols, dating back thousands of years, without excluding or marginalizing any period. Moreover, the status of the Amazigh language in educational curricula needed to be restored, to enable learners to grasp their culture and civilization adequately and deeply, in order to focus and deepen their awareness of the Amazigh identity in their personality.

In the Field of Public Culture

The institute set to work, according to the strategy set by the board of directors, via its various centers, to issue dozens of publications in various fields of Amazigh culture and civilization, including historical, literary, intellectual, and creative books, both by researchers at the institute and by accomplished outside authors. This is not to mention the many educational books or those related to the integration of Amazigh into educational systems. This surge of productions and publications was able to fill a significant gap that had long afflicted Moroccan libraries, particularly in relation to history and geography. Most of our historians had focused on writing the history of the elites and the cities where they reside, totally ignoring our rural history, for political reasons that need not be mentioned here. This interest in historical and geographical writings fits with a policy of rewriting national history and correcting what has been written about it as well as filling the gaps within it.

Communication and Interaction with the Surrounding Environment

The institute's board adopted a clear policy in this area based on the need to interact with its environment, including civil society associations, especially those interested in Amazigh affairs, as the main bridge enabling the implementation of the institute's strategy in these fields, whether by supporting its cultural, communications, or training activities. These communications activities have made a significant contribution to expanding interest in Amazigh culture and language, encompassing vast and remote areas of the national territory, thanks to the institute's interest in them. This has helped break the cultural and developmental siege on these areas, which to this day have not enjoyed their share of development and infrastructure.

As part of its communications strategy, the board adopted a policy of communicative diplomacy aimed at creating channels of communication and dialogue with various government departments and political bodies, from parliamentary groups to influential social bodies, in order to bring the Amazigh issue, in its official framework, closer to such bodies and to urge them to do what was needed in their respective spheres for the benefit of Amazigh culture. This included the development of Amazigh language and culture and its integration into public life, as per royal directives expressed in the decree establishing the institute, which amounted to a new policy in managing the Amazigh issue as a national responsibility, or within the framework of supporting cultural diversity in the country in general.

The institute's approach to communicating with various bodies and institutions drove an institutionalization of relations on the Amazigh issue, transcending frameworks of protocols between institutions. This strategy was also able to make an effective contribution to integrating the Amazigh language into public life, via institutional cooperation with both governmental and nongovernmental sectors.

Over its first eight years—which is a short period considering the wide scope of its interventions in the fields of education, communication, the media, and culture—the institute has not fully been able to correct the country's path or address what had been overlooked in all these areas over many decades. However, even in this short period, it made achievements that are worthy of appreciation, both in terms of their quantity and in terms of laying out strategies of action and setting priorities, as well as laying the initial foundations for managing the Amazigh question at the institutional level, by setting clear strategies in the fields of education, the media, communications, and in public life. It has also imposed itself by working and interacting with its natural environment, including cultural associations, official state bodies, and unofficial organizations, as well as various national and international educational bodies and universities. It has also rapidly marked itself out as a reference point on everything related to Amazigh language, culture, and civilization, thanks to the efforts of the board, which has operated with a sense of the historical responsibility on its shoulders and its national awareness of the scale of this responsibility. Indeed, over these eight years it has worked hard to prove that it is capable of bearing this responsibility and worthy of the trust placed in it by His Majesty, to complete this massive project, a unique one in the modern history of the Maghreb.

However, we must not overly inflate our optimism about the foreseeable future of the Amazigh language, unless this interest in managing the Amazigh question evolves into an institutional matter that concerns all ministries, government bodies, quasi-government institutions, and economic sectors of our country, an institutionalization able to express the political will of all parties to engage to make this national project, established by royal decree, a success. By contrast, in the absence of effective action to integrate Amazigh into public life, and enrich and development it, the institute will turn into an academic institution with little real impact on the ground, or in the daily life of the citizen; its publications will sit forgotten on library shelves, the graveyards of books, and the efforts of the institution and its staff will be wasted. To avoid the institute suffering this painful fate, it is vital that political forces and civil society, including human rights bodies, the Amazigh movement, labor unions, and women's organizations step up their efforts, sacrifices, and solidarity, to institutionalize and bring about constitutional protection of the Amazigh language, formalizing it as an official language alongside Arabic and enshrining the Amazigh component as a fundamental element of the national identity, in order to guarantee its right to grow and develop.

If we consider the importance of the civilizational and political initiative represented by the establishment of the Royal Institute alone, in the context of pioneering scholarly, cultural, and democratic transformations, as well as its many achievements, we must make some observations and suggestions that I believe could help develop the work of this young but important institution.

Firstly, all the recommendations issued by the cultural, educational, and communication committee of the board of directors must be implemented and registered, as they reflect the committee's experience and its accumulated knowledge of monitoring and supporting research centers.

Secondly, the institute should place special emphasis on training researchers at its centers to help them to fully understand its strategy in all fields, as well as enhancing their ability to write in the Tifinagh script, as it has been observed that most of the researchers and staff do not fully understand how to write in this script.

Thirdly, the institute must develop the performance of its centers, especially the center for history, the environment, and anthropology, to pay more attention to the little-known ancient history of Morocco, to restore the esteem due to its political and cultural figures and to Moroccan civilization, and to remove erroneous perceptions. Researchers should not merely recount history as it is taught in universities or related in certain books by ideologically biased historians. Rather, it is the duty of these centers to make the necessary corrections to the contents of historical books, to rewrite our history from the necessary national and academic perspectives, and to expedite the publication both of historical research and of anthropological books and research, given their fundamental importance when it comes to understand the self and its relationship with its surroundings, along with historical research.

Fourthly, in its dealings with its environment, the institute must transcend its current focus on quantity and numbers as concerns its support of Amazigh cultural associations, to elevate these interactions to a level that takes into account their qualitative nature, so this support and these partnerships can transform from solidarity to seeing to fruition major projects that serve the Amazigh language, culture, and civilization. After all, the institute's mission is to develop and nurture these areas, not simply to provide solidarity and cooperation. The current partnerships give the impression that they are only intended to win over to the institute as many collaborators, drawn from the associations, as possible. If this continues, it will be detrimental to the process itself because it will not achieve the cultural goals for which this support was created, as it has so far been mainly for show rather than for production and accumulation.

Therefore, it is time to separate the support system that has hitherto been dedicated to associations to help them integrate and make effective contributions to Amazigh cultural work in their respective regions, and to provide them with the necessary training material resources to play an educational role there, based on a program of partnership with certain institutions or leading figures to carry out national or regional activities concerning the development of Amazigh language and culture. These partnerships should not be subject to the same conditions for support, but rather to other procedures, determined by the administration and obligatory on both parties, in execution of clear obligations on each. Through these contracts and partnerships, the institute must, in the future, implement clearly defined and cost-effective projects, through cultural training, elevating Amazigh language and culture to the high status they deserve. It must also organize festivals for all kinds of Amazigh cinema, theater for adults and children, and major literary gatherings that can showcase and disseminate new creations in all genres, as well as widespread teaching of Amazigh to children and young people, with material support to spread the culture of summer cultural camps with high-quality Amazigh educational content.

I believe if these observations are taken into account, provided the institute carries out the necessary, objective evaluation of its important and useful experience, it will be able to assert its presence as a reference and be effective in playing its pioneering role in full harmony with the royal decree establishing it. This will create a dynamic with its social environment that will enable it to contribute effectively to the development, advancement, and dissemination of the Amazigh language, culture, and identity in our country.

In conclusion, I would like to express my great pride in the achievements in which I have played a role through my membership of the board of directors of the Royal Institute of Amazigh Culture, since its establishment by His Majesty King Mohammed VI. I have made every effort to fulfill my duties, whether as chairman of the Committee on Cultural Affairs, Education and Communication, or as a member of the committees on which my fellow board members gave me the honor of having a seat. I have made sure to perform these tasks and not to miss a single board meeting, as I felt the responsibility placed upon all of us as members of the council, especially during this foundational period of the life of the institute.

I also wish all the best to those who will come to serve as members of the council, as they continue the great work that awaits them, that of serving and developing the Amazigh language and culture, for the public good, and to advance desires of His Majesty, King Mohammed VI, may God assist him.

NOTES

1. The following associations attended: the Confederation of Amazigh Associations in the North, represented by Professor Mohammed El-Chami and Ahmed El-Ziyani; the Tamaynut Association, represented by Hassan Id Balkassam and Abdellah Hitous; me, and Abdelaziz Bourass representing AMREC; and Ibrahim Akdime representing the Liaison Committee for Cultural and Developmental Associations in Tafraout.
2. The following associations and organizations endorsed the statement: the Association for Research and Cultural Exchange, represented by me and Abdelaziz Bourass; the Confederation of Amazigh Cultural Associations in Northern Morocco, represented by Mohammed El-Chami and Mohammed Al-Zayani; Tamaynut Ifous, represented by Ahmed Barchil; and the Tafraout Coordination Committee of Cultural and Developmental Organizations, represented by Muhammad Aqdim.
3. The following represented their organizations and spoke at the conference: Abderrahman Ben Amrou, Ibrahim Yassine, Ahmed Bedaoui, Ali Ammar, Bouchaib Ouabbi, Abdellah Hitous, Abdullah al-Bakkali, El Houssain Ouazi, Ouchen, Tariq Mohammed, Bijaja, Al-Radi, Ahmed Rakiz, Hmid Farid, Mustapha Moatassim, Said Fakak, Mohammed Hafidh, and Hmid Bouz.
4. Translator's note: El-Othmani went on to be prime minister of Morocco, from March 2017 to October 2021.

CONCLUSION

As I draw to the end of this autobiography, I should point out that while it narrates stages of my life, from childhood until today, it also reflects the lives of millions of Amazigh-speaking people from Morocco, whose economic and social circumstances have forced them to migrate within and beyond the country and to deal with unfamiliar cultures and lifestyles, into which they have had to integrate. This memoir also demonstrates the form of the struggle chosen by an elite group of intellectuals who emerged as a result of these new transformations, experienced by Amazigh speakers in particular and Moroccan society in general, to protect their cultural, linguistic, and civilizational gains in order to face down a cultural challenge that targeted their identity in all its manifestations. In the midst of this cultural struggle, an Amazigh speaker hailing from one area of Morocco who was forced to move to another, urban area could be unaware that the person imposing this new culture upon him, speaking a different language, and practicing this behavior of humiliation and condescension, had been, once upon a time, nothing other than an Amazigh like him—but one who had been robbed of or lost his original language, taking on another one unlike that of his forebears, coming to believe, over successive generations, that he belonged to a different people from that of the Amazigh-speaking newcomer to the cities.

As the reader will notice, my story has mainly followed the trajectory of the Amazigh movement, of which AMREC, founded in 1967, is a fundamental component and was, for some, the "Mother Association" of the movement. Since the founding of the association, along with the many activists mentioned above, my life and that of the association have become intertwined. It is hard to separate between the two paths, as the Amazigh cause has occupied me as a national issue, and the association has occupied me as the framework through which I and my comrades who share my concern for its destiny have managed the fate of this cause. I do not claim credit for any of the ideas I have presented in these memoirs; rather, they are the fruits of our collective effort. They are not merely personal viewpoints but have become the basis of our strategic work within this framework, which has enabled us to unify, stay disciplined, and maintain continuity. We have transcended our selfishness and intellectual individualism in furthering our cause, which is greater than all of us, being the cause of our entire people and a pivotal issue for future generations.

However, what distinguishes me from the rest of my brothers in the organization and throughout this path is the extent of the responsibility that I bore due to my presidency of the association, since its establishment, and what this responsibility required in terms of good crisis management and the need to ensure continuity, as well as initiative and courage to bear the consequences. This meant that I was more exposed and targeted than others in the attempts of our opponents and the authorities to block our path to achieving our goals.

The Amazigh issue, in its content and philosophy, is a profound cultural revolution and, as such, is a civilizational and political revolution, as it aims to change things from the inside, altering mentalities and reevaluating concepts and behaviors. It does not seek the kind of change seen in armed coups, which aim to bring about superficial changes from the outside but also rob agency from the people, who become overwhelmed and unable to contribute to deciding their fate. The Amazigh cause is a revolution in which individual selfishness becomes the selfishness of love for the nation, a revolution against history, aiming to correct and rewrite it as the history of a people, not as the history of regimes and individuals. This is a political revolution for the supreme interest of the nation, not for narrow sectarian or regional interests. It is an intellectual revolution seeking to allow intellectuals to rid themselves of cultural domination and self-contempt, and to be transformed into scholars who think for themselves, based on the reality of their people, rejecting intellectual and civilizational subjugation, and thus becoming creative and innovative rather than being consumers of the thoughts of others. This is the revolution in which we are engaged, and this is the style of struggle we have chosen, as an intellectual elite, to address the cultural issue in our country. It aims to bring about deep change, by shedding all outdated and unrealistic concepts that govern our minds and frame our thinking to this day, due to the nation-less educational curricula set out by subjugated political elites who want to use these curricula to erase our civilization, history, and identity, and put others in their place. This is a policy that targets our national entity in its existence and continuity, diverting it from its natural and historical path.

I have long believed in this revolution and in the need to contribute to its success with all the strength I possess, including the sacrifices it required from me, because it is a revolution that we wanted to spring from the depths of Moroccan society and its reality so that it would be in the interests of the people, serving its welfare, continuity, and growth. I also believed in it because it is a revolution for and by every citizen, without racial, regional, or religious discrimination, transcending all political ideologies. I believed and engaged with all my strength in this great undertaking for our society, because for the first time in the history of North Africa, Moroccan Amazigh intellectuals were devoting their thinking, through the Amazigh movement, to promoting their own language and culture, and restoring the status of their national identity, rather than serving and devoting their thought to foreign languages and cultures. Such impositions had, throughout history, been met with a total readiness to perform this service for no compensation, placing the components of the country's own culture and civilization at risk of being lost, by neglecting them and depriving them of any effort to develop them and make them prosper. This, then, is a peaceful cultural revolution that we are waging, working to deepen our people's awareness of its Amazigh identity so that it might arise, renew its thoughts, and wake up from its slumber, mobilizing all its capabilities to correct this historical path and its intellectual and political choices.

Moreover, despite all these observations, which sometimes amount to historical criticisms of our ancestors and an intellectual policy concerning our present, I feel that if each of us seeks radical national solutions to this issue, a vital one for our people, there is no option but to be convinced of and recognize the Amazigh nature of Morocco and its people, and to move urgently to give the Amazigh language its status as a national and official language and to confirm the equal status of the Amazigh and Arabic languages, as a necessity if we are to achieve equality among all members of the Moroccan nation. Otherwise, as officials, intellectuals, and people active on this matter, we will guide the people into the unknown, because the Moroccan nation, and the Amazigh nation, will not settle for less than an assertion of its Amazigh identity, thus freeing itself from the intellectual and ideological subjugation that has long dominated it.

Now that the seeds of this consciousness have sprouted and evolved in our society, through the struggle of the Amazigh movement over more than four decades, and through the bold initiatives and the new policies of the young King Mohammed VI in favor of the Amazigh cause, as well as the efforts of various components of civil society to recognizing our distinctive identity, with its deep roots in history, the fruits of all this will inevitably appear soon, thanks to this shared desire of king and people.

Any approach that runs counter to this direction will inevitably go against the will of the people, and its fate will be the same as that of other forms of domination and unpatriotic behavior through history, which have all ended in failure and collapse. My confidence in our imminent reconciliation with our Amazigh self, both officially and as a people, grows stronger along with my growing trust in this people to which I belong, in its strength, and in its desire to complete its quest for sovereignty on its land by honestly recognizing its Amazigh identity through language, culture, and civilization, and by practicing this culture in all linguistic manifestations, alongside the Moroccan *dārija* and *ḥassaniyya* dialects of Arabic.

In this memoir, I have discussed the contributions I have been able to make, both intellectually and as an activist, throughout my struggle, as well as the difficulties and risks I faced, which varied in intensity over time, according to the political circumstances of each period. However, it never once occurred to me, even for a moment, to abandon this national duty, which was never directed against anyone, whether institutions or individuals. Nor did it cross my mind to use it to achieve political ends or my own personal interests.

However, throughout this long experience, I became convinced—through practice and my personal feelings—that divine power was continuously on our side, and that in everything we set out to achieve, success and fortune accompanied us. This was also clear in the fact that the Amazigh movement achieved the significant gains that it did with minimal losses and suffering, compared to the harm suffered by other movements, although this is primarily because we did not target the regime or the royal institution during the "Years of Lead,"[1] as our revolution sought to change minds, not the regime. That said, we still faced all kinds of harassment and provocation, as I have related, not only from the authorities but also from many political organizations and intellectual figures who attacked us with all forms of intellectual terrorism.

Indeed, we in the Amazigh movement made a number of respectable political gains, even if we differ on how we evaluate them. However, they must be seen as fundamental shifts, considering the relatively short period over which they were achieved. First and foremost, the highest authority in the country recognized the legitimacy of Amazigh demands, and the Amazigh question was acknowledged as a national responsibility that falls equally to all citizens, whether they are Amazigh speakers or not. We also settled the issue of the Tifinagh script and the unity of the Amazigh language, as well as seeing the start of its integration into the curriculum for all Moroccans, as well as in the media. We saw the establishment of the Royal Institute for Amazigh Culture, as an institution concerned with managing the Amazigh question, nurture the language and regulate its grammar. However, our greatest political gain was the increasing popular engagement in the process of taking care of this language, whether by associations, political organizations or individuals, a manifestation of the fact that that the Amazigh question is a national responsibility, in contrast to the long-dominant, reductionist view that wanted to confine the Amazigh question to the struggle of Amazigh associations, or argued that it only concerned the Royal Institute and the royal court.

Despite this optimism, the main demands of the Amazigh movement still await realization. These relate to the constitutional recognition of the Amazigh language as an official and national language, and its integration into public life, something that is not limited to education and the media, but also pertains to every aspect of state institutions and the daily life of the citizen. This requires the collaborative efforts of all parts of the Amazigh movement, state institutions, political parties, and civil society organizations, all of which are responsible and concerned with the issue. Therefore, we in the Amazigh movement must live up to our responsibilities by choosing our discourse and defend our legitimate cause by adopting a method based on persuasion and the strength of argument, avoiding all provocative methods that could harm the Amazigh cause. We must avoid policies that exclude the other, and refrain from monopolizing the Amazigh issue as we defend it, being tolerant among ourselves and with our interlocutors, creating opportunities for solidarity and collaboration among associations so they can be an effective force in the arenas of politics and civil society, working to expedite the achievement of our legitimate demands, rallying around the many things that unite us, and postponing that on which we are divided so that it does not drive us apart and clash with our goals.

To ensure the success we desire, for the Amazigh cause and for the nation, we must ensure that our behavior and our discourse are characterized by the spirit of unity: the unity of the Moroccan people, the unity of the nation, and the unity of the Amazigh language, which we want to be the language of all Moroccans, the language of writing, creativity, and study, so it can rise and transcend its current status as the vernacular of the people, and become a language of scholarship, able to meet our linguistic needs and live up to the challenges of the era. In calling for national unity, I am not defending a system of administrative centralization to manage the national territory—the kind of centralization exploited by special interest lobbies to exclude and marginalize certain regions from development, by depleting their resources and discriminating between regions and citizens in terms of opportunities, meaning that the inhabitants of these areas are excluded from managing their affairs or benefiting from their wealth in ways that achieve human, economic, and cultural development. Rather, I support any form of territorial management of Morocco's regions that achieves comprehensive development for these areas and ensures equal opportunities for its people to exploit their resources both for their benefit and for that of the nation, by handling their local affairs with a greater degree of autonomy, within the framework of national unity, the unity of the people, and the unity of the Amazigh language for all Moroccans, all within the context of a structured integration among all regions, to achieve an economic balance and to ensure social peace for this nation.

We must not forget that the most important guarantee of the preservation of our language and culture is its use in writing and artistic creation, because it can have no future unless it is used for creativity and imagination in all fields of literature and thought. Its practical application in theater and cinema are a means of cultural and intellectual communication between creators and the audience. Moreover, Amazigh activists, if they truly want to follow this path, must be well-read and trained theoretically and practically in all fields, so they can be skilled and equipped with all the mechanisms and means to defend their cause and convince their interlocutors, being simultaneously prepared to give, create, and bear responsibility.

In concluding this memoir, I wish to confirm to everyone that I have sincerely attempted to relate events and positions to reflect the true nature of what happened, without introducing personal bias over my relations with any activist, participant, or association in the movement. I believe that these events and their consequences belong to the movement and to the Moroccan people as a whole. Therefore, I have aimed to write with honesty and integrity, out of respect and appreciation for those who shaped these events, both the living and the deceased, and due to my deep belief in the nobility of the cause and my sense of responsibility toward all these matters. From this firm conviction and sense of responsibility, I want to assure everyone that I have never intended, even for a moment, to offend anyone mentioned in this memoir, whether friends, activists, or figures who might be embarrassed by my opinion on a position they took, or due to our differing views on an issue. I can assure them that the position I have expressed rises from the values that govern me and from which I cannot deviate. They are not personal or self-serving, but rather principled and patriotic. Despite any differences in opinion or behavior, what remains is friendship, respect, and appreciation for these individuals, because I always value those with differing opinions, and respect their courage in expressing them.

NOTE

1. Translator's note: The "Years of Lead" refers to the rule of King Hassan II, from 1956 to 1999, which saw heavy repression of political dissent, widespread use of torture, and the enforced disappearance of hundreds of individuals.

POSTSCRIPT FROM THE TRANSLATOR

In 2011, following a wave of anti-government protests inspired by uprisings across the Middle East and North Africa, Morocco passed a constitution that officially recognized the Amazigh component of the country's identity.

While it preserved the status of Arabic as "the official language of the state," it added:

> "Tamazight also constitutes an official language of the State, being common patrimony of all Moroccans without exception."

INDEX

ABOUT THE AUTHOR AND THE TRANSLATOR

Brahim Akhiate (1941–2018) was a central figure in the struggle for Amazigh linguistic and cultural rights in Morocco. Born in a remote Tamazight speaking village, Akhiate became keenly aware of the marginalization facing Amazigh culture when he joined his older brother to pursue his studies in the capital Rabat. In 1967, he cofounded the Association marocaine de recherche et d'échange culturel (AMREC), serving as its secretary-general until his death in 2018.

Despite threats and intimidation—particularly during the oppressive "Years of Lead" under King Hassan II—Akhiate and his colleagues worked relentlessly to bring Amazigh language and culture from the margins of Moroccan official culture into schools and the mass media. In 2011, the Tamazight language was finally recognized in the country's constitution.

The success of decades of activism by Imazighen—Amazigh people—in Morocco stands at odds with the experiences of Amazigh activists elsewhere in Tamazgha, notably Algeria and Libya. It also serves as a template for linguistic and cultural struggles of Indigenous people elsewhere around the globe.

Paul Raymond is an Australian-British translator, journalist, and musician. He studied Arabic in Amman, Fes, and at the University of Leeds, before honing his Palestinian dialect on the streets of Jerusalem and the West Bank.

In 2012, he moved to Istanbul and into journalism, first covering the Syrian revolution then reporting from across the MENA region, from Beirut to Timbuktu.

After several years as a newswire journalist with Agence France-Presse (AFP)—including in Tunis as Maghreb Correspondent—he returned to his first love, Arabic. He now translates and edits for research institutes, academia, and NGOs, focusing on history, biography, political science, and current affairs. He also translates from French.